Theatre and AutoBiography

Mavor Moore and Joy Coghill at the "Putting a Life on Stage" workshop, University of British Columbia, Vancouver, February 2004. Photograph by Gabriele Helms.

Theatre and AutoBiography

Writing and Performing Lives in Theory and Practice

Edited by

Sherrill Grace & Jerry Wasserman

Talonbooks

Talonbooks
278 East First Avenue, Vancouver, British Columbia, Canada V5T 1A6
www.talonbooks.com

Second printing: March 2015

Typeset in Scala
Printed and bound in the U.S.A.

Cover design by Adam Swica
On the cover: Linda Griffiths as Pierre Trudeau in *Maggie & Pierre* by Linda Griffiths with Paul Thompson; photograph by James Gilmore

Talonbooks gratefully acknowledges the financial support of the Canada Council for the Arts, the Government of Canada through the Canada Book Fund, and the Province of British Columbia through the British Columbia Arts Council and the Book Publishing Tax Credit.

Library and Archives Canada Cataloguing in Publication

Theatre and autobiography : writing and performing lives in theory and practice / edited by Sherrill Grace and Jerry Wasserman.

Includes bibliographical references.
ISBN 0-88922-540-0

1. Biographical drama—History and criticism. 2. Autobiography in literature. 3. Dramatists in literature. 4. Canadian drama (English)—20th century—History and criticism. 5. American drama—20th century—History and criticism. 6. English drama—20th century—History and criticism. I. Grace, Sherrill E., 1944– II. Wasserman, Jerry, 1945–

PN2039.T52 2006   822'.91409351   C2005-906200-2

ISBN-10: 0-88922-540-0
ISBN-13: 978-0-88922-540-4

Actors, although vain and nervous,
Do perform a social service,
Showing in their gilded mimes
A mirror of our life and times.

This image of our age would look
Far better in the history book
If it did not expose to view
The lives and times of actors too.

—Mavor Moore, *And What Do You Do?:*
A Short Guide to the Trades and Professions

Contents

List of Illustrations 9

Preface and Acknowledgements 11

Theatre and the AutoBiographical Pact: An Introduction
    Sherrill Grace 13

Part One—Theorizing AutoBiographical Theatre

3-D A/B
    Susan Bennett 33

Documemory, Autobiology, and the Utopian Performative in Canadian Autobiographical Solo Performance
    Ric Knowles 49

Theorizing the Gendered Space of Auto/Biographical Performance via Samuel Beckett and Hans Bellmer
    Richard J. Lane 72

(Un)Covering the Mirror: Performative Reflections in Linda Griffiths's *Alien Creature: A Visitation from Gwendolyn MacEwen* and Wendy Lill's *The Occupation of Heather Rose*
    Katherine McLeod 89

Part Two—AutoBiographical Plays: Stage, Page, or *Real* Life?

Tremblay's Impromptus As *Process*-driven A/B
    Louis Patrick Leroux 107

The Shape of a Life: Constructing "Self" and "Other" in Joan MacLeod's *The Shape of a Girl* and Guillermo Verdecchia and Marcus Youssef's *A Line in the Sand*
    Joanne Tompkins 124

Resonant Lives: The Dramatic Self-Portraiture of Vincent and Emily
    Anne Nothof 137

Auto/Biography and Re/Vision: Betty Lambert's *Under the Skin*
    Cynthia Zimmerman 152

A Ship of Fools in the Feminine: Six Characters in Search of Self
    Louise Forsyth 167

Part Three—Theatre Lives: From Autobiography to Biography

Autobiography, Gender, and Theatre Histories: Spectrums of Reading British Actresses' Autobiographies from the 1920s and 1930s
    Maggie B. Gale 185

Untold Stories: [Re]Searching for Canadian Actresses' Lives
    Paula Sperdakos 202

Totem Theatre: AutoBiography of a Company
    Denis Johnston 225

David Mamet: Life Without an Archive
    Ira Nadel 249

Behind the Scenes: Irish Theatre, Irish Lives, and the Task of the Biographer
    Ann Saddlemyer 261

Sharon Pollock's *Doc* and the Biographer's Dilemma
    Sherrill Grace 275

Part Four—Creating AutoBiography on Stage

Writing and Performing Lives: Ten Playwrights Speak
    Jerry Wasserman 291

Playwright: Parasite or Symbiont
    Sharon Pollock 295

I Am a Thief ... Not Necessarily Honourable Either
    Linda Griffiths 301

Fact Does Not Interest Me Near As Much As Fantasy
    Tomson Highway 306

The Malcolm X School of Playwriting
    Lorena Gale 309

How in Hell Did She Do It?
    Joy Coghill 313

I'm Not God's Gift to Black People
    Andrew Moodie 317

I Always Stick to Facts
    Sally Clark 321

Never Not Narrative
    R. H. Thomson 324

In the End You Are Made Accountable
    Marie Clements 329

Blahblahblahblah Mememememe Theatreschmeatre
    Guillermo Verdecchia 332

Playwrights' Selected Bibliography 336

Contributor Biographies 338

Index 344

Illustrations

1. Mavor Moore and Joy Coghill . . . . *frontispiece*

2. Djanet Sears in *Afrika Solo* 59

3. Guillermo Verdecchia in *Fronteras Americanas* 65

4. Gwendolyn MacEwen 95

5. Linda Griffiths as Gwendolyn MacEwen in *Alien Creature* 95

6. Production photograph from *Encore une fois, si vous permettez* 111

7. Production photograph from *Le vrai monde?* 114

8. Production photograph from *Vincent in Brixton* 141

9. Production photograph from *Song of This Place* (2004) 147

10. Production photograph from *Song of This Place* (1987) 148

11. Production photograph from *Under the Skin* 161

12. Constance Collier in "At the 'Gaiety'" 191

13. Constance Collier as Cleopatra 191

14. Catherine Proctor in *A Midsummer Night's Dream* 207

15. Judith Evelyn in *Angel Street* 208

16. Ida Van Cortland in *Pygmalion* 208

17. Elizabeth Jane Phillips 210

18. Margaret Bannerman 214

19. Charlotte Nickinson Morrison and family 216

20. Thor Arngrim and Stuart Baker, Totem Theatre 231

21. Totem Theatre production of *A Streetcar Named Desire* 236

22. Thor Arngrim and Norma Macmillan 238

23. Thor Arngrim and Stuart Baker with Suzie the elephant 245

24. Sharon Pollock as Shipman in *Moving Pictures* 296

25. Linda Griffiths as Pierre Trudeau in *Maggie & Pierre* 302

26. Production photograph from Tomson Highway's *The Rez Sisters* 307

27. Lorena Gale as "Lorena Gale" 310

28. Joy Coghill as Emily Carr in *Song of This Place* 315

29. Andrew Moodie in *A Common Man's Guide to Loving Women* 318

30. Sarah Ireland as Frances Farmer in Sally Clark's *Saint Frances of Hollywood* 323

31. R. H. Thomson and his great-uncle Arthur from *The Lost Boys* 325

32. Production photograph from Marie Clements's *The Unnatural and Accidental Women* 331

33. Guillermo Verdecchia in *Fronteras Americanas* 333

Preface and Acknowledgements

This volume of essays and interviews has been both a labour of love and a labour of many hands. The script began with "Putting a Life on Stage: A Theatre and AutoBiography Exploratory Workshop" held at the University of British Columbia in February 2004, and that event brought an invited group of playwrights, academics, actors, directors, artists, and drama publishers together to share three intense days of debate, meals, wine, coffee, and theatre discussion, and to witness the kind of ephemeral, magic moments that can only happen with theatre. From the start we all knew we could never recapture that atmosphere, which lingers now for us in personal memory. Therefore, this book is a collection of post-memories, among other things, through which we have tried to trace and recreate that event for our readers within the limits of the printed page, the photograph, and the interview. We also hope that in this *solid* form the volume will contribute to the increasingly collaborative work being done between the theatre and the academy and between Theatre Studies and AutoBiography Studies.

Neither the workshop nor this book could have happened without a great deal of help, and we would like to thank all our participants and contributors, not least those who are not represented in this volume: Mavor Moore, Robert More, Veda Hille, David Fancy, Michelle Laflamme, and Gabriele Helms. Mavor Moore, one of Canada's preeminent men of letters and of the theatre, honoured us by speaking at our closing banquet; Robert More spent weeks away from home to rehearse the play *Song of This Place*; Veda Hille blew us all away with her extraordinary songs about Emily Carr; David Fancy read a fine paper and entertained us all at the banquet; and Michelle Laflamme created our stunning web site. Gabriele Helms, our very dear young colleague and co-organizer, died in December 2004 from cancer, and in preparing this book we have kept her always in mind.

It is a more formal but nonetheless sincere thanks that we extend to Dianne Newell, Director of the Peter Wall Institute of Advanced Studies, and to the institute staff who made us so welcome and helped to finance our research; to the Theatre Department of the University of British Columbia, which mounted the play and helped behind the scenes in many ways; and to the Hampton Fund at the university, which welcomes applications from scholars undertaking unusual, interdisciplinary research that cannot be supported through more traditional agencies. A project such as ours simply could not have been imagined without this financial and intellectual support. And we do not forget the many kindnesses we have received from those who provided the illustrations; they are named in the captions. In a few cases we were unable to identify or contact the photographer, despite having made all reasonable attempts to do so. We would be happy to include these names in a new edition of the book.

Finally, it is our special pleasure to thank Linda Morra for her practical help with the preparation of the manuscript; she made time in her own busy research and teaching schedule to get us over a number of memory lapses and forgotten lines. To Davinia Yip our thanks for her care and attention to details in the production stage. To Karl and Christy Siegler of Talonbooks, once more, thank you. If this performance has legs it is because of your commitment to publishing.

Sherrill Grace and Jerry Wasserman

Theatre and the AutoBiographical Pact: An Introduction

Sherrill Grace

I

If "acting and autobiography go hand in hand," as Evelyn Hinz suggests (200), can we also think of playwriting and AutoBiography, or more specifically of the playwright and the auto/biographer, as doppelgängers? Hinz's proposal and my question raise a host of further questions and open up enticing possibilities, many of which are explored in this book. Our collective purpose in *Theatre and AutoBiography* is to identify, analyse, and debate the issues that arise when contemporary drama meets biography and autobiography on stage or page because variations on these relationships (one set of which is signalled by the double capitalization in AutoBiography or by the slash in auto/biographical to indicate the interdependence of the two genres) seem extraordinarily popular amongst today's artists, theatre practitioners, readers, and audiences. Something is going on out there in front of the lights; someone's *real* life story is being staged, performed, revealed, or re-discovered, and we have been invited to watch, participate in, and discuss the show.

But just what are these so-called *real* life stories? Why are they popping up so frequently? How do these stories, when created in a play and presented in live performance, differ from the many other forms of contemporary life writing that enjoy such immense popularity today, at least in Western culture? How does the playwright function as an auto/biographer and what challenges does the auto/biographical playwright create for his or her own biographer? And where, in all this life-storying, does the theorist, theatre historian, or critic fit in? In this brief introduction I cannot hope to answer these questions or even identify all the issues—that is the work of the following chapters. What I can do, to some small degree, is set the stage, move a few key props into position, and provide you with a quick cue-to-cue.

That both autobiography and biography have acquired a position of unprecedented importance over the past thirty years is now obvious (see, for example, Gilmore 2001, 1, and Alpern et al. 5). Less obvious, or less often examined, are the reasons for this phenomenon. Theorists and students of AutoBiography, a research subject now viewed as respectable in academic circles, have mapped the contours and shifting parameters of the autobiographical and, to a lesser degree, the biographical processes, thereby contributing to the profile and stature of both. This collection contributes to current debates in both Theatre and AutoBiography Studies by clarifying the role of AutoBiography in the theatre. For me, the most exciting contribution these chapters make to our thinking about AutoBiography lies in their critical attention to the creative conjunction of theatre and the auto/biographical; not only is this critique fairly new and innovative (certainly in such a sustained and multifaceted manner), but, I believe, theatre enables us to investigate the current appetite for AutoBiography from new angles and, therefore, to gain fresh insight into the underlying reasons for its popularity. There is something about the live performance of a play before a witnessing, reacting, participating audience that accentuates what is crucial in life stories *and* unique to theatre. And there is something fundamental to the life and work of an actor or playwright that foregrounds the performance of living and thereby complicates the biographical recreation of that life.

In general terms, AutoBiography—whether as prose memoir, biography, feature film or documentary life story (another hugely popular form in Europe and North America at present), portraiture, photography, "reality TV" programs, online diaries (blogs), performance arts, and auto/biographical plays—appeals to audiences because we live in a culture of *me* or *I* at a time when access to this cultural production is easy. But there are other much more interesting and complex explanations for our obsession with the personal. Auto/Biographies satisfy our desire for story at the same time as they promise to give us *truths* (if not Truth), to provide meaning, identity, and possibly even order, in an otherwise incoherent, arbitrary, and often violent world. They seem to put a human face on the abstract, impersonal forces of globalization, terrorism, and the corporatism of our so-called post-national condition. (Just reflect for a moment on the box-office success of films like *Supersize Me* or *Fahrenheit 9/11*.) They are, moreover, more democratic than many other forms of communication, and this is especially true of autobiography. While it is not accurate to claim that *anyone* can write a memoir or keep a diary or create a blog or stage a performance piece on their life (economics, access, and education are not equally available), the autobiographical voice and eye/I are available to minorities and to groups, such as women, who have been excluded from the dominant discourse and whose stories have been dismissed as worthless. With the post-postmodern return of the author and the waning of a deep-seated anti-humanism associated, in Western culture, with modernist ideology and aesthetics, a desire for agency, voice, visibility, and subjectivity has surfaced, clamouring for attention and seeking ways to create meaningful identity (personal and public, individual and communal) in the face of contemporary dehumanization, fragmentation, trauma, and commodification. While this predilection for AutoBiography no doubt satisfies a basic voyeuristic impulse (and does well in the marketplace), it also represents a crucial site for inscribing and preserving cultural memory. Indeed, AutoBiography and memory are inextricable, no matter what genre or medium is doing the auto/biographical work.

It is my contention, shared by the contributors to this volume, that the relationship between AutoBiography and Theatre Studies is a highly productive one and that over the past thirty years, at least in the English-speaking world, we have seen a proliferation of plays and performance works that take biography and autobiography as their subjects. From Michael Frayn's *Copenhagen* and *Democracy* or Pam Gems's *Stanley* to several plays by Adrienne Kennedy and Michel Tremblay to Edward Albee's *Three Tall Women* or Sharon Pollock's *Doc* and *Moving Pictures*, major playwrights have put the lives of real people or aspects of their own life stories on stage. Or perhaps I should say that they have *created* life stories about themselves and others that portray familiar historical figures or explore personal identity within a wider socio-historical context that resonates with audiences. To be sure, playwrights have written auto/biographical plays before—*The Glass Menagerie* (1945), *Long Day's Journey into Night* (1956), *Krapp's Last Tape* (1958), *After the Fall* (1964), and *Betrayal* (1978) are all, to varying degrees, just such plays. However, Samuel Beckett and Arthur Miller would reject this categorization of their plays, no matter how nuanced and carefully argued the claim.[1] The more contemporary playwrights whom I have mentioned, along with many others who are discussed in the following chapters, are less likely to reject, or even resist, the notion. While they will dismiss narrow labels and express concern over reductive analogies, they know they are working with life stories, creating biographical fictions, openly exploring auto/biographical concerns, and often inventing new ways of presenting biography within autobiography, of dramatizing autobiography through biography, or of illustrating how the performance of a life story can constitute, as well as represent, the life-as-lived.

When performed, these auto/biographical plays become what Elin Diamond has called "the site in which concealed or dissimulated conventions might be investigated" (5). In Jill Dolan's phrase, they often "*reveal* performativity" (431), and by doing so they examine a number of intertwined contemporary questions about identity, subjectivity, truth, and memory. At their best, auto/biographical plays are profoundly philosophical; they probe and weigh what it means to claim a personal or national identity—to use the first person pronoun and assert *I* (or even *not I*)—to make ethical choices that affect, or have affected, the actual lives of other real people, and they challenge the social construction of identity by staging processes of identity formation that invite audiences to see themselves and others as able to recreate identity and to reassert personal agency. At their best, these plays use the facts of a personal story to make us rethink the concept of *self* and the relationship of *self* to other.[2] That they can do all this while also remembering individual and collective pasts or giving voice and embodiment to marginalized, forgotten, or devalued lives only adds to their significance. And, at their best, these plays are deeply engaging (for readers and audiences); they entertain, as theatre must do, and they are often funny as well as, at times, harrowing.

In trying to understand how auto/biographical plays work and where to locate the source of their wide appeal, I return to Philippe Lejeune's concept of the autobiographical pact with which a reader, viewer, or participant must comply (1989, 124–26). As Lejeune explains, when we sign on to this pact we expect to be told the truth about someone's life, we believe that the people we encounter are *real*, that they live outside the text and go to the bank and grocery store as we do, and we bring this expectation to autobiography and biography (as to portraiture, documentary film, blogs, and family photograph albums) *despite our realization that we are engaged with art, not life.* Furthermore, additional expectations arise when the AutoBiography takes place on stage because the identities being performed live are inescapably embodied and performative, as several recent theatre theorists engaged in the performance/performativity debate have demonstrated.[3] It is surely no coincidence that so much of the recent theory in both AutoBiography and Theatre Studies has been feminist in orientation, even when it can be usefully applied to non-feminist issues and texts, because such an approach recognizes the erasure of certain identities, voices, and bodies and exposes the interpellation, within a dominant Western ideology, of all identity—to the advantage of some and the great disadvantage of others. But this is precisely where auto/biographical plays, at least in performance, hold out such promise: if Diamond, Dolan, and Geraldine Harris are correct (as I believe they are), then what Harris calls the "performativity of performance" (23) facilitates change by identifying essentialized and constructed conditions of self production, by *playing* with these conditions and, in the process of performance, by recreating identities. While some performance work may have "a basis in autobiography" (37) and therefore, as Harris argues, be *especially* responsive to performative reconfigurations of the self, I believe that many auto/biographical plays *also* invite us to re-think who we are and how we come to see ourselves—and others—as changing human beings with some degree of agency and the capacity to remember.

But just as playwrights find innovative ways to dramatize life stories and, in the process, question the nature of identity, so too are contemporary biographers and autobiographers reinventing genres that have been around in Western culture for a very long time, in fact, since Augustine with his auto/biographical *Confessions* or Agnellus, a Roman biographer who proudly claimed of his biographees, "I invented lives for them and I do not believe them to be false" (quoted in Gould and Staley 90). Biography is simply not written as it was in Dr. Johnson's day, or even in Virginia Woolf's, although her *Orlando* would have satisfied Agnellus. Today, biographies are not restricted to famous male politicians, military leaders, or artists, and they no longer presume to capture and fix the unchanging essence of their subject any more than they impose rigid teleologies on the shifting sands of a life story. Some of the best biographies are of minor figures within a larger cultural scene, and the remembering of that scene is as important as the individual life. Playwright-biographer Ken Mitchell goes so far as to insist that the lesser known the figure, the safer (indeed, more free) the playwright is when constructing a successful *drama* from the facts, and the more conventional and flawed, or basically human, the subject is, the more appealing and culturally resonant his or her dramatic recreation will be (265–72). As yet, the *art* of biography has been less studied and theorized than the art of autobiography, but the two genres have never existed entirely independently; any biographer worth her salt knows the importance (and the seductive dangers) of autobiographical materials like letters, diaries, journals, and personal memoirs.[4] And no autobiographer can tell his personal story without infringing on the biographies of others, without, in fact, tacitly acknowledging what Paul John Eakin calls the relationality of identity (43–44). Thus, to a significant degree, the theory of autobiography informs the biographer's task, and the constraints on the biographer (even the playwright-biographer) highlight the fabrications and the fictional process (of selected detail, repressed facts, tricks of memory, a created voice) of the autobiographer, who, after all, should never be trusted entirely.

Underlying and informing all AutoBiography, then, are two basic tools that are also deep-seated needs: story and memory. Narrative desire both motivates and structures life writing, so it is not surprising to find a great deal of critical attention paid to the narratology of all life writing (see Bal, Caruth, Eakin, Lejeune, Gilmore 1994, Marcus, Nadel, and Olney). Narrative has the capacity to reveal, organize, and create meaning. To speak of culture without story is a contradiction. It is through stories that we isolate facts, build histories, and contextualize events; it is through story that we strive to make sense of experience, discover what we accept as truths, and come to know ourselves and others (insofar as we ever do that). But without memory we cannot have recognizable narrative, stories that cohere, and contemporary Western culture strikes me as virtually obsessed with memory and acts of remembering.[5] This wide-spread obsession with memory surfaces in the private, public, local, and national attention to commemorative and physical sites of memory; recent cultural work on the First and Second World Wars in plays, films, books, art exhibitions, television programs, memorial buildings, and museums is a case in point. It is apparent in the prominence and resources granted to medical research on the brain and on the neurochemistry and physiology of memory, research no doubt spurred on by the prevalence of diseases like Alzheimer's. If we judge (and I do) by the current interest in prose memoirs, films depicting cultural memory, trauma narratives, and auto/biographical memory plays, then we are, right now, in Europe and North America, experiencing a crisis of remembering.

Various generic parallels for AutoBiography have been posited in attempts to contain what often seems like a scurrilous monster with a dubious genealogy and spurious claims to legitimacy. The most common comparison for both forms is with the novel, although historiography and portraiture are invoked by some theorists, but I am less convinced by these analogies than by the one with drama because, for a start, AutoBiography, like a play, demands a dramatic plot even when the facts must be rearranged to achieve that end. Evelyn Hinz, with whom I began this introduction, calls "drama the 'sister-art'" (196) of AutoBiography because in both endeavours it is the unfolding story *as lived*, embodied, and enacted by individuals (including actors), communities, and nations that draws us in and holds our attention. Moreover, the drama of living, much like the actual performance of a life on stage, *is a process*, subject to the vagaries of memory, scripted and experienced relationally by many participants. The play, like all auto/biographical activity, is reproducible but always different, always open to reinterpretation, at least until the final curtain ends the life. To speak this way of theatre performance, of course, is to speak in metaphors. But when such metaphors are grounded in auto/biographical plays, then they underscore the theatre's representation of what I call performative autobiographics: the creation of identities that exist in performance, that challenge fixed notions of the *self* and of *subjectivity*, and that are new each time the life story is performed.[6]

II

The discussion presented in this collection of essays began with a February 2004 workshop on Theatre and AutoBiography called "Putting a Life on Stage." Sponsored by the University of British Columbia's Peter Wall Institute for Advanced Studies (PWIAS) and supported by the PWIAS and a Hampton Research Grant, this event brought an invited group of scholars from Canada, England, and Australia together with a number of Canadian playwrights, actors, and biographers (one person often embodying all roles). Our chief goals were to discuss the scope and nature of auto/biographical work in theatre and to consider why and how Theatre Studies contributes to and advances our understanding of AutoBiography. In conjunction with this workshop, *Song of This Place*, an auto/biographical play by Joy Coghill, was produced at the Frederic Wood Theatre and all workshop participants attended a performance and contributed to the discussion of the play. We were fortunate to be able to bring Robert More to Vancouver to direct this production because, in addition to being a talented director, More had worked with the large puppets required for the play at its premiere in 1987, and he was able to train the student actor/puppeteers in this new production.[7] Coghill, who had performed in the premiere (as Frieda, the actor/playwright whose personal struggles to create the life story of painter Emily Carr constitute the play we watch), attended rehearsals, performances, and workshop sessions, and her reflections on the creative process are included in part 4 of this book. For Coghill the challenges of writing and performing *her* story of Carr's life arose from the fact that Carr is famous and her biography well known; several biographies have been written about her and many plays and documentary films already exist.[8] To further complicate matters, Carr wrote her own autobiography and maintained a jealous control over her life story; she was never a cooperative biographee, a characteristic that Coghill finally used dramatically in the play.

The workshop organizers (Jerry Wasserman, Susanna Egan, Gabriele Helms, Linda Morra, and myself) deliberately planned to throw the cats among the pigeons by bringing a small group of artists and theatre practitioners together with a small group of academics. As anyone working in the theatre or the academy knows, this kind of mixing occurs infrequently and can be problematic because we do not always speak the same language. But the purpose of the PWIAS is to promote interdisciplinary, innovative research on the assumption that the crossing of disciplinary borders and professional divides can work and can also lead to new knowledge, to shared perspectives on current issues, and to the identification of new directions for continuing creative and scholarly work.

As we expected, our debates were lively—at times heated—but we quickly settled into the realization that we were all engaged in a common endeavour and that our different approaches greatly enriched our shared experience. To be sure, the three days of the workshop were intense. But they were also fun and at times moving. When the playwrights read from their auto/biographical works, which as actors they had often performed themselves, the energy in the room was palpable. No one fortunate enough to be there will soon forget R. H. Thomson's eloquent reflections on the young men in his family whose letters home from the Great War inspired his rediscovery of these men—and of himself in them—through the writing and performing of *The Lost Boys*, or Lorena Gale's passionate memories of her mother and of her own growing up as an anglophone girl-of-colour in Montreal that led her to create and perform *Je me souviens*. For a few electrifying moments Linda Griffiths recreated *her* Gwendolyn MacEwen for us, and those moments transformed a sun-filled meeting room into the dark, tormented, and haunted space of an artist's mind.

If the academics were less mesmerizing, they were nonetheless eloquent, totally engaged with the questions before them and, at times, even theatrical. They explored a wide range of plays, theories, and themes in a collaborative effort to better identify, define, and analyse just what theatre, performance, and playwriting do with AutoBiography. As the following chapters demonstrate, the line between a life lived and the staging of a life is central to any auto/biographical play, but it is not a sharp, clear line. It is often blurred or wavering, highly ambiguous or deliberately problematized. The inescapable corporeal fact of the body as a living signifier and archive of identity presents performers, writers, and theorists alike with many fascinating questions. And there is also the live audience to consider: what does an audience expect of an auto/biographical play? What—or who—do they think they are looking at? How is the audience's role constructed by the performers, and how much knowledge can a playwright anticipate that his or her audience will bring with them to such a play? In the live theatre of AutoBiography, truth claims, the function of memory, the distinctions between fiction and non-fiction, and the creation, re-creation, or discovery of self acquire an urgency and immediacy, a capacity to engage or confront, that are unique to theatre and difficult, if not impossible, to realize in any other auto/biographical medium or genre.

Several of the contributors analyse what I see as the timely conjunction of feminist theory and AutoBiography studies, and once again this conjunction carries new force for discussions of theatre in part because of the debate surrounding the appropriation of terms like performativity and performance by theorists from other fields. Working *inside* theatre or performance studies or, more centrally still, *in the theatre*, practitioners, writers, and scholars see the theatre's representation of auto/biographical selves and the distinctions between living and acting or between a socially constructed gender identity and a rediscovered or subversive performance of gender in ways not available, or at least not as clear, to those working in other disciplines. There is no easy substitute for the living, embodied selves who meet in a theatre. And if we are trying to articulate the complex dynamic of that meeting and its potential for refashioning auto/biographical truths about subjectivity, memory, and identity, then it is, as many of the following authors note, because of the prominence today of the auto/biographical play and the solo performance. Whether they are monologues, or multi-character memory plays, or self-reflexively theatrical plays that stage the process of acting a life story or creating—before our eyes—the shared life story of a group, these plays are sites of memory (*lieux de mémoir*) that collectively help us to see who we are as individuals, communities, and nations.[9]

As the critical focus of our analysis shifts from the auto/biographical play itself to the playwright or actor *as* autobiographer and biographer or to the biographer and theatre historian writing the life of an actor, a playwright, or even a theatre company, new practical sight lines and ethical dilemmas open up. Not surprisingly, auto/biographical playwrights stress the importance of their preliminary research as well as its aesthetic transformation from something called facts into a work of art—a fiction—whose *truth* will convey meaning well beyond any personal reference. And this process of transformation, which occurs in all the arts, is especially sensitive in auto/biographical art for several reasons. Until fairly recently, the anti-personal bias of modernism dismissed the auto/biographical as self-indulgent, effeminate, and thus as a failure of art itself. Moreover, the ethics of using one's life and, inevitably, the lives of others as material for storytelling, especially when that life story is publicly staged, raises a host of concerns and places constraints on artist and scholar alike; the playwright, like the biographer, must try to assess how much of a life story is already well-known, historically documented, or considered *true*, and then decide how to shape the narrative, where to invent motivation or event, and when to abandon fact for the greater dramatic power of artistic truth. Time and again, the published auto/biographical play will carry caveats and explanations of the sort Vern Thiessen provides for *Einstein's Gift*, his award-winning play about German scientist Fritz Haber: "I am a playwright, a storyteller," he insists, and "I don't care much about breaking ... the sacred seal of historical fact" (105).

The biographer (as distinct from a biographical playwright) must likewise embrace the need for story, role-playing, invention, and the *art* of biography, while doing due diligence with research and facts. And this Catch-22 of biography may be especially ominous for a biographer who is writing the life of an actor or a playwright because these artists know what it means to perform a role far better than any politician, army general, scientist, or painter. How does the biographer respect this performativity while creating a life story that represents the theatre artist without taking the play(ing) for the life or reducing one to the pale facsimile of the other and both to a *tableau mort*? Or, when the actor/playwright creates a play that is overtly auto/biographical, how hard can the biographer lean on such a fiction before falling victim to the facts? Although the art of biography has received less theoretical scrutiny than autobiography, one idea that does surface periodically is that biography at its best, as I noted earlier, is more like a play than a novel. Thus, the challenge for today's theatre biographer may well be to dramatize the story (to show rather than merely to enumerate the facts) by establishing the socio-historical context as a set and by lighting key events, through what Ira Nadel calls "anecdotes" (9), to achieve a heightened effect. And before I drop the metaphor, which despite being metaphor does carry instructive value here, the biographer must remember—as the playwright and actor do—that the people in the story are, in important ways, characters, *dramatis personae*, each with his or her own life story, in another's drama that grants them secondary, supporting, or even walk-on parts. At the same time, these bit players are important and must be cast as interactive, dialogic presences. They are needed, in a biography as in a play, for the plot to be dramatic, for the through line to emerge clearly, and for the biographee to acquire an identity at all, to become the subject of a life story.

In my work on auto/biographical plays I have developed the hypothesis that these plays illustrate a performative auto/biographics, by which I mean that the playwright uses the theatre to embody and perform a process of self-creation, recreation, and rediscovery. If I am correct, or if this formulation is at least helpful in understanding the aesthetics, philosophical challenges, and socio-political promises of such plays, then I would go further to suggest that contemporary biography in general and theatre biography in particular can, even should, attempt a performative auto/biographics for its subject. A prose biography can never do what a live performance does. But to strive for that process, to resist the fixing and reduction of identity to formulaic, essentialized stereotypes, and to fashion a life story that defies, as Dolan says of theatre, "with gestic insistence" (435) the conventions of the socially prominent, public, singular, linear life, is surely worth the effort.

III

This book has been edited and organized by Jerry Wasserman and myself, with the assistance of Linda Morra, into four sections, but these groupings, while they reflect the shifting emphases of the chapters, are by no means prescriptive. Anyone reading straight through or back and forth across the chapters (or why not begin with part 4?) will see how congruent the arguments are and how persistently certain questions and issues arise. Part 1, "Theorizing Auto/Biographical Theatre," with contributions from Susan Bennett, Ric Knowles, Richard J. Lane, and Katherine MacLeod, focusses closely on theories of the body in performance, of personal and cultural memory, of gender and the "third space" of the actor, and of the improvisation of the self through "mirror talk" (the term is Susanna Egan's). But this theorizing is always taken back to the theatre—for Bennett, with the monologues of Spalding Gray, Karen Finley, and Adrienne Kennedy; for Knowles, with a set of "minoritized" plays and performances by artists such as Lorena Gale, Monique Mojica, and Guillermo Verdecchia (to name just three); for Lane, with an almost anti-auto/biographical play like Beckett's *Not I*; and for MacLeod, with two key monologue plays by Wendy Lill and Linda Griffiths. Part 2, "Auto/Biographical Plays," reverses the emphasis of part 1 by examining several plays within the context of theories drawn from several different sources. Thus, Patrick Leroux examines key works, impromptu plays, and autofictions by Michel Tremblay to demonstrate how extensively he stages remembered versions of his own and his family's life; and Joanne Tompkins explores "the construction of self and subjectivity" in Joan MacLeod's prize-winning play *The Shape of a Girl* and Guillermo Verdecchia and Marcus Youssef's *A Line in the Sand*, two recent Canadian plays that draw on factual accounts and contemporary events to portray the personal cost of violence.

Anne Nothof shifts from contemporary scenes of domestic and political violence to consider some of the ways in which playwrights (one British, one Canadian) portray the biography of a painter on stage; the painters are Vincent Van Gogh and Emily Carr, whose life stories test the skills of any writer brave enough to tackle them and, in the case of Coghill's *Song of This Place*, perform them *in propria persona*. Cynthia Zimmerman shifts our focus once more, this time from biography to thinly disguised—transformed might be a better term—autobiography through her discussion of Betty Lambert's *Under the Skin*, a fictional re-creation of the 1976 kidnapping of a child that made headlines in local and national newspapers and was followed avidly by other media. For Zimmerman, the questions are not only why but *how* the playwright grasps such difficult, traumatic material and uses it to carry auto/biographical weight: How does the playwright stage personal trauma, clothed in public fact, so that it gathers meaning beyond the narrowly personal? This, of course, is a question fundamental to much auto/biography, regardless of genre or medium. The last chapter in part 2 is by Louise Forsyth, who returns us to performance and to some of the issues at centre stage in part 1, but this time the performance is multiple rather than solo, an interconnected set of voices in monologues that enact auto/biography for a group of women, as much as for the individual writers and actresses on stage. Forsyth's chosen text, the 1976 Québec feminist, collaborative play called *La nef des sorcières* (literally "Ship of Witches"), was strikingly ahead of its time as an early example of innovative performance art in which a *feminist* auto/biographical pact revealed, not a series of disconnected, solitary "I's" but a collective identity produced through the voicing of shared, overlapping experiences.

Given the prominence of the actor as creator in *La nef des sorcières*, Forsyth's discussion provides a provocative entrée to part 3, "Theatre Lives," which begins with Maggie Gale's analysis of early twentieth-century autobiographies by British actresses. Gale's feminist, theatre-historical approach to these real lives requires her to examine concrete documents and social history that help her recuperate the autobiographies themselves as well as the women who wrote them. Paula Sperdakos performs a similar task for a number of long-forgotten North American actresses, several of whom disappeared behind changes in name and national affiliation. Both Gale and Sperdakos make an additional move that is strategic and theoretical; they speak emphatically in their own first person voices as women and theatre historians, thereby underscoring (as the playwrights so often do) the embedding of the autobiographical imperative within the biographical project. Denis Johnston pushes the real life investigation further in his study of a Canadian theatre company. For Johnston, the story of Totem Theatre is like a biography, for which he serves as biographer by interviewing the lead actors, combing archives and newspaper files for facts and dates, and reconstructing the story of their victories and defeats. Moreover, he is present throughout; his own story (at least where it coincides with his search for Totem Theatre) is revealed through theirs. Part 3 closes with the reflections of three biographers, Ira Nadel, Ann Saddlemyer, and myself. Nadel's singular subject is David Mamet; Saddlemyer's composite one is of George Yeats, W. B. Yeats, and the Abbey Theatre; and mine is Sharon Pollock and her family as recreated in *Doc*. But these theatre biographers share a number of common concerns, despite the differences in time, place, and biographical subject (could the arch American individualist Mamet be more sharply contrasted than with the collective creativity of the Yeatses and the Abbey?). As Nadel and Saddlemyer demonstrate, a theatre biographer, like a playwright or theatre historian, must research the facts, must have an archive—or create one—must conduct extensive detective work on his or her elusive, possibly reluctant, subject, and must then decide which skeletons to leave in the closet before raising the curtain on their (auto?) biographical performance. My challenge, as Pollock's biographer, is to determine what auto/biographical trust I can put in a play like *Doc* that resists simple truths and complicates notions of identity.

Part 4, "Creating AutoBiography on Stage," speaks for itself. Or, more precisely, the playwrights get the last word. Pollock's "Playwright: Parasite or Symbiont" is the text of the plenary lecture she gave at the workshop. Her reminder that "it is impossible to write or portray a life [because] it can only be lived" comes as an ironic Cassandra-like warning to anyone who dares to think (as Pollock has herself, after all) that they can undertake such a presumptuous, prodigious task. And yet what she describes in her own work is true for all theatre art: in the final analysis, "the only life on stage is that of the play." Jerry Wasserman conducted and introduces nine interviews that follow Pollock's piece, and in his introduction he describes the process and identifies the issues addressed by the playwrights who have contributed to this discussion of AutoBiography. It is no exaggeration to say that we are especially pleased with the artists' contributions. Their reflections on the challenges presented by their work with the stories of actual people, their often contradictory views about what constitutes *truth*, their differing assumptions about audience expectations, the ethical choices they make when writing auto/biographical plays, and the need to do extensive research, which must then be allowed to sink beneath aesthetic choices and practical theatre requirements, all provide unique and stimulating insights into the creative process. We thank them for sharing these reflections with us and with you, our readers, while emphasizing our understanding that the true life story of an auto/biographical play is the play itself in performance.

Throughout this introduction I have tried to highlight some of the broader contexts within which our collective and collaborative study takes its bearings, but no summary here can do justice to the wealth of argument and example contained in the chapters that follow. Many questions are spotlighted from different sides of the stage and with varying intensities, and some stimulating answers are presented for consideration. The playwrights discussed could scarcely be more broadly representative of British and North American drama in the twentieth and early twenty-first centuries than those gathered here, either for analysis or because they speak in their own voices: from Yeats and Beckett to Tremblay, Pollock, and Mamet; from Spalding Gray and Karen Finley to Linda Griffiths; and from Orlan to Sally Clark, R. H. Thomson, Monique Mojica, and George Seremba, the range of styles, performances, and subjectivities is extraordinary. What brings these writers and those who study or discuss them together, at least in this volume, is the auto/biographical pact, that agreement we have made with each other to believe—if only for the sake of argument—that we are being told and are watching a *real* life story. What we have collectively illustrated, I think, is that the conjunction today of AutoBiography and Theatre is more than a mere coincidence and is much more productive than the occasional self-performance might imply. For some of the reasons I have outlined, the *subject* has returned to the stage, as it has to all other forms of art (notably portraiture) and cultural expression, with a renewed vigour and passion, and it behooves us to pay close attention to what these subjects are saying. One of the messages so artfully conveyed by these plays is that personal identity matters and that it is not necessarily fixed by a set script we learn from birth. Another message that is unavoidable in these plays is that memory is rampant among us, and we should be asking ourselves why this is so.

But it would be a mistake to close on a portentous note. If AutoBiography, in all its forms, enjoys great popularity today, it is because it entertains, and auto/biographical plays are no exception. One of the most delightful reflections on this phenomenon that I know of comes from Guillermo Verdecchia's *Fronteras Americanas*, in which the playwright performs his immigrant story using two voices—his own and that of his Latino avatar, "Wideload." In the scene I am thinking of, "Verdecchia" has just told us about his first day as a small boy in a Canadian school. The teacher, a "Miss Wiseman," stumbles over the pronunciation of the child's name while the boy shrinks in mortification, imagining that he has sprouted "antennae and gills where everyone else has a mouth." [10] "Verdecchia" is about to continue his sorry life story when he hesitates— "but I don't want to go on about myself all night"—whereupon he is immediately and unceremoniously interrupted by "Wideload," his fast-talking, stereotypical Latino alter ego, who swaggers forth to pronounce,

> Thank God. I mean I doan know about you but I hate it when I go to el teatro to de theatre and I am espectin' to see a play and instead I just get some guy up dere talking about himself—deir life story—who cares? Por favor ... And whatever happened to plays anyway—anybody remember plays? Like wif a plot and like a central character? Gone de way of modernism I guess and a good thing too. (317)

And so on with the show.

Notes

1. Miller was especially hostile to descriptions of *After the Fall* as autobiographical; see Gottfried 345, 352–71. See also Knowlson on Beckett, 406–07.

2. This relationality is central to Eakin's thinking about autobiography and identity, and he does not see relationality as an exclusively feminist or feminine condition; see chapter 2 of *How Our Lives Become Stories*. See also Egan, and Smith and Watson.

3. See the arguments made by Claycombe, Diamond, Dolan, Harris, Holledge and Tompkins, Postlewait, Sidnell, and Worthen. In *Interfaces*, Smith and Watson explore issues of performance and performativity, but not in terms of theatre; for them, "the autobiographical is a performative site" (11), but this formulation ignores the discipline of theatre performance by merging it in a broader concept of performance.

4. A small number of studies of biography have appeared to date, but the theorizing of biography still lags behind that of autobiography. See Alpern et al., Epstein, Gould and Staley, Pachter, Rhiel and Suchoff, and Wagner-Martin.

5. Paul Fussell may have sparked this academic interest in memory and culture, but numerous critical studies, explicitly on memory, have appeared since 1975 when *The Great War and Modern Memory* was published. One of the more comprehensive is Peter Middleton and Tim Wood's *Literatures of Memory*, but most recent work in autobiography theory deals centrally with the connections among trauma, memory, and identity; see also Malkin, Marcus, and Sturkin. Several recent novels, plays, and films might well be described as memory-texts due to the structural and thematic stress placed on memory, or on the loss or disruption of memory: films like *Rosenstrasse* (2003), *A Very Long Engagement* (2004), and *Mémoires affectives* (2004) come immediately to mind.

6. I have discussed my concept of performative autobiographics in "Performing the Auto/biographical Pact." The term "autobiographics" is Gilmore's and I have adapted it to identify how the self is expressed and articulated—in short, *performed* in an auto/biographical play. However, the debate about performance and performativity has been closely addressed by feminist theatre specialists such as Harris, Diamond, and Dolan, and I am indebted to their analyses.

7. The play was performed in February 2004 under the direction of Robert More with sets by Robert Gardiner and puppets and masks by Trish Leeper, and with Donna White as Frieda and Barbara Pollard as Millie. The September 1987 premiere in Vancouver starred Coghill as Frieda, with Joan Orenstein as Millie Carr. It was directed by Robert More and Roderick Menzies.

8. See Anne Nothof's essay (137–51) for a discussion of this work.

9. In *Performing Canada*, Alan Filewod explores the ongoing connection between theatre and nation in Canada. He argues that "Canadian theatre can as a whole be considered as a meta-performance that literally enacts crises of nationhood" (xvii). I am increasingly interested in the way created places, or *sites*, are being invested with *imagined* national and historical significance, not just in Canada but elsewhere. See Cavell, Hirsch, and Young on this subject.

10. Although this is a decidedly autobiographical play, and at its premiere and other productions Verdecchia played himself, the role of "Verdecchia/Wideload" has been performed by other actors. I have only seen Verdecchia himself in the role (at which he was superb), so I cannot compare

productions, but I frankly find it difficult to imagine the play without him. This raises some interesting questions about authenticity, audience expectation, and identity that are inseparable from any autobiographical play which cannot always and forever be performed by its creator.

Works Cited

Abbott, H. Porter. *Beckett Writing Beckett: The Author in the Autograph*. Ithaca: Cornell University Press, 1996.

Alpern, Sara, and Joyce Antler, Elizabeth Isreals Perry, and Ingrid Winther Scobie, eds. *The Challenge of Feminist Biography: Writing the Lives of Modern American Women*. Urbana and Chicago: University of Illinois Press, 1992.

Bal, Mieke. "Memories in the Museum: Preposterous Histories for Today." In *Acts of Memory: Cultural Recall in the Present*, ed. Mieke Bal, Jonathan Crewe, and Leo Spitzer. Hanover, N.H.: University Press of New England, 1999. 171–90.

Caruth, Cathy. *Unclaimed Experience: Trauma, Narrative, and History*. Baltimore: Johns Hopkins University Press, 1996.

Cavell, Richard. "Architectural Memory and Acoustic Space." *Architecture in Canada* 29, nos. 1–2 (2004): 59–66.

Claycomb, Ryan. "Playing at Lives: Biography and Contemporary Feminist Drama." *Modern Drama* 47, no. 3 (2004): 525–45.

Coghill, Joy. *Song of This Place*. Toronto: Playwrights Canada, 2003.

Diamond, Elin. *Performance and Cultural Politics*. London and New York: Routledge, 1996.

Dolan, Jill. "Geographies of Learning: Theatre Studies, Performance, and the 'Performative.'" *Theatre Journal* 45, no. 4 (1993): 417–41.

Eakin, Paul John. *How Our Lives Become Stories: Making Selves*. Ithaca: Cornell University Press, 1999.

Egan, Susanna. *Mirror Talk: Genres of Crisis in Contemporary Autobiography*. Chapel Hill: University of North Carolina Press, 1999.

Epstein, William, ed. *Contesting the Subject: Essays in the Postmodern Theory and Practice of Biography and Biographical Criticism*. West Lafayette: Indiana University Press, 1991.

Filewod, Alan. *Performing Canada: The Nation Enacted in the Imagined Theatre*. Kamloops, B.C.: Textual Studies in Canada, 2002.

Fussell, Paul. *The Great War and Modern Memory*. New York and London: Oxford University Press, 1975.

Gale, Lorena. *Je me souviens*. Vancouver: Talonbooks, 2001.

Gilmore, Leigh. *Autobiographics: A Feminist Theory of Women's Self-Representation*. Ithaca: Cornell University Press, 1994.

———. *The Limits of Autobiography: Trauma and Testimony*. Ithaca: Cornell University Press, 2001.

Gottfried, Martin. *Arthur Miller: His Life and Work*. Cambridge, Mass.: Da Capo, 2003.

Gould, Warwick and Thomas E. Staley, eds. *Writing the Lives of Writers*. New York: St. Martin's, 1998.

Grace, Sherrill. "Performing the Auto/biographical Pact: Towards a Theory of Identity in Performance." In *Tracing the Autobiographical*, ed. Marlene Kadar, Linda Warley, Jeanne Perreault, and Susanna Egan. Waterloo: Wilfrid Laurier University Press, 2005. 65–79.

Griffiths, Linda. *Alien Creature*. Toronto: Playwrights Canada, 2000.

Harris, Geraldine. *Staging Femininities: Performance and Performativity*. Manchester: Manchester University Press, 1999.

Hinz, Evelyn. "Mimesis: The Dramatic Lineage of Auto/Biography." In *Essays on Life Writing: From Genre to Critical Practice*, ed. Marlene Kadar. Toronto: University of Toronto Press, 1992. 195–212.

Hirsch, Marianne. *Family Frames: Photography, Narrative, and Postmemory*. Cambridge: Harvard University Press, 1997.

Holledge, Julie and Joanne Tompkins. *Women's Intercultural Performance*. London and New York: Routledge, 2000.

Jeunet, Jean-Pierre, dir. *A Very Long Engagement*. Warner Brothers, France/U.S.A., 2004.

Knowlson, James. *Damned to Fame: The Life of Samuel Beckett*. London: Bloomsbury, 1996.

Leclerc, Francis, dir. *Mémoires affectives*. Montreal: Palomar, 2004.

Lejeune, Philippe. "The Autobiographical Pact (bis)." In *On Autobiography*, ed. Paul John Eakin, trans. Katherine Leavy. Minneapolis: University of Minnesota Press, 1989. 119–37.

Malkin, Jeanette R. *Memory-Theatre and Postmodern Drama*. Ann Arbor: University of Michigan Press, 1999.

Marcus, Laura. *Auto/biographical Discourse: Theory, Criticism, Practice*. Manchester: University of Manchester Press, 1994.

Middleton, Peter and Tim Woods. *Literatures of Memory: History, Time and Space in Postwar Writing*. Manchester: Manchester University Press, 2000.

Mitchell, Ken. "Between the Lines: Biography, Drama, and N. F. Davin." In *Biography and Autobiography: Essays on Irish and Canadian History and Literature*, ed. James Noonan. Ottawa: Carleton University Press, 1993. 263–72.

Nadel, Ira. "Biography and Theory, or Beckett in the Bath." In *Biography and Autobiography: Essays on Irish and Canadian History and Literature*, ed. James Noonan. Ottawa: Carleton University Press, 1993. 9–17.

Olney, James. *Memory and Narrative: The Weave of Life Writing*. Chicago: University of Chicago Press, 1998.

Pachter, Marc, ed. *Telling Lives: The Biographer's Art*. Philadelphia: University of Pennsylvania Press, 1985.

Postlewait, Thomas. "Autobiography and Theatre History." In *Interpreting the Theatrical Past: Essays in the Historiography of Performance*, ed. Thomas Postlewait and Bruce A. McConachie. Iowa City: University of Iowa Press, 1989. 248–72.

Rhiel, Mary and David Suchoff, eds. *The Seductions of Biography*. New York and London: Routledge, 1996.

Sidnell, Michael. "Authorizations of the Performative: Whose Performances of What, and for Whom?" In *The Performance Text*, ed. Domenico Pietropaolo. New York, Ottawa, and Toronto: LEGAS, 1999. 97–112.

Smith, Sidonie, and Julia Watson, eds. *Interfaces: Women, Autobiography, Image, Performance*. Ann Arbor: University of Michigan Press, 2002.

Sturken, Marita. "Personal Stories and National Meanings: Memory, Reenactment, and the Image." In *The Seductions of Biography*, ed. Mary Rhiel and David Suchoff. New York and London: Routledge, 1996. 31–41.

Thiessen, Vern. *Einstein's Gift*. Toronto: Playwrights Canada, 2003.

Thomson, R. H. *The Lost Boys: Letters from the Sons in Two Acts 1914–1923*. Toronto: Playwrights Canada, 2002.

Verdecchia, Guillermo. *Fronteras Americanas (American Borders)*. Vancouver: Talonbooks, 1997.

Von Trotta, Margarethe, dir. *Rosenstrasse*. Los Angeles: Samuel Goldwyn Films, 2003.

Wagner-Martin, Linda. *Telling Women's Lives: The New Biography*. New Brunswick, N.J.: Rutgers University Press, 1994.

Worthen, W. B. "Drama, Performativity, and Performance." *PMLA* 113, no. 5 (1998): 1093–1107.

Young, James E. *At Memory's Edge: After-Images of the Holocaust in Contemporary Art and Architecture*. New Haven and London: Yale University Press, 2000.

PART ONE

Theorizing AutoBiographical Theatre

3-D A/B

Susan Bennett

> The self that is the center of all autobiographical narrative is necessarily a fictive structure.
>
> —Paul John Eakin, *Fictions in Autobiography*

I start with a quotation that has become axiomatic for contemporary critics and theorists of autobiography because, since Paul John Eakin's definitive statement, studies of autobiography have paid particular attention to the strategic fictions that the representation of a life must necessarily incur. We are by now thoroughly familiar with the interrogatory and skeptical stance that we realize ought to characterize our reading of print autobiographies. Notwithstanding this monumental overhaul of reading practice in the field of autobiography, there has remained, I want to suggest, a fundamental difficulty for—and a challenge to—our conviction that "fictions and the fiction-making process are a central constituent of the truth of any life as it is lived and of any art devoted to the presentation of that life" (Eakin 5). This is, quite simply, the body.

In print autobiographies, where the presentation of a life is substantially textual, readers inevitably give special attention to any photographs supplementing the words on the page. "The regime of visuality," as Sidonie Smith and Julia Watson remind us, "has come to play an ever larger role in written autobiographical narratives, incorporated as another mode of telling within the text" (Smith and Watson 8). Or, more directly, by Roland Barthes: "The photograph is literally an emanation of the referent" (80). Barthes's meditation on the photograph's intrinsic claim as the "that-has-been" turns on his looking at photographs of his mother, shortly after her death:

> Hence I was leafing through the photographs of my mother according to an initiatic path which led me to that cry, the end of all language: "There she is!": first of all a few unworthy pictures which gave me only her crudest identity, her legal status; then certain more numerous photographs in which I could read her "individual expression" (analogous photographs, "likenesses"); finally the Winter

Garden Photograph, in which I do much more than recognize her (clumsy word): in which I discover her: a sudden awakening, outside of "likeness," a *satori* in which words fail, the rare, perhaps unique evidence of the "So, yes, so much and no more." (109)

Of course, Barthes's exclamation notwithstanding, we know just as well that the photograph is no less manufactured than a word-based text, yet not only do we often have what seems to be an unavoidably emotional response to the content of the image, to its apparent ability to capture the "real" person, but we are also culturally trained to accept its evidentiary value. The photograph has "legal representational status, as can be seen in driver's licenses, bank cards with photographic identification, medical records, crime photographs, and passports" (Adams 6). To cite Timothy Dow Adams, "Apparently no amount of appealing to logic about the obvious distortions of photographs can quite sway viewers from the popular idea that there is something especially authentic or accurate about a photographic likeness" (4). In short, the photograph, in its representation of the autobiographical subject, has a distinctive claim to referentiality, to what we, despite everything, think of as *the real*.

If the sight of the human body in a photograph underwrites such a claim and the viewer's response substantiates it, then the moving bodies of film make this production/reception exchange even more likely. Again, as with theories of autobiography and theories of photography, recent theories of the documentary film have insisted on the genre as an essentially constructed medium, so we might expect an appeal to logic to throw the same suspicion on film's ability to autobiographize, as much as its print and photography equivalents. This is hardly so. Programmers for television channels know particularly well that the audiences for documentaries are compelled by the Barthesian "that-has-been" of filmic bodies, by the certain, evidence-based knowledge that the bodies rendered on screen are those of the people to whom these things happened, for whom these represented events were lived experience. For this reason, the autobiographic documentary is powerfully persuasive in that, even if the material has been shaped, selected, adapted, and edited, what we see—the bodies on the screen— affords us some special insight into the history under review. This brief rehearsal of the camera's relationship to the body is to prepare the way for my topic of live performance for, if we credit the filmic body with a privileged referentiality that rarely fails to intensify signification, then the sheer dimensionality of the body in live, autobiographical performance provides what might easily be seen as a frenzy of signification.

I acknowledge here Philip Auslander's persuasive impatience with unexamined ideals of "liveness"—the residual notion that "television cameras give you only 'images,' and theatre gives you living truth"—but would suggest, as with other examples already given, that Auslander's appeal to logic is quickly forgotten in the moment of autobiography rendered live in performance (42). The very quality of liveness accentuates the problem of the body for autobiography, displaying that body along an axis of two orders of signification. The first is the signification of identity, not primarily the identity that the writer constructs for him- or herself as the autobiographical project, but the identity that is a production of the body's exteriority. In its three-dimensionality, the body is not, ever, simply those identities it claims for itself, but also those identities claimed on its behalf. In live performance, there is an explicit statement of the scriptural economy that "transforms individual bodies into a body politic," as Michel de Certeau would put it (142). It is not—or at least not just—the fiction of the author, but the regulatory fiction of identity that the law requires.

On the other axis is the signification of the body as archive, the literal vessel of a somatic history. The body archives a history that may or may not be part of the performance narrative, explicitly or implicitly; it also enacts that history irrespective of the other constituents of performance and irrespective of the autobiographer's intentions for it. The live, performing body renders the script three-dimensional but it has itself been scripted, as it were, prior to its subject matter. Its very physicality—indeed, its liveness—is an account of all experiences leading to the present moment, the archive of a life lived. When there is a coincidence between the subject of the autobiographical performance and the body of the performer for that script, then the frenzy of signification produced along this axis has, for audiences, an unusually strong claim to authenticity. The fictive structures familiar to autobiographical narrative are always already written on this body and the body is always already more than the sum total. Furthermore, the lamination of signifier to referent not only stimulates a density of signs, but also raises the question "what here is real?"

In this context, the dramatic monologues of Spalding Gray are exemplary: his performance work is created out of what Gray would have the audience see as his everyday life, the quotidian experiences that make up his autobiography. As David Savran explains, "For Spalding Gray, all performance is autobiographical, not because it recreates the performer's past, but because the performer can play only himself, can project only the diversity within" (63). Gray's monologues address stories and details to constitute a sense of self, in his work as an actor as well as in his family life; cumulatively his performances explore how what might otherwise be construed as the mundane and typical becomes dramatic and exceptional. This transformation relies on a particular representation of the body—one that suggests in its appearance and demeanour that Gray is as much an everyman as his narratives would insist. Of course, this is just the kind of self as fictive structure that consumers of autobiography have long been warned against, even if the live presence of the performer's body works to disavow such a caution. For this reason, it is important to examine Gray's creative practice and his own particular development of autobiographical performance.

Gray had trained as an actor at Emerson College and had worked in mainstream American theatre (notably the Alley Theatre in Houston) before exploring the more experimental work for which he is well-known (for example, his contributions to the

Performance Group and then the Wooster Group). It was here that Gray discovered: "I no longer wanted to pretend to be a character outside myself. The streets where I encountered this other were in my body and mind" (35). His autobiographical performances are concerned, then, with that productive tension between self and other, body and mind, somatic memory and psychic recall. Gray's dissatisfaction with the impersonation of characters others had created translates, in his own compositions, to a fundamental concern with the personal.

With the Performance Group Gray first wrote dramatic pieces based on his own life—a trilogy co-written with then partner Liz LeCompte, *Three Places in Rhode Island*. The trilogy's first two pieces were multi-character, but the third in the series, *Nayatt School* (1978), took the form of a direct address to the audience by Gray. Perhaps provoked by that experience, certainly soon afterwards, Gray started on his career as a monologist with *Sex and Death to the Age 14*.[1] Gray admits that after performing *Sex and Death*, he thought, "Oh my god, I have found something, I have found a form for myself that I didn't know I was looking for" (quoted in Schechner 163). The process for that form, Gray suggests, is necessarily based in recollection: "[T]hat's a very loose and open thing, a creative thing. So my memory is my first structure. Then I listen to a tape of what I said and wonder how I can make it a little more dramatic and funny by juxtaposing a little hyperbole here and play with it a little bit there" (166). In this sense, then, Gray's work is all about identity and archive.

This dynamic of signification is exemplified in his 1993 monologue, the wittily dubbed *Gray's Anatomy*. The piece, by way of its title, takes as its starting point not only the standard reference work on the human body, consulted by all students of biology and medicine, but also the body of the performer—or, as Gray would have it, a recollection of the body of the performer. Explicitly, the title names the subject of the performance and the subject who acts on stage. This self-conscious "autoperformance," to use Deborah Geis's term (4), scrutinizes one particular bodily failure—sight problems with his left eye, eventually diagnosed as a macula pucker[2]—as the occasion for *Gray's Anatomy*; its narrative is a collection of Gray's reactions to this diagnosis. The monologue opens: "*I think it all began when* I was doing a storytelling workshop in upstate New York. I had about fifteen people I was working with. I asked them to sit in a circle as a kind of centering exercise before we began telling stories, and just look into each other's eyes. Not to speak but to just look into each other's eyes—and when they got tired of looking into one person's eyes they could move on to someone else's" (3).[3] Thus the telling of stories—as Gray has defined it, the business of his dramatic monologues—is inspired not by words but by bodily action, on the premise that looking into the eyes of another will reveal something (about the self, about the other). This is a paradoxical truth for Gray the performer, to suggest the power of looking into the eye, the very organ that has, for him, failed. It is telling, too, that the monologue opens in a workshop Gray is teaching so that *Gray's Anatomy* starts with creative strategies for story composition, a reminder to the audience of the constructedness of his monologues at the very same time his authenticity (this is the body that taught that class) is underwritten. What Gray stages in *Gray's Anatomy* is a conflation of past and present to certify his own brand of autobiographical performance.

On stage, Gray is unprepossessing and unremarkable in many ways—a white man in late middle age, with more or less conventional appearance and attire. He creates drama from a body before the audience that seems like an unlikely companion for the hysterical and obsessive stories of his monologues. In *Gray's Anatomy*, the audience witnesses a series of manoeuvres by Gray to avoid the truth of his failed eye—or, at least, to delay the inevitable medical treatment that it requires. Rather than go through the recommended scraping of his macula, Gray looks to a Christian Science practitioner, his therapist, a Native American sweat lodge, a Californian self-healing guru, a raw vegetable diet opthalmologist, and a healer in the Philippines known as the "Elvis Presley of psychic surgeons" (60). Each is, not surprisingly, ineffective in addressing his eye problem and finally Gray goes for the macula scraping operation, the success of which he celebrates by drinking, eating, and smoking a cigar, *"everything* that could make me blind" (80).

An obsessive interrogation of selfhood permeates *Gray's Anatomy*. For instance, when Gray first sees the opthalmologist and goes through a battery of tests, he waits anxiously for the results:

> Finally the doctor comes back, but he does not come over to me. Instead he goes
> over to the telephone and calls Dr. Schecter, my optometrist, who's not in but
> has an answering machine. So Dr. Mendel begins dictating this message into Dr.
> Schecter's answering machine. He begins by saying, "Hello, Dr. Schecter, this is
> Dr. Mendel calling. First of all, I want to thank you for sending over your patient
> Gary Spalding." (8)

Here the rendition of the performer as third person object as well as the misnaming by the opthalmologist points to an always-present potential for the failure of identity. In performance, the audience is reassured by their own recognition that this is Spalding Gray, and we are asked to share both the humour and the fear provoked by a reduction of the self to a body part, rather than any fuller recognition of the individual.

When Gray realizes that the treatment for a macula pucker is an invasive "scraping," he immediately looks for other doctors and/or treatments to avoid the surgery. Significantly, he also journals about what might have caused his condition—a strategy that demands an autobiographical turn:

> First of all, I thought it might be the book—the book that I was writing, *Impossible
> Vacation*. It was simply too painful. It was about my mother's suicide, and I felt I
> really had never properly grieved for her, or mourned her, and what happened

was, my eye—my left eye just cried in a big way.... And then I began to think, no,
it was because the book was written in the first person. It was too much, *I, I, I, I,
I, I I I I I I I I I iiiiii!* (10–11)

Gray's monologue cites the body that performs it and at the same time self-
psychologizes. This sequence, as with the doctor's mistake about his "real" identity,
functions as an improvisation on subject/object relations.

Eventually, of course, Gray is persuaded to undergo the macula scraping and, despite
his extraordinary level of fear, the operation is a success: "The doctor gave me a videotape
of the operation to take home. He titled it 'Swimming to Macula Pucker.' He had a great
sense of humor" (72). The opthalmologist's archive of the operation in *Gray's Anatomy*
plays on an earlier Gray monologue, *Swimming to Cambodia* (itself based on another Gray
performance, in Roland Joffé's film *The Killing Fields* about the Pol Pot regime in
Cambodia); it fuses both the reality of the body (what he did to Gray's eye) with the nature
of performance (apparently "Swimming to Macula Pucker," as much as *The Killing Fields*,
requires players, action, and audience for its success). For all the insistence on everyday
life as the fundamental premise of the monologue, Gray reminds the viewer, again and
again, of the necessary artifice in any presentation of autobiography. Nonetheless, critics
and audiences alike have been persuaded to see his monologues as very close to the truth,
an issue Gray addressed in the context of a later work: "I am in a sticky place now because
Morning, Noon, and Night is about my family—so I am both living in it and telling about
it, which makes things extremely claustrophobic. Also, once it's done, where do I go?
How can I be a family man and do new material? Because to do new material would be
to make an ongoing soap opera of the family—which I don't want to do" (quoted in
Schechner 164).[4] The problem, Gray suggests, is how to continue to live a life rather than
direct it all toward autobiographical performance.

Gray's Anatomy provides a useful illustration of the difficulties the body creates for
autobiographical performance. It insists, persuasively, on its ability to represent what
really happened and to mitigate both the performer's and the audience's inclination to
remember the rules of fictive structure. The monologue rehearses the body's role in the
expression and claims of identity and, at the same time, insinuates a particular purchase
on its referent, "real life."

If Gray's anatomy, or at least a temporary failure of part of it, is the occasion for his
dramatic monologue, then Karen Finley's *The American Chestnut* is an explicit
territorializing of the (female) body. Like other Finley performances, this is a show with
autobiographical investments. During *The American Chestnut* the audience sees Finley
interact with and perform against both slide images and film. In one such sequence,
projected behind Finley are giant four-by-six-foot slide images of a baby's head crowning
and emerging from the mother's vagina, pictures given to Finley by a gynecologist friend.
At once these images dwarf Finley's actual body as well as hyper-realize a reductive

signification of woman as only her sexual and reproductive capacities. This, for Finley, was long overdue social commentary:

> And pregnant women today are given extensive instructions and coaching geared toward allowing them to give birth without expressing pain. There are relaxation exercises, Lamaze techniques, yoga, meditation. The idea of being serene and relaxed during childbirth is absurd to me. Labor was the most excruciating, painful experience my body has ever gone through. I had a natural childbirth and I broke my tailbone pushing my nine-pound daughter out of the birth canal. The idea that pain should not be expressed during childbirth is a cultural misogyny, a way of trying to control women's emotions. (187)

So the body in live performance can provide a critique of an assigned identity that assumes such submissive behavior at the behest of social norms, the denial of pain as proof of an appropriately docile and, indeed, female body. But it is also absolutely the case that the body in front of the audience is that one with the presumably now-healed tailbone. This is a body that has given birth in and against the medical, social, and cultural economies that *The American Chestnut* aims to resist. Its extra-performance history is available to us in every movement and gesture, whether or not these are consciously scripted acts. Indeed, it is at the very moments when Finley appears not to "act" that we believe we see the body's autobiographical and authentic past. We know, if only from the preview articles in the local newspapers, that Finley travels with her young daughter as well as her mother and thus as a daughter herself. It makes a difference, at least it does to me, that part of the archive that is Finley's performing body is a complex relationship of mothers and daughters, work and motherhood, giving birth and making art. What is generously available is the "that-has-been" from where the performance derives.

The American Chestnut also incorporates a video (first used in Finley's installation piece "The Relaxation Room") that shows Finley "squirting breast milk onto black velvet." "I am in my studio," she says, "and I take my 40 D milk-laden breasts out of my smock and lactate on to the velvet in an abstract pattern. It's hysterical. It is my response to Jackson Pollock's film *I Am Nature*" (189). This may have been an intention—to parody Pollock's work—but it also invokes other autobiographical points of reference. One of these is obviously the maternal body; another is her public identity—or, perhaps better put, notoriety—as the performance artist defunded by the National Endowment for the Arts on account of her "indecency." Both in video representation and live performance, her body carries the archive of the chocolate-smeared woman of an earlier piece, *We Keep Our Victims Ready*. And Finley recognized, too, that this last autobiographical fact would impact any reading of her new work (especially because of all the media interest in the court case). It was for this reason she sought out the American Repertory Theatre at Harvard for *The American Chestnut*'s premiere performance—she had performed there before and felt that the Theatre's personnel would provide the kind of support she would need. They not only agreed to do the show, but gave Finley access to the libraries for her research and writing. Nevertheless, Finley's anxieties were well-founded: "Before the show premiered, someone from the NEA called the American Repertory Theatre, inquiring about my nursing video, asking for a detailed description of it. The NEA wanted to know if this new show was 'indecent.' The ART staff considered it odd. They had never had inquiries about other shows" (193–94). On the day *The American Chestnut* was to open, Finley was told that a death threat had been received and that she was to have a police escort:

> There were going to be police in the wings during the performance, in the entrance to the theater, and in plain clothes in the audience. I was beside myself. I didn't know if I could go through with the show. I sat with my husband and talked it over. It's still difficult to look back and remember that this was the decision I was being forced to make on the opening night of the show—whether to risk my life or not.
>
> I decided that I had to perform—if I didn't, it would be like letting them kill me in a different way. (193–94)

For audiences who know this story, how is it possible to ignore the reality of that threat to Finley's performing body? The content of her monologue, its intentionality— autobiographical and otherwise—is radically overdetermined by what that body has done before. Finley's performances are, as Geis has noted, "notorious for … their intensely visceral/corporeal emphases" (160).

Finley had created the sequence where she covered her body with chocolate as a way to talk about the Tawana Brawley case—in which a sixteen-year-old African-American female had been found semi-conscious in a trash bag, covered in human excrement. Brawley said she had been raped by white police officers—an accusation she was soon accused of inventing. Finley writes: "I knew that I could never go emotionally where Brawley had been…. In the piece that grew out of this [case], I smeared my body with chocolate, because, I said in the piece, I'm a woman, and women are usually treated like shit" (84). But irrespective of what she *said* in *We Keep Our Victims Ready* or how she explained the performance thereafter, the NEA deemed it offensive and her public body came to signify all that was indecent and inappropriate about contemporary and especially feminist art. Finley was demonized by the Right in many different venues far outside of either art or theatre: "[Rush] Limbaugh said that I had sex and masturbated on stage, that I used real feces in my work. I eventually had to take legal action to put him on notice that what he was saying about me was untrue, and that, if he persisted in saying such things, it could legally be considered 'with malice' and slanderous. He shut up" (150).

All of this is to illustrate that Karen Finley's body is itself in public circulation, primarily because of her insistence in her performance work that she has a body, and that its effects are borne significantly in her life. The body is not protected by the contextual framework of art, nor can it escape from its accumulation of signification outside the aesthetic practice itself, and, thus, there can hardly be a more explicit example of a body rendered as the culmination of the identities claimed for it in the larger social/cultural domain. Even in a friendly press, in an attempt to lodge a countervailing image of Finley's body, *New York Times* writer Mel Gussow can only find different stereotypes to do this work. In an article published to coincide with the PS 122 run of *The American Chestnut*, Gussow commented,

> Just off the main street of this small Hudson River town [Nyack] is a large, rambling house, a converted barn built in 1886. In the garden, a gray-haired woman is puttering and pruning. Inside the house is a catacomb of rooms filled with old and antique furniture. It is a jumble of work and play, the play area belonging to a 4-year-old named Violet, who attends school nearby. The homey environment and the three generations of occupants—grandmother, mother and daughter—are like an image of Victoriana thrust suddenly into the modern age.
> With her long hair and her blouse and long skirt, the 41-year-old lady of the house looks as if she might have been posing for a portrait by Sargent. She is, however, Karen Finley, the performance artist whose name is synonymous with controversy, the "chocolate-smeared woman" of Senator Jesse Helms's nightmares. (E1)

Apparently, the only available corrective to the explicit body of rank indecency perpetuated by Helms, Limbaugh, and others is a differently reductive recuperation of her body for a myth of bourgeois American life. Gussow's portrait just as certainly (and with a lot more charm, to be sure) instates those regulatory fictions that insist, in so-called real life, that women's bodies behave according to a few limited scripts.

The singularity of autobiographical subject, author, and performer can hardly fail to create, as I have suggested, an over-investment of spectatorial response in corporeal evidence against which we might better understand the narrative, by sifting through its more or less fictive truths. If there is only one speaking/moving body, then it is hardly surprising that it is the focus of our interpretive energies. And it seems to me self-evident that the body has the ability to produce signification that the autobiographical subject, author, and performer cannot necessarily restrict, far less control. Thus, the body instates the problematic of identity as well as its own physical presence, and that somatic history, past and present, inspires an unusually deep field of signification. Geis has, for example, criticized scholarship on Karen Finley's "oeuvre [that] has focus[sed] on these visual elements almost to the exclusion of their verbal texts" (161)—but this only demonstrates how emphatically the body drives narrativization in Finley's work, as it does so often in the solo autobiographical performance.

An autobiographical play that is highly unlikely to put the autobiographer's actual body in front of a theatre audience might, then, seem to be entirely different. The shaping of the autobiography as a script for more than one actor, the constituents of dramatic realization—the set, the design, the costumes, the lighting, and so on—as well as the embodiment of real-life subjects by actors would seem, at first glance, to allow, even more than print autobiographies, for a critical distance from the subject him- or herself. I am not sure, however, if this is necessarily so. Even in the case of a non-coincident body, the capacity remains, by virtue of both the dimensionality of the performing bodies and their "liveness," to work along the same axis of signification: of identity and of archive.

My example here is Adrienne Kennedy's Obie-winning play *Sleep Deprivation Chamber*—a play Kennedy co-wrote with her son Adam based on an event in his life. In short, the autobiographical detail is this: one evening Adam Kennedy had been driving home to his father's house in Virginia when he was pulled over by a police officer for a broken tail light on his car. A block from his father's home, Kennedy had slowed to fifteen miles an hour and then turned into the driveway where he was subsequently beaten by the police officer. Kennedy was arrested for assault and battery. *Sleep Deprivation Chamber* is, then, an autobiographical meditation on the events of that night.

One reviewer described the play's "unsettling power" as follows: "It is indeed as if the demons that have long inhabited Ms. Kennedy's artistic imagination have been given grotesque external form, as if real life had confirmed her darkest intuitions" (Brantley C11). *Sleep Deprivation Chamber* is, in any case, an example of the latest installment of Kennedy's autobiographical dramas where she has used the character Suzanne Alexander—whose family exactly mirrors Kennedy's own. The play's first full description of what has happened to Teddy Alexander (Adam Kennedy) comes from Suzanne (Adrienne Kennedy) in epistolary form, to the state governor on her son's behalf:

> Dear Governor Wilder:
>
> My name is Suzanne Alexander. I am a black writer. I have written you once before in February. I am writing to you again about the Arlington, Virginia, Police Department.
>
> (*Scene of Teddy and Police Officer. Flashing red and white lights and the image of a car. A white Officer moves towards Teddy.*)
>
> TEDDY: Officer, what seems to be the problem? Can I help you?
>
> OFFICER: Get back in the car.
>
> TEDDY: Officer, what seems to be the problem? I live here, this is my house. Can I help you? (*Fade.*)
>
> (*Light on Suzanne.*)
>
> SUZANNE: (*Continues letter to Governor Wilder.*)
> We are an outstanding black American family. My former husband, David, is head of Africa/USA. My plays and stories are published and taught widely.

> We are now a grieved family. Our son is being persecuted by the Arlington
> Police Department just as surely as happened in the Deep South in the 1930s or
> during Emmett Till's time. (8–9)

Suzanne's letter continues with a description of the incident and their complaint of persecution, pointing out, "My son has never been in any trouble at all. He is a fine citizen and student at Antioch College." She is also clear about the family's demands—that they want the "false charges dismissed" (8–9). Because this is the first account of the events that constitute the autobiographical content of this play, it is important to pay attention to the strategies mobilized both in the description and the defence that the letter attempts. Its opening is precisely a recourse to identity, those attributes that Suzanne claims for herself and her family: "We are an outstanding black American family." It also claims for Teddy the narrative of his college success and ambitions (a postscript to the letter outlines his successes as a theatre practitioner as well as a published scholar), a palpable statement of class. Events are described from his perspective and contextualized by black American history (lynchings in the 1930s, the murder of Emmett Till in the 1950s). Suzanne's letter insists on historicizing what is otherwise an incident the effects of which are felt only in the immediate domestic circumstances of the Alexanders.

Sleep Deprivation Chamber uses a remarkable range of what Derrida would call "prostheses for so-called live memory"—letters, flashbacks, dream scenes (which is to say, nightmares—one recurring for Teddy as an interrogation by a character identified in the play as the "Unseen Questioner"), interactions between family members, interviews with police, interviews with lawyers, and a representation of the trial itself. No single mode is given authority in its retrieval of events; in fact, in most cases, the representations cut across each other as they did in the sequence quoted above. Together they combine to give the audience a multi-perspective picture of the events of 11 January as well as some sense of the felt experience for all the family members in the aftermath of that night.

Sleep Deprivation Chamber also elaborates on Teddy's trial with a cross-examination of the police officer in a substantial scene (some fifteen pages in print form), but this sequence seldom develops the kind of flow that might allow the audience to become absorbed in the presentation of evidence. Instead the trial is interrupted first by a memory/flashback sequence of Teddy's—an earlier occasion when he and his cousin were pulled over by police in Beverley Hills, wondering what they were doing in that part of town (a scene of graphic verbal violence which turns on the police officers' assumption that two young black men driving a Jaguar in Beverley Hills must be criminals). Other interruptions to Officer Holzer's testimony are another dream of Teddy's involving interrogation by the Unseen Questioner, two dreams of Suzanne's about her Cleveland childhood and her own father's campaigns for the betterment of Negro life, and, finally, a flashback scene with Teddy that recreates three-dimensionally on stage the events of the night. In this sequence, the audience witnesses the officer beating Teddy as Teddy's brother runs out of the house to discover what is happening and hears the voice of David Jr. (presumably on a cellphone): "Police, a police officer is beating up my brother, please send help. 5943 Riverdale Road. (*Yells*.) Dad, the police are beating up Teddy" (56). A following stage direction reads:

> *Spotlight shines on Teddy. After dragging Teddy diagonally across the cement drive Officer Holzer slams Teddy's face down to the ground. Teddy lands on the dirt and wet leaves, his head just inches away from smashing into a cluster of large rocks. Officer Holzer pulls Teddy's right arm upward and kicks him several more times in his chest and then places the handcuffs on him. Another officer appears and helps Officer Holzer pull Teddy up. David Alexander follows David Jr. out of the house and stands in the front yard. The officers place Teddy spread-eagle, his upper body placed flat on the car, his face turned sideways, his legs spread wide open, on top of the front of a police car. Two more officers surround Teddy, pinning him down on the hood of the car. Teddy is dazed and can barely breathe. David Jr. in background quietly films this with camcorder.*

Like Suzanne's letter to Governor Wilder, this passage bears examination for the multiplicity of identities it invokes. This provides evidence that Teddy is the victim of the police officer's unnecessarily violent acts—behavior that turns, we are to understand, on racial hatred, the white police officer's fear and contempt for the black male body. Yet, the framework for this critique is the Alexanders' class privilege: David Jr. uses his cellphone to summon help, ironically the help of the very police force attacking Teddy, and then switches technologies to the camcorder so that he may collect reliable evidence (the camera does not lie).

The play, in the end, is about a surfeit of evidence that indicates, in the eyes of the law, insufficient evidence to prosecute. In Adam Kennedy's case, the judge dismissed the charges and Kennedy later won a civil suit against Arlington County (Brantley, C11). In *Sleep Deprivation Chamber*, the action ends after the judge dismisses the case, with a stage direction: "*Bright light on Teddy, sitting alone in courtroom. He remembers his family at the table in Edelstein's [his lawyer's] office watching film of his beating. The film is very dark and filled with the sounds of his screams*" (59). De Certeau wonders, "Perhaps all experience that is not a cry of pleasure or pain is recuperated by the institution" (149), and all of my autobiographical performance examples perhaps demonstrate that to be true. But, unlike the solo performances of Finley and Gray, we must remember here that *Sleep Deprivation Chamber* relies on actors to whom the literal events have not happened—their cries of pain are substitutes for the real thing. And the play itself makes precisely this point in its insistence on a metatheatrical context for the autobiographical history. Suzanne's letter to Governor Wilder is the first description of those brutal events of 11 January, but *Sleep Deprivation Chamber* does not start here. It starts instead in the rehearsal room.

Winter. Antioch College Theatre Department. Backstage with a view of the rehearsal hall and stage. In the rehearsal hall is a long table. The Student Cast sits with scripts and books, their voices are muted. The rehearsal hall and backstage are almost dark. Suzanne sits at a dressing table writing.

STUDENT CAST: Ophelia, betrayal, disillusionment.

(Suzanne looks toward doorway at the end of the rehearsal hall, she's an African-American writer mid-fifties. She wears winter coat, scarf.)

Ophelia, betrayal, disillusionment.

(Through the door at the end of the rehearsal hall comes Teddy, Suzanne's son. He is a slight young man, twenty-one, sallow skin like his mother's, black hair already thinning, glasses, wearing rehearsal clothes. He joins Student Cast at table. He is the director.)

The murder of the sleeping king.

(Suzanne puts her head down on the dressing table.)

Asleep at the moment of his murder. (7)

The play, then, starts in the theatre—or, more accurately, in that incubator for performance, the rehearsal. For my purposes here, let me just underscore two elements of this opening strategy—the first is its reference not to the events of 11 January but to Shakespeare's tragedies (*Othello* then *Hamlet*) and the second its metatheatrical framing of evidence (that the bodies here are only impersonations of those to whom these things happened). On the one hand, I think, this opening summons a common humanity among all of us, the very quality we understand to have given Shakespeare's tragedies their longevity; on the other hand, that Adam Kennedy and his mother are presented as the prosthetic characters Teddy and Suzanne Alexander, embodied by actors, suggests a chain of identification that mobilizes shared experience and lived history between African-American bodies. This embraces the actors, of course, some or all of whom may have found the events remarkably familiar; it also extends, obviously, to African-American spectators. For this audience and the actors alike, they are only a broken tail light away from the reality *Sleep Deprivation Chamber* explores. Kenneth Mostern, in his study of African-American autobiography, has noted that the field of African-American studies has "tended to place autobiography in a relatively stable location in the field: where 'I' tends to have a determinate relation to a specifically racial 'we'; and where the text provides for its audience a way to symbolize racialization as a version of the real" (30–31). The Alexanders—or the Kennedys—of *Sleep Deprivation Chamber* produce the body as archive, only to make it a rehearsal for those scripts of the law that, in the act of instantiation, require certain bodies to be punished. The autobiographical project is at once personal yet committed to a larger field of signification. We are not yet beyond the need to remind ourselves that the personal is political.

Each of these autobiographical performances, in different ways and against different bodies, draws on a relationship between individual life experiences and those scripts that constitute normative performances in our contemporary culture. The criss-crossing of the law and the stage marks their similarities in that these autobiographical performances circulate on regulated and prohibited identities. The body, above all else, makes these performances both more and less reliable than their written equivalents, for it claims a special purchase on the real, incites the evidence of the past, and promises, for the audience, a three-dimensional text. We witness identity in all of its legislation and in all of its constructedness. Against this complexity of signification, there is the ever-present archive on which the performing body must depend. This is, in the end, live performance's contribution to autobiographical praxis. As Derrida says of the archive: "One will never be able to objectivize it with no remainder. The archivist produces more archive, and that is why the archive is never closed. It opens out of the future" (68)—and so, it seems to me, does performance.

On 7 March 2004, Spalding Gray's body was found in New York's East River, almost two months after he had been reported missing by his wife. The performer's battles with depression, seriously exacerbated after a terrible car crash during a vacation in Ireland in 2001 (a trip to celebrate Gray's sixtieth birthday), had been well documented and he appears to have committed suicide by jumping from the Staten Island Ferry. This awful conclusion to Gray's disappearance makes the title of the last monologue he had worked on, *Life Interrupted*, seem tragically predictive. But Gray's monologues (in print and in video/DVD formats) remain when his body cannot. The recordings are literally and compellingly an archive but they are a reminder, too, that, detached from live performance, the self of autobiography is, emphatically, always a fictive structure.

Notes

1. In an interview, Gray suggests that the title was not his but was suggested by either Richard Schechner or Liz LeCompte. See Schechner 163.

2. The macula is the area at the centre of the eye's retina and it allows for clear vision. If the macula is damaged (and the macular pucker indicates a wrinkle on the macula), then some vision loss can occur and straight lines often appear as wavy. Surgery is recommended if the macular pucker interferes with normal daily activities. See the American Academy of Ophthalmology web site: www.aao.org.

3. The DVD version of Gray's *Gray's Anatomy* (published in 2002 from a 1997 recording) has both small editorial and more significant changes to the book version. It is also of note that the DVD is described as based on the monologue by Gray and Renee Shafransky (his first wife). The book names only Gray as author.

4. *Morning, Noon, and Night* was published in 1999 (New York: Farrar, Strauss & Giroux).

Works Cited

Adams, Timothy Dow. *Light Writing and Life Writing: Photography in Autobiography*. Chapel Hill: University of North Carolina Press, 2000.

Auslander, Philip. *Liveness: Performance in a Mediatized Culture*. London: Routledge, 1999.

Barthes, Roland. *Camera Lucida*. Trans. Richard Howard. New York: Hill & Wang, 1981.

Brantley, Ben. "Righting a Wrong in a World out of Joint." *New York Times*, 27 February 1996, C11.

de Certeau, Michel. *The Practice of Everyday Life*. Trans. Steven Rendall. Berkeley: University of California Press, 1984.

Derrida, Jacques. *Archives Fever: A Freudian Impression*. Trans. Eric Prenowitz. Chicago: University of Chicago Press, 1996.

Eakin, Paul John. *Fictions in Autobiography: Studies in the Art of Self-Invention*. Princeton: Princeton University Press, 1985.

Finley, Karen. *A Different Kind of Intimacy: The Collected Writings of Karen Finley*. New York: Thunder's Mouth Press, 2000.

Geis, Deborah R. *Postmodern Theatric(k)s: Monologue in Contemporary American Drama*. Ann Arbor: University of Michigan Press, 1995.

Gray, Spalding. "About *Three Places in Rhode Island*." *The Drama Review* 23, no. 1 (1979): 31–42.

———. *Gray's Anatomy*. New York: Vintage Books, 1994.

Gussow, Mel. "The Other Life of Karen Finley: 'I Try to Fix Things,' Says a Startling Performance Artist." *New York Times*, 22 September 1997, E1.

Kennedy, Adrienne and Adam P. Kennedy. *Sleep Deprivation Chamber*. New York: Dramatists Play Service, 1996.

Mostern, Kenneth. *Autobiography and Black Identity Politics: Racialization in Twentieth-Century America*. Cambridge: Cambridge University Press, 1999.

Savran, David. *The Wooster Group 1975–1985: Breaking the Rules*. Ann Arbor: UMI Research Press, 1986.

Schechner, Richard. "My Art in Life: Interviewing Spalding Gray." *The Drama Review* 46, no. 4 (Winter 2002): 163.

Smith, Sidonie, and Julia Watson, eds. *Interfaces: Women, Autobiography, Image, Performance*. Ann Arbor: University of Michigan Press, 2002.

Documemory, Autobiology, and the Utopian Performative in Canadian Autobiographical Solo Performance

Ric Knowles

In the intimate confines of Mount Allison University's Windsor Theatre, on a bone-chillingly cold night in February 2002, Emily Taylor stood alone on a stage that was empty except for a single porcelain toilet, stage centre.[1] As the lights came up for her autobiographical solo show, *Bathroom*, she walked "*confidently downstage*" and confided, "I've spent my life in a bathroom" (1). The show continued, genially at first, as the audience was taken on a tour of public and private washrooms, focussing on degrees of convenience and cleanliness and on familiarly awkward situations in which public washrooms are locked, or, once opened, the stalls *won't* lock; the place is filthy, the toilet seats are scarred with cigarette burns, the toilet paper dispenser is ripped off the wall, or the cubicles are etched with innocuous, gratuitous, informational, or "philosophical" graffiti. As the tour continued, however, our empathetic intimacy with the performer having been established, the criteria upon which each washroom was judged—its privacy, the quality of its soundproofing, the availability of sturdy paper towels, and the capacity of its toilets to resist backing up—surfaced gradually as those of a bulimic. The performance proceeded through increasingly graphic first-person accounts of the obsessive ingestion and regurgitation of vast quantities of food; of a roller coaster of weight gain and loss over ten years; of the lies, evasions, excuses, and other strategies used to avoid detection; of the parents, friends, boyfriends, psychologists, psychiatrists, nutritionists, counsellors, workbooks, diet plans, and twelve-step programs that had been tried but had failed to help; and of the ravages that the body we were watching had suffered and continued to be marked by.

At least initially, the show presented itself as the familiar confessional narrative of someone who has gone through hell and come out on the other side. It staged a powerful critique of the societal policing of the female body image, and it was not without its entertainment value, including black humour: "Bless me Father for I have binged. / It has been one half hour since my last concession stand" (10). This particular example, not incidentally, parodied the autobiographical confessional form that is both the object of Foucault's analysis in *The History of Sexuality* (61) and the familiar genre in which the show itself participated. But the show's ending was unusual and extraordinarily powerful. After delivering a heart-wrenching account of her "unforgiveable" mistreatment of her parents, friends, family, and partner, including an acknowledgement of her condition's relationship to alcohol and drug addiction (14), and in the immediate wake of a powerful and abusive address to her own unruly, abjected body (an address to which I will return), Taylor retrieved a large, gooey apple fritter from a paper bag that had been pre-set inconspicuously downstage right, returned to centre stage, and devoured it with what the stage directions call *"evident and uncouth enjoyment"* in a split second that seemed to a rapt audience like an eternity. The donut finished, she looked up, paused, and politely delivered the show's final line: "[E]xcuse me. I have to go to the bathroom" (17).

The moment carried with it a phenomenological *frisson* similar to that of witnessing the high-school-visit recovery narrative of an alcoholic or "reformed drug addict" that ended with the speaker taking a drink or shooting up.[2] It represented a particularly graphic and powerful example of the phenomenological challenge to semiology's dictum that "everything on stage is a sign," an instance of the way in which the embodied "real" can exceed representation, or, in the late Bert States's terms, not be "consumed in its sense" (27). In some ways the moment recalled the more graphic and sensational efforts of performance artists such as Chris Burden and Vito Acconci in the 1970s to embrace "liveness," eschewing the theatre's supposed entrapment in mimesis, representation, repetition, and the always already performed—Burden's *Shoot*, for example, involves his anti-mimetically being shot in the arm with a rifle. "[G]etting shot," he said, "is for real" (quoted in Carlson 103). But *this* moment *gained* in impact through its very repeatability. For of course the audience knew that that same recovering, bulimic body would ingest that donut, in that fashion, *every time the show was performed.*

But it is also important to note that the moment did not simply or unproblematically reinscribe what Philip Auslander has called "liveness," what Ann Wilson has referred to as "the nostalgic belief that theatre involves presence" (1994, 35), or the naïve faith, still inscribed in the most progressive actor training, that "the body cannot lie." Indeed, the show turned on a confrontation between the discursive "I" as social and grammatical "subject" and the *culturally and discursively produced and abjected* body. In the monologue that immediately preceded the ingestion of the donut, Taylor staged, almost equally shockingly, what might best be understood as a graphic autobiographical moment of self-alienation, of separation between the self as it is produced through language and the material, explicitly sexualized, abjected female body:[3]

> [Y]ou're out of here, bitch, whore. I'm going to torment you until you leave my
> body you fat fuck because you can't do this to me you fuck, not this time, you can't
> take me back there you self-indulgent bitch because I will not go, not this time I

will not ever again I am going to starve you until you are dead and I can be free, and if God has any mercy he will let me out and away from you, you cunt. Get out of my fucking body you whore. I will kill you this time you fucking whore, so help me God get out. You're going to die. I won't allow you to do it, not this time, you can't turn me into that again. This time I'm in charge and you DIE. (16)

"I've never told this to anyone before," she continued. "I really haven't."

Oh God. It's too fucking easy to lie!

(*Silence.*)

(*She finally gets an idea. Looks up. She takes a deep breath.*) (17)

The eating of the donut that followed—"*this* is not a lie," she asserted (17)—was introduced as both a claim to embodied truth in the face of untrustworthy language— "lies"—and as itself a lie, a "confession" (with the audience constructed as potentially coercive interlocutors [Foucault 61]), at once a rehearsed, mediated *coup de théâtre* and a moment of powerful bodily presence. Like performance, it functioned to provoke, in Josette Féral's formulation, a "synaesthetic relationship between subjects" (179)— performer and audience; like theatre, it functioned semiotically as representation. *As* theatre, the moment seemed to represent a failure of resolve, a return to bingeing. But as *performance*, whatever it represented and however horrifying that seemed, it functioned as a powerful moment of what Jill Dolan calls intersubjectivity between audience and stage, an example of Dolan's "utopian performative" (2001, 455). "[P]erhaps," she argues, moments such as this "aren't moments of defeat, but moments of relief" that might "herald the new" (475–76) through their fleeting and tentative glimpse of the possibility of "*communitas*," and through the dangerous, visceral power of presence and "the transformations it makes possible" (473, 469).[4]

In this paper I want to focus on a number of Canadian autobiographical solo shows from the last decade or so in order to trace some aspects of the relationships among the performative construction of embodied subjectivities, embodied cultural memory (what Susan Bennett, invoking Derrida, calls the body as "archive" in her essay in this collection [35]), and potentially transformative moments of Dolan's utopian performativity. A useful starting point for this investigation is Ken Garnhum's 1994 performance piece *Pants on Fire*, another remarkable autobiographical solo show that hinged on a movement between lies and embodiment and that included another startlingly synaesthetic moment of intersubjectivity. In solo shows such as *Beuys Buoys Boys* (1989) and *Surrounded by Water* (1991), which he wrote, designed, and performed, Garnhum had established himself as a provocative and fiercely independent multimedia artist whose subject was consistently the intersection of his sophisticated autobiography as an artist—invoking Bruegel, Brecht, Beckett, and Beuys—and his folksy autobiography as a gay man growing up in Prince Edward Island—invoking buoys and boys. *Pants on Fire* was an extension of this work. Like *Bathroom*, the show started with humour and the establishment of an empathetic identification between the performer and the audience, and like *Bathroom*, it addressed the question, crucial to solo performance, of lying. In fact, *Pants on Fire* begins, as reviewer Kate Taylor says, "as a monologue about naming"—a subject to which we will return—in which "Ken tells us that his name is Liar Liar Pants on Fire and that his favourite of Augustine's eight types of lies is number four, a lie told solely for the pleasure of deceiving—like theatre":

> Slowly, in his chat about his past, the self-portraits he has painted and the big painting that he has yet to finish, Ken reveals that he is one of those who have always had to lie about their love. He is gay.
>
> While Ken tells us all this, Gabe [who, as Ann Wilson points out, "serves as an aspect of himself" (1994, 35)] fights to get on stage. His gloved hand rises up from a trap door and attempts to set Ken's pants on fire; he starts cutting a hole through the stage with a saw; he pulls up a plank from underneath and sends in a Trojan cat who carries inside a one-word message for Ken: "Liar."
>
> Finally, Gabe just lays down a plank on stage left and walks into the action.... First, Gabe hijacks Ken's story and repeats it to us, but gradually the two actors come to a *modus vivendi* on stage. Gabe presses Ken to show us his unfinished painting, an image of the Tower of Babel.... And ultimately, under Gabe's prodding—"Is not telling lying?"—Ken reveals what he hasn't been telling us: that he is HIV positive. And so his show becomes a play about that which he didn't want it to be about: AIDS. Ultimately, Gabe's presence onstage in what Garnhum has labeled a one-man show for two becomes a powerful metaphor for Ken's new fragility. While the inevitable loss of privacy and independence may be bitter, Gabe also shows Ken how the acceptance of others' help and the reliance on human love offer hope. (C5)

The audience, in 1994 when HIV-positive status was closer to a death sentence than it is as I write, watched Ken's "confession" in stunned silence similar to that of the audience that watched Taylor's ingestion of the donut. Garnhum's first public revelation of his HIV status—which was represented as the body, invaded by disease, forcing a confessional moment of self-alienation (and the need for the Other)—shifted the scene from the realm of representation, or theatre, into that of performance. The moment's fragile sense of *communitas* and human inter-reliance deepened into utopian performativity that depended on the form of autobiographical performance.

In a frequently cited passage Herbert Blau addresses the issue of presence in acting by reminding us of "the one inalienable and arcane truth of theatre, that the living person performing there may die in front of your eyes, and is in fact doing so" (105).[5] In this instance, in 1994, our awareness of that fact, together with that of our *shared* mortality, was exponentially heightened by Ken's "confession." As Dolan says, "however differently we live, our common, flesh-full cause is that in performance, we're dying together"

(2001, 459), and she locates the utopian performative in the theatre explicitly as a "space of desire, of longing, of loss, in which I'm moved by a gesture, a word, a glance, in which I'm startled by a confrontation with mortality (my own and others')" (456).

Pants on Fire played off an opposition between "Lying and Dying" (to cite the title of Wilson's article on the similar concerns of the Daniel MacIvor/Daniel Brooks collaborative solo show *Here Lies Henry*): lying as text, and fearful embodiment as rupture; text as the Word of the unified autonomous subject as Author, embodiment as the realm of divided, interpenetrable subjectivity and dis-closure: representation as lying, dying as truth. Like *Pants on Fire*, Garnhum's subsequent 1997 solo show also involved two people, but in *One Word* the two performers—"Chairman" and "Walkman"—were not only explicitly identified as aspects of the same psyche, but were explicitly split between almost disembodied text and almost exclusively embodied non-verbal performance: Chairman, played by the white author, Garnhum, *talked* a lot—autobiography as narrative—but was confined to a chair, perched high on the back wall of the stage, false legs extending uselessly and absurdly far to the ground beneath him; Walkman, played by African-Canadian dancer Learie McNicholls, was mute except for the final "one word" of the show, but he moved fluidly and eloquently about the space—autobiography as embodied performance. In addition, there were periodic voice-overs, totally disembodied, in the conflated voice of Garnhum and author-ity. At first legible in conventional, racially and textually hierarchical terms—white ego controlling Black Other, text asserting itself over performance—the show moved towards a kind of reconciliation of different aspects of the autobiographical subject through what the Chairman, in his last words, called "chang[ing] strategies" in the face of the silence, darkness, stillness, and inevitability of the "tomorrow" that "we're afraid of" (60). "Yes," says Walkman, his only word in the show, its final line, and, as its affirmative utopian "*One Word*," its "title role."

If the work of Taylor and Garnhum point towards some sort of utopian reconciliation of—or perhaps productively tense ambivalence between—the autobiographical self as constituted through language and through embodiment, a range of autobiographical solo performances by Canadians from various racially and ethnically minoritized groups have performed similar work at the level of community. But before turning to them I want to take a detour to France. I have no wish to claim the French performance artist Orlan as Canadian, but a brief look at her life/work might serve to clarify some of the concerns that are driving my argument. Like Garnhum, if in a very different manner, Orlan undertakes autobiographical solo performances that require the assistance of others. Like his, but more graphically, her work involves the transformation of the self in both linguistic and material ways. But her work also problematizes the borders between live and mediatized performance, and it literalizes the question of permeable and transformable subjectivities in ways that may be useful here. Many are now familiar, at least by report, with the series of "surgical performances" Orlan has undertaken since her first, significantly, on her birthday in May 1990. The series has two titles, *Image(s) Nouvelle(s) Image(s)* and *The Reincarnation of Saint Orlan* (1998, 316).[6] In these performances, broadcast "live" to galleries around the world, Orlan has employed plastic surgeons to transform her own body and face, initially into a collage of features lifted from representations of idealized female beauty in canonical works of Western art, "appropriating," as she says, "the religious images of madonnas, virgins, saints" (316). She re-designs the operating room, provides costumes for the surgical staff, and remains unanaesthetized and in control of the proceedings throughout the performance/surgery, reading aloud from philosophical, psychoanalytic, and theoretical texts. She then documents and exhibits the process of her recovery and healing, displaying and even selling the residue from the operations, including bottles of her own fat removed during liposuction (Augsberg 302–3). Recent operations have included the insertion of "the largest implants possible for [her] anatomy" into her temples, "the kind usually used to enhance the cheeks" (Orlan 1998, 323), and future plans include the acquisition of "the largest [prosthetic] nose technically possible (in relation to [her] anatomy) and ethically acceptable for a surgeon of this country [Japan, where the operation will take place]." "This nose," she says, "must start at the forehead in the manner of a Mayan sculpture" (323). In spite, or perhaps because, of the thoroughly mediated nature of Orlan's surgical performances—involving both medical technologies and implants, but also the mediations of video-casting and of the various writings by herself and others through which most know her work—that work also, as Auslander notes in another context, "asserts the body's materiality" (1990, 188): viewers witness and respond viscerally to the cutting and peeling back of living flesh, and they do so in full knowledge of the performance's permanent material consequences, its performativity, in Austinian terms, and its "force" (see Worthen).

Orlan's work, as Tanya Augsberg says, is "meant to be transformative" (288), but Orlan is not only concerned with the transformation of her body, a body that, as her "body of work" extending from the 1960s to the present suggests, intervenes directly into the social and discursive as well as medical/cosmetic production of embodied female subjectivities.[7] Indeed, the article on her work that Orlan contributed to the collection *The Ends of Performance* is entitled "Intervention" (which, as she notes, "also means 'operation'" in French [1998, 315]). The homepage on the official Orlan web site is bifurcated: the top of the page consists, on a red background, of an image of Orlan's surgically altered head on a silver disk, her hair divided between equal shocks of black and silver, her face marked by what seem to be computerized tracings of proposed surgeries (one of which bears a startling resemblance to Homer Simpson), her forehead displaying vaguely plastic veining reminiscent of *Star Trek*'s Klingons, and her eyes confronting the viewer (returning the gaze) directly. Enhanced by her trademark dark lipstick, it all looks surprisingly elegant in a cyborg-ish kind of way. Beneath this image, however, against a white background, is the title, "Orlan," in red lettering, which gestures towards another story.

Less often told, that story is also about what Augsburg calls "Orlan's Performative Transformations of Subjectivity" (285). For, of course, "Orlan" was not her birth name. It was adopted by the artist in what Augsberg calls "a twofold gesture of self-creation and self-autonomy" as an assertion that "we need to consider her art in relation to her autobiography" (292). This gesture also signalled, predating her surgical transformations, Orlan's transformational (re)invention of herself *in discourse*. In 1971 she "baptized herself *Saint* Orlan" (emphasis added) and the name has been read as a reference both to Genet's self-destruction as a subversively sacrificial martyrdom[8] and to Virginia Woolf's transformational story of gender identification, *Orlando* (Augsberg 294), although the resonances of "Orlan" with Nylon, Teflon, Alcan, and other "brands" also suggest, to me at least, a parodic affiliation with the world of marketing. What's more, Orlan has announced, "When the operations are finished, I will solicit an advertising agency to come up with an artist's name and logo; next I will retain a lawyer to petition the Republic to accept my new identity and my new face. It is a performance that inscribes itself into the social fabric, that challenges the law, that moves toward a total change of identity" (1998, 326). As a coming together of discursive and embodied rebirth, *The Reincarnation of Saint Orlan* could hardly be more explicit. If its postmodern parodic quality, together with its ambivalent "liveness," would seem to remove it from the realm of the utopian performative—there is no "synaesthetic relationship between subjects" here, at least insofar as no energy is directly exchanged between the performer and her audiences, who watch on video—it nevertheless effectively models embodied and discursive transformation through autobiographical solo performance, and it seems undeniably to function as a performative intervention.

Joseph Roach defines performance as "the kinaesthetic and vocal embodiment of social memory and self invention" (23). I want to turn now to this intersection of social (or cultural) memory and self invention, specifically in relation to autobiographical solo performances by members of minoritized cultural groups within Canada. Many of these works use performance to map resistant and transformational continuities with a suppressed cultural past, and attempt to embody more than individualized subjectivities. In his seminal 1989 book, *How Societies Remember*, Paul Connerton distinguishes between "inscribed" memory (4) and incorporating practices such as "commemorative ceremonies" (41), "bodily practices" (72), and habits transmitted from generation to generation as cultural practices. He discovers "an inertia in social structures" that is attributable to the sedimentation of memory in such embodied "performative" practices (5). In Marita Sturken's term, suggestive both for its theatrical resonances and its insistence on the discursive nature of such embodied practices, these are societally "prescripted" (236). Connerton's work effectively demonstrates not only the *persistence* of embodied memory, but also the ways in which such memory tends to "legitimate a present social order" (3), and from a very different angle to reinforce the most deterministic readings of Judith Bulter's work on the performativity of gender (and other subjectivities)—readings that Butler herself tends to favour.[9] Arguing that gendered subjectivities are *composed* through repetition and reiteration—through "*a stylized repetition of acts*" (1990b, 270)—Butler suggests that the primary social function of performativity is to police appropriate, hegemonic behaviours, though some of her work, particularly *Gender Trouble*, holds out some hope for a more subversive repetition *with a difference*, since reproduction can never be totalizing or absolute. I want here to place a reading of the subversive potential of Butler's performativity within the context of a reading of Connerton by African-American scholar Sandra Richards that shifts the ground somewhat to find resistant potential in the very *persistence* of embodied memory. Citing the survival of diasporic African culture in the wake of the slave trade, Richards has suggested that embodied memory, habit, and social ritual are mechanisms through which minoritized cultures can in fact survive in the face of repression. Indeed, it was precisely this bodily transmission of cultural memory as a mechanism of cultural survival that the Canadian residential school system and the enforced removal of Native children from their families through adoption and foster parenting—the "scoops"—were designed to interrupt, by operating as technologies of Canada's culturally genocidal project of assimilation.

In the last ten or fifteen years Canadian theatre has produced a remarkable number of autobiographical solo performances by members of minoritized groups, and a significant number of these performances include moments of phenomenological *frisson* similar to, if less spectacular than, the ones I've been discussing. Most rely on the audience's knowledge that the body they are watching perform is the one to which the events on which the show is based happened, and to which, as "bodily archive" in Bennett's Derridean sense, the shows refer for a kind of authentication, or author-ization. Thus, Lorena Gale's Black, bilingual, female, expatriate (in Canada), "Montréalaise" body seems more performatively to *present* than theatrically to *represent* the tensions that she enacts, at least as much socially as theatrically, in her autobiographical solo show *Je me souviens*, which she considers to be more performance art than theatre; Djanet Sears's anatomically diasporic body—she finds her history in "my thighs, my behind, my hair, my lips" (91)—is subject and defining object of her quest for a homeland in *Afrika Solo*; Monique Mojica's autobiographical embodiment of a whole history, or memory, of First Nations and mixed-blood women in Turtle Island, *Princess Pocahontas and the Blue Spots* (another solo show for two), is introduced through the embodied biological fact of the blue spot that appears at birth at the base of the spine as "a sign of Indian blood" (20), and the show is literally grounded in Mojica's "wide, square, brown feet" (58).[10]

Guillermo Verdecchia's *Fronteras Americanas* is similarly grounded in the almost schizophrenic embodiment of the conflicted, border-dwelling Argentinian-Canadian body of its creator and performer; Shirley Cheechoo's account in *her* communal autobiography, *Path with No Moccasins*, of her period of alcoholism in the wake of her residential school trauma is made graphic through the voice and presence of her recovering body; and George Seremba's *Come Good Rain* includes not only a graphic narrative of his having been shot several times and left for dead in the infamous Namanve Forest by the Ugandan military under Milton Obote, but in performance it grounds that account in his visibly scarred body as archive.

In looking at these shows I am particularly interested in what I am calling "documemory," in which the "marked" (see Phelan) performing body as archive serves up embodied traces—scars—as documents of both individual and cultural memory; I'm interested in stories about gaining, losing, choosing, changing, or earning names as social identifiers and cultural markers; I'm interested in what I am calling "autobiology," performances of the social and cultural assemblage of the body becoming itself; I'm interested in the Butlerian question of the performativity of gender, race, and other social identities, particularly hybrid identities; and I'm interested in the question of the different roles that embodied cultural memory might play in different cultural contexts within Canada, where the continuities of embodied memory might be understood to replace misrepresentation—or indeed lack of representation—in dominant Western historiography.

Each of the plays I have cited here involves some attempt to return to a home— Montreal, Argentina, Africa, and so on—that is not in any real sense *there*; each involves a body that is in some sense both physically and discursively "marked" (Phelan); each involves a more or less direct statement that the autobiography being performatively constructed is not simply that of its individual author but of its historical and continuing cultural community; and each moves towards a moment of what might be called transformative utopian performativity.

In many ways the clearest example is Sears's *Afrika Solo*, which begins with the problem signalled in the preface to Gale's *Je me souviens* (the title of which claims participation *as* Anglo-African-Québecoise in Québecois cultural memory.)[11] "It is a legacy of the African diaspora," argues Gale, "to become rooted in a land where one is always seen as 'other'" (11). Two of the epigraphs to the published script of *Afrika Solo*— "Swing low, Sweet Chariot / Coming for to carry me home" (13) and "Beam me up, Scotty" (14)—signal its project, structure, and cultural hybridity:[12] in spite of one passage in which the central autobiographical subject, "Janet," briefly considers plastic surgery, providing a curious connection to Orlan's *Reincarnation* (28), the show is in fact about attempting to construct or perform a coherent subjectivity by going "home," one way or another, to Africa. Home, of course, is proverbially where the heart is, but the African-

Canadian-Caribbean protagonist of *Afrika Solo*, born in the U.K., finds her heart divided: "What the hell am I doing here in my ancestral homeland, my cultural birthplace," she asks, "feeling homesick" (78). But she does "find" or reconstruct herself, in part through performative embodiment. She recognizes in West Africa that the women's bodies resemble hers: "I began to notice that a lot of the women, well—had behinds that were just like mi—very well developed" (63). She proceeds to see "familiar faces" in Togo and Benin, of people who might be, or might have been, her relatives (65–66), and she is recognized there as having come back: "They always said that you would return," a West African woman tells her. "The legends say that those who where [sic] taken away by the European [sic] on their big ships would return one day" (66). But when she ultimately returns, to *Canada*, she does so with "all my history on my back. The base of my whole culture would be forever with me. And funny thing is, it always had been. In my thighs, my behind, my hair, my lips" (91).

She does not return, however, without having undergone a performative transformation, one that recognizes her hybridized identity as "African Canadian. Not coloured, or negro.... Maybe not even black. African Canadian" (88). Her transformation most significantly involves choice, and agency, in the construction of her social identity, one that the show seems not only to represent, but to *perform*. In the wake of a story about the so-called "discovery" and "naming" of Victoria Falls—"you know, nothing exists until a white man finds it!" (53)—the character *and actor* hitherto known as "Janet" visits the Saharan oasis town of Djanet and its nearby African rock paintings. The experience is transformational (see figure 2). As she writes in a postcard to her parents,

> [T]he rock paintings in Djanet are ten thousand year [sic] old. That's four hundred generations ago. Three hundred and ninety eight point two grandmothers ago. Can you imagine, people lived ten thousand years ago in Djanet? Love Janet.
>
> *She crosses out her signature and replaces it with:*
>
> D.J.A.N.E.T

Then she breaks into rap:

> Though Janet rhymes with planet,
> what's in a name?
> I'll add a "D" to the beginning and it's
> Djanet again.
>
> Djanet with a "D" not Janet with a "J,"
> Djanet with a "D" not Janet with a "J,"
>
> I changed my being and spirit this way!! (54–55)

In a telling final moment at the airport, the newly baptized Djanet (an Arabic word meaning "paradise")[13] sees her reflection in a glass door, dons her newly acquired West

Figure 2. Djanet Sears as Djanet in
Afrika Solo, first produced at Factory
Theatre, Toronto, 1987. Photograph
by Peter Freund.

African Babou, and comments on something I have elsewhere called a postcolonial
Lacanian mirror-stage moment of cultural identification/alienation: "[Y]ou know,
sometimes when you look into the mirror and you sorta'—catch your own I" (93; see also
Knowles 2004, 17). "*Her metamorphosis ... complete*" (93), she ends the show singing
"That's love" "*in her own Canadian/Caribbean/British style over the intense African rhythm,*"
followed by a communal African song to a Sunnu rhythm. The two other
performer/musicians join her, "*releasing the incantation and ending the play*" (94) that
matches the "incantation" with which the show began (15), and that functions *in*
performance as a utopian performative across the gap between audience and stage.

Joanne Tompkins has argued persuasively that the "metamorphosis" performed here
is not, in fact, "complete," that what *Afrika Solo* represents is the *rehearsal*—"repetition
with change" (35)—of a shifting African, Guyanese, Jamaican, British, and Canadian

processual subjectivity that refuses to settle into "identity" understood as something complete and finished. "The 'real' performance," Tompkins argues, "is endlessly deferred, the construction of identity is always in progress" (36). But perhaps, at least in Butler's sense, the real performance has just begun, as "Djanet" returns to Canada to (re)iterate performatively her new subjectivity on stage (in *Afrika Solo*), in life, and in labour. In a very real sense, it was with this show that Sears shifted from being an *actor* to being not just a writer, but, individually and culturally, a *performer*. The utopian performative with which *Afrika Solo* concludes has served to mark not only Sears's own transformation-in-progress (she has spelled her name "Djanet" since that show) but the beginning, too, of her performative transformation of the African-Canadian theatrical community, not only as a prominent playwright bringing African-Canadian work into the mainstream, but also as the founding director of the biennial AfriCanadian Theatre Festival, the editor of the two volumes of *Testifyin'*, the first "national" anthologies of African-Canadian plays, the editor of the first collection of audition monologues for African-Canadian actors, and the co-editor of a *Canadian Theatre Review* special issue on African-Canadian theatre.

Another Canadian playwright of African descent, George Seremba, has produced a very different sort of autobiographical solo performance about his relationship to his African homeland, but in the case of *Come Good Rain* the narrative is not about his return to Africa; rather it deals with his life in and escape *from* his Ugandan homeland under Idi Amin and Milton Obote.[14] Seremba is explicit about his play as the autobiography of a community, and about his responsibility to the people of Bweyogerere village, who he feels, in rescuing him on 11 December 1980 from the Namanve Forest at huge risk to their own lives, had "commissioned" him to "[t]ell my story, my country's story…. Tell our history together" (11). The performer also presents himself as the embodiment of his ancestors in a way that is much more explicit than Sears's sharing of physical characteristics as documemory, but that anticipates Monique Mojica's performance of embodied cultural memory in *Princess Pocahontas and the Blue Spots*.[15] Early in the life narrative he provides an account of a visit to his grandmother in Rubaga, including a detour past the palace where his father tells him that his great-grandmother's father had been King of Buganda, recounting his subsequent lineage. Touching the ancient walls of the palace, George says, "My ancestors were no longer just names. They began to throb in my bones. I could touch and feel the country as if it had flesh and blood" (19). Later, left for dead in the Namanve Forest, he invokes this ancestry, calling upon his ancestors by their (African) names in a kind of ritual incantation:

> You my ancestors, all of you from Kabaka Kalema whose remains lie in Mende, Kakungulu and Mugujula the two valiant warriors. My grandparents back in Masaka. My grandmother, Bulaliya Nakiwala, you who always danced agile as a

duiker without touching a drink in your entire life. Yekoniya Zirabamuzale, you who
lost your sight and never your wisdom and legendary charity. My stillborn brothers,
you who never left the void, please pave my way and ease my transition. (47)

This invoking of the African names of his ancestors at the moment of his (presumed) death is a reclamation of subjectivity that the colonial system at the beginning of the show had done its best, like Canadian residential schools, to erase. At the preparatory school where he was educated, George and his fellow students were required to use their Christian names (20), to forget their "vernacular" languages, and, in a stereotypically racist phrase, their sense of "African time" (21). "[A]ll under thirteen. All ours to shape and mold," as the schoolmaster says. The students were taught to obliterate their African subjectivities, and a foreign language was encouraged to invade their very bodies and imaginaries: "From now on you must speak English. *Eat* English, sleep English, and *dream* English" (21, emphases added).

But like *Afrika Solo*, *Come Good Rain* is a performance of rebirth and transformation: it opens with a musical "invocation," and it is framed by a parallel story of rebirth from the Ugandan oral tradition, as well as by embodied ritual (15); it also evokes community in part by involving an onstage musician, including, here, ceremonial drumming, in a supposed one-person show. The key moment of phenomenological *frisson* in the play, and the one that produces its most powerful synaesthetic transfer of energies between the audience and the stage, is the extended account, to which I have already pointed, of the shooting of Seremba's still-marked body. But the narrative itself is marked by the language of self-alienation, as if at the moment of death Seremba reverses the Lacanian mirror-stage experience of separation between the self speaking and the self as represented in discourse (Lacan 1–7). As he undergoes his torture and intended murder, Seremba moves between first person references to the self and a third person account of what is happening to "*the* body," as bullets hit "*the* right leg," "*the* left arm," "*the* right thigh," and "*the* head" but another finds "*my* right hand at an angle just over *my* heart" (44–45; emphasis added). As one soldier aims a rocket-propelled grenade at him, "*I* stared at him in disbelief. Oh God, there goes the rest of *the* body" (45; emphases added). Once the soldiers leave, he makes detached references to "the husk that was my body" (47) and even to "the corpse" (46) that he hopes will not be lost.

Seremba's survival is recounted in the familiar literary tropes of rebirth and healing rain that are signalled by the show's title, but such tropes do not fully apply to "the body"; in fact, after the surgery that saves him, his family complains that "they stitched our son up like a gunny bag. Only post-mortem surgeons do that. It's for dead bodies" (52). Indeed, it is his escape from Uganda, and Africa, that is figured as a rebirth. After a Christmas dinner at which he again pays tribute to his "African extended family" (53) and particularly his ritually named grandmother—"no amount of oppression will remove the inner dignity and proverbial wisdom of Semei Kakungulu's daughter and granddaughter of a noble King of Buganda" (54)—he begins his long journey to Kenya, then Canada, with his "new identity card." "For the first time I use the name Seremba," he says (54). But the body we watch telling this story remains visibly marked by scars, the embodied traces of his ordeal—"documemory" in its most literal sense. And in spite of Marc Maufort's argument that the show "enables the protagonist to come to terms with painful memories by re-enacting them" (94), Seremba explicitly figures his performance in his "Playwright's Note" as *not* a therapeutic journey of "getting over it" or "coming to terms," but as a struggle resistantly to *hold on* to his memories, as a "fight to *keep* some of my emotional and psychological scars—just like my country" (11–12; emphasis added). He stresses, then, the systemic, social, and representative rather than the personal or psychological nature of his ordeal and recovery. As Modupe Oloagun argues, "*Come Good Rain* underscores the transformational potential of certain *communal* acts" (2000, 333, emphasis added), among them the potentially resistant, constitutive, utopian act of *communitas* that is involved in storytelling and performance.

Guillermo Verdecchia's *Fronteras Americanas*, at first blush at least, seems a very different kind of show from the others I have been discussing, and in fact, with the partial exception of Anne Nothof (204–05), few scholars who have written about the play discuss it *as* autobiographical performance.[16] Ann Wilson does characterize it as "a type of confession, but one which views the individual as a social being and so emphasizes individual identity as produced within the context of ideologies." It "does not," she argues, "acquiesce to notions of bourgeois individualism which characterize much solo performance" (1996, 8). Indeed, the play's politicized poststructuralism eschews the type of sequential, continuous narrative that sutures story to autobiographical subject, actor to character in *Come Good Rain*. In fact, where several of the one-person shows I am discussing are enacted by more than one person, *Fronteras* is a one-person, two-persona show, in which the solo author-performer-autobiographical-subject himself stages the fragmentation of his subjectivity: he plays both "Verdecchia," who is "lost" (20) and like "Janet" Sears wants to perform a homecoming, and "Wideload," a deconstructive, abject embodiment of media imaginings of "Latino" stereotypes. But *Fronteras* also shares many of the features of the shows I have been discussing, and ultimately moves, perhaps more clearly than most, towards a synaesthetic moment of utopian performativity.

As Nothof has noted, and like Garnhum in *Pants on Fire*, "Verdecchia begins his play with naming" (204), and the trope recurs throughout. Its early instances are comparable to Seremba's account of his prep school experience. "Verdecchia" recounts his formative grade-school experience at the appropriately named (for its anglo-colonialist implications) "Anne Hathaway Public School" in the similarly appropriately named Kitchener, Ontario. His teacher, otherwise effortlessly reading the roll-call, comes to an unfamiliar name:

> Minutes, hours, a century passes as the teacher, Miss Wiseman, forces her
> mouth into shapes hitherto unknown to the human race as she attempts to
> pronounce my name.
> "Gwillyou—ree—moo ... Verdeek—cheea?"
> I put my hand up. I am a miniscule boy with ungovernable black hair,
> antennae and gills where everyone else has a mouth.
> "You can call me Willy," I say. The antennae and gills disappear. (33)

Wideload, Verdecchia's alter-ego, goes through a similar, if much more self-assertive transformation on *his* arrival in Canada, one that, however parodically, invokes his ancestry in a way similar to that of Seremba:

> My name ees Facundo Morales Segundo. Some of you may know me as de
> Barrio Tiger. I am a direct descendent of Túpac Amaru, Pancho Villa, Doña Flor,
> Pedro Navaja, Sor Juana and Speedy Gonzalez. I am de heads of Alfredo García and
> Joaquín Murrieta. I am de guy who told Elton John to grow some funk of his own.
> Now when I first got here people would say, "Sorry what's de name! Facoondoe?"
> "No mang, Fa-cun-do, Facundo."
> "Wow, dat's a new one. Mind if I call you Fac?"
> "No mang, mind if I call you shithead?"
> So, you know, I had to come up with a more Saxonical name. And I looked
> around for a long time till I found one I liked. And when I found the one I
> wanted I took it. I estole it actually from a TV show—"Broken Badge" or
> something like that.
> I go by the name Wideload McKennah now and I get a lot more respect, ese.
> (24)

Taken together, these passages illustrate, according to Urjo Kareda in his foreword to the play, "[h]ow we betray ourselves, giving away our very *names* for the quick trade-off of pronunciation ease and acceptance" (11).

And in spite of the play's sophisticated poststructuralist location of identity in discourse (ideologically encoded)—which in Wilson's formulation becomes an almost deterministic capitulation to the identity structures of late capitalism—*Fronteras* shares with the other shows I am discussing a focus on the *embodied* performance of ancestral memory as potentially effective performative resistance. One encoding of this in the show comes as a humorous digression, as Verdecchia visits a doctor in an attempt, through "X-rays, brain scans" (52), to map "the precise coordinates of the spirit, of the psyche, of memory" (51). "They didn't find anything," he reports. But "I wasn't fooled. I am a direct descendant of two people who once ate an armadillo—armadillo has a half life of 2000 years—you can't tell me that isn't in my bloodstream. Eva Perón once kissed my mother and that night she felt her cheek begin to rot. You can't tell me that hasn't altered my DNA" (52). Verdecchia, then, does place his autobiography, as part of the problem, within history—specifically, a three-page "Idiosyncratic History of America" that locates "Latin America" in the context of Western colonialism and nascent capitalism (29–33)—but he also locates his "self," as part of the solution, within the realm of embodied cultural memory. Again humorously, he envisions the material traces he has left behind—a sock in Mendoza, a Zippo lighter in Chile, a toenail in Pougnadoresse, a combful of hair in Venice—as "slowly crawling towards each other ... and arranging to meet in my sleep" (68–69).

In his sleep, in his grandmother's bed in Buenos Aires, he has dreams of Argentinian flora, fauna, and tradition:

> Mount Aconcagua, of Iguacú, of Ushuaia and condors, of the sierras yellow and green, of bay, orange, quebracho and ombu trees, of running, sweating horses, of café con crema served with little glasses of soda water, of the smell of Particulares 30, of the vineyards of Mendoza, of barrels full of ruby-red vino tinto, of gardens as beautiful as Andalusia in spring. I dream of thousands of emerald-green parrots flying alongside my airplane.... (50)

In his waking hours, he claims to have "memories of things that never happened to me—I feel nostalgia for things I never knew—I feel connected to things I have no connection with, responsible, involved, implicated in things that happen thousands of miles away" (69), but he sees this as symptomatic of his identity problem, "the division between two cultures and two memories" (21). When standard therapy fails to help, moreover, he finally visits the suspect Latino healer "El Brujo," "en la frontera" (70) at Bloor and Madison in Toronto, where he confronts, incredulously at first, embodied memories including scars from events long past—what Holocaust memory theorists have referred to as "postmemory" (Hirsch 9):

> El Brujo said, "I remember the night Bolívar burned with fever and realized there was no way back to the capital; the night he burned his medals and cried, 'Whosoever works for the revolution ploughs the seas.'"
>
> * * *
>
> El Brujo said, "I remember the Zoot Suit Riots. We were beat up for our pointy shoes and fancy clothes. I still have the scar." And he lifted up his shirt and showed me a gash. It was ugly and ragged and spotted with freshly dried blood. (71–72)

"What do *you* remember," El Brujo asks (72, emphasis added), which leads Verdecchia into a confessional litany of memories that move from the cultural/historical to the personal/confessional, and that show, as did El Brujo's and George Seremba's, *his* personal and cultural scars, the embodied traces of his hybrid cultural memory:

> "I remember the French invasion of Mexico; I remember the Pastry War.
>
> * * *

"I remember a little boy in a red snowsuit who ran away whenever anyone spoke to me in English. I remember la machine queso.

"I remember a gang of boys who wanted to steal my leather jacket even though we all spoke Spanish, a gang of boys who taught me I could be a long-lost son one minute and a tourist the next.

"I remember an audition where I was asked to betray and insult everything I claim to believe in and I remember that I did as I was asked.

"I remember practicing t'ai chi in the park and being interrupted by a guy who wanted to start a fight and I remember thinking, 'Stupid drunken Mexican.' I remember my fear, I taste and smell my fear, my fear of young men who speak Spanish in the darkness of the park, and I know that somewhere in my traitorous heart I can't stand the people I claim are my brothers. I don't know who did this to me. I remember feeling sick, I remember howling in the face of my fear...." (72–73)

His embodied memories of "tasting and smelling"—his performative social identities—are both "Latin" and mainstream Anglo-Canadian (see figure 3).

Figure 3. Rehearsal photo of Guillermo Verdecchia as Wideload in *Fronteras Americanas,* first produced at Tarragon Theatre, Toronto, 1993. Photograph by Roger West.

On his journey of discovery, "Going Home" to Argentina (36), Verdecchia, like Sears, had found himself in his homeland paradoxically wanting to go home—"but I'm already there—aren't I?" (50)—and returning to Canada to perform an identity that is hybrid. As he learns from El Brujo, "The Border is your [home]" (74).[7] But the maps and definitions, "metaphors and not the territory," with which the show had started (20) and which prove unsatisfactory—what *are* "the precise coordinates of the spirit, of the psyche, of memory" (51)—are literalized in a conclusion that asks us to "throw out the *metaphor* of Latin America as North America's 'backyard' because your backyard is now a border and the metaphor is now *made flesh*" (77, emphasis added). Similarly, where the show had started with division—between the personae of Verdecchia and Wideload within the representation, and between the Spanish speakers and the anglo members of the "Saxonian community" (40) within the audience—at the end the personae are sutured together (as in *Pants on Fire* and *One Word*), Verdecchia and Wideload speaking for the first time in one voice (77). Verdecchia then turns to the audience and performs a similar operation—"Did *you* change your name somewhere along the way?... Do *you* have a border zone? Will you call off the Border Patrol?" (78; emphasis added): "Ladies and gentlemen, please reset your watches. It is now almost ten o'clock on a Friday night—we still have time. We can go forward. Towards the centre, towards the border." And Wideload invites us, to the music of Mano Negra (a "Latin" group from France who perform in Spanish), to "let the dancing begin" (78).

It is a consciously utopian moment of "intersubjective illumination" (Turner 48, as quoted in Dolan 2001, 473), a rehearsal (in Tompkins's terms) and performance (in Butler's) of a divided, intranational subjectivity that is communal. Wilson finds this resolution sentimental, asking, given the hegemonic technologies of capital, "Can the Border Patrol ever be called off?" (15). But if the operations of hegemony are not to be read deterministically (and pessimistically) as closed and monolithic, and if theatre can be used as an agent of social change, as I believe it can, then one of its own most powerful technologies is to marshal, synaesthetically, the felt potential of something different, something better. As Dolan says, "I know I'm risking sentiment here; I know that community and theatre, like utopia, can be coercive, that nothing exists outside of ideology, and that nothing is ever, truly perfect" (478–79). But as she also says, she believes in the achievement of fleeting moments of grace such as this one, "generous" moments of "spontaneous communitas," "when we can believe in utopia. These are moments," she argues, "[that] theatre and performance make possible" (479).

Notes

1. I am grateful to Sherrill Grace, Jerry Wasserman, and the committee who organized the "Putting a Life on Stage" exploratory workshop at the Peter Wall Institute for Advanced Studies, University of British Columbia, for the invitation that served as the impetus for the writing of this paper. I am also grateful to Jill Dolan, who generously read and commented on an earlier draft.

2. Linda A. Carson's similarly autobiographical solo show about bulimia, *Dying to Be Thin*, also stages the bulimic body eating, and both shows were explicitly autobiographical, using post-show discussions with the author as autobiographical subject and survivor. In Carson's case, too, the script is published with an extended apparatus including an authorial "Diary of a Bulimic" (41–48), and in the case of Taylor, the "Artist's Note" in the program refers explicitly to "what [she] had been living through while coping with bulimia" (n.p.). It is odd, then, that unlike the other shows discussed here (but like Margo Kane's foundational autobiographical First Nations show, *Moonlodge*), both used a fictionalized name for the autobiographical central character. I am grateful to Sherrill Grace for reminding me about *Dying to Be Thin*.

3. In Lacanian terms, what she staged so graphically was the Oedipal suppression, by language and the Law of the Father, of the Lacanian "imaginary," a suppression followed, in the eating of the donut, by the body's abject and rebellious return.

4. Dolan is drawing on Victor Turner's concept of "spontaneous communitas" as "a direct, immediate and total confrontation of human identities," a "deep rather than intense style of personal interaction" (Turner 47–48), and is citing a classroom discussion with performance artist Peggy Shaw on "the power of presence." Dolan elsewhere discusses a different kind of intersubjectivity that is achieved in multiple-character solo performances, or "monypolylogues," where the subject is inhabited by a variety of subject positions, a variety of "Others," and in the process is "radically destabilized," in Elin Diamond's terms, and "transformed by such identifications" (Dolan 2002, 498 passim; Diamond 391, 396).

5. Dolan (2001, 459) and Ann Wilson (1994, 35; 1997, 40) both cite this passage from Blau, and I am indebted to them for reminding me of it.

6. *Image(s) Nouvelle(s) Images* is the title for the series listed on Orlan's official web site ("Orlan"). She translates it as *Image—New Images* in her article "Interventions." Orlan gives the date of her birth and of her first surgical performance in "Interventions" (316).

7. For a tour of Orlan's history as a performer, as well as bibliographies of her own writings and writings about her, see her official web site ("Orlan"). A retrospective of her work was mounted jointly by Le Centre National de Photographie and Le Centre de Création Contemporain in Paris, 17 March–6 June 2004.

8. Julia Kristeva notes, in Kim Solga's summary to which I am indebted here, that "[i]n biblical tradition ... sacrifice is the very act that establishes and authorizes the sacred and, thereby, like all aspects of abjection, threatens radically to disturb the very order it enforces: in destroying itself, sacrifice renders momentarily visible the sacred's dependence upon it" (Solga 349, citing Kristeva 90–112).

9. I am drawing here on Butler's essay, "Bodily Inscriptions, Performative Subversions," in *Gender Trouble* (128–41) and on her more deterministic revisiting of that essay in *Bodies That Matter*.

10. I have written extensively about *Princess Pocahontas and the Blue Spots* elsewhere (see Knowles 2001; 2003, 252–56; 1999, 148–50), so I won't focus on it here. It is, however, perhaps the autobiographical solo show that least risks sentiment in its movement towards a utopian performative explicitly based on political solidarity across difference. It begins, like many of the shows I'm discussing, with a quest for home (19); the central autobiographical subject— "Monique" in the first published version in *Canadian Theatre Review* 64 (Fall 1990): 66–77, "Contemporary Woman #1" thereafter, revealing its autobiographical base and its refusal to speak as an autonomous individual—autobiographically embodies an entire history of mixed-race Native women in the Americas (22; also see Knowles, 2001, 262–63 and 2003, 255); the action turns on ancestral documemory (38–39); and it moves towards a performative moment of solidarity with other women "word warriors" (such as Gloria Anzaldúa, Paula Gunn Allen, Cherríe Moraga, Chrystos, Diane Burns, "sisters, guerilleras" [59]) as well as towards community, and intervention. It ends with a utopian performative as "Blind Faith leaps in the dark" (60).

11. "Je me souviens"—which translates inadequately into English as "I remember," without the self-reflexive overtones of "remembering" one's self—has, since the first accession to power of the nationalist Parti Québecois, been the motto of the Québec "nation," inscribed on every licence plate in Québec (replacing the earlier tourist lure, "la belle province"). Gale uses it to disrupt the discourses of *pûr laine* nationalism which exclude what then Québec premier Jacques Parizeau, in the wake of the narrowly lost vote on Québec sovereignty in 1995, notoriously labelled "money and the ethnic vote," including, presumably, Québecois of African origin.

12. Another is from Malcolm X on African-Americans' internalized self-hatred through exposure to negative Western representations of Africa (12).

13. According to Sears in the play (49). Joanne Tompkins provides the same translation, but says the word is Swahili (39).

14. For an account of *Come Good Rain* in the context of other plays about Idi Amin's Uganda see Oloagun 2002.

15. See note 8.

16. See Harvie and Knowles (Knowles 1999, 206–07), Gomez, Maufort (86–93), Nothof, and Wilson.

17. The published script omits the final word, which is implied, but Mayte Gomez reports that it appears in the original production script (Gomez 37).

Works Cited

Augsburg, Tanya. "Orlan's Performative Transformations of Subjectivity." In *The Ends of Performance*, ed. Peggy Phelan and Jill Lane. New York: New York University Press, 1998. 285–314.

Auslander, Philip. "Vito Acconci and the Politics of the Body in Postmodern Performance." In *After the Future: Postmodern Times and Places*, ed. Gary Shapiro. Albany: SUNY Press, 1990. 185–95.

———. *Liveness: Performance in a Mediatized Culture*. London and New York: Routledge, 1999.

Bal, Mieke, Jonathan Crewe, and Leo Spitzer, eds. *Acts of Memory: Cultural Recall in the Present.* Hanover, N.H.: University Press of New England, 1999.

Bennett, Susan. "3D A/B." Paper presented at "Putting a Life on Stage: A Theatre and Autobiography Exploratory Workshop." Peter Wall Institute for Advanced Studies, University of British Columbia, Vancouver, B.C. 20 February 2004.

Blau, Herbert. *Blooded Thought: Occasions of Theatre.* New York: Performing Arts Journal Publications, 1982.

Butler, Judith. *Gender Trouble: Feminism and the Subversion of Identity.* New York and London: Routledge, 1990a.

———. "Performative Acts and Gender Constitution: An Essay in Phenomenology and Feminist Theory." In *Performing Feminisms: Feminist Critical Theory and Theatre,* ed. Sue-Ellen Case. Baltimore: Johns Hopkins University Press, 1990b. 270–82.

———. *Bodies That Matter: On the Discursive Limits of "Sex."* New York and London: Routledge, 1993.

Carlson, Marvin. *Performance: A Critical Introduction.* London and New York: Routledge, 1996.

Carson, Linda A. *Dying to Be Thin.* Winnipeg: Scirocco, 1993.

Cheechoo, Shirley. "Path with No Moccasins." In *Canadian Mosaic: 6 Plays,* ed. Aviva Ravel. Toronto: Simon & Pierre, 1995. 9–42.

Connerton, Paul. *How Societies Remember.* Cambridge: Cambridge University Press, 1989.

Diamond, Elin. "The Violence of 'We': Politicizing Identification." In *Critical Theory and Performance,* ed. Janelle G. Reinelt and Joseph R. Roach. Ann Arbor: University of Michigan Press, 1992. 390–98.

Dolan, Jill. "Performance, Utopia, and the 'Utopian Performative.'" *Theatre Journal* 53, no. 3 (October 2001): 455–79.

———. "'Finding Our Feet in the Shoes of (One An) Other': Multiple Character Solo Performers and Utopian Performatives." *Modern Drama* 45, no. 4 (Winter 2002): 495–518.

Féral, Josette. "Performance and Theatricality: The Subject Demystified." *Modern Drama* 25, no. 1, (March 1982): 170–81.

Foucault, Michel. *History of Sexuality.* Vol. 1. Trans. Robert Hurley. New York: Vintage, 1990.

Gale, Lorena. *Je me souviens.* Vancouver: Talonbooks, 2001.

Garnhum, Ken. *Beuys, Buoys, Boys: A Monologue.* In *Making, Out: Plays by Gay Men,* ed. Robert Wallace. Toronto: Coach House, 1992.

———. "Pants on Fire." Production at the Extra Space, Tarragon Theatre, Toronto, Ont. Staged by Duncan McIntosh, with Ken Garnhum and Andrew Massingham, 29 March–17 April 1994a.

———. *Surrounded by Water.* In *Solo,* ed. Jason Sherman. Toronto: Coach House, 1994b.

———. *One Word.* In *Canadian Theatre Review* 91 (Summer 1997): 47–60.

Gomez, Mayte. "Healing the Border Wound: *Fronteras Americanas* and the Future of Canadian Multiculturalism." *Theatre Research in Canada/Recherches théâtrales au Canada* 16, nos. 1–2 (1995): 26–39.

Grace, Sherrill, and Albert-Reiner Glaap, eds. *Performing National Identities: International Perspectives on Contemporary Canadian Theatre.* Vancouver: Talonbooks, 2003.

Hirsch, Marianne. "Projected Memory: Holocaust Photographs in Personal and Public Fantasy." In *Acts of Memory: Cultural Recall in the Present,* ed. Mieke Bal, Jonathan Crewe, and Leo Spitzer. Hanover, N.H.: University Press of New England, 1999. 3–23.

Kane, Margo. *Moonlodge.* In *Singular Voices: Plays in Monologue Form,* ed. Tony Hamill. Toronto: Playwrights Canada, 1993. 77–107.

Kareda, Urjo. Foreword to *Fronteras Americanas (American Borders),* by Guillermo Verdecchia. Vancouver: Talonbooks, 1997. 9–12.

Knowles, Ric. *The Theatre of Form and the Production of Meaning: Contemporary Canadian Dramaturgies.* Toronto: ECW, 1999.

———. "Translators, Traitors, Mistresses, and Whores: Monique Mojica and the Mothers of the Métis Nations." In *Siting the Other: Re-visions of Marginality in Australian and English-Canadian Drama,* ed. Marc Maufort and Franca Bellarsi. Brussels: P.I.E-Peter Lang, 2001. 247–66.

———. "The Hearts of Its Women: Rape, Residential Schools, and Re-Membering." In *Performing National Identities: International Perspectives on Contemporary Canadian Theatre,* ed. Sherrill Grace and Albert-Reiner Glaap. Vancouver: Talonbooks, 2003. 245–64

———. *Shakespeare and Canada: Essays on Production, Translation, and Adaptation.* Brussels: P.I.E.-Peter Lang, 2004.

Kristeva, Julia. *Powers of Horror: An Essay on Abjection.* Trans. Leon S. Roudiez. New York: Columbia University Press, 1982.

Lacan, Jacques. "The Mirror Stage as Formative of the Function of the I." In *Écrits: A Selection.* Trans. Alan Sheridan. New York: Norton, 1977. 1–7.

Maufort, Marc. *Transgressive Itineraries: Postcolonial Hybridizations of Dramatic Realism.* Brussels: P.I.E.-Peter Lang, 2003.

———, and Franca Bellarsi, eds. *Siting the Other: Re-visions of Marginality in Australian and English-Canadian Drama.* Brussels: P.I.E-Peter Lang, 2001.

Mojica, Monique. *Princess Pocahontas and the Blue Spots.* Toronto: Women's Press, 1991.

Nothof, Anne. "Canadian 'Ethnic' Theatre: Fracturing the Mosaic." In *Siting the Other: Re-visions of Marginality in Australian and English-Canadian Drama,* ed. Marc Maufort and Franca Bellarsi. Brussels: P.I.E-Peter Lang, 2001. 193–215.

Oloagun, Modupe. "The Need to Tell This Story: George Seremba's Narrative Drama, *Come Good Rain.*" In *Testifyin': Contemporary African Canadian Drama: Volume 1,* ed. Djanet Sears. Toronto: Playwrights Canada, 2000. 331–35.

———. "Dramatizing Atrocities: Plays by Wole Soyinka, Francis Imbuga, and George Seremba Recalling the Idi Amin Era." *Modern Drama* 45, no. 3 (Fall 2002): 430–48.

Orlan. "Intervention." In *The Ends of Performance,* ed. Peggy Phelan and Jill Lane. New York: New York University Press, 1998. 315–27.

———. "Orlan." http://www.orlan.net. 8 February 2004.

Phelan, Peggy. *Unmarked: The Politics of Performance.* New York and London: Routledge, 1993.

Phelan, Peggy and Jill Lane, eds. *The Ends of Performance*. New York: New York University Press, 1998.

Richards, Sandra. "'Snapshots of the Great Homecoming': Memorializing the Slave Trade in Ghana." Paper presented at the Cultural Memory Colloquium, Centre for Cultural Studies/Centre d'études sur la culture, University of Guelph, Guelph, Ont., 10 November 2000.

Roach, Joseph. "History, Memory, Necrophilia." In *The Ends of Performance*, ed. Peggy Phelan and Jill Lane. New York: New York University Press, 1998. 23–30.

Sears, Djanet. *Afrika Solo*. Toronto: Sister Vision, 1990.

Seremba, George. *Come Good Rain*. Winnipeg: Blizzard, 1993.

Solga, Kim. "*Mother Courage* and Its Abject: Reading the Violence of Identification: Toward an Epic Feminine." *Modern Drama* 46, no. 3 (Fall 2003): 330–57.

States, Bert O. *Great Reckonings in Little Rooms: On the Phenomenology of Theater*. Berkeley: University of California Press, 1985.

Sturken, Marita. "Narratives of Recovery: Repressed Memory as Cultural Memory." In *Acts of Memory: Cultural Recall in the Present*, ed. Mieke Bal, Jonathan Crewe, and Leo Spitzer. Hanover, N.H.: University Press of New England, 1999. 231–48.

Taylor, Emily. "Bathroom." Unpublished script. Halifax, 2001.

———. "Artist's Note." In program of "Bathroom," by Emily Taylor, directed by Andrew Gillis. Windsor Theatre, Mount Allison University, Sackville, New Brunswick, 18–19 February 2003.

Taylor, Kate. "A Tiny, Perfect Piece of Theatre." Review of *Pants on Fire*, by Ken Garnhum, staged by Duncan McIntosh at Tarragon Theatre, Toronto, Ont., 29 March–17 April 1994. *Globe and Mail*, 30 March 1994, C5.

Tompkins, Joanne. "Infinitely Rehearsing Performance and Identity: *Afrika Solo* and *The Book of Jessica*." *Canadian Theatre Review* 74 (Spring 1993): 35–39.

Turner, Victor. *From Ritual to Theatre: The Human Seriousness of Play*. New York: Performing Arts Journal Publications, 1982.

Verdecchia, Guillermo. *Fronteras Americanas (American Borders)*. Vancouver: Talonbooks, 1997.

Wilson, Ann. "Bored to Distraction: Auto-performance and the Perniciousness of Presence." *Canadian Theatre Review* 79/80 (Fall 1994): 33–37.

———. "Border Crossing: The Technologies of Identity in *Fronteras Americanas*." In "Theatre and the Canadian Imaginary," special focus issue edited by Joanne Tompkins. *Australasian Drama Studies* 29 (October 1996): 7–15.

———. "Lying and Dying: Theatricality in *Here Lies Henry*." *Canadian Theatre Review* 92 (Fall 1997): 39–41.

Worthen, W. B. *Shakespeare and the Force of Modern Performance*. Cambridge: Cambridge University Press, 2003.

Theorizing the Gendered Space of Auto/Biographical Performance via Samuel Beckett and Hans Bellmer

Richard J. Lane

The slash placed between "auto" and "biography" indicates a contemporary awareness, as Sherrill Grace has pointed out, of the chiasmus between autobiography and biography: in other words, notions of authorial self-presence and biographical command are undermined by giving all forms of life story equal epistemological status (Grace 2005). With performative auto/biographics, Grace also notes that the concept of a "version" of a life story *detaches* it from prior notions of the auto/biographical performance perceived as a secondary event, i.e., these notions are deconstructed. In relation to the diverse, relatively new theories of performative auto/biographics, there are two main questions that I will explore and attempt to answer: first, in the wake of numerous theories of the divided subject, and in some ways the subject's *self-inaccessibility*, which element or component of *autos* is performed? Second, while we may *read* the English "auto" as *autos*, do we also *hear* the sound "auto" which is commonly used as shorthand for that other Greek word, *automatos*, acting independently, spontaneous, and self-moving: in other words, the automatic? Is it possible that life writing can be translated as "automatic writing," and, furthermore, that auto/biographical performance can be translated as "automatic performance"? If so, then there is a radical shift away from conceiving of auto/biographical performance as the performance of an authentic self, and a concomitant move towards conceiving of auto/biographical performance as the expression, via specific theatrical strategies, of the divided, *eccentric* subject. Various "theatrical resources" (Grace 2003, 122) can be deployed to create a zone of hybridity, a transformative space which happens in the present time of the performance yet also presents other times, places, fantasies, or memories on stage. In this chapter I will focus on the spatial and temporal aspects of the zone of hybridity—the term, of course, comes from Homi Bhabha's work on postcolonial theory, i.e., the "third space"—especially where the use of masks, veils, and puppets generates the uncanny: appearing both dead and, through artistic manipulation, profoundly alive, these veiled figures, masks, and/or puppets function via synecdoche (a part for a fantasized whole), transference, fetishization, memory, and, problematically, sadism. Is this *substitution* of the human subject in the zone of hybridity gendered? Can there be a neutral deployment of uncanny theatrical resources in the production or performance of the auto/biographical subject? Or is the auto/biographical subject always "subject to" gender performance? By juxtaposing Beckett and Bellmer, I will foreground the chiasmus between Bellmer's artistic manipulation of puppets or dolls and Beckett's manipulation of his female protagonists to attempt an answer to these theoretical questions.

The Auto/biographical Subject Is *Not I*

Beckett's plays occupy an unusual position in the study of auto/biographical performance: they are regarded in one theoretical tradition (loosely called liberal humanism) as auto/biographical and in another, more recent tradition (loosely called poststructuralist) as deconstructive of auto/biographical concepts. Working critically within the first tradition, Katherine Kelly argues that Beckett's "Mouth" in *Not I* is one in a series of "autobiographers," the others being Krapp (*Krapp's Last Tape*), Hamm (*Endgame*), Maddy (*All That Fall*) and Winnie (*Happy Days*) (122). However, these "autobiographers" or "fictionalizers," as she also calls them, do not form a unified continuum: "In contrast to these earlier fictionalizers, Mouth's storytelling is not metaphorical. The elements of her story, from her premature birth to something very like death, constitute the actual shape of her life in her consciousness" (123). There is a struggle going on in this play: between the projection of a third person subject and the actual shaping and manifestation on stage of the first person "I." Kelly argues that while Mouth wants to be "not I," the deployment of theatrical resources forces a coincidence between the third and first person: "In spite of all her efforts to insist that she is not telling her own story, the identity of Mouth with 'She' comes slowly into focus in the first part of the monologue" (123). Kelly puts this another way by arguing that the coincidence is a failure of the fictionalizing process: "Mouth fails in her attempt to fictionalize herself by revealing, perhaps unwittingly, that her heroine's predicament is identical to her own as the audience perceives it" (124). Finally, Kelly provides a key formulation of the experience of Beckett's "heroines":

> One of the effects of Mouth's transparent denial of her fragmented self is to attach to that denial the aspect of suffering; to give her, even in this eccentric and austere work, the status of a feeling being. The first person pronoun, in itself unimportant, is associated with a series of hurts and disappointments; specifically, with the absence of love and the exception that "tender mercies" will alleviate the pain of existing. The particular kind of hell inhabited by Beckett's heroines is created by their eternally thwarted desire for love, mercy, and renewal. (124)

I will return to the notion of a Beckettian "hell" being a particularly gendered experience after a detour through an example of the second critical tradition through which Beckett is read, that of poststructuralism. Simon Critchley, in his *Very Little ... Almost Nothing: Death, Philosophy, Literature*, asks, "Who speaks in the work of Samuel Beckett?" (172). It is via this question that I wish to interrogate the first critical tradition:

> [T]o ascribe the voice that speaks in the work with the author Samuel Beckett, or
> to identify the narrative voice with a controlling consciousness that looks down
> upon the drama of Beckett's work like a transcendent spectator, is to fail to
> acknowledge the strangeness of the work under consideration and to read the
> work as an oblique confession or, worse still, a series of case studies in a reductive
> psycho-biography. (Critchley 172)

For Critchley, there is a strangeness and then there is a strangeness: the liberal humanist recognition of strangeness is ultimately defused by the reining in of its effects/affects (say, the Classical or canonical tradition which enframes and encloses Kelly's essay); the poststructuralist recognition of strangeness is, allegedly, completely open to a subsequent overpowering force, perhaps the dispossessing "I":

> This is Blanchot's hypothesis—in Beckett's work we approach an experience, a
> *literary* experience, that speaks to us in a voice that can be described as
> impersonal, neutral or indifferent: an incessant, interminable and indeterminable
> voice that reverberates outside of all intimacy, dispossessing the "I" and delivering
> it over to a nameless outside. Beckett's work draws the reader into a space—the
> space of literature—where a voice intones obscurely, drawn on by a speaking that
> does not begin and does not finish, which cannot speak and cannot but speak,
> that leads language towards what Blanchot calls with reference to *Comment c'est*
> "an unqualifiable murmur." (172–73)

In other words, "I do not speak, it speaks" (174), this spectre or ghost that constantly and continually disturbs the desire for a self-present voice (Spivak 1976). At this point in Critchley's analysis of this spectral voice in relation to *The Unnameable* and Beckett's work as a whole, *Not I* interrupts or punctures his text: it forms a "connection" between itself and *The Unnameable*, and it is "a distilled redrafting of *The Unnameable*" (Critchley 174); but it is also quite different: "As Beckett laconically points out in the only note to *Not I*, the Mouth is engaged in 'vehement refusal to relinquish the third person.' Although it should be noted that this third person is 'she' rather than 'he,' and it is here that one might want to raise the question of gender and challenge the alleged neutrality of the narrative voice" (174–75). The auto/biographical voice in *Not I* is both eccentric and "outside" of the control of the humanist self-present subject: now the subject is spoken by "the insomniac narrative voice that opens like a void in the experience of literature" (175). What both of these exemplary readings from antithetical critical traditions recognize is that the space of auto/biographical performance in or through *Not I* is gendered; it is also a hellish space, one of sadism and torture (see O'Gorman). The latter is not an arbitrary interpretation or reading of the play, rather it is based upon the recorded experiences of the women who have played Beckett's characters.

Another figure in *Not I* that I argue is of importance here is the "Auditor": "*[D]ownstage audience left, tall standing figure, sex undeterminable, enveloped from head to foot in loose black djellaba, with hood, fully faintly lit*" (Beckett 376). In James Knowlson's insightful biography of Beckett, *Damned to Fame*, this figure is quite specifically traced (quoting Enoch Brater) to Beckett's visit to El Jadida: "Sitting in a café, Beckett observed: 'a solitary figure, completely covered in a djellaba, leaning against a wall. It seemed to him that the figure was in a position of intense listening.... Only later did Beckett learn that this figure ... was an Arab woman waiting there for her child who attended a nearby school'" (Knowlson 589). While Beckett's Auditor in the published version of the play is of "sex undeterminable" and, as noted intriguingly, appears to be based upon an "Arab woman," the majority of the commentators on the play shift *her* back to the masculine pronoun "he." The Auditor is a compassionate figure, who watches the tortured Mouth, but this torture is not metaphorical; for example, Jessica Tandy "found the experience of acting *Not I* terrifying" and "had to be wheeled on [to the stage] in a sort of black box.... In this 'contraption,' she stood holding on to two iron bars on either side of the box" (Knowlson 592). Knowlson writes more approvingly of Billie Whitelaw's acceptance of the physical constraints of the play—Tandy modified the "technology" to "fit her needs as a person" (597)—noting that she sat on a chair which "looked disquietingly like an electric chair and, in late rehearsals, it seemed as if she was being prepared for some medieval torture.... [H]er body was strapped into the chair with a belt around her waist; her head was clamped firmly between two pieces of sponge rubber ... and the top part of her face was covered with black gauze with a black transparent strip for her eyes" (597). During rehearsals, because of the strain and family problems, Whitelaw had a "breakdown," although she "quickly pulled herself together," Knowlson writes (597). Rosemary Pountney, in her essay "On Acting Mouth in *Not I*", notes that

> When eventually we began to rehearse on stage, my head was encased at our first attempt at blacking out the face in a Ku Klux Klan-type hood, with a hole for the mouth alone. This proved hot, claustrophobic, and enormously difficult (with eyes gone) to judge how much voice was required to fill the auditorium. We therefore removed the hood, working up to what we felt to be a satisfactory pitch and pace for the performance, while I simply sat on stage. But I was aware of reinforcing mouth with eyes—and dreaded being blacked out again. (84)

Auditor and Mouth can be regarded as fragmented doubles: Mouth in this case is a synecdochic double of Auditor, a part for the veiled or covered whole, be that part a mouth or a vagina (O'Gorman 88).

If Auditor and Mouth are considered as entirely separate entities, radically different readings occur. An agonistic relationship between the two has been posited by critics; for example, John Calder argues that Mouth is actually being interrogated by Auditor (36). Richard Begam suggests that the sense of interior disconnection expressed in the play "is further dramatized by the framing device, in which Mouth and Auditor appear as distinct entities"; thus the resistance of the first person "is an emptying out of the *cogito*, an admission not of self-knowledge but of self-ignorance" (29). For Ulrika Maude, the important process at play in *Not I* is that of memory and "phantom limb experiences" where "what is distinctly Beckettian about the memories is the plainly corporeal nature of the recollections" (119). Maude's argument returns conceptual models of Beckett to the body:

> Triggered not by mere intellectual memory but by the body's own recollection of sensory experience, the strange time and place sequences in works such as *Company*, the four novellas, *That Time* or any other Beckettian haunting of the present by the past, become explicable in so far as the past is sedimented in the body itself, in a perpetual present continuous tense that leaves what has once been experienced and what can never truly be left behind irreversibly echoing in the characters' bodies. The bodies in Beckett seem not only to exist in several tenses, but to have both a time-arresting stative aspect and an active, dynamic one that is almost time itself. It is as if the paradoxes present in Beckett's account of involuntary memory were in fact aspects of continuity and discontinuity embedded in the very notion of bodily existence. (119)

The "subject" in *Not I* has a bodily experience regardless of the critical models brought to bear (see Gray); further, the women who play Mouth do not just have to train themselves to speak rapidly, they are in turn constrained, strapped in, bound, fragmented, and in many respects sadistically tortured. The "babble" that bursts forth from this tortured Mouth functions like a piece of disembodied automatic writing: it is both eccentric to the body and somehow, arguably, more essential. The automatic writing repeatedly returns Mouth to her formative experience of premature delivery, and it is in turn bound and marked or divided by the four auditing interventions, the silent *witness* in the play (Lane 2002, 175).

Performing Gender: Beckett and Bellmer

Automatic writing does not liberate the subject, rather it embeds her in a repetitive enunciative compulsion (Foster 11). The controlling *cogito* is replaced and surpassed by the "mouth of unreason," to use Victor Hugo's phrase (quoted in Polizzotti 103). As André Breton puts it in his *Manifesto*: "we were trying to obtain ... a monologue spoken as rapidly as possible without any intervention on the part of the critical faculties, a monologue consequently unencumbered by the slightest inhibition and which was, as closely as possible, akin to *spoken thought*" (23). In *Not I* the "mouth of unreason" is gendered—perhaps she is an "Irish bag lady" as diverse commentators suggest—and, as I argue, perhaps the Auditor is an Arab woman; both women are manipulated as if they were puppets or dolls, or to use the German surrealist Hans Bellmer's term, *poupées*. As Hal Foster notes, Bellmer's *poupées* were "made of wood, metal, plaster pieces, and ball joints" and they "were manipulated in drastic ways and photographed in different positions" (102). While Bellmer is sometimes placed on the margins of critical accounts of Surrealism, Foster presents his *poupées* as having far more importance; they are

> uncanny confusions of animate and inanimate figures, ambivalent conjunctions of castrative and fetishistic forms, compulsive repetitions of erotic and traumatic scenes, difficult intricacies of sadism and masochism, of desire, defusion, and death. With the dolls, the surreal and the uncanny intersect in the most difficult desublimatory ways—which is one reason why Bellmer is marginal to the literature on surrealism, devoted as it mostly is to the sublimatory idealisms of Breton. (101)

The representation, manipulation, dismemberment, and repositioning of the female subject via the *poupées* create an aesthetic of sadistic intensity; Bellmer audits his own scenes by appearing, ghostlike, in some of the photographs, where he is no less mastering the scene than witnessing the dissolution of the female body. Such an aesthetic has been related to Bataille, especially the "play of *altération*" whereby "the formation of an image is its *de*formation, or the deformation of its model. For Bataille, then, representation is less about formal sublimation than about instinctual release" (Foster 113). Foster suggests that this can help explain Bellmer's *poupées*, which are driven "not by sublimatory *transpositions* but by desublimatory *altérations*" (113). In the case of Beckett's *Not I*, the recourse to the subject (Adorno 30), either as a resisting subject of traditional auto/biographical expression, or as a fragmented subject deconstructing auto/biographical self-presence, may be more accurately perceived as an enactment of fluctuating intensity, what Pierre Klossowski calls in his *Nietzsche and the Vicious Circle* a "tonality" (vii). In other words, to argue, for example, that Mouth's own *assertion* that she has "no idea what she's saying" (Begam 28) is proof that she really does have no idea "what she's saying" is still to assert a self-present interpretive subject, even if she is denying her self-presence via the eccentric, always separated, third person.

I regard the linguistic outpouring as a fluctuating intensity that situates Mouth within the sadistic scene of the play, whereby Mouth and Auditor are constricted and disarticulated. Relating such a disarticulation to Bataille's theories of representation and eroticism, especially the link to the death-drive, Foster asks, "But again, why is it played out on the compulsively (dis)articulated image of a female body?" (114). Even Lacan's description of the fragmented body, as exemplified for him by the paintings of

Hieronymus Bosch and described by Lacan in gender-neutral terms as the appearance in the form "of disjointed limbs, or of those organs represented in exoscopy, growing wings and taking up arms for intestinal persecutions" (4), gets transmuted into the unacknowledged gendered space of *Not I* in Wright's commentary: "Mouth is reliving the trauma of the primordial moment when the body senses its split from the Real. This experience can neither be included in the Imaginary, the realm of illusory wholeness, nor can it be part of the Symbolic, the domain which grants a conditional identity" (5). What appears to be foreclosed in this transmutation of Bosch into Beckett is gender difference itself, as nowhere does Wright mention that Mouth articulates a particular woman's experience. This may be due to an earlier binary opposition constructed in Wright's text, where Beckett is opposed to Artaud: "The plays of Samuel Beckett graphically present us with images of bodies, or parts of bodies, sometimes comically, sometimes desperately, struggling to channel their desire through speech. Conversely, the theatre of Antonin Artaud assaults us with images of the body's violent refusal to become entrapped in language" (5). There is no doubt that Mouth is part of a body, but Auditor is a whole (covered, veiled) body that presents us with a minimal but nonetheless active presence on stage; Mouth appears to be separated from the subject of the stream-of-utterance, refusing to be "entrapped" by the identification with one's self that would occur with the use of the first person. This refusal may be a resistance to *being spoken*: the fluctuating intensities or levels of memory have an existential import that a stream-of-signs undermines or reduces in vitality.

My reading therefore opposes Klossowski's "tonalities" with his "everyday code of signs" (1997, vii–xiii), where the latter, to put it simply, represents Lacan's Symbolic order, and the former his Imaginary. The Symbolic is the realm of language and the law of the father; Foster tentatively argues that Bellmer's *poupées* are aimed at the law of the fascist father and state, leading to a notion of "second-degree" reflexive sadism. As he says, this may not render the *poupées* "any less problematic (the ground of this 'Oedipal' challenge remains the female body, and 'woman' remains a trope for other things), but it does suggest what they seek to problematize" (115). Bellmer's assault on fascist "armouring" via his *poupées* also links them with the "degenerate art" of modernism(s) that the Nazi male (body and psyche) had to be shielded from (Foster 115–20). Is it possible that the performative self-denial of the auto/biographical narrative in *Not I* is representative of a combined foreclosure of gender *and* a "second-degree" reflexive sadism in Beckett's work as a whole? If so, this may have further implications for both humanist and poststructuralist readings of auto/biographical performance, suggesting that a "third space" is needed here.

The Conjectural Order: The Auto/biographical "Third Space"

Nisha Sajnani, in her essay "Strategic Narratives: The Embodiment of Minority Discourses in Biographical Performance," argues that Bhabha's concept of the "third space" is useful for understanding hybrid auto/biographical identities: "This space represents the in-between zone, in which individuals who were born between cultures or raised in a multicultural environment can articulate their lived experience in order to create the meaning of their multiple and contingent identities" (33). While it has become commonplace in postcolonial theory to automatically refer to the "third space" without necessarily examining what Bhabha means by this term, it is still a productive and useful concept: the "third space" of enunciation is *a general condition of cultural production*: "It is only when we understand that all cultural statements and systems are constructed in this contradictory and ambivalent space of enunciation, that we begin to understand why hierarchical claims to the inherent originality or 'purity' of cultures are untenable" (Bhabha 37). Bart Moore-Gilbert expresses the conundrum this way: "Precisely because of his attempt to avoid polarities, to stress contiguity and the productive dynamics of cultural 'translation,' as well as on the grounds of plain common sense, Bhabha is forced to admit that *all* cultures are impure, mixed and hybrid" (129).

If hybridity and the "third space" are a general condition of cultural production, one which is complicated further by focussing on "the parallel processes of Othering of women and subordinate classes in the domestic sphere" (Moore-Gilbert 129), and if theatre critics such as Sajnani have found these concepts useful in exploring auto/biographical minority discourses in performance, can the "third space" be applied to a general theory of auto/biographical performance? Bhabha regards an "enunciative split" as central to expression within the "third space," quite simply, the subject's enunciation being constituted, disrupted, and made eccentric via writing, literally the necessary shift via *différance* to the "not I": "The implication of this enunciative split for cultural analysis that I especially want to emphasize is its temporal dimension. The splitting of the subject of enunciation destroys the logics of synchronicity and evolution which traditionally authorize the subject of cultural knowledge" (Bhabha 36). In other words, it is important to think of the "third space" not just as a complex interlacing of identities and a spatial mapping-out of these new formations, and not just as something that occurs in writing (since the speech/writing opposition is here deconstructed), but also, if not primarily, as a complex temporality:

> It is often taken for granted in materialist and idealist problematics that the value
> of culture as an object of study, and the value of any analytic activity that is
> considered cultural, lie in a capacity to produce a cross-referential, generalizable

unity that signifies a progression or evolution of ideas-in-time, as well as a critical self-reflection on their premises or determinants....

The intervention of the Third Space of enunciation, which makes the structure of meaning and reference an ambivalent process, destroys this mirror of representation in which cultural knowledge is customarily revealed as an integrated, open, expanding code. Such an intervention quite properly challenges our sense of the historical identity of culture as a homogenizing, unifying force, authenticated by the originary Past, kept alive in the national tradition of the People. In other words, the disruptive temporality of enunciation displaces the narrative of the Western nation which Benedict Anderson so perceptively describes as being written in homogenous, serial time. (Bhabha 36–37)

Through this "disruptive temporality of enunciation" then, the "third space" of auto/biographical performance can be perceived as a desublimatory convergence of fluctuating intensities or tonalities with the auto/biographical investment. In other words, instead of regarding auto/biographical performance as a liberal humanist attempt to re-stage and recover the "truth" about a subject, *and* instead of the subject being regarded in the poststructuralist sense as being spoken or performed *by* language, I suggest that there is a third position where the creation of the auto/biographical subject is a creative experience *and* a proleptic investment: what the subject *was* coincides with what the (representing, or acting) subject wants, desires, or could be. This experience is not purely representational: it is a *lived experience* for the actor, the performance of situations and intensities that also functions as a form of cathexis or *Besetzung*, in the Lacanian sense of investment. The auto/biographical performance is thus a "proleptic investment of energy in a representation" (Ragland-Sullivan 218), where the desire to structure the past meets the intention and existential action of staging this desire itself. As Ellie Ragland-Sullivan puts it, "the link of Desire to signifier as trace [is] a narcissistic action that aims at constancy, mastery of the body, and recognition" (218). *Besetzung* is both the commonplace "concentration of psychic energy on a single goal" (*Collins Dictionary*) and a "discharge" of fluctuating intensities in the auto/biographical performance *as* investment. I call this "third space" of auto/biographical performance the "Conjectural order," that is to say, it crosses Lacan's Imaginary and Symbolic orders (or it functions by traversing both orders), but it is always an investment *and* a projection, in other words a *creation* of the auto/biographical subject through this combined investment/projection. Re-staging the subject is a process of re-staging subjectivity *per se*, one which occurs in everyday life when a crisis point has been reached or a transformational event occurs.

Does this Conjectural order account for the fragmented body, especially the *sadistic manipulation* of the fragmented female body? To use Deleuze and Guattari's phrase concerning Beckett here, "*everything divides, but into itself*" (76). In the desublimatory convergence of fluctuating intensities or tonalities which occurs with the auto/biographical investment, perception is in turn divided, sometimes fragmented, at other times simply interrogated, and then folded back upon itself. Deleuze gives, as a concrete and more structured example of this, Beckett's *Film*, which appears to be about an attempt to escape perception. Deleuze structures the "Condition of the Problem" in Beckett's *Film* according to a fold whereby the unbearable fact of being perceived by a third party is replaced by a recoil that ends with self-perception (1998, 23). This recoil goes through three phases: Action, Perception and Affection. In the first phase the perception of action can be simply "neutralized" by stopping action; in the second phase the perception *of* all objects, i.e., their uncanny ability to double and in turn perceive the human subject, is neutralized by a process of veiling and expulsion; in the third phase, the camera "surpasses the angle" (which maintains an acceptable distance between subject and camera) to reveal its "perception of affection, that is, the perception of the self by itself, or pure Affect" (Deleuze 1998, 25). It is this revelation that is terrifying: "that perception was the perception of the self by itself" and which is also the terror of Mouth in *Not I* (25). In *Cinema 1: The Movement-Image*, Deleuze names these three phases of Beckett's *Film* the perception-images, action-images, and affection-images. Together, they comprise the "assemblage" or "centre of indetermination" that is the human subject (1997, 66). With their extinguishing in *Film*, Deleuze argues that "Beckett ascends once more towards the luminous plane of immanence, the plane of matter and its cosmic eddying of movement-images" (68). This extinguishing action is also regarded as the condition of possibility of experimental cinema. In the notes to *Film*, Beckett writes that with "[a]ll extraneous perception suppressed, animal, human, divine, self-perception maintains in being" (323). Deleuze goes beyond this maintenance to arrive at the "pure" movement-image; in the auto/biographical investment, the shock value resides in the third phase: the recognition that the "biographical" performance coincides with the perception of the self, however much the latter is constrained, disfigured, or resisted. The desublimation processes that Foster regards as at work in Bellmer also lead to a resistance of the perception of the fragmented body as being necessarily a projection of patriarchy; in postmodernism, which should also be considered here, this desublimation is key. As Linda Nochlin argues, "The female sex organ is irrevocably de-fetishized in the entirely apotropaic prothesis [sic] photographs of Cindy Sherman and the de-sublimation—and, dare I say, domestication—of the male organ effected in the seductive and fragmented photographs of Robert Mapplethorpe" (54–55).

Towards a Theory of "Third Space" Auto/biographical Performance

The "third space" of auto/biographical performance perceived as a desublimatory convergence of fluctuating intensities or tonalities has been revealed as a gendered space, and one which negotiates two antithetical critical traditions. A poststructuralist reply to this summary would be to say that there is still a trace of the metaphysics of presence at work in this "third space." This is correct, as Anthony Easthope has pointed out: "I would invoke Lacan's notion of the imaginary to sanction the view that some provisional identity is necessary for the subject, that the ego must maintain for itself some permanence, some identity, some unity, some presence, some fixity of position" (147). For the purposes of auto/biographical performance, this "provisional identity" is *each* theatrical event, the necessary repeat play of identity, repetition, and difference. Easthope compares Derrida's and Lacan's competing concepts of the subject and notes that "while Derrida begins with a subject *already* foreseen from the side of language, a subject as a proper name, Lacan starts with a 'particularity' which precedes language altogether" (148). In asking how this Lacanian position can be possible, linking Darwinian science and the mirror-stage, Easthope argues that "[f]or Lacan, scandalously, there is indeed a pre-linguistic self, the particular materiality of the body as shaped by its place in the family. The subject is defined by the attempt to re-find this self within culture and language" (149).

There are a number of directions which a new theory of auto/biographical performance could take at this point: for example, creating a synthesis of the Conjectural order with Kristeva's concepts of geno- and pheno-text (and the relevant feminist gyno-criticism), or countering the law-of-the-father as a limit or boundary-experience and a shift into the Symbolic with the often understudied and marginalized formative mothering relationships that occur during this stage and beyond (see the critical essays edited by Abbey & O'Reilly). Work on "testimony" could also be dovetailed here (Anderson 126–133), and more literal notions of performance and law considered (Lane 2003b, 275–76). However, to conclude this chapter by remaining focussed on Beckett and Bellmer, I will return to the "not" in *Not I* and its homophone, or "knot," which Derrida explores at the beginning of *Glas*, that of *Sa* (*savoir absolu* or absolute knowledge), *Sa* (*significant* or signifier), and *Ça* (Id). This "knot" is an "interweaving of philosophical discourse with its 'remains' or 'debris'" (Lane 2003a, 106). As Hartman notes,

> That the word "knot" may echo in the mind as "not" is one of those small
> changes that analyst or exegete are trained to hear.... There are so many knots:
> Donnean, Penelopean, Lacanian, Borromean, Derridean. At the beginning of
> *Glas*, the similarity in sound of *Sa* (acronym for "savoir absolu") and *Sa*
> ("signifiant") is such a knot with a positive philosophic yield. Yet because of the
> equivocal, echo-nature of language, even identities or homophonies sound on:
> the sound of *Sa* is knotted with that of *ça*, as if the text were signaling its
> intention to bring Hegel, Saussure, and Freud together. *Ça* corresponds to the
> Freudian Id ("Es"); and it may be that our only "savoir absolu" is that of a *ça*
> structured like the *Sa*-signifiant: a bacchic or Lacanian "primal process" where
> only signifier-signifying-signifiers exist. (60–61)

Hartman's performance of Derrida here is exemplary, with the philosophical-theoretical knot—Hegel, Saussure, Freud—being transformed into the Lacanian "primal process." I argue that in performing auto/biography the humanist desire to gather absolute knowledge (*Sa*) of the subject is countered with the postmodernist and poststructuralist play of difference, the arbitrary Saussurian signifier (*Sa*). With my contention that there is a recovery of the *automatic* in auto/biographical performance (the performance of Surrealist automatic writing, or the automatic enunciation which "speaks the subject," and so on), the unconscious is perceived as structured like a language, or, as Hartman puts it, "*ça* structured like the *Sa*-signifiant." The concept of a Conjectural order stops the knot from being a new binding which would otherwise replace a contradiction (humanist vs. poststructuralist views of the auto/biographical subject) with a new chain of slippery signifiers (Lacan's "primal process"). Instead, the Conjectural order (the re-staging of the subject, of equal power to the mirror-stage but as occurs in later life) treats each auto/biographical performance as a determinate event, and it binds competing theories of subjectivity together. In Lacan's use of the Borromean knot, for example—"three rings, no two of which actually intersect, but which are kept knotted together"—the analogy was made with his three orders: "if one ring is cut, all three fall apart" (Wright 112). Similarly, in the Conjectural order, a new vision of subjectivity is produced, however fragmentary or broken, yet still as a determinate event.

This is not just a spatial theory, since as noted in relation to Bhabha, time is reconceived here—in the plays of Beckett linear time is reconceived via *life-rhythms*: "eating, breathing, sleeping-waking, night-day, the seasons, the phases of the moon, etc. These rhythms do not have beginnings, middles, and ends in the Aristotelian sense. One rhythmic cycle is completed only to begin again: nothing is resolved" (Schechner 21–22). These pulsations, these fluctuating intensities, are not decoupled or left unbound. The subject is not sublimated in *Not I*, or in Bellmer; rather the utilization of a "rhythmic cycle" is a desublimation. Gender in Beckett can be covered or veiled (Auditor), or reduced to an essentialist sexual difference (Mouth), but it is not in itself repressed. Gender is ejected, foreclosed by the critical denial of sadism in the performance of *Not I* and other plays, but this is to exile gender difference to the Lacanian Real, not to simply ignore it. As Spivak notes, it is the foreclosure of difference that is needed to charge the "reflexive judgment" of *Sa* (*savoir absolu* or absolute knowledge) and send it off in its homogenous, serial time or teleological movement (1999, 6).[1] As Laplanche and Pontalis note, such foreclosed signifiers re-emerge in the Real (166). In other words, not only does the "exile" of gender in the critical denial of sadism *not* lead to its total effacement from the critical scene, but this "exile" becomes the condition of possibility for the recuperation and re-examination of the role of gender in performing auto/biography.

Spivak's wider point is that the voracious dialectic of "absolute knowledge" (i.e., Western systems of knowledge) can be interrupted and re-engaged from a feminist and/or postcolonial perspective precisely through an awareness of the foundational nature of those subjects that are foreclosed.

Adorno's comment that Beckett's plays "put meaning on trial" (and "unfold its history") (153) is relevant to the auto/biographical Conjectural order: the investment here is not simply generative of meaning or signification (as an existential experience), but it places "meaning" under erasure; i.e. the word is crossed out but it remains of necessity legible (see Spivak 1976). This is less a bracketing-out of "meaning" and more a suspicion of the production of any universal truth in the theatrical event. The auto/biographical subject is thus brought to, or immersed in, a limit or boundary situation, where new creative possibilities both present themselves and are made (Jaspers 179). These situations are not arbitrary, and they are not commutable (although they can be repeated in performance, re-lived *and* re-performed). With Beckett and Bellmer, the sadistic play also approaches a limit or boundary situation, which, as with the work of de Sade, may simply reinforce conservative gender formations and relations as normative (Klossowski 1992, 20–21), or may have a more transgressive objective (as in the work of Bataille).

Another way of formulating this heightened creativity and intensity of the boundary situation in Beckett and Bellmer is via Benjamin's interpretation of Surrealist "profane illumination" (Benjamin 1999a, 209), that is, not an attempt to transgress, but dialectically and materially to transfigure the subject (see Lane 2005). Modified by Benjamin with his "dialectics at a standstill," "profane illumination" becomes *Das Jetzt der Erkennbarkeit* or the "now of knowability" or (re)cognizability. In other words, Benjamin picks up on the Surrealist shift from aesthetics to politics, just as Foster regards Bellmer's "second-degree" reflexive sadism as a critique of the fascist law-of-the-father and state. But again, is this use of Jaspers and Benjamin somehow too metaphysical, even as it draws attention to the potential political import of the auto/biographical performance? I argue that the "third space" of auto/biographical performance perceived as a desublimatory convergence of fluctuating intensities or tonalities is also one which utilizes a *radical metaphysics* in the sense of Fanon's development of Jasper's work. For example, Fanon refuses to re-stage the colonial subject as normative, so in *Black Skin, White Masks* he begins with embedded situations and deconstructs them via a constitutive, *disturbing, dislocating* series of propositions, statements, and questions concerning being and identity. The deconstructive-destructive (Benjamin 1999b, 470) analysis of the psychoexistential complex of colonialism is also an analysis of the "time of" subjectivity. This brings us full circle (again) to Bhabha's comments concerning temporality in the "third space."

In conclusion, the performance of auto/biography presents a formidable challenge to theorists, regardless of the critical tradition they work within; by focussing in this essay on Beckett and Bellmer, I argue that gender formation and performance re-emerges from the Real in complex, disturbing, but always central ways. I have shown how the divisions of the *eccentric* subject in the "automatic" expression of life writing and performance are not arbitrary; rather, they function via gendered processes that can be explored using post-Freudian concepts, as with the work of Foster and/or Spivak. Theorizing the gendered space of auto/biographical performance has also led me to the notion of a *radical metaphysics*, whereby questions concerning lived experiences coincide with a reworking of contemporary theory from a feminist and postcolonial perspective. Thus Beckett's and Bellmer's female "characters" or puppets emerge from a sadistic "zone of nonbeing," to use Fanon's term, via an interrogation of the aesthetic traditions within which they have been embedded and via which they have been foreclosed.

Notes

1. As with the previous links established between Bhabha's work and performing auto/biography, Spivak's notion of foreclosure is also drawn from work on postcolonial theory. In this case, Spivak's adoption of "foreclosure" in relation to the "native informant" and the ways in which the erasure of the latter, for Spivak, is an exemplary Western move (creating a condition of possibility for Western thought), followed by the re-emergence of the "native informant" in the Real. The gendered space of auto/biographical performance is therefore closely linked with notions of ethnicity and race.

Works Cited

Abbey, Sharon and Andrea O'Reilly, eds. *Redefining Motherhood: Changing Identities and Patterns.* Toronto: Second Story Press, 1998.

Adorno, Theodor W. *Aesthetic Theory.* Trans. Robert Hullot-Kentor. Minneapolis: University of Minnesota Press, 1997.

Anderson, Linda. *Autobiography.* London and New York: Routledge, 2001.

Bataille, Georges. *Visions of Excess: Selected Writings, 1927–1939.* Trans. Allan Stoekl, with Carl R. Lovitt and Donald M. Leslie, Jr. Minneapolis: University of Minnesota Press, 1985.

Beckett, Samuel. *The Complete Dramatic Works.* London: Faber & Faber, 1990.

Begam, Richard. "Beckett and Postfoundationalism, or, How Fundamental are those Fundamental Sounds?" In *Beckett and Philosophy,* ed. Richard Lane. New York: Palgrave, 2002. 11–39.

Benjamin, Walter. "Surrealism: The Last Snapshot of the European Intelligentsia." In *Selected Writings: Volume 2, 1927–1934.* Ed. Michael W. Jennings. Trans. Rodney Livingstone et al. Cambridge, Mass. and London: Belknap Press of Harvard University Press, 1999a. 207–21.

————. *The Arcades Project.* Trans. Howard Eiland and Kevin McLaughlin. Cambridge: Belknap Press of Harvard University Press, 1999b.

Bhabha, Homi K. *The Location of Culture.* London and New York: Routledge, 1994.

Breton, André. *Manifestoes of Surrealism.* Trans. Richard Seaver and Helen R. Lane. Ann Arbor: University of Michigan Press, 1972.

Calder, John. *The Philosophy of Samuel Beckett.* London: Riverrun, 2001.

Critchley, Simon. *Very Little ... Almost Nothing: Death, Philosophy, Literature.* London and New York: Routledge, 1997.

Deleuze, Gilles. *Cinema 1: The Movement Image.* Trans. Hugh Tomlinson and Barbara Habberjam. London: Athlone, 1997.

————. "The Greatest Irish Film (Beckett's 'Film')." In *Essays Critical and Clinical.* Trans. Daniel W. Smith and Michael A. Greco. London: Verso, 1998.

—, and Félix Guattari. *Anti-Oedipus: Capitalism and Schizophrenia*. Minneapolis: University of Minnesota Press, 1989.

Easthope, Anthony. "Homi Bhabha, Hybridity and Identity, or Derrida Versus Lacan." *Hungarian Journal of English and American Studies* 4, nos. 1–2 (1998): 145–51.

Fanon, Frantz. *Black Skin, White Masks*. Trans. Charles Lam Markmann. London: Pluto, 1986.

Foster, Hal. *Compulsive Beauty*. Cambridge: MIT Press, 1993.

Grace, Sherrill. "From Emily Carr to Joy Coghill … and Back: Writing the Self in *Song of This Place*." *BC Studies* 137 (Spring 2003): 109–30.

—. "Performing the Auto/biographical Pact: Towards a Theory of Identity in Performance." In *Tracing the Autobiographical*, ed. Marlene Kadar, Linda Warley, Jeanne Perreault, and Susanna Egan. Waterloo: Wilfrid Laurier University Press, 2005. 65–79.

Gray, Katherine M. "Troubling the Body: Toward a Theory of Beckett's Use of the Human Body Onstage." *Journal of Beckett Studies* 5, nos. 1–2 (1995–96): 1–17.

Hartman, Geoffrey H. *Saving the Text: Literature, Derrida, Philosophy*. Baltimore and London: Johns Hopkins University Press, 1985.

Jaspers, Karl. *Philosophy*. Vol. 2. Trans. E. B. Ashton, London and Chicago: University of Chicago Press, 1970.

Kelly, Katherine. "The Orphic Mouth in *Not I*." In *The Beckett Studies Reader*, ed. S. E. Gontarski. Gainesville: University Press of Florida, 1993. 121–28.

Klossowski, Pierre. *Sade My Neighbour*. Trans. Alphonso Lingis. London: Quartet, 1992.

—. *Nietzsche and the Vicious Circle*. Trans. Daniel W. Smith. Chicago: University of Chicago Press; London: Athlone, 1997.

Knowlson, James. *Damned to Fame: The Life of Samuel Beckett*. London: Bloomsbury, 1996.

Lacan, Jacques. *Écrits: A Selection*. Trans. Alan Sheridan. London: Tavistock, 1977.

Lane, Richard J. "Beckett and Nietzsche." In *Beckett and Philosophy*, ed. Richard J. Lane. London: Palgrave, 2002. 166–76.

—. *Functions of the Derrida Archive: Philosophical Receptions*. Budapest: Akadémiai Kiadó, 2003a.

—. "Performing History: The Reconstruction of Gender and Race in British Columbian Drama." In *Performing National Identities: International Perspectives on Contemporary Canadian Theatre*, ed. Sherrill Grace and Albert-Reiner Glaap. Vancouver: Talonbooks, 2003b. 265–77.

—. *Reading Walter Benjamin: Writing Through the Catastrophe*. Manchester: Manchester University Press, 2005.

Laplanche, Jean and J.-B. Pontalis. *The Language of Psycho-Analysis*. Trans. Donald Nicholson-Smith. New York: Norton, 1973.

Maude, Ulrika. "The Body of Memory: Beckett and Merleau-Ponty." In *Beckett and Philosophy*, ed. Richard J. Lane. London: Palgrave, 2002. 108–22.

Moore-Gilbert, Bart. *Postcolonial Theory: Contexts, Practices, Politics*. London: Verso, 2000.

Nochlin, Linda. *The Body in Pieces: The Fragment As a Metaphor of Modernity*. London: Thames and Hudson, 1994.

O'Gorman, Kathleen. "'but this other awful thought': Aspects of the Female in Beckett's *Not I*." *Journal of Beckett Studies* 1, nos. 1–2 (1992): 77–94.

Polizzotti, Mark. *Revolution of the Mind: The Life of André Breton*. London: Bloomsbury, 1995.

Pountney, Rosemary. "On Acting Mouth in *Not I*." In pt. 1 of a section on "Practical aspects of theatre, radio and television." *Journal of Beckett Studies* 1 (Winter 1976): 81–85.

Ragland-Sullivan, Ellie. *Jacques Lacan and the Philosophy of Psychoanalysis*. Urbana and Chicago: University of Illinois Press, 1987.

Sajnani, Nisha. "Strategic Narratives: The Embodiment of Minority Discourse in Biographical Performance." *Canadian Theatre Review* 117 (Winter 2004): 33–37.

Schechner, Richard. *Performance Theory*. London and New York: Routledge, 1994.

Spivak, Gayatri Chakravorty. Translator's preface to *Of Grammatology*, by Jacques Derrida. Trans. Gayatri Chakravorty Spivak. Baltimore and London: Johns Hopkins University Press, 1976. ix–lxxxvii.

———. *A Critique of Postcolonial Reason: Toward a History of the Vanishing Present*. Cambridge: Harvard University Press, 1999.

Wright, Elizabeth. *Psychoanalytic Criticism: Theory in Practice*. London: Methuen, 1984.

(Un)Covering the Mirror: Performative Reflections in Linda Griffiths's *Alien Creature: A Visitation from Gwendolyn MacEwen* and Wendy Lill's *The Occupation of Heather Rose*

Katherine McLeod

Improvisation as a critical term rarely enters into auto/biographical discourse, yet improvisation offers a method of self-performance deserving of our critical attention, specifically through the multifaceted intersections among improvisation, pedagogy, and dramaturgical processes. At the forefront of these intersections lies the question of how improvisation becomes a performative tool for writing a *self*—a self that is not a mirror image but rather an unfixed *self* engaged with its own representation. Voice slips out of the mirror's grasp, pushing us out of mimesis and into the realm of diegesis—and it is through this medium of voice that I offer a repositioning of Susanna Egan's auto/biographic theory of "mirror talk" in relation to performativity.[1] Egan herself gestures towards this paradigm shift when she refers to "listening as performative dialogism" (25), and I would like to pursue her idea of listening as a participatory act, particularly regarding how participation itself constitutes a medium of self-representation within mirror talk. What I will call "performative mirror talk" refers to a method of auto/biographic representation that foregrounds its own *process* of making—particularly through its attentiveness to the voice as enabling linguistic reflections, or rather linguistic reiterations—of a *self* in flux. Integral to the voice as medium through which to perform this sounding of self is Leigh Gilmore's "autobiographics": a term referring to a self-representational and reading practice "concerned with interruptions and eruptions, [and] with resistance and contradiction as strategies of self-representation" (42). Building upon these theoretical frameworks provided by Egan and Gilmore, I will explore how performative mirror talk underlines the construction of an auto/biographic *self* in two recent Canadian dramas—Linda Griffiths's *Alien Creature: A Visitation from Gwendolyn MacEwen* and Wendy Lill's *The Occupation of Heather Rose*—both of which involve a female character whose story is not so much about reflecting her life in a narrative as it is about engaging with the improvisatory and performative processes that perform her life on stage.

Improvisation allows us to consider how self-representations that emerge through performative mirror talk continue to be in flux—not only because they are expressed through the ever-shifting medium of speech but also because of their continuous engagement with the representational process itself. Recent criticism in improvisational studies points towards theoretical readings of an improvised self; most notably, cultural theorist Ajay Heble argues that improvisation offers "a particularly resonant framework of analysis for the (per)formative power of self-representational strategies" (92). For Heble, autobiographies such as Billie Holiday's *Lady Sings the Blues*, Duke Ellington's *Music Is My Mistress*, and Charles Mingus's *Beneath the Underdog* exemplify "performance-oriented models of improvisation to engage complex questions of agency and identity" (96). This notion of "performance-oriented models" applies to my reading of Griffiths's and Lill's plays as improvisatory in the sense that their structure foregrounds an improvisatory process even though the words themselves are scripted on the page. In re-contextualizing the work of Anthony Frost and Ralph Yarrow on dramatic improvisation in the realm of jazz studies, Marshall Soules makes an important observation on how both jazz and dramatic improvisations share the common ground of improvising identity: "[B]oth jazz and improv acting are procedural systems that challenge restricting constructions of character; both seek to open up character to greater expressive potential, wider freedoms and responsibilities" (284). Griffiths and Lill employ these "procedural systems that challenge restricting constructions of character" to the extent that their plays enable the transformative aspect of character that is central not only to Egan's mirror talk but also to Soules's understanding of improvisation: "[T]he actor involved in transformations is riffing like the jazz musician, a channel for a dialogic mix of cultural voices unencumbered by reifications of personality or place" (293). While neither Griffiths nor Lill explicitly calls for improvisation in the script, their plays are versions of Heble's performance-oriented models that do call for the performer and her audience to hear how improvisation informs the structure of each play, whether through the improvisatory sessions that shaped Griffiths's writing process or through the way in which Lill scripts Heather Rose as if she is improvising herself through the multiple voices of her past.

In conversation with Kathleen Gallagher, Griffiths explains how *Alien Creature* was "written—about 70 per cent of it—through improvisation" (128). Griffiths's reflection on her writing process suggests that improvisation provides a *performative* interaction between herself and her subject, Gwendolyn MacEwen. I call their interaction performative in the sense that it enacts Judith Butler's understanding of performativity "not as a singular or a deliberate 'act,' but, rather, as the reiterative and citational practice by which discourse produces the effects that it names" (2). Not only does the performative element of their interaction call for the continuous reflection, or rather reiteration (to mark the shift beyond the visual and into linguistic and acoustic terms), of selves, but the improvisatory element of their interaction further indicates that these selves are in flux. Relating back to Heble's integration of autobiography and improvisation, the refusal of a stable auto/biographical "I" signals a departure from self-representation that claims to know itself fully. Improvisation plays a critical role in performative mirror talk because the audience is intimately part of this process of performing a self—a self that reverberates somewhere within this negotiatory process between performer and audience, as implied through Heather Rose's admission that, despite her efforts to transfer her story from herself to the audience, her story still exists within herself in as much as it exists in its telling: "It's inside me now" (Lill 330). The character of Heather Rose is fictional—her "auto/biography" is scripted by Lill—yet I would like to suggest that this construction of self does not have any less validity for being fictional because it presents us with a model through which to question the possibilities and limitations of self-representation through a voice-based medium. It is through voice that we hear how both Griffiths's and Lill's plays exemplify what Heble describes as performance-oriented texts that attempt to unsettle the auto/biographical "I"—but these two plays unsettle the "I" even further by being live performances themselves, enabling us to hear the voice as if it engages in mirror *talk* without the visual mirror, in darkness.

Haunting Performances: From Poetry to Stage

Linda Griffiths held a glass of water to her lips, hesitated, and then lowered it while keeping her eyes fixed on us, a spellbound audience. The stage directions in her play have their own description of this moment—"*She raises the glass to her lips, then lowers it untouched*" (47)—but the magic woven by Griffiths, performing this scene at the "Putting a Life on Stage" workshop (UBC 2004), surpassed any description, even stage directions written by the playwright herself. Sitting alongside other playwrights on a conference panel, Griffiths managed to create a space of magic like the one that she alludes to at the beginning of her play: "Come into my beautiful basement" (16). Winner of the 2000 Chalmers Award, *Alien Creature* is a monologue written and performed by Griffiths in which the spirit of Gwendolyn MacEwen attempts to re-educate us as to who she *really* was: "I want you to know I was brave. I want you to know I fought hard. I want you to know I loved beauty, that I laughed. I want you to know I was a coward. I wish ... I wish" (15). Important to Griffiths in explaining MacEwen's myth is explaining her death: "But I did not commit suicide. I drank myself to death, it's different. Don't Sylvia Plath me and I won't Sylvia Plath you" (13). While Griffiths's conjuring of MacEwen clearly identifies MacEwen's myth as emanating from her spirit, it is told through collaborative language that makes it a myth of two women rather than of one. The audience witnesses an interaction between artists whose reflections of *self* seem deeply rooted in the language of one another. Although Griffiths writes the majority of the play in her own words, there are thirteen direct quotations from MacEwen's poetry, and the play itself concludes with one of these quotations that reminds both Griffiths and the audience of how MacEwen's words haunt the words of the play: "I am starting to haunt you. I am starting right now" (50). Upon hearing these words, we might suggest that the mirror talk between Griffiths and MacEwen is one of haunting; however, as much as the poetics of the play foreground the presence of such a hauntology, Griffiths refuses to be passively "haunted" by MacEwen. Rather than surrendering her agency to the power of MacEwen's "ghost," Griffiths positions herself as an active participant in this reflective haunting. Therefore, the "I" in the last line of the play can be heard as either Griffiths's or MacEwen's because their haunting reflects both ways, and perhaps even a third way as the audience too leaves the theatre haunted.

MacEwen's presence haunts the final words of the play because they are, in fact, her own words. Among the nine quotations from MacEwen's poetry in the play, the lines quoted to end the play literally and thematically foreground this act of poetic haunting:

"Past and Future Ghosts"

Everything is already known, but we proceed as though we know nothing. I have lived in houses haunted by ghosts from the future as well as the past—ghosts of my future and past selves as well as ghosts of others. It's very simple; we all just move from room to room in these time-houses and catch glimpses of one another in passing. As a child in one house I used to see this older woman who was myself grown up, and thirty years later I went back there and met the child, who was waiting for me to come. Who is haunting whom? Right now some future ghosts are re-decorating the house I live in; I see them out of the corner of my eye, tearing down certain walls and inventing new ones. Look out—you who inhabit those rooms of my future—I'm coming after you. I'm starting to haunt you, I'm starting right now.

(MacEwen 91)

MacEwen's poem anticipates her own self-haunting while also reiterating the dialectics of haunting that underscore Griffiths's play. With reference to "my past and future selves," MacEwen articulates her own negotiation of selves—a negotiation that remains unresolved at the end of the poem. Her question "Who is haunting whom?" moves the poetic voice from descriptive to dialectic, engaging the listener in a dialogue that moves from the "I" to the "you." But rather than marking an "ending," this move to the second-person address signals a beginning—"I'm starting to haunt you, I'm starting right now"—which defies the notion of ending the complex conversation already occurring among the audience, Griffiths, and MacEwen. The fact that Griffiths chooses to end her play with MacEwen's own negation of an ending indicates that Griffiths intends to continue a haunted conversation between speaker and listener.

Poetic Mirrors

MacEwen's question, "Who is haunting whom?", applies to Griffiths's play because of its complex audience-performer dynamics: are we watching Griffiths perform, or are we watching Griffiths perform as MacEwen? Or is Griffiths watching MacEwen perform through her own body just as much as we are watching Griffiths perform? The words of MacEwen's poems provide space for the otherwise temporally disparate words of each artist to touch hands upon the page. When these words are corporealized through bodily utterances, Griffiths embodies the juxtaposition of her improvised voice and MacEwen's textual voice. Reading this transference of voice as an auto/biographical act, we can read Griffiths's embodiment of the biographical subject as autobiographical, especially when we recall her comment on how she was drawn to writing this play because MacEwen "could have been me."[2] As much as the play is *about* MacEwen, Griffiths's play refuses to be *only* about MacEwen—as we watch Griffiths slipping back and forth between her own words and MacEwen's, we realize that this endless dialogue of haunting is, perhaps, *who* the play is *about*.

At the end of the published text of *Alien Creature*, Griffiths lists thirteen quotations from MacEwen's poetry that appear throughout the play. Although they are unidentified by the speaker in the play, these quotations provide moments of audible recognition for audience members familiar with MacEwen's poems: as if suddenly we are *hearing* MacEwen herself (even though one supposedly hears Griffiths speaking as MacEwen throughout the play). The inclusion of MacEwen's own words creates points of rupture within the speaker's voice, thereby amplifying the multiple voices being performed through a single body. The quotations foreground the limitations of the play as biographical drama: Griffiths must fill in the spaces between these quotations with words that can never be MacEwen's, yet these spaces provide Griffiths with an opportunity to insert herself. In doing this, Griffiths writes a play that is as much about MacEwen's words as it is about the interplay between Griffiths's words and MacEwen's. As Griffiths acknowledges in her "Playwright's Notes" preceding the script of *Alien Creature*, those familiar with MacEwen will realize that there is another voice present in this telling of MacEwen's life: "I want to say, 'This may not be your Gwen, or you may find glimpses of her when you least expect it. Then there might be times when you think, "she would never say that."' The person that is present that you don't know is me. She and I are doing this play. And only both of us can speak" (10). The notion that "only both of us can speak" prepares the reader, or the audience in the case of performance, for a script that is self-conscious about its vocal layers, gesturing towards the idea that MacEwen and Griffiths depend upon each other in order to speak for themselves. In the Playwrights Canada edition of Griffiths's play, the reader is further invited to regard Griffiths and MacEwen as mirroring aspects of each other through the inclusion of photographs: a haunting close-up of MacEwen's eye on the cover and frontispiece, a shadowy picture of Griffiths performing MacEwen in *Alien Creature*, and a photograph of MacEwen at the end of the text, leaving the reader looking into her thoughtful gaze as if speaking the last lines through her eyes: "I am starting to haunt you. I am starting right now" (50). The inclusion of these photographs invites the reader to consider how both Griffiths and MacEwen are visually, linguistically, and acoustically present and how, in fact, the play itself exists in the literal space between these photographs. Even though the textual representation of voice lacks the embodied acoustics of voice in performance, the fact that the voices of MacEwen and Griffiths are scripted between their visual reflections structurally engages a process similar to the performative mirror talk that takes place on stage between the selves of MacEwen and Griffiths (see figures 4 and 5).

The performative mirror talk that takes place within Griffiths's play emerges primarily out of improvisation. In the context of Canadian theatre, Linda Griffiths's improvisatory work in both acting and writing offers exemplary glimpses into the practical and pedagogical practices of improvisation; moreover, Griffiths's improvisations directly relate to the overall aim of this discussion: to focus on improvisation not only as a theatrical technique but also as an autobiographical tool—a tool namely for articulating the process of writing a *self* in flux. Griffiths herself has explored what the word "process" itself means in relation to auto/biographical writing, especially regarding the question of whether the audience expects a process or a product. In her article "Process?" Griffiths suggests that the emphasis on either process or product depends on personal preference; for Griffiths, the emphasis falls on the former, as she comments that "process is a live thing, with no rules but instinct and the desire to offer something" (61). Before outlining her own writing and acting processes, Griffiths questions what exactly she means by process: "Am I talking about the process of improvising a play, the process of writing, of collaborating with directors, other writers, audiences? Am I talking about what happens behind the closed doors in the rehearsal room or about what the audience sees? I realized that I'm actually talking about all of this and more" (56). Her conclusion that process involves "all of this and more" makes a salient point considering how process has, in fact, been the product in nearly all her plays: ranging from her improvisational collaboration with other young artists in *Heartbreak Hotel*, to improvisations on political figures with Paul Thompson that pulled her towards writing *Maggie & Pierre*, to her attempt at translating improvisation into a "paper play" for *O.D. on Paradise*, to her intensive collaboration with Maria Campbell on *Jessica* (resulting in a documentation of the process

Figure 4. Gwendolyn MacEwen. Photograph by John McCombe Reynolds, courtesy of Kari Reynolds.

Figure 5. Linda Griffiths as Gwendolyn in *Alien Creature*, first produced at Theatre Passe Muraille, Toronto, 1999. Photograph by David Kinsman.

itself in their co-authored book, *The Book of Jessica*), to developing a complex connection to the audience in *The Darling Family* and *A Game of Inches*, and then to a ten-day improvisational workshop in which Griffiths wrote and re-wrote a draft of *The Duchess: a.k.a. Wallis Simpson* (57–61).

Griffiths construes her history of writing and acting as a history of processes that she continues to participate in, especially since she had not yet written *Alien Creature* at the time of her article's self-reflection. Nonetheless, Griffiths mentions her next project as a piece about MacEwen that she plans to improvise in front of an audience: "The idea for the Gwendolyn MacEwen play is to immerse myself in her work and life, make a loose map, then go out and improvise in fifteen-minute segments at events throughout the city for the next year" (61). As jazz theorist John Corbett explains about the risks of improvisation, musicians can either eliminate risk through improvisation (as there is no such as thing as a "mistake") or take a risk through improvisation. In taking a risk, Corbett cites three pitfalls for the musician exploring the improvisatory unknown: stagnation, insanity, or completion (223). For Corbett, these pitfalls combine to form the ultimate risk of improvisation: that in attempting to destabilize normative codes, the musician ends up re-inscribing the improvisation that was once "new" (223). Although Griffiths's improvising on MacEwen's life functions in somewhat different terms than Corbett's, Griffiths does perform a destabilizing of the MacEwen known to the general public, at the same time performing a MacEwen that cannot be codified and cast aside as a self that is "known." Moreover, when looking ahead to her MacEwen play, Griffiths describes her own improvisational practices in terms of risk—"I've never worked quite so much without a net in front of audiences, but I believe that this is the best way to get around the traps of inherent literary material" (1998, 61)—which raises the question of what is at risk in such a performance: artistic integrity or integrity of self? Risk reminds us that the "success" of theatrical improvisation relies primarily upon the audience—a reliance that Griffiths herself understands in terms of her own audience-performer relationship between herself and MacEwen. Upon recognizing the risks involved in improvising, Griffiths concludes her article with a depiction of herself as an audience to MacEwen: "Hopefully, if I listen to Gwendolyn, she'll answer" (61).

Griffiths's *Alien Creature* approaches the condition of musical improvisation because the quotations from MacEwen's poetry function as melodies upon which Griffiths improvises.[3] Especially considering Griffiths's technique of improvising for fifteen minutes upon a phrase from the poetry, one might say that she riffs upon these phrases. Her physical actions provide evidence of this riffing, such as when the stage directions call for her to pull "a series of gauzy cloths" from an empty glass immediately before speaking these lines from MacEwen's poem "The Magician": "Finally then do all my poems become as crazy scarves / issuing from the fingers like a coloured mesh / you, magician ... " (2000, 17). In addition to these embodied improvisations, Griffiths's words riff upon MacEwen's words. A poignant example occurs after the story of Wonder Woman, a mythic figure whom Griffiths weaves into an elaborate story of how she saves the Amazons from the Eve of Destruction. The story itself reads as an improvised narrative, but what I would like to highlight is the song between the story's initial tragic ending and the heroic ending that she includes after realizing, "But that's no way to sell comics! And so what happens is, with a mighty feat of strength, courage and training, Wonder Woman throws off the creature" (24). Before this ending, the story of Wonder Woman fades into a song of despair as she falls asleep in the grasp of the creature:

> (*Singing*) You're nothing but a nothing,
> A nothing, a nothing.
> You're nothing but a nothing.
> You're not a thing at all.
> Not a thing at all ... (24)

In this song, we hear reflections of MacEwen and Griffiths in the fictional reflections of Wonder Woman and the creature—each singing of herself as a nothing. But another voice enters into this multivocal reflection: a voice from MacEwen's poem "Animal Spirits," which ends with a lingering on this word "nothing":

> Lord,
> Teach me to be lean, and wise. Nothing matters,
> nothing *matters*. (64)

In keeping with the jazz terminology of improvisation, we might say that MacEwen *riffs* upon the word "nothing" (or, to use the terminology of classical music, she performs a *variation* on the word "nothing"). We can hear how, echoing the structure of this poem, Griffiths employs a similar structure of "theme and variations" or jazz riffing on a melody to interact with MacEwen herself and also with her texts. In her preface to the play, Griffiths calls these riffs "theatre-poems": "I start writing the script and these poems come, little rhyming pieces that said a certain thing I need to be said at a certain time" (10). Her improvisation upon MacEwen's own words in writing these theatre-poems provides a space through which Griffiths can write herself. Her improvisation enacts performative mirroring—a mirroring that acknowledges its citation of the subject and its reinterpretation of the subject into the terms of the performer. Keeping in mind Griffiths's own awareness of the citationality of the theatre-poems—"there are these theatre-poems mixed in with the poetry of this real poet" (10)—the linguistic underlies the performative interaction between Griffiths and MacEwen. For Griffiths and MacEwen, the word "nothing" provides a space for their languages to touch, leaving tangible traces in this seemingly empty space—a negative poetics that offers a place for *nothing*, indeed, to *matter*.

(Un)Covering—Acoustic Mirrors

Performative mirroring between MacEwen and Griffiths in *Alien Creature* enables the representation of self to manifest itself not as a visual, mimetic reflection but rather as a kinetic, corporeal performance. Building upon this shift away from reflections and towards reiterations and embodiments, Wendy Lill's *The Occupation of Heather Rose* offers voice as a medium through which to understand performative mirroring. Lill's play involves a vocal mirroring that refuses mimetic constraints, a refusal best represented in Heather Rose's eventual covering of her mirror. Covering the mirror implies a denial of self-knowledge, and yet I would like to explore how this act of covering the mirror leads to an *uncovering* of self.[4] In particular, I would like to consider how such an act privileges the oral/aural over the visual, thereby enabling the "performative mirroring" that I have been arguing for in Griffiths's *Alien Creature*. In recounting the situation in which she literally covers the mirror, Heather Rose thematizes a rejection of the visual; but Lill's play goes beyond mere thematization by structurally emphasizing how Heather Rose's multiple voices acoustically perform a self in flux—a self that calls for a rethinking of mirroring itself. Heather Rose herself finally comments on the state of her story, "It's inside me now" (330), as if disappointed that her story cannot be removed from her to be examined like a reflection; but we as listeners can realize that the process of her performance is the material through which we experience this self named Heather Rose.

In *The Occupation of Heather Rose*, the title character delivers a monologue composed not only of her voice but also of the voices of three other characters.[5] These voices construct a story of self, or rather a story of self-destruction, as we hear of Heather Rose venturing North as a young nurse only to realize that she is disastrously unprepared for the cultural and social challenges of living within the First Nations community of Snake Lake.[6] In her article, "Language and Racism: Wendy Lill's *The Occupation of Heather Rose*," Jacqueline Petropoulos argues that the multiple voices of the play can be described by Mikhail Bakhtin's term "dialogic." In fact, I would argue that this play embraces dialogism to the point that it becomes what Jennifer Harvie and Ric Knowles call "a dialogic monologue," a term that challenges Bakhtin's notion of drama as striving through an individual speaker towards unitary language and, instead, posits drama as enabling a dialogic monologue that conveys "a fractured, incoherent or self-alienated subject through which various *voices* are heard" (140). Far from being monologic in Bakhtinian terms, *The Occupation of Heather Rose* refuses to speak from a single position of authority. Even though the character of Heather Rose is the only one who speaks, she keeps her auto/biographical "I" in a state of slipperiness, circling around her story while speaking from the many voices implicated in it. Her character vocalizes the "dialogic monologue" that Harvie and Knowles theorize in their critical discussion of the term; yet, in this conversationally structured article, Harvie dismisses Lill's *The Occupation of Heather Rose* as "not notably dialogic" (140). Although critics such as Petropoulos have argued for Lill's play as dialogic—and I too would argue that dialogism informs the play's self-representational structure to the extent that Harvie's unqualified dismissal certainly calls for an explanation—what I propose as to why Harvie overlooks the dialogism within the play is that she does not take into account the performativity of Heather Rose's voice, particularly how this performativity augments the play's attempt to produce itself as a dialogic monologue. Building upon Petropoulos's understanding of our own participation in hearing the play's dialogism, I would like to reposition this dialogism in the realm of performativity, keeping in mind Egan's aforementioned phrase, "listening as performative dialogism" (25). I find that *The Occupation of Heather Rose* provides an opportunity for the audience to listen *actively*, and I would like to amplify the concept of the voice itself as it pertains to this active listening because it is through our attention to how this voice performs through mirror talk that we hear Heather Rose's monologue as dialogic.

In Egan's theory of mirror talk, the mirror is constructive rather than reflective, and its constructivism emerges from its dialogism (23). Through the monologue form of Lill's play, we hear Heather Rose constructing a dialogic mirror to which we may listen. To take Egan's privileging of construction over reflection one step further, I would argue that Lill's portrayal of mirroring strongly critiques the monologic reflection of the visual—in other words, her play pushes us to do what Heather Rose so poignantly does, cover the mirror: "After being witty, with Leslie Walters, or just with myself—I thought I was the best audience of all—I put a towel over the bathroom mirror. It made the mornings easier" (319). This covering of the mirror follows Heather Rose's re-enactment of presenting herself as an authority on the community of Snake Lake to a newcomer, Leslie Walters: "What d'you want to know? Heather Rose tells all" (319). Before beginning this re-enactment, Heather Rose tells us that she "desperately needed an audience," and at first we assume that this audience refers to Leslie Walters; but once we hear Heather Rose's admission—"After being witty, with Leslie Walters, or just with myself—I thought I was the best audience of all"—we realize that she performs for herself. With this perspective, we can understand not only how she tries to convince herself even more so than Leslie Walters that "it's not a bad place" (319) but how her entire performance involves herself as audience, trying to piece together a *self* out of the dissonant reflections in the same way that we attempt this process as audience members.

Although I speak of Heather Rose as an audience to *herself*, I use this word loosely since we hear a fragmented self, as if instead of her mirror fracturing, Heather Rose's voice fractures acoustically. In fact, this scene presents us with an acoustic mirror that is more self-reflective (or rather self-reflexive) than the visual mirror. With the words "I put a towel over the bathroom mirror," we hear the oral/aural replace the visual while witnessing a character's desperate re-conceptualization of herself as an audience that she wishes to erase. However, what Heather Rose does not realize is that the *hearers* of her voice are, perhaps, the ones able to effect change. Although she considers her story untold—"But what did I think would happen here? That I would somehow be able to unload this. I can't" (330)—the audience hears her embodied story through her voice, telling us an oral tale of broken reflections and interruptions. Nevertheless, if we hear this story through Egan's notion of "listening as performative dialogism," then we must recognize ourselves as active participants in this oral/aural mirror that Heather Rose speaks herself into. But when her voice fades into the darkness of an unreflecting auditorium, will we speak back?

Performative Voice—Listening

In relation to both Lill's *The Occupation of Heather Rose* and Griffiths's *Alien Creature*, I have been applying the concept of performative mirroring, which combines Egan's mirror talk with Judith Butler's notion of a bodily, citational performance of identity. As previously mentioned, Egan's description of listening in mirror talk as "performative dialogism" anticipates an intersection between her theories and theories of performativity, a combination of which explains how one's attempts to reflect a story of *self* are rooted in both the body and language. In Lill's play, we see and hear how Heather Rose's language cannot uproot her story from her body: "It's inside me now" (330). Her story is *inside* her. There are many forms of occupation in this play, ranging from Heather Rose's occupation as a nurse to Camilla Loon's occupation of the nursing station in protest, but the most relevant occupation to this discussion of self-representation is the story that occupies Heather Rose's body. As the plays ends with the lines, "That's about it. The occupation of Heather Rose" (330), we as audience members pause to consider how easily the word "occupation" in the title, *The Occupation of Heather Rose*, could be interchanged with the word "autobiography."

The corporeal occupation of Heather Rose's autobiography raises the question of whether her story can ever be told. In other words, can language sufficiently deliver a story from one's body or, as in the case of Heather Rose, will there always be parts of the self that are unspeakable? Similarly, the improvisational process of writing *Alien Creature* raises the question of whose voices are speaking, and how the improvisational process itself places the limitations of speech itself at the forefront. Butler's understanding of the speakable and the unspeakable provides insight into how to *hear* the performative and improvisational voices in both of these plays: "The normative force of performativity—its power to establish what qualifies as 'being'—works not only through reiterations, but through exclusion as well. And in the case of bodies, those exclusions haunt signification as its abject borders or as that which is strictly foreclosed in the unliveable, the nonnarrativizable, the traumatic" (188). Performative mirror talk then must be understood as a self-reflection articulated through both its sound and its silence—for the moments of silence speak of that which is unspoken. In the case of Heather Rose, we *hear* the nonnarrativizable through the ruptures, interruptions, and disruptions amid her Bakhtinian heteroglossia of voices. When Heather Rose's bleak, jaded voice interrupts her bubbly, naïve voice, then interrupts herself again to impersonate her cynical friend Lorraine's voice or to mimic herself phoning home while blaming the phone lines for her "gloomy" voice (314), we *hear* a character defining herself through Gilmore's notion of autobiographics, through interruption and disruption. The performance of self through interruption reiterates the importance of oral/aural mirroring, thereby suggesting that whatever definition of self emerges through this process of interruption will be fluctuating within the sound waves of the auditorium.

Performative mirror talk as a concept risks reinscribing the mimetic mirroring that it attempts to critique; nevertheless, the performative element maintains a self-awareness of the bodily and linguistic mirroring processes, resulting in a mirroring that is reflective yet indefinite and permeable in its reflections. The basis for such a re-conception of mirroring aptly emerges from within Egan's theory itself, as reflections in mirror talk "do not reflect life so much as they reflect (upon) their own processes of making meaning out of life" (8). Particularly through self-reflexive structures of improvisation, the performative process itself comes to the forefront, never allowing the audience to forget that a dialogue is ongoing between the *auto* and the *biography*. Voice in both Griffiths's *Alien Creature* and Lill's *The Occupation of Heather Rose* provides a medium through which improvisation and performativity both foreground the processes of telling an auto/biographical story while at the same time reminding us that these very processes can defer parts of the story from ever being told. Through this negotiation of the speakable and unspeakable, the voice in both plays allows us to *hear* how performative mirror talk negotiates its own liminality. In recalling what Knowles proposes in a transferring of listening skills from jazz improvisation to theatrical improvisation in order "to hear the unusual, the unexpected, the silenced, the *other*" (2002, 15), what I propose in a hearing of autobiographics within mirror talk involves this act of engagement on behalf of the performers and audience with the practice of listening itself. When we listen to the plays of both Griffiths and Lill, inasmuch as they speak through the otherwise untold silences, these breakages—between voices and within breaths—outline the limits of language to perform a self. Yet if we listen closely enough, we can *hear* them, living.

Notes

1. Although my focus on theatre naturally involves an awareness of the theatrical element of the performative, I would like to emphasize how Griffiths and Lill extend the theatrical into the realm of performative identity, particularly through their self-reflexive exploration of the limits and possibilities of spoken language. In the broader context of auto/biographical studies, Sidonie Smith and Julia Watson summarize the role of performativity in autobiographical theory: "A *performative* view of life narrative theorizes autobiographical occasions as dynamic sites for the performance of identities.... In this view, identities are not fixed or essentialized attributes of autobiographical subjects; rather they are produced and reiterated through cultural norms, and thus remain provisional and unstable" (140).

2. This comment was made by Griffiths during the workshop "Putting a Life on Stage" at UBC in February 2004. Furthermore, Brent Wood's review of *Alien Creature* in *Canadian Theatre Review* (Summer 2000) makes an intriguing parallel between Griffiths and MacEwen: "The first thing one notices is that Griffiths bears a superficial resemblance to MacEwen in build, hair colour and age. More significantly, during early work on the play, Griffiths, by her own admission, began to feel as though she were possessed by MacEwen's spirit. Most of Griffiths's own poetic contributions to the script were created spontaneously while experiencing this sense of identity. The result is a theatrical performance that is neither Gwendolyn MacEwen nor Linda Griffiths but a new being produced by their union. As Griffiths writes in the program notes, 'She and I are doing this play, and only both of us can speak'" (103).

3. For a comparison, see Rosemary Sullivan's biography of Gwendolyn MacEwen, *Shadow Maker*, that offers a recounting of conversations with MacEwen in a more narrative structure than Griffiths's improvisational "visitation."

4. Although Heather Rose's occupation resembles Lill's own position as a young woman working for the Canadian Mental Health Association in Kenora, what I mean by auto/biography in this play is the self-performance of the character Heather Rose.

5. The appropriation of voice is at issue in Heather Rose's speaking *for* characters who are meant to represent specific socially and racially marked roles, and yet the multi-voiced structure of the play foregrounds the limitations of voice while also implying that all of these voices are dialogically part of who Heather Rose *is*. As Jacqueline Petropoulos argues, the play seeks to deconstruct its racially and socially marked language: "Lill's critique of the language of racism opens up a space for considering the larger question of how this discourse produces certain material and ideological effects that benefit the status quo, defined in the play as white middle-class Canadians" (39). One result of this deconstruction, according to Petropoulos, is the decentring of the colonial ideology that informs the "white" discourse of Heather Rose's education. Significantly, Petropoulos points out that the audience hears this deconstruction of language while Heather Rose does not.

6. Lill structures the play around Heather Rose as she waits for a Miss Jackson who never appears, echoing Samuel Beckett's *Waiting for Godot*. Aside from this literary echo, the epigraph contains quotations from Lewis Carroll's *Alice in Wonderland* and Joseph Conrad's *Heart of Darkness*. With respect to concerns about voice appropriation, these quotations complicate the politics of the play by othering the space into which Heather Rose travels—an othering that augments the play as a psychological drama but problematizes the play's construction of a

northern, rural setting. At one point in the play, Heather Rose writes the words "Indians" and "Whites" on a blackboard; as audience members, we are left with the troubling question of if and how the space between these two words can ever be bridged. Resonating with this question is Ric Knowles's suggestion that listening practices provide ways to hear ourselves between and among these words. He argues that we can learn from jazz improvisations how to hear the structural layers of voice and silence within theatre as they speak powerfully and politically about their own representation: "This involves learning *how* to listen, and learning, as part of a workshop, course or rehearsal process's conscious structure, how to listen *collaboratively* rather than competitively— including learning how to hear the unusual, the unexpected, the silenced, the *other*" (15).

Works Cited

Bakhtin, Mikhail. *The Dialogic Imagination.* Ed. Michael Holquist. Trans. Caryl Emerson and Michael Holquist. Austin: University of Texas Press, 1981.

Butler, Judith. *Bodies That Matter: On the Discursive Limits of "Sex."* New York: Routledge, 1993.

Corbett, John. "Ephemera Underscored: Writing Around Free Improvisation." In *Jazz among the Discourses*, ed. Krin Gabbard. Durham and London: Duke University Press, 1995. 217–40.

Egan, Susanna. *Mirror Talk: Genres of Crisis in Contemporary Autobiography.* Chapel Hill: University of North Carolina Press, 1999.

Frost, Anthony and Ralph Yarrow. *Improvisation in Drama.* London: MacMillan, 1990.

Gilmore, Leigh. *Autobiographics: A Feminist Theory of Women's Self-Representation.* Ithaca: Cornell University Press, 1994.

Griffiths, Linda. "Process?" *Canadian Theatre Review* 97 (Winter 1998): 57–61.

———. *Alien Creature: A Visitation from Gwendolyn MacEwen.* Toronto: Playwrights Canada, 2000.

———, and Maria Campbell. *The Book of Jessica: A Theatrical Transformation.* Toronto: Coach House, 1989.

———, and Kathleen Gallagher. "Improvisation and Risk: A Dialogue with Linda Griffiths." In *How Theatre Educates: Conversations and Counterpoints with Artists, Scholars, and Advocates*, ed. Kathleen Gallagher and David Booth. Toronto: University of Toronto Press, 2003. 114–30.

Harvie, Jennifer and Ric Knowles. "Dialogic Monologue: A Dialogue." *Theatre Research in Canada* 15, no. 2 (Fall 1994): 136–63.

Heble, Ajay. *Landing on the Wrong Note: Jazz, Dissonance, and Critical Practice.* New York: Routledge, 2000.

Knowles, Ric. *The Theatre of Form and the Production of Meaning: Contemporary Canadian Dramaturgies.* Toronto: ECW Press, 1999.

———. "Impro: Improvisational Practices in Theatre and in Jazz Are Examined, Compared, and Questioned." *Canadian Theatre Review* 112 (Fall 2002): 13–15.

Lill, Wendy. *The Occupation of Heather Rose.* In *Staging the North: Twelve Canadian Plays*, ed. Sherrill Grace, Eve D'Aeth, and Lisa Chalykoff. Toronto: Playwrights Canada, 1999. 293–330.

MacEwen, Gwendolyn. *Afterworlds.* Toronto: McClelland & Stewart, 1987.

Metcalfe, Robin. "Letters Out: Profile of Wendy Lill." *Books in Canada* 19, no. 2 (March 1990): 21–24.

Petropoulos, Jacqueline. "Language and Racism: Wendy Lill's *The Occupation of Heather Rose.*" *Canadian Theatre Review* 114 (Spring 2003): 38–41.

Smith, Sidonie, and Julia Watson. *Reading Autobiography: A Guide for Interpreting Life Narratives.* Minneapolis: University of Minnesota Press, 2001.

Soules, Marshall. "Improvising Character: Jazz, the Actor, and Protocols of Improvisation." In *The Other Side of Nowhere: Jazz, Improvisation, and Communities in Dialogue*, ed. Daniel Fischlin and Ajay Heble. Middletown, Conn.: Wesleyan University Press, 2004. 268–97.

Sullivan, Rosemary. *Shadow Maker: The Life of Gwendolyn MacEwen.* Toronto: Harper Collins, 1995.

Wood, Brent. Review of *Alien Creature: A Visitation with Gwendolyn MacEwen*, by Linda Griffiths. Directed by Simon Heath, Theatre Passe Muraille, Toronto, Ont., 11 November–12 December 1999. *Canadian Theatre Review* 103 (Summer 2000): 88–89.

PART TWO

AutoBiographical Plays: Stage, Page, or *Real* Life?

Tremblay's Impromptus As *Process*-driven A/B

Louis Patrick Leroux

"Sandra, c'est moi," proclaimed Michel Tremblay in a 1980 interview (quoted in Piccione and Lacroix).[1] He was referring, of course, to the eponymous character from his play *Damnée Manon, Sacrée Sandra* (first produced 1977).[2] Before Sandra's eventual degeneration, his/her name was Michel and he had grown up on the immortalized Fabre Street of Tremblay's own youth in Montreal. In an interview with Marie-Lyne Piccione almost twenty years later, Tremblay stated that *Les anciennes odeurs* (*Remember Me*, first produced 1981) was his favourite play because it was his "first real autobiographical work" (Piccione 1999, 189). Aside from a few shared themes and character traits in both plays that might refer to the author's life—homosexual characters, narcissistic tendencies, authorial aspirations—we can only believe the author's claim to their autobiographical origins because he has declared it so. The intimate events or emotions detailed in both works cannot be authenticated by anyone other than the author because neither work makes *explicit* its autobiographical nature. How then can we analyse these plays as *autobiographical* drama? Should we? Is it even possible? Does it matter?

Tremblay has admitted to purposefully and playfully establishing false leads so that no one will ever find him in his writings: "Je fais exprès de multiplier les fausses pistes" (quoted in Cloutier 68). He insists that it would be an impossible challenge for us to uncover the *truth* in his large puzzle, as he has consciously blurred the clues, over the course of twenty-five years, "pour que personne ne me trouve jamais moi en fin de compte" (68).[3] This avowed masking and inventing of truths seems to me a thinly veiled challenge to textual geneticists and autobiography scholars.

Significantly, Tremblay's writings ring most true and he articulates his intentions most eloquently when he is playing with form and using his creative licence to establish false leads—as we will see with his impromptu plays and autofictions. The function of the autofiction, in the specific case of *Encore une fois, si vous permettez* (*For the Pleasure of Seeing Her Again*, first produced 1998), is to bridge the fictive and real worlds through a hybrid work linking the life stories, the novels, and the plays. His impromptus, self-conscious works staging the writer as a writer, reveal much of his creative process and inform some of his moral and social positions. I will argue that his oft-ignored impromptus (*Ville Mont-Royal ou Abîmes*, *L'Impromptu d'Outremont*, *L'Impromptu des deux "Presse," Le vrai monde?*, and—to a lesser extent—*En circuit fermé* and *L'État des lieux*)[4] work as a veritable *ars poetica* informing us, through autobiographical anecdote or allusions, of his writing process and the formation of his artistic and social discourse. Most of these plays refer back to the banner work *Les Belles-Sœurs* and could not exist without it. In a way, these plays unveil the backstage workings of the playwright and enable us to make an *a posteriori* series of adjustments in the author's discourse about his own work.

Autobiography/Autofiction

Tremblay's characters are often liberal in their interpretations of truth. In his novels Tremblay has them utter such truisms as "all artists are liars" (*Quarante-quatre minutes, quarante-quatre secondes*) and "experience doesn't count for anything, it's the well crafted lie that counts" (*Des nouvelles d'Édouard*, 1984, *News from Édouard*) (quoted in Piccione 1999, 14).[5] Many of his protagonists are writers or artists finding ways to express themselves while being distracted by the inevitable task of translating and transcribing the world around them. His protagonists are essentially tellers of tall tales. The tales have their basis in fictional reality—for instance, the Duchess who appears in the play *La Duchesse de Langeais* (first produced 1969) and the novel *La Duchesse et le roturier* (1982, *The Duchess and the Commoner*) did in fact spend thirty-six hours in Paris—but the way she tells it, she spent years in Parisian inner circles being courted and amusing the elite there. Tremblay has Marcel state, "I've chosen mendacity" ("J'ai choisi le mensonge"), as if expiating the creative licence he has taken (quoted in Piccione 1999, 18). *Le mensonge* isn't necessarily untruthfulness; it can also be joyful deceit or necessary peripeteia.

The term "autofiction" was coined by Serge Doubrovsky in 1977. He used it on the back cover of his hybrid autobiographical fiction, *Fils*. Replying to Philippe Lejeune's *Le pacte autobiographique* published two years earlier, Doubrovsky wanted to question Lejeune's schematic organization of various types of autobiography. Where do we fit the impossible genre, that which is bound by an autobiographical pact but which accepts that, for the sake of art, the writer might tinker with the truth? Many of Marguerite Duras's works could also fit in this category, as do most purely autobiographical works of drama which, after being interpreted by actors who add multiple degrees of separation and interpretation, rarely conform to the original "authentic" autobiographical objective. We have here the Platonist definition of the rhapsode: "interpretations of interpretations," to which I would add the Aristotelian "of a representation of life/action." This self-reflective paradox essentially describes the nature of *autofiction*. Doubrovsky's flash of wit would later be "consecrated" as theory by the novelist in his scholarly works (see 1980, 1988): "Neither autobiography nor fiction, in the strict sense, autofiction rather functions as a go-between in the undefined interstice—that place which is impossible and which can only exist in writing" (Doubrovsky 1988, 70). Accepting that pure autobiography can only be, as Pascal claimed, *un sot projet* (a futile endeavor), Doubrovsky proposes a non-dogmatic, inclusive appellation which more closely resembles much of the work to be found in the gray zone where autobiography and fiction blend. O'Neill, Tennessee Williams, Proust, and countless others might very well have agreed with this hermeneutic definition. Hadn't Aristotle stated that a text's literary quality depends on the degree of its fictionalization? Following this logic, Sébastien Hubier in *Littératures intimes* suggests that autofiction might be a strategy to make autobiographical writings into legitimate literature. Herein lies the very foundation of what Hubier calls the Oxymoric Pact in a playful take on Lejeune's original Autobiographical Pact.

With *For the Pleasure of Seeing Her Again*, Tremblay formally created a link between the three genres he produces: drama, fiction, and autobiographical non-fiction. This link is, in fact, a work of autofiction, an instrument of legitimization through literature.

For the Pleasure of Seeing Her Again

The three forms of autobiographical drama, as defined by Patrice Pavis, are the *life story* (for example an actor-cum-playwright relives the highlights of his life on stage), the *confessional play* (generally about a terminal disease or a troubling admission to the audience), and the *identity-play* (where one toys with gender and identity-bending, questioning the very sense of self) (361–62). As I have suggested before,[6] productions over the course of the past ten years have led me to believe that, in addition to various forms of self-representation not considered by Pavis (including the impromptu),[7] there is indeed a fourth form of autobiographical drama: autobiography as memory-play, or, more precisely, a specified spatio-temporal representation of Self: "un espace mémoire permettant un lieu des retrouvailles avec soi" (Leroux 2004b, 82–83; see also Leroux 2002). The memory-play is in fact, in this case, the recreation for the benefit of the author (where the audience is also invited as voyeurs) of a time/space continuum where self and former self can meet. If, as Ricoeur suggests, identity is the "maintaining of self across time" (1996–97, 11–12), then the memory-play's function is to act as a fertile ground for the meeting of self and former self.[8]

The title *For the Pleasure of Seeing Her Again*, originally *Encore une fois, si vous permettez* (literally "once again, if you'll bear with me"), indicates its palinodic intentions.[9] Tremblay will, once again, revisit the character of his mother, but would this play have been possible without the preceding life stories? His three explicitly autobiographical tales, published between 1990 and 1994—*Les vues animées* (*Bambi and Me*), *Douze coups de théâtre* (*Twelve Opening Acts*), and *Un ange cornu avec des ailes de tôle* (*Birth of a Bookworm*)—all inform and define the Narrator and Nana in a way that the previous novels have not. Nana—also known as Michel's mother, Rhéauna, and the Fat Woman Next Door—appears in more than a dozen works of Tremblay's fiction and in all of the life stories (see "Nana" in Barrette 137–39). The shared name, physical description, language, appetite, fierce motherly instincts and camaraderie with her bookish, affectionate son certainly contribute to the blurring of boundaries between the fictive Nanas and the real one. The meeting on stage between mother and son is a tender, gracious, unpretentious one. Just like old times: they are enveloped in endless discussions, articulating the world to better appropriate it. Doubrovsky further defines autofiction as the "fiction of real events and facts," where the "language of an adventure" is given up to the "adventure of language" (1988, 70). In Tremblay's autofiction, the dialogue does indeed convey the sense that we are engaged in an adventure of language—through language and a stage with a few props and actors, the playwright is transported to the space that makes memory-plays possible.

In the original French production at the Théâtre du Rideau Vert in 1998, the Narrator was played by André Brassard, Tremblay's *de facto* director since *Les Belles-Sœurs*. Interestingly, this was a strategy somewhat similar to the one used by Jean Giraudoux when he cast his accomplice, director Louis Jouvet, as a character aptly named ... Louis Jouvet. Significantly, Jouvet would become the stage spokesman for the playwright's ideas in *L'Impromptu de Paris*. Rather than a professional actor playing the role, Tremblay's director and long-time associate stood in for the author's persona on stage. Was this a further play of mirrors or a simple substitute for a shy or busy playwright? One could argue that the author isn't a professional actor and shouldn't have been expected to play his own role on stage, but neither is André Brassard. To achieve a truly staged autofiction, the author himself should have played the part of the Narrator. This is precisely what he did in writing the play, yet it nevertheless remains a textual autofiction rather than a theatrical one.

The story of *For the Pleasure of Seeing Her Again* had been known to Tremblay enthusiasts before he transformed it into a play. As Piccione (1999) and Pascal Riendeau (2002–03) have both suggested, one need only compare it with "Patira," a life story from the explicitly autobiographical *Birth of a Bookworm*, to realize that a substantial piece of the story, plot, and even dialogue has been reproduced almost word for word in the play. The peritextual supports, such as publicity and the back cover of the original French-language edition of the play, while alluding to "autobiographical *accents*" or *touches*, do not explicitly present this work as autobiography or autofiction, but rather as a "comedy in one act." Can we read this as autobiography? Given the textual lifting of his own life story, I believe we can consider it to be autofiction, at the very least. This precise moment staged between mother and child might never have happened precisely as depicted in the text, but in essence, it recreates many similar moments.

As Ibsen, Kantor, and Genet previously did, Tremblay establishes a dialogue with the dead. French director Antoine Vitez was convinced that the dialogue with the dead remained one of the foundations of theatre (see Borie). He suggested that this dialogue would enable us to resurrect them if only momentarily—which is what Tremblay has done over and over again with the mother figure. In spite of the title, which suggests a palinodic address to the audience, we are summoned to a relational spectacle, one featuring ghosts: the ghost of the author as a young boy and that of his mother.

By the end of the play, Nana is brought to a *trompe-l'oeil* stage rendering of her native Saskatchewan prairie and hooked up to a fly with angel wings. This echoes the final scene of Giraudoux's *L'Impromptu de Paris* and Tremblay's own Manon being lifted up to the sky as Sandra eggs her on in *Damnée Manon, Sacrée Sandra*.[10] The narrator, as does the playwright, bids his mother farewell. The obvious stage markers remind us that she has crossed into the realm of theatre and that she plays her part there. Final adieu? Maybe, as far as the stage goes, but further variants of her character might still haunt Tremblay's fiction and life stories.

Figure 6. Rita LaFontaine as Nana and André Brassard as *le narrateur* in Michel Tremblay's *Encore une fois, si vous permettez* at Théâtre du Rideau Vert, Montreal, 1998. Photograph by Pierre Desjardins.

Impromptus or Extemporaneous Plays

In the French tradition, the impromptu or "extemporaneous" play is an exercise mimicking what is composed or performed on the spur of the moment. Ever since Molière staged himself as himself and explained the inner workings of his theatre troupe, defining his position in response to attacks on his previous plays in *L'Impromptu de Versailles*, we have periodically seen playwrights attempt a number of variations on Molière's self-representational theme. The impromptu play *appears* improvised; it simulates the act of creating a play (quite explicitly in Ionesco's *Impromptu de l'Alma*, 1956) and generally features the author or his substitute (as in Giraudoux's *L'Impromptu de Paris*, 1937), exposing his social, political, and, especially, aesthetic conceptions. Variations on the impromptu play, such as Cocteau's *Impromptu du Palais-Royal* (1962) and many of Tremblay's own impromptus, feature the author, not as a stage presence but as a metatextual organizing force. These plays are meant to express the author's *art poétique*.

The first self-conscious impromptu Tremblay wrote was *L'Impromptu d'Outremont* (*The Impromptu of Outremont*, first produced 1980), a play that offers a view into the elitist world that negates everything he and his writing represent. However, this play was preceded by its primitive source, an *ur*-play if you will, *Ville Mont-Royal ou Abîmes* (1972, untranslated). It was an ironic answer to the then Minister of Culture who intervened to ensure that *Les Belles-Sœurs* did not receive a touring grant to France because, according to the minister, the play was badly written and unrepresentative of Québec's cultural aspirations. *Ville Mont-Royal* was published in *Le Devoir* and produced by the Centre des auteurs dramatiques (CEAD) at a support rally. Containing no direct references to *Les Belles-Sœurs* nor to the scandal at hand, *Ville Mont-Royal* is a focussed attack on the cultural elite of the day who opposed the use of *joual* and other plebian devices.

The theme would remain the same for *The Impromptu of Outremont*, although the setting would change slightly to another bourgeois neighbourhood. Molière's *Les Précieuses ridicules* is not very far off in the audience's mind as Tremblay exhibits his upper-crust version of sibling rivalry in the Beaugrand sisters' family house.

The bitter, snobbish, castrating *outremontaise* Fernande Beaugrand-Drapeau is the dominant sister, keeping her siblings in thrall (except for Loraine who married beneath her station and now lives with an Italian man in St-Léonard). Fernande is a well-born and bred Lisette de Courval (of *Les Belles-Sœurs* fame), yet her mother, interestingly enough, remains a Mme. Tremblay of modest origins who has married well. As if to hide her parvenu origins, she becomes more intransigent than is necessary, retreating into Upper Outremont, avoiding the plebes, maintaining decorum, distinction, and a treasure-trove of intimate writings which she believes would astound the reading masses, if only she published them. Aside from the emancipated Loraine who has managed to leave the moneyed and staid ghetto, the other sisters have trouble coping with their lives of leisure and senselessness. These are the very women who reacted violently to *Les Belles-Sœurs* at the Théâtre du Rideau Vert in 1968. Tremblay actually quotes them in the play as having been there and having thought that the vandals and barbarians were at the gates.

Tremblay explained part of his motivation for writing this play in an interview with *Canadian Theatre Review*: "I have a theory," he says, "that the elite has unfortunately always spoken a written language, they've never had a spoken language so [the play] was very hard to write, it's a language which is totally *bland*, as you would say, without a personality. It's difficult to make the characters human, because of that language" (Usmiani 28). The language isn't actually all proper—variations in register are to be heard, and constant corrections and admonishments are delivered. Loraine and Lucille eventually chastise Fernande for speaking too well to have any imagination. The shadow of the playwright's hand crosses the page and the stage. This play emphatically marks the end of "high society" culture and the beginning of its democratization in Tremblay's oeuvre, in spite of Fernande's retrograde insistence that "theatre should move from the kitchen back into the drawing room" (Tremblay 1980, 100). The entire play is a vicious satire, a negative of the play and world view they are mocking.

In *L'Impromptu des deux "Presse"* (1985, untranslated), more of a short conceptual exercise than anything else, the author stages himself when he was twenty and as his current forty-year-old self. When the authors meet in 1985, they are both reading their respective contemporary editions of *La Presse*, the Montreal daily newspaper. This third impromptu, like his latest, *L'État des lieux* (*Impromptu on Nuns' Island*, first produced 2002), strikes a tone of bemused resignation. The mature author accepts that nothing much changes over the decades and assures his younger self that everything will turn out. A wink and a nod are given to Tremblay's banner play when the younger man says to the author, "I think that I have a really good idea for a play.... And I'd like to know if I'll actually finish it, and especially ... will anyone like it? It's about these fifteen women who gather in a kitchen to lick stamps. Do you remember it?" (296). The seasoned professional remembers it well. In those twenty years, he has gone from a manual worker aspiring to become a writer to a known and respected playwright and novelist. The Parti Québécois has since been created and elected, and has proposed and lost a referendum on the separation of Québec. The world around him has ostensibly altered, but nothing appears to have changed much. This impromptu could have transcended trite retrospection had the author seized the opportunity, but something has kept him from truly taking the stage. The author, so exposed, reminds us of Claude's prudish position in *Le vrai monde?* (1987, translated as *The Real World?*)

The Real World? is Tremblay's only true impromptu, in the very strict sense of the term as I defined it earlier. A Pirandellian play on play-making, it features aspiring playwright Claude and his family as well as their doubles, caricatures of themselves. Their doubles, existing only in Claude's play-within-a-play about his family, are trapped in a kitchen-sink melodrama that portrays them as caricatures of the original characters. Otherwise, the overall play addresses the writer's responsibility to his subjects, the limits of creative interpretation of reality, and the difficulties of depicting the real world and having that real world react to one's depiction. It is an eloquent reflection on the role of the writer and the necessity (and danger) of "getting it right."

Claude's defined characteristics closely identify him with the Tremblay of 1965—they are both twenty-three years old, both typesetters in a printing plant, they both write realist plays and live in the Plateau Mont-Royal neighbourhood, and their families are eerily similar. Claude will become a writer, like the young boy in the novel *La grosse femme d'à côté est enceinte* (1978, translated as *The Fat Woman Next Door Is Pregnant*), like Jean-Marc in *Remember Me*, *Le Coeur à découvert* (screenplay, 1986, *The Heart Laid Bare*) and *Le Coeur éclaté* (1993, untranslated), but especially in *La maison suspendue* (first produced 1990). The scribe of his family's trials and tribulations, he presents a monist and tainted view of his world, which he then shares with his mother, Madeleine, who reacts violently to what she considers her son's treason. "It's as though," she says, "my life has been disfigured ... Have I raised a spy? A spy who recorded our lives so that he could mock us later?" (*The Real World?*, *Théâtre* I, 407). That the family members have become caricatures is unnerving to her, but worse still, they retain their own names in Claude's revisionist rendition of their lives. Madeleine immediately identifies the major flaw in Claude's play: while he is caricaturing the family, he himself has chosen to hide. Is it the

Figure 7. A scene from Michel Tremblay's *Le vrai monde?*, first produced at Théâtre du Rideau-Vert, Montreal, 1987. Photograph by Pierre Desjardins.

"historian's" discretion or the logic of two-body psychology—discovering oneself through the knowledge of others—that prevails? Again, as was the case with the three preceding impromptus (*Ville Mont-Royal*, *The Impromptu of Outremont*, and *L'Impromptu des deux "Presse"*), this play revisits the effects of *Les Belles-Sœurs* on the playwright's life and attempts to explain in part the author's aesthetic and social motivations in writing his signature play.

En circuit fermé (1994, untranslated) and *L'État des lieux* (*Impromptu on Nuns' Island*) are less reflections on Tremblay's writer's craft than thesis plays enabling the playwright to gripe and to expound on what is wrong with today's society. The earlier play, *En circuit fermé*, meaning "closed circuit" (in reference to television but also to a closed, tight clique), deals with the corrupt system behind French-language national television. Tremblay exposes the pettiness, corruption, and cultivated mediocrity that is rampant in those running our public television. The tone is that of a bitchier, sleazier *L'Impromptu d'Outremont*. In fact, Fernande's well-born, well-bred son, Nelligan, has been catapulted into power to reshape the nation's broadcasting network in spite of his lack of experience and credentials. Labelled a "pamphlet" by the author-cum-pamphleteer, the play was never produced in Montreal but it did receive a single staged reading at the Théâtre du Nouveau-Monde. Truly polemical and enjoyably sardonic, this manifest declaration is very much the antipode of the more recent *Impromptu on Nuns' Island*. The French title, *L'État des lieux*, suggests an exposé of the societal elements up for review in the next revolutionary "Estates General." Yet the play is in fact an inoffensive impromptu, a thesis-less *pièce à thèse*, unless one considers "compromise" a valid political and cultural argument. Tremblay here shows the same resignation his forty-year-old counterpart showed in the 1985 *L'Impromptu des deux "Presse."* His characters are each modelled in part on his conflicting selves and they are all right in their own way.

The Banner Play

Les Belles-Sœurs has been, as Micheline Cambron has suggested, a centripetal force for many of the metatexts created by Tremblay. His impromptu plays, from *Ville Mont-Royal* to *The Real World?*, all refer in implicit or explicit ways to *Les Belles-Sœurs*. In *Ville Mont-Royal*, the referent play is not mentioned per se, but the author proposes a negative or ironic "antidote" to *Les Belles-Sœurs* for the benefit of the minister who refused to fund its tour in France. There are direct references to the 1968 premiere in *The Impromptu of Outremont*, a reworking of the first impromptu. The tribulations of the Beaugrand sisters are not those of the assembled "sisters-in-law," but one could argue that the later play is a self-conscious and self-referential Outremont version of *Les Belles-Sœurs*. In *L'Impromptu des deux "Presse"* the two versions of the author are kept separate by the knowledge and the experience of the success of his Big Play. With *The Real World?*, Jean-

Pierre Ryngaert suggests that Tremblay has become "a spectator of his own audacity" (205). By describing and "artistically distorting" his milieu in his banner play twenty years before, Tremblay, through Claude, ponders the difficulty of speaking of oneself through mouthpieces, let alone without them. With *En circuit fermé* and *Impromptu on Nuns' Island*, he uses the more traditional form of impromptu as political and social credo. In these plays, the author's discourse becomes the only true voice emerging from the multiple voices of his characters. In Tremblay's world, where drama, fiction, and life stories share common traits, the characters, locales, and events inform us of the interpretive gaps in his labyrinthine oeuvre. How else can we define his impromptu plays other than as the author's discourse? Here, I am tempted to borrow Michel Tournier's recent neologism, "extimate," from his *Journal extime*, as in the opposite of "intimate." The term expresses the notion that one observes and interprets the world through others. This is not quite altruism, nor is it empathy, but rather the act of describing the world and oneself through other people and exterior events. In this sense, Tremblay's impromptu plays are prime examples of "extimate" writing—the antithesis of his growing number of life stories, but complements his more assuredly "autofictional" works.

Though analysing different works by Tremblay, Dominique Lafon and Jean-Pierre Ryngaert have arrived at similar conclusions: the saga at which the author has been toiling away is in fact a quest for personal and societal identity. Tremblay described his younger alter ego in *The Fat Woman Next Door Is Pregnant* as the "multiple child." The child will be multiple in that he will carry everyone's voices: "Cet enfant est celui qui va empêcher la famille de sombrer en la réhabilitant et en la fixant par l'écriture" (Piccione 1999, 189) ("This child is the one which will keep the family from foundering by reinstating its reputation and by setting the story straight through writing").

In this respect, one is not tempted painstakingly to excavate Tremblay's palimpsestic opus in order to prove its autobiographical origins, but rather to read it as a myth of self-creation: the writer actually defining himself through memory, real and fictive family, and generative creation—"Sandra, c'est moi." Indeed, as are Jean-Marc, Claude, and all the others. Yet, one might wonder what autobiographical impulse is behind Tremblay's forays into autofiction, his outright biographical stories, and, as we have just seen with his impromptus, the running commentary on his own work and place in society.

Why Autofiction?

Robert Folkenflik in *The Culture of Autobiography: Constructions of Self Representation* argues that the autobiographical impulse is most often provoked by the desire to tell about success stories. But what about confessional, conversion, and trauma-related tales? These clearly do not fall into his conception of autobiography. However, Susanna Egan speaks, more appropriately it seems, of a sense of *crisis* as being central to the autobiographical act. I would argue that the success story Tremblay is writing about is his transcending of his own initial social and cultural condition. The immediate success of *Les Belles-Sœurs*, followed by constant and renewed success over the course of the 1970s, consolidated his position as *the* modern-day success story in Québec theatre.[11] This early consecration might have enabled him to tempt fate, as it were, by venturing onto the murky grounds of autobiography.

Interestingly, with *Les Belles-Sœurs*, Tremblay was hailed by Jean-Claude Germain and other notable critics at the time as the spokesman for *otherness* rather than the Self. Critics were baffled by the sheer strangeness of a playwright seemingly absent from the plot and the discourse of the play. It was as though, wrote Germain in his famous preface to the published play ("J'ai eu le coup de foudre" [3–5]), Tremblay had looked into Germaine's kitchen window and had jotted down what he saw and heard—as though he were a foreigner peeking in and taking notes, just as the author would self-reflectively represent his alter ego Claude as doing in *The Real World?*

By associating himself with the *querelle du joual*, a modern-day "Ancients vs. Moderns" battle on the grounds of the propriety of language, Tremblay—in spite of the occasional wink and nudge pointing to his actual writing strategy—would be seen as championing the emerging polyphonic voices of Québec society. Both abroad and as close as English Canada, he would become the fetishistic voice of Québec rather than a singular voice from Québec.

The illusion of Tremblay's fictional world remained fictional—in spite of his constant teasers (through interviews alluding to autobiographical content, and through his impromptu works, culminating in *The Real World?*)—until, of course, he published actual avowedly autobiographical tales. As we have seen, his life stories were published starting in 1990 with *Bambi and Me*, *Twelve Opening Acts* (1992), *Birth of a Bookworm* (1994), and *Bonbons Assortis* (2002, not yet translated). Published along with a string of less significant dramatic works, these texts lent a new texture to his drama. From 1990 onward, it became difficult to dissociate his fiction from his autobiography because many of his life stories were accurately reflected in his fiction, the prime example being the parallel between "Patira" and *For the Pleasure of Seeing Her Again*.

If the autobiographer is really writing the story of two lives—his own life, as it appears to himself and as it appears to others (see Grace)—Tremblay's own ventures into autobiography mirror this dichotomy, not simultaneously as one would expect, but sequentially. The first is reflected before the publication of his life stories, the second after they appeared. His first forays into autofiction seem, in retrospect, to be variations on fantastical readings of his own life. Manon and Sandra concede that they have been "invented" by "Michel." Tremblay insists that Sandra—that very character whose name was Michel before his/her degeneration—is in fact himself. He admitted in an interview on Radio-Canada (Montreal, October 2003) that Albertine was his godmother and that her death and the guilt he felt at having staged her persona motivated his writing of *The*

Real World? Piccione has suggested that the Carmen-Sandra-Claude trio forms the triad of a potential self. The triumvirate remains a concrete attempt at an "autobiography of what is possible" (1999, 92–97). It also helps define the emergence of a virtual "I" in a more interesting and more eloquent way than the original. Tremblay's youthful alter egos, in his plays as in his novels, all confront the limits of their speech, and the lameness of their culture, so they are either engaged in self-destruction or self-betterment. Writing serves as salvation and redemption for many of the characters, as one suspects it has for the author. In this world, perfect articulateness exists, and it exists in a street-smart language.

Since Tremblay has published the life stories, tying up many loose ends and retroactively renaming characters of previous plays in order to establish a stronger concordance between the stories, his narratives can no longer sustain the illusion of fiction; thus, most of his works will fall into the grey zone of autofiction, in spite and because of himself. The genealogical exercise becomes a veritable enterprise in constructing one's own self-mythology. Along with Jovette Marchessault's dramatized biographies of notable women and Victor-Lévy Beaulieu's self-referential mytho-poetic world, Tremblay's work has become, as Ricoeur would say, a dialectic of self and other than self (1992, 140–168). The Self—that is, the constant tension between sameness (*idem*) and selfhood (*ipse*), or consistency and identity—is defined in opposition and in dialogue to other than self. Self-accomplishment and transcendence of one's condition remain the core issues of these three playwrights.

A Case for "*Process-driven* Autobiography"

Anyone working on autobiography and drama in Québec is confronted with Tremblay's paradoxical, omnipresent role. The playwright who was once said to have given voice to Québec's man-on-the-street has turned out to have been more interested in creating his own world, recognizing his own achievements, and building his own myth. He has written a biographical play on the poet Émile Nelligan (*Nelligan*, 1990); a memory-play, *For the Pleasure of Seeing Her Again*, which is firmly ensconced in fantastical autobiography; and many genealogical works stemming from and informing *Les Belles-Sœurs*. He has also written a few autofictional works based on role-playing and identity, notably *Damnée Manon, Sacrée Sandra*; *Sainte-Carmen de la Main* (*Sainte-Carmen of the Main*, first produced 1976); and *Remember Me?* And, as we have seen, he has written a series of impromptu plays extolling his ideas on drama and exposing his craft.

His multifaceted oeuvre spans the wide spectrum from biographical drama to the autobiographical memory plays, with his impromptus the central works linked to and explaining his process. These impromptus, in addition to being lively manifestos, are exercises in self-representation and interesting metaphorical examples of *replication* or "mirror talk" (see Egan). Along with Jean-Pierre Ronfard's numerous exercises in self-representation, Tremblay's impromptus are at the centre of the process-oriented auto/biographical enterprise of Québec drama. I would argue not only that they bridge his fiction, drama, and life stories, but that they are necessary to understand his ongoing Balzacian genealogical process. If *Les Belles-Sœurs* remains the referent or banner play for the plots and themes of his opus, the impromptus are the referent plays for his writing process and artistic and social discourse.

Notes

1. This chapter brings together two previous papers on Tremblay. The first, focussing on his autofictions and impromptu plays, was presented at the Congress for the Humanities and Social Sciences in Halifax in May 2003. The second paper, elaborating on the impromptus and focussing on the context of Tremblay's work in Québec, was presented at the "Putting a Life on Stage" exploratory workshop at the Peter Wall Institute for Advanced Studies at UBC, Vancouver, in February 2004.

2. I use the English title followed in parentheses by the original French title. Some of the plays, such as *Damnée Manon, Sacrée Sandra*, kept their original French title when translated into English. In these cases, only one title is given. Untranslated work will be identified as such. Subsequent references to the works will use the English titles when they exist. All translations are mine.

3. "'Tout tourne effectivement autour des relations familiales, celle de mes personnages autant qu'avec ma porpre famille,' raconte Michel Tremblay. 'La différence entre les deux n'est pas tranchée au couteau, parce que je fais exprès de multiplier les fausses pistes.... Mais je défie quiconque de trouver la vérité maintenant parce qu'après 25 ans de ce puzzle-là je sais que j'ai assez de fausses pistes pour que personne ne me trouve jamais moi en fin de compte.'" ("'[In my work,] everything effectively deals with family relations, as much with my fictional characters as with my own family,' says Michel Tremblay. 'The difference between the two isn't easily discernible because I seek to confuse by creating multiple false leads.... But I challenge anyone to find out what exactly is true. Because after twenty-five years, I know that I've laid out enough false leads to make sure that no one, in the end, will find me'" (quoted in Cloutier 68).

4. *Ville Mont-Royal ou Abîmes*, untranslated; originally published in *La Presse* in 1972 and read at a Centre des auteurs dramatiques (CEAD) event that same year. *L'Impromptu d'Outremont*, translated as *The Impromptu of Outremont*, was first produced in 1980. *L'Impromptu des deux "Presse,"* untranslated, published in 1985 as part of a collection celebrating the CEAD's twentieth anniversary. *Le vrai monde?*, translated as *The Real World?*, was first produced in 1987. *En circuit fermé*, untranslated, was first produced as a staged reading in 1994. *L'État des lieux* was translated as *Impromptu on Nuns' Island* and originally produced in 2002.

5. See Piccione 1999, especially chapter 3, "Quand l'autre est le même," for an exploration of the artist as *bonimenteur* and *double* in Tremblay's œuvre.

6. I first proposed this fourth category of autobiographical play in a paper given at the Congress for the Humanities and Social Sciences, ACTR section, in May 2002 in Toronto (Leroux, 2002). I then further elaborated on the matter in a subsequent article on autobiographical drama in *Cahiers de théâtre JEU* (Leroux, 2004b).

7. I addressed the issue of non-explicitly autobiographical forms of staged self-representation, particularly the case of Jean-Pierre Ronfard, in a recent article in *L'Annuaire théâtral*. See Leroux 2004a.

8. For further elaboration of this conception see Ricoeur 2000.

9. I'm referring here to the palinode (or epanorthose) as a discursive trope. The palinode, when applied to discourse, operates as an *a posteriori* corrective or retroactive correction of previously stated facts by the author.

10. Not only is Manon in virginal holy ascension mode, as with Nana in the later play, but she refers to having been but a doubly fictional character: invented by Michel (alias Sandra in drag-queen garb) but also, by implication, by Michel Tremblay, the author: "MANON: J'crois en vous! Croyez donc en moé! Même ... si ... j'ai ... été ... inventée ... par ... Michel. SANDRA: Monte ... plus haut ... monte! MANON: Oui ... plus haut!" (306) ("MANON: I believe in you! Why can't you believe in me! Even ... if ... I ... was ... invented ... by ... Michel. SANDRA: Rise ... rise above it all ... rise! MANON: Yes ... higher and higher!").

11. Gratien Gélinas had laid claim to the original title of home-grown "success story," but he wouldn't have the same impact on subsequent writers that Tremblay had. If modern *French-Canadian* drama is often seen as originating with Gélinas's 1948 moralizing post-war *Tit-Coq*, contemporary *Québecois* drama is generally dated twenty years later, from *Les Belles-Sœurs* onward.

Works Cited

Barrette, Jean-Marc. *L'Univers de Michel Tremblay. Dictionnaire des personages.* Montreal: Presses de l'Université de Montréal, 1996.

Boire, Monique. *Le fantôme ou le théâtre qui doute.* Arles: Actes Sud, 1997.

Boulanger, Luc. *Pièces à conviction. Entretiens avec Michel Tremblay.* Montreal: Leméac, 2001.

Cambron, Micheline. "Le cycle centripède: l'univers infini des *Belles-Soeurs*." In *Le Monde de Michel Tremblay.* Montreal: Cahiers de théâtre Jeu; Carnières: Éditions Lansman, 1993. 241–57.

Cloutier, Guy. "Michel Tremblay: une affaire de famille." *Magazine Littéraire* 317 (January 1994): 68–70.

Cocteau, Jean. *L'Impromptu du Palais-Royal.* Paris: Gallimard, 1962.

Doubrovsky, Serge. "Autobiographie/Verité/Psychanalyse." *L'Esprit créateur* 20, no. 3 (Fall 1980): 87–97.

———. *Autobiographiques de Corneille à Sartre.* Paris: Presses Universitaires de France, 1988.

———. *Fils.* Paris: Gallimard, 1997.

Egan, Susanna. *Mirror Talk: Genres of Crisis in Contemporary Autobiography.* Chapel Hill: University of North Carolina Press, 1999.

Folkenflik, Robert. "The Self As Other." In *The Culture of Autobiography: Constructions of Self-Representation,* ed. Robert Folkenflik. Stanford: Stanford University Press, 1993. 215–34.

Germain, Jean-Claude. "J'ai eu le coup de foudre." Preface to *Les Belles-Sœurs,* by Michel Tremblay. Montreal and Toronto: Holt, Rinehart & Winston, 1968. 6.

Giraudoux, Jean. "L'Impromptu de Paris." In *Théâtre Complet.* Paris: Gallimard, 1982. 687–724.

Grace, Sherrill. "Creating the Girl from God's Country: From Nell Shipman to Sharon Pollock." *Canadian Literature* 172 (Spring 2002): 92–111.

Hubier, Sébastien. *Littératures intimes. Les expressions du moi, de l'autobiographie à l'autofiction.* Paris: Armand Colin, 2003.

Ionesco, Eugène. "L'Impromptu de l'Alma." In *Théâtre I*. Paris: Gallimard, 1958.

Lafon, Dominique. "Généalogie des univers dramatique et romanesque." *Le Monde de Michel Tremblay*. Montreal: Cahiers de théâtre Jeu; Carnières: Éditions Lansman, 1993. 309–33.

Lejeune, Philippe. *Je est un autre. L'autobiographie, de la littérature aux medias*. Paris: Seuil, 1980.

———. *Le pacte autobiographique*. Paris: Seuil, 1993.

Leroux, Patrick. "Première esquisse pour une réflexion portant sur l'auteur-rhapsode comme figure d'auteur et de protagoniste dans les dramaturgies subjectives inspirées de faits reels." Paper presented at the Congress for the Humanities and Social Sciences to the Association for Canadian Theatre Research (ACTR), University of Toronto, Toronto, Ont., 2002.

———. "Me! Me! Me! Autofiction and Confessional Drama in Montreal." *Canadian Theatre Review* 118 (Winter 2004a): 71–3.

———. "Jean-Pierre Ronfard en auto-représentation." *L'Annuaire théâtral* 35 (Spring 2004b) 55–72.

———. "L'alchimie de la transformation totale. Pol Pelletier et son récit de conversion." Paper presented at the International Colloquium, "Figures du Monologue," Laval University, Québec City, Quebec, 2004c.

———. "Le récit de conversion de David Fennario." Paper presented at the Congress for the Humanities and Social Sciences to the ACTR, University of Manitoba, Winnipeg, Manitoba, 2004d.

———. "Théâtre autobiographique: quelques notions." *Cahiers de théâtre Jeu* 111 (June 2004e): 75–85.

Molière. "L'Impromptu de Versailles" and "Critique de l'École des femmes." *Oeuvres complètes 2*. Paris: GF-Flammarion, 1965. 103–68.

Olney, James. *Metaphors of Self: The Meaning of Autobiography*. Princeton: Princeton University Press, 1972.

Pavis, Patrice. "Théâtre autobiographique." *Dictionnaire du theatre*. Paris: Dunod, 1996. 361–62.

Piccione, Marie-Lyne. "Du masque au visage: la conquête du 'Je' dans l'oeuvre de Michel Tremblay." In *Littérature autobiographique de la francophonie*, ed. Martine Mathieu. Paris: L'Harmattan, 1996. 31–43.

———. *Michel Tremblay, l'enfant multiple*. Talence: Presses universitaires de Bordeaux, 1999.

Piccione, Marie-Lyne and J. M. Lacroix. "Entrevue avec Michel Tremblay dans la Maison de Radio-Canada, 15 avril 1980." *Canadian Studies* 10 (1981): 203–08.

Richard, Hélène. "Narcisse sur scène: itinéraire de creation." In *Le Monde de Michel Tremblay*, ed. Gilbert David and Pierre Lavoie. Montreal: Cahiers de théâtre Jeu; Carnières: Éditions Lansman, 1993. 405–23.

Ricoeur, Paul. *Oneself As Another*. Trans. Kathleen Blamey. Chicago and London: University of Chicago Press, 1992.

———. "Entre mémoire et histoire," *Projet* no. 248. 1996–97.

———. *La mémoire, l'histoire et l'oubli*. Paris: Seuil, 2000.

Riendeau, Pascal. "La dramaturgie autobiographique de Michel Tremblay: *Encore une fois, si vous permettez.*" *Québec Studies* 34 (Fall 2002–Winter 2003): 69–85.

Ryngaert, Jean-Pierre. "Fait-il faire parler le vrai monde?" In *Le Monde de Michel Tremblay*, ed. Gilbert David and Pierre Lavoie. Montreal: Cahiers de théâtre Jeu; Carnières: Éditions Lansman, 1993. 197–205.

Tremblay, Michel. "Ville Mont-Royal ou Abîmes." *Le Devoir*, 28 October 1972, xvii.

———. *L'Impromptu d'Outremont*. Montreal: Leméac, 1980.

———. *L'Impromptu des deux "Presse." 20 ans du CEAD*. Montreal: VLB éditeur, 1985. 285–97.

———. *La maison suspendue*. Montreal: Leméac, 1990a.

———. *Les vues animées*. Montreal: Leméac, 1990b.

———. *Théâtre I*. Montreal: Leméac; Arles: Actes Sud-Papiers, 1991. Includes: *Les Belles-Sœurs*; *La Duchesse de Langeais*; *À toi, pour toujours, ta Marie-Lou*; *Hosanna*; *Bonjour, là, bonjour*; *Sainte-Carmen de la Main*; *Damnée Manon, Sacrée Sandra*; *Les anciennes odeurs*; *Albertine en cinq temps*; *Le vrai monde?*.

———. *Douze coups de théâtre*. Montreal: Leméac, 1992.

———. *Un ange cornu avec des ailes de tôle*. Montreal: Leméac; Arles: Actes Sud, 1994a.

———. *En circuit fermé*. Montreal: Leméac, 1994b.

———. *Encore une fois, si vous permettez*. Montreal: Leméac, 1998.

———. *Bonbons assortis*. Montreal: Leméac; Arles: Actes Sud, 2002a.

———. *L'État des lieux*. Montreal: Leméac, 2002b.

———. *L'impératif présent*. Montreal: Leméac, 2003.

Usmiani, Renate. "Where to Begin the Accusation?" Interview with Michel Tremblay. *Canadian Theatre Review* 24 (Fall 1979): 28.

The Shape of a Life: Constructing "Self" and "Other" in Joan MacLeod's *The Shape of a Girl* and Guillermo Verdecchia and Marcus Youssef's *A Line in the Sand*

Joanne Tompkins

She's a regular girl.

—Joan MacLeod, *The Shape of a Girl*

A lot of people back home have questions about this. They need some answers. Good answers.

—Guillermo Verdecchia and Marcus Youssef, *A Line in the Sand*

Theatrical representations of seemingly inconceivable (but nevertheless documented) actions generally aim to decipher how such events could come to pass. The two plays at the centre of this chapter focus on infamous events, but their more significant achievement is their attention to the construction of the self and subjectivity generally, beyond the composition of the individual self in question. Joan MacLeod's *The Shape of a Girl* and Guillermo Verdecchia and Marcus Youssef's *A Line in the Sand* also have implications for the staging of a self in less disastrous auto/biographical circumstances.

Neither play hides the incidents that generated it: Jerry Wasserman's introduction to MacLeod's play refers directly to the Reena Virk case in which a teenager, bullied by her female peers, was found murdered (8); the alternate act 2 that is published with *A Line in the Sand* refers equally explicitly to the 1993 death of the sixteen-year-old Somali, Shidane Arone, killed by Canadian peacekeepers (107). Each play stands alone, but it also carries traces of the original, "real" life story: each encourages its audiences to read the fictional characters in their own context but neither isolates that context from the "real" life models which partly precipitated them. This combination of fiction overlapping with the "real" world may provide the basis for the "good answers" of which the Colonel speaks in this paper's second epigraph, referring to the inevitable questions about horrifying real-life events that do not seem to fade from public view: several of the people charged in connection with Reena Virk's death continue to make headlines with related and unrelated court appearances and trials.[1] The second Gulf War has made the hero pictures that *A Line in the Sand* describes (photos of soldiers humiliating and/or torturing prisoners, and used as war trophies) a common—if tragic and macabre—feature in newspapers and broadcasts around the world. Fiction permits both actors and audience to achieve a level of critical engagement with terrible events that would be difficult to sustain in auto/biographical accounts of shocking events, since "reality" is trapped to some extent by authenticity. Equally, techniques of the auto/biographical can come to bear on the development of fiction: the genres of both fiction and biography contribute to the shaping and expressing of subjectivity and subject positions in these plays.

My yoking of these two genres, fiction and "reality," is not meant to suggest that fiction is unreal while auto/biography remains the realm of the "real" and "true." Susanna Egan is not alone in maintaining that autobiography is inevitably fictional: the four patterns of autobiography that she identifies "have very little to do with life as it is lived; they are all imaginative verbal constructs; all of them are fictions" (1984, 5). Sidonie Smith also argues that

> the cultural injunction to be a deep, unified, coherent, autonomous "self"
> produces necessary failure, for the autobiographical subject is amnesiac,
> incoherent, heterogeneous, interactive. In that very failure lies the fascination of
> autobiographical storytelling as performativity.... It is as if the autobiographical
> subject finds him/herself on multiple stages simultaneously, called to
> heterogeneous recitations of identity. (110)

Smith is mobilizing theatre as a metaphor in a specific way, although the actual performance of such multiply configured auto/biographical identities on stage is more complex than she pursues here. For Philippe Lejeune, auto/biographies "are *referential* texts ... Their aim is not simple verisimilitude, but resemblance to the truth. Not 'the effect of the real,' but the image of the real" (22). Such attention to the "image of the real" permits plays like *A Line in the Sand* and *The Shape of a Girl* to explore theatrically and productively the multiple ways in which the (fictional) subject can be (re-)configured on stage.

These plays are, of course, designed for performance, and as such they must be analysed using theatre-specific interpretations of subjectivity, since theatre inevitably shifts auto/biography theory somewhat. The act of performance by an actor who is not the "true" self affects how audiences view and interpret the subject being depicted. The focus in theatre auto/biographics tends to be a binary examination of the relationships between actor/role, stage/audience, real/fiction, etc. Work on theatre auto/biographics by Evelyn Hinz and Sherrill Grace, among others, has focussed on the distinction between actor and the role or persona performed. Hinz maintains that "[i]n the same way that an actor/actress assumes the role of another, so autobiography involves coming to terms with another self.... In both cases, a sacrifice of ego is involved, and the degree of pleasure is in proportion to the amount of conflict" (200). Further, as Grace has argued, "performative auto/biographics returns agency to the theatre by producing identities for all who sign the theatrical pact" (76–77). As Grace makes clear in a move that stretches performative auto/biographics beyond the binary of actor/role, the signatories to the theatrical pact can be numerous. My own attempt to look beyond the foundational actor/role relationships to just one aspect of subject formation in theatre is to analyse the substantially unexamined construction of the "other" to the self.[2] This self is the fictional self that is constructed in/for/via the narrative, a self that in the case of these two plays relies also on real events. This self also crucially relies on the other which helps define that self. This self that is shaped by the other is, of course, further complicated by performance.

Those critics who do explicitly establish the relationship between the other and the self do little beyond acknowledging the fact. Amelia Jones's examination of feminist performance art and photography is a notable exception: "[T]he performance of the self is not self-sustaining or coherent within itself, not a pure, uni-directional show of individual agency, but always contingent on otherness" (86). In fact, she insists that "the performative posing of the self, whether photographically documented or 'live,' is always already a performance of the other" (83). Taking Jones's cue, I would like to read these two plays not in terms of the construction of the self as authentic in relation to the "real" subjects that sparked the plays, but in terms of the establishment of a self as obviously contingent and reliant on the "real" self, on a fictional construct, and on performance. In theatre the distinction between self and other is usually figured as being between role and actor, but the examination that I am proposing shifts the focus so that "self" and "other" both become part of the development and portrayal of a character's basic subjectivity, a subjectivity that will become further developed in performance. *A Line in the Sand* and *The Shape of a Girl* explore the necessary contingency of otherness, using narrative and performative tactics that can also apply to more conventional autobiographical writing for theatre. While both plays focus on young people who are actively attempting to establish a workable subjectivity by trying on, as it were, different personas (MacLeod 23; Verdecchia and Youssef 30), they foreground the nature of the self as a construct that inevitably relies on otherness.

Jacques Lacan provides one of the best-known descriptions of the subject as constituted by a relationship between the self and the other. For Lacan, "[t]he Other is the locus in which is situated the chain of the signifier that governs whatever may be made present of the subject—it is the field of that living being in which the subject has to appear" (203). Emmanuel Levinas pursues this relationship in the context of the face. In explaining Levinas's theory of the place of otherness, Simon Critchley argues that "the deep structure of subjective experience ... is structured in a relation of responsibility or, better, responsivity to the other" (21). Levinas determines that "the subject arises in the response to the other's call" (22). It is in the face-to-face meeting that the self-other relationship makes its presence felt and is differentiated from the overwhelming presence of "just" the self. This cannot be a fixed encounter in each play, since, as Elizabeth Hallam and Brian Street argue, perceptions of self and otherness "are not stable unitary categories but shifting and sometimes contradictory constructs" (5). Nevertheless, the self is established in these plays in relation to the other: through their consideration of how a subject who could perpetrate such real-life events comes to be constituted, both plays negotiate the construction of the self and the different effects of ignoring the other. Levinas's use of the face to understand the other is helpful in theatre's "facing" of actors against audience, since (according to Bernhard Waldenfels's explanation of Levinas) "[w]e can certainly contradict what the other says because the other is not a dogmatic authority, but we cannot contradict the call and demand of the other's face which precedes any initiative we may take" (71). Yet the self-other relationships exhibited in *A Line in the Sand* and *The Shape of a Girl* are, in the first instance, less between the audience and the performer(s) and more between the characters themselves. To return to Lejeune's "image of the real," these two plays permit the examination of facets of subjectivity by addressing the construction of the other literally in the self. At the core of my discussion is an analysis of the construction of self and other in the main characters of *The Shape of a Girl* and *A Line in the Sand* with a view to articulating some aspects of identity formation that apply to fictional and auto/biographical subjectivities, and to performance.

MacLeod's monodrama *The Shape of a Girl* focusses on fourteen-year-old Braidie, who speaks to her absent brother. The play spans the course of two weeks in which she refuses to go to school and in which her world, as she has always known it, disintegrates. She remembers seven events from the past, from ages eight to fourteen, with one memory repeated and told in two different ways. During her two weeks of truancy, she follows keenly the press coverage about the girls charged with killing Reena Virk (also fourteen years old) in nearby Victoria. Wasserman maintains that "[i]n MacLeod's plays the self is ineluctably connected to the world. The personal and political intertwine" (7). This is certainly true of *The Shape of a Girl*, as Braidie works up to both telling her absent brother about Sofie, who has been brutally bullied over a six-year period, and deciding to do something about it. More than just an exercise in courage, Braidie's decision involves redefining her entire identity once she begins to read subjectivity in terms of self and otherness, instead of just "self."

Shelley Scott quotes Anne Nothof's comment that MacLeod's plays "imagin[e] the possibility of crossing psychological borders to effect a transformation" (275). Scott asserts that "Braidie must cross the border between seeing herself as someone outside the situation of bullying and violence and seeing herself as someone who is implicated and responsible" (275). Braidie, who is faced with redefining her own identity by reconfiguring the nature of self and other, "watches" events from her past accumulate to make up her life. These events pass in front of her own eyes, in effect, as well as the eyes of the audience (MacLeod 28). Braidie comes to acknowledge the collaboration of self and other in the "performance" of herself. Wasserman maintains that "MacLeod's monologists aspire to dialogue" (2003, 102), but Braidie in this case dialogues first with herself, even though her absent brother is supposedly the receiver of her confession. She writes the script of her life (backwards and forwards), replaying and actively attempting to work out how it happened, as she works up the courage to do something about it.

In the course of the play, Braidie discovers how sound works: "I am acutely aware for the first time that sound carries across water BOTH ways" (22).[3] In a move that forces her to understand the other and its place in the construction of the self, she realizes that not only could she hear the campers at the camp for blind children across the water from her house on an island near Victoria, but that the campers can also hear her. This turning of the tables is a revelation to her, well beyond the physics of sound waves. At roughly the same time, another incident forces her to rethink the nature of identity at the deepest level. She sees on the television news herself and her friends, but then she realizes that the faces are obscured: the faces that are under erasure belong not to her group but to "those" girls facing trial over Reena Virk's death. The blank spaces in place of the faces of the girls on TV give her unconscious an opportunity to insert the faces of her own friends—and, more importantly, herself—before she is aware of what she is doing (26). She is alternately horrified and unsurprised that she has replaced those faces with hers and her friends'. In dealing with the conundrum that this clarity of vision has just provided her, she forces herself to re-view her memories of past events. The two-way traffic of sound and vision connects her, personally, to the girls who are charged with killing Reena Virk, as she puts herself in the identity-threatening position of Sophie, the girl she helped to bully. She comes to see "that she could be, that maybe she already is, one of them: a monster in the shape of a girl" (Wasserman 2002, 10). She tells her brother that "what scares me, what freaks me right out Trevor is that I know the way in. I don't know how else to put it. I know the way in" (33).

Braidie's revelation should perhaps not be as overwhelming as it is for her because it reflects the standard role-play of subject formation that she goes on to describe. Yet when she places herself in the position of the other and realizes the otherness that generates her own subjectivity, she finds the process shocking. *The Shape of a Girl* is framed by a world of watching and performing: each girl knows her role and place, watching the others to make sure that she maintains it. Girls make and unmake their lives and the lives of others. Adrienne, the leader of the group, determines and even names their world, while the others look on and follow. To go against Adrienne is inconceivable. Adrienne's actions are planned, even if the logic is beyond anyone else's grasp. And these are the "good girls" (38), not the "wipe out girls" (33) from the news coverage of the trial. Braidie's realization that there is no difference between these types of girls is what she finds impossible to reconcile.

Sofie, the girl targeted to be othered, "never cares about who sees" (30), and to some extent that is her "crime," although Braidie explains, "I don't know why it was Sofie. It just was" (31). Sofie is not contingent on otherness: bullying forces otherness on her as she learns well before Braidie that subjectivity is not just about the self. Sofie, however, is not as othered as Lorna. Braidie explains: "We don't even think of Lorna as an actual person" (41). Lorna is denied even the status of human by her peers, othered beyond other, for no other reason than she is Lorna. Sofie, meanwhile, "doesn't know, doesn't get the plot, doesn't understand her part" (50). Sofie comes to be so conditioned by her unsought role as scapegoat that she loses her sense of self in that otherness. She takes on, in Braidie's words, "statue mode, uninhabited. No doubt Sofie's entire school life is an out of body experience" (54). Finally, the abuse is so extensive that Sofie "smashes her head into the side of the [toilet] stall. We did a good job. Even Sofie hates Sofie" (56). Even if Sofie "doesn't get the plot," the others do and behave in such a way that they will avoid being next to be othered.

Just as the sound waves are returned, the other watches back, but in this monodrama the return gaze leads, in the first instance, to no action at all. Braidie explains: "I watch Adrienne watching Sofie…. Sofie is watching me. She has no idea my body has turned to concrete. I can't move and I can't shout. All I can do is see" (29). Braidie's conditioning allies her with Adrienne and, while she cannot always understand the reasons for Adrienne's vilification of Sofie, she accepts them because to do otherwise would have compromised Braidie's own identity as Adrienne's best friend. Braidie explains that "[y]ou do what you have to do. You look down" (55). While she knows that the girls who "merely" watched Reena Virk being bullied and injured are not considered by the police to be as complicit as the girls who took more of an active role, Braidie comes to interpret watching *as* complicity. She then takes drastic action in terms of her own identity: she breaks the bonds of identity construction through Adrienne and in the process is exiled from "self" as she has known it. Her close identification *with* Adrienne has been identification *as* Braidie so her actions mean that she is cutting herself off, in effect, from herself: "This is me without my friends. I am nothing, zero, zip. A black mark on the horizon" (43). Equally, Adrienne's subjectivity comes to be compromised: "And she's gone. The friend I loved is gone. All that's left is the shape of a girl" (56).

Another other (so to speak) in the form of the audience emerges to trigger a chain reaction effect: the audience provides an additional perspective against which the staged self is contingent. The powerful image of watching as complicity challenges the position of the audience, itself watching, itself also placed in the position of acting as a surrogate Trevor (supposedly the recipient of the play's confession) and a surrogate Braidie who plays out the confession more for herself than for Trevor. Braidie's complicit, concrete-like "looking down" forces the audience to consider its own complicity. The audience has almost as awkward a relationship with Braidie as Braidie has with the girls on television: the audience alternatively identifies with and is repulsed by Braidie. Just as

Braidie's construction of self is tempered substantially when the other is inserted into the equation, so the audience's assumed position is complicated because it reflects the play's exploration of subjectivity as a delineation of self and other.

The characters exist by role-playing in parts determined by Adrienne, but the reality of Reena Virk remains a backdrop to the lives that are shaped here, as Braidie's monologue establishes an identity that acknowledges the other in the self, outside of the hopelessly inadequate stereotype of the "good girls." Braidie singles out in the television coverage one of the girls charged with Reena Virk's murder, who is, she says, "just a regular girl" (49). Braidie also uses the same words to describe Sofie (53). The good girls who were actually misbehaving on the school bus are also the "perfect girls" (60). They are the bullies and the victims and, in the case of Braidie, the ones who eventually fit into neither category. *The Shape of a Girl* deals with "the necessities and possibilities of the strictly human" (Wasserman 2002, 8), as opposed to relegating identity formation to the broad realm of the imagination. MacLeod concludes the play with Braidie remembering how, at eight years old, she and her friends speculated about "all these possibilities" (60). But the play's dialogue between self and other narrows those possibilities that Braidie had interpreted as endless: as it plays many of them out from the perspective of the "other," they are reinterpreted before the audience. *The Shape of a Girl* performs the working out of an identity that necessarily acknowledges both self and other, within Braidie's own subjectivity.

While Braidie is desperate to understand her identity-threatening situation, Paul Mercer in Verdecchia and Youssef's *A Line in the Sand* demonstrates no productive way of dealing with the otherness that threatens to overwhelm him and little concern for the effects of his actions. Private Mercer is a twenty-one-year-old Canadian peacekeeper in Qatar in the first Gulf War, but Mercer's other in this play also insists on being heard in the form of Sadiq, the almost seventeen-year-old Palestinian purveyor of black market goods, particularly pornographic photographs. Like *The Shape of a Girl*, this play centres on the role-playing that is part of self-identification, but whereas Braidie bares her soul about the pretence of the "good girls," Mercer reveals very little, forcing the audience to draw conclusions themselves, however grim they may be. The details emerge through various strategies, including the narrative of the first act in which Mercer needs to be coaxed into conversation, then a military interrogation, then finally a one-sided phone call; cumulatively, these scenes articulate how we understand subjectivity, the construction of the self, and the creation of lives in theatre.

A Line in the Sand follows the relationship between two young men: it is initially a commercial deal, then a friendship of sorts, then a sexual relationship, before one is tortured and murdered with the help of the other. The second of three acts departs from the relatively naturalistic narrative to expose in quasi-documentary format the racism and cliché in the construction of a stereotypical "Arab" in politics and popular culture.[4] This act explores the problematic construction of "Arab" in popular culture, from politics to the Disney depictions in the film *Aladdin*. The rest of the play's narrative is set against this act. In act 3, Mercer is questioned by his Colonel about his role in the torture and murder of Sadiq at the Canada Dry One base. Back in Canada, the penultimate scene sees Mercer talking on the phone with his girlfriend, while in the final scene the dead Sadiq finds himself in Sudbury, passing bitter judgment on Mercer.

It is tempting to concentrate on Sadiq, since his self-construction is so clear and he demonstrates some understanding of the two-way traffic that so intrigues Braidie: the nationless and motherless Sadiq plans to reconstruct himself as a Hollywood ideal when he earns enough money to go live with his uncle in Kansas. Sadiq says, "I live in Qatar. In America I will be born" (43). Sadiq's engaging—if plastic—recreated identity contrasts with Mercer's inability to frame a self. As the second act illustrates, such an identity is hardly going to serve Sadiq well, but Sadiq at least possesses an understanding of the self-other relationship, even if he might be disappointed in Kansas.

Mercer appears to have no such self-awareness, either real or imagined. He joined the army to "get my shit together" (24), and the recent death of his mother who had been mentally ill since he was a child has interfered with his goal of achieving discipline. In a rare outburst of emotion, Mercer tells Sadiq, "I'm not anything. It's like nothing there. Like a hole. It's just a hole. And it fucks me up 'cause my mother is dead and I don't give a shit and you're supposed to give a shit when your mom dies but I don't" (51). He hopes that the army will produce subject formation for him, as it has historically in American recruitment rhetoric. He is particularly taken with the televised image of discipline and restraint in a Canadian soldier when an Oka protester yelled at him: "[N]othing could touch that guy" (26). Further, enlisting differentiates him from his estranged father, the "Assistant Deputy Minister with responsibility for the UN Peacekeeping Operations" (74).

If Mercer has difficulty with reading his own subjectivity, he not surprisingly faces problems when forced to acknowledge otherness. This inability to deal with otherness is first evident in his interactions with Sadiq. Mercer's difficulty is all the more ironic since the similarities between the two men are established from the beginning. Sadiq picks these up instantly, but Mercer needs to have them spelled out: both lost their mothers, both disagree with their fathers, who wanted them to be educated, and both are learning, as Sadiq says, from "real life" (25). Sadiq even suggests that both are in Qatar in order to anger their fathers. Mercer is quick to insist on distinguishing Canadians from Americans, but he has a greater difficulty with the otherness that Sadiq represents to him, particularly since the similarities between them are more substantial than the differences that are supposed to characterize all Arabs. Mercer almost unconsciously enacts the Saidean Orientalism that act 2 describes as he constructs the Arab as subservient—financially, intellectually, politically, sexually—to his own position as the superior Western protector and adventurer (who, true to the Orientalist model, exhibits a staggering ignorance about the land he is supposedly protecting). The first part of the play structures "us and them" as if attempting to sideline difference, but the final act demonstrates how much Mercer has absorbed Western culture's construction of the Arab as classic "other" when he labels Sadiq a sneaky, dangerous thief in order to get off the murder charge: "He's n-n-nobody. He's only a fucking Arab. That's what we're here for. To kill a bunch of Arabs. He doesn't count. He's here illegal anyway. Who needs to know?" (88).

The sexual relationship between the two men only serves to unsettle Mercer even more. His confusion is clear when he tells the Colonel, "It gets in. It got in. I kissed him. I sucked his cock. We—he. We fucked. He melted me like an explosion like a Big Blue 82. He evaporated who I was, disintegrated me. He put his hands on my stomach and that hole in my gut ... he filled it up with his brown hands. I broke his teeth. I cracked his ribs. I kissed his lips. Put that in your report sir. There's nothing else. That's all. It's over" (96).

Instead of making the move that Braidie chooses—dismantling the assumptions of self-other—Mercer appears to be compromised by Sadiq's otherness to the extent that he feels "evaporated" and "disintegrated." It is as if his self has disappeared in the other. Mercer retreats into standard operating mode and participates in the killing of Sadiq to reset the more familiar boundaries between self and other, particularly in front of his colleagues.

A principal way in which Mercer comes to reveal himself as a self defined without substantial attention to otherness is through photography: he insists that he is seeking control, which he attempts to assert by photographing the people and events around him, even though he comes to be shown to be out of control. In an effort to obtain the elusive discipline he seeks, he says, "The camera lets me control everything" (34), referring to more than the camera's technology. This play displays snapshots of the self rather than a three-dimensional, fleshed-out self. Mercer's photos (as opposed to Sadiq's) nevertheless provide a way of telling the course of a life, and even Mercer recognizes that they also frame the self in the context of the other: he photographs Sadiq to understand himself. Snapshots are, however, an impossibly limited way to determine subjectivity. Later, the Colonel takes a photo of Mercer while talking about Mercer's most infamous photo (which documents the torture and murder of Sadiq), reprehensibly known as a "hero photo," a genre which has more recently created public relations problems for the American army in Iraq, not to mention the torture they memorialize for the Iraqis depicted in them. In the instant of being photographed by the Colonel, Mercer is forced to change positions: no longer a subject who may be attempting to recognize otherness, he is now othered himself. The othering accomplished by the investigation—no matter how benign an interrogation it actually is—puts Mercer in a subservient position. He briefly and reluctantly takes on the role of other in relaying to the Colonel the details of the sexual encounter with Sadiq but Mercer drops this role almost as soon as he tries it out. The play concludes with Mercer in Vancouver, apparently not seriously punished for his role in Sadiq's death: Mercer escapes the literal objectivity of the Colonel's photograph, whereas Sadiq remains captured forever in the photo and, in Mercer's eyes, in otherness itself.

One aspect of subjectivity that both characters respond to as they reveal aspects of their personal identities is the fear that they will appear to be a child, rather than a man: both insult the other with references to being young. Sadiq in particular sees Mercer as a lost little boy, although both admit that losing their mother makes them lost children (52). In the final scene, the dead Sadiq appears in Sudbury and explains that he retains a photographic image of Mercer as a little boy. It's that image that will remain with Sadiq, as the play suggests the need for Mercer—and all that he represents—to grow up to deal with limiting images, beyond just photographic ones. Sadiq is reconstructed once more at the end: he announces, "I am new again" (99), while on the other side of the stage, in Vancouver, sits the same old Mercer, unable or unwilling to respond to Sadiq.

The play seems to give Mercer the opportunity to face his other, and he does attempt to do so in a cursory way by photographing his surroundings in order to establish his own subjectivity. He appears, however, to be unable to accommodate otherness in any meaningful way: he is certainly unable to articulate it, having developed a stammer while he is under interrogation. The audience, however, must face the self-other relationship more directly and must piece together the connections within the sequence of events. While Mercer appears to have escaped a murder charge, "responsibility" is transferred to the audience, not for the murder of Sadiq but for general cultural complicity in the construction of "Arab" and "Canadian" in politics and popular culture.

Both the narrative action and the non-narrative act 2 reinforce the need for investigating the complexities of the self-other relationship, even if Mercer continues to misunderstand the boundaries of and between self and other. In fact, the second act shifts the action and the dynamic substantially, forcing the audience to engage on a completely different (non-narrative) level. The audience has less opportunity to misunderstand, having had the lesson in act 2 in entrenched racism and anti-Arab trends that extend to the influential Disney corporation and well beyond. Yet Mercer's absence of understanding, responsibility, or remorse, and his effective closing off from others do not automatically encourage audience association with Sadiq: the structure of the play prevents simple audience identification with Sadiq, since after the first act he does not reappear until the final scene, except in the photo that the audience does not actually see. The interrogation scene also toys with an audience unlikely to wish to be associated with either Mercer or the Colonel, whose interrogation tactics and plan for dealing with the torture and murder appear to be questionable, to say the least. Once again, the audience is forced alternatively to identify with and dissociate from each of the characters so that the simplistic views that Mercer espouses are made to seem demonstrably untenable, and a range of self-other relations becomes apparent to the audience. Both Mercer and Sadiq demonstrate inadequate constructions of self, but Sadiq does at least permit the possibility of otherness as part of the establishment of self: his generation of the persona that he will adopt when he goes to Kansas is based on an understanding of self and other, even if the United States would likely cause him disappointment and/or disillusionment. *A Line in the Sand* presents various perspectives on how to understand subjectivity and the construction of the self. Its confronting of narrative, and the uncomfortable place in which it leaves its audience, encourages that audience to rethink its assumptions about self and other, whether Arab or not.

While the audience is conscripted to play a part in these plays, the construction of the self in and through the characters themselves interests me most. Nevertheless, the way in which the audience is encouraged to "participate" in the action—even if it is to be repelled by it—suggests a personal interaction that is equivalent to Levinas's face-to-face relationship. The self-other relationship *on* the stage frequently takes place between aspects of a single character, but in the evolution of that character the face-to-face reinforces the significance of theatre in formulating subjectivity. Levinas talks about the "ethical" importance of a "relation ... where I *face* the other person" (quoted in Critchley 26). Certainly, as Blanchot argues, "In the relation of *myself to the Other*, the Other [may] exceed ... my grasp" (19), but an interaction with otherness is nevertheless essential to subjectivity for fictional and auto/biographical subjects. *A Line in the Sand* and *The Shape of a Girl* explore the paradoxical closeness of the relationship between the self and the other, using narrative and performative tactics that have relevance beyond fiction to more conventional autobiographical writing in theatre as well. Both plays negotiate the construction of the self, trying to understand how a subject who could perpetrate the real-life events comes to be constituted. Both plays reflect the other back at the self: they ask what the role of otherness is in the construction of identity and of collective lives, and they demystify the other by demonstrating the other's similarity to the self. Both plays consider the response of the self when confronted with/by the otherness that shapes that self. They provide a range of examples of successful and unsuccessful constructions of the self in an attempt to resemble—but not replicate—the "real." These "images of the real" (Lejeune 22) offer ways of coming to terms with horrifying real events and with subject formation outside the theatre. Both plays echo Levinas's construction of the "inter-human" (165), which recognizes a basic responsibility of one person toward another and what happens when that responsibility is abrogated. *A Line in the Sand* and *The Shape of a Girl* assess the possibilities and problematics of the self-other representation, as they explore real-world disasters of subjectivity and the implications therein for (re-)shaping lives and communities.

Notes

1. See Scott for an extensive exploration of the particular ways in which crimes by girls capture the public imagination.

2. Susanna Egan explores otherness in the context of the reader to whom an autobiographer speaks: "Autobiographers who, within one text, are both subject and object of speech and regard, becoming in turn self and other for each other, play out the politics of lived experience as a realistic trope for exploring, defining, and expressing just who they are" (1999, 8). Further, she discusses the role of dialogism that her concept of "mirror talk" provides, particularly in the context of autobiographies that emerge from contexts of diaspora: "The narrators of these autobiographies [of diaspora] position themselves with more confidence in relation to other people" (157). While she does explain that contemporary autobiography is "[n]ot privileging one perspective over another, but transforming the narcissistic by means of the corrective lens of the other" (25), mirror talk appears to refer to the construction of the self in dialogue with the other, rather than exploring the construction of the other within the self.

3. All further references to this play will be to this edition, indicated in the text by page number.

4. This format is one with which Verdecchia is familiar. See Daniel Brooks and Guillermo Verdecchia's *The Noam Chomsky Lectures* and Verdecchia's *Fronteras Americanas*.

Works Cited

Blanchot, Maurice. *The Writing of the Disaster*. Trans. Ann Smock. Lincoln: University of Nebraska Press, 1995.

Brooks, Daniel, and Guillermo Verdecchia. *The Noam Chomsky Lectures*. Toronto: Coach House, 1991.

Critchley, Simon. Introduction to *The Cambridge Companion to Levinas*, ed. Simon Critchley and Robert Bernasconi. Cambridge: Cambridge University Press, 2002. 1–32.

Egan, Susanna. *Patterns of Experience in Autobiography*. Chapel Hill: University of North Carolina Press, 1984.

———. *Mirror Talk: Genres of Crisis in Contemporary Autobiography*. Chapel Hill: University of North Carolina Press, 1999.

Grace, Sherrill. "Performing the Auto/biographical Pact: Towards a Theory of Identity in Performance." In *Tracing the Autobiographical*, ed. Marlene Kadar, Linda Warley, Jeanne Perreault, and Susanna Egan. Waterloo: Wilfred Laurier University Press, 2005. 65–79.

Hallam, Elizabeth, and Brian Street. "Introduction: Cultural Encounters—Representing 'Otherness.'" In *Cultural Encounters: Representing Otherness*, ed. Elizabeth Hallam and Brian Street. London: Routledge, 2000. 1–10.

Hinz, Evelyn J. "Mimesis: The Dramatic Lineage of Auto/Biography." In *Essays on Life Writing: From Genre to Critical Practice*, ed. Marlene Kadar. Toronto: University of Toronto Press, 1992. 195–212.

Jones, Amelia. "Performing the Other as Self: Cindy Sherman and Laura Aguilar Pose the Subject." In *Interfaces: Women/Autobiography/Image/Performance*, ed. Sidonie Smith and Julia Watson. Ann Arbor: University of Michigan Press, 2002. 69–102.

Lacan, Jacques. *The Four Fundamental Concepts of Pscyho-analysis*. Trans. Alan Sheridan. Ed. Jacques-Alain Miller. Harmondsworth: Penguin, 1979.

Lejeune, Philippe. *On Autobiography*. Vol. 52, *Theory and History of Literature*, ed. Paul John Eakin, trans. Katherine Leary. Minneapolis: University of Minnesota Press, 1989.

Levinas, Emmanuel. "Useless Suffering." In *The Provocation of Levinas: Rethinking the Other*, ed. Robert Bernasconi and David Wood. London: Routledge, 1988. 156–67.

MacLeod, Joan. *The Shape of a Girl*. In *The Shape of a Girl / Jewel*. Vancouver: Talonbooks, 2002. 15–60.

Said, Edward. *Orientalism*. New York: Vintage, 1979.

Scott, Shelley. "Hell Is Other Girls: Joan MacLeod's *The Shape of a Girl*." *Modern Drama* 45, no. 2 (2002): 270–81.

Smith, Sidonie. "Performativity, Autobiographical Practice, Resistance." In *Women, Autobiography, Theory: A Reader*, ed. Sidonie Smith and Julia Watson. Madison: University of Wisconsin Press, 1998. 108–15.

Verdecchia, Guillermo. *Fronteras Americanas (American Borders)*. Vancouver: Talonbooks, 1997.

———, and Marcus Youssef. *A Line in the Sand*. Vancouver: Talonbooks, 1997.

Waldenfels, Bernhard. "Levinas and the Face of the Other." In *The Cambridge Companion to Levinas*, ed. Simon Critchley and Robert Bernasconi. Cambridge: Cambridge University Press, 2002. 63–81.

Wasserman, Jerry. Introduction to *The Shape of a Girl/Jewel*, by Joan MacLeod. Vancouver: Talonbooks, 2002. 7–11.

———. "Joan MacLeod and the Geography of the Imagination." In *Performing National Identities: International Perspectives on Contemporary Canadian Theatre*, ed. Sherrill Grace and Albert-Reiner Glaap. Vancouver: Talonbooks, 2003. 92–103.

Resonant Lives: The Dramatic Self-Portraiture of Vincent and Emily

Anne Nothof

Life cannot be written or portrayed; it can only be lived.

—Sharon Pollock

Nothing is not narrative. You inevitably reveal yourself.

—R. H. Thomson

Performing the lives of artists has long constituted "the fascination of what's difficult," to quote the title of W. B. Yeats's poem on the challenges and frustrations of making Irish theatre (40). The dramatic portrait of an artist assumes an attempt at accuracy and authenticity, or at least at a recognizable likeness; it typically includes iconic anecdotes and demonstrates a creative genius in formation and in action. Too often portraits of artistic genius succumb to clichés and exploit the eccentricities and "abnormalities" of the artist that result in a distorting caricature. As *Edmonton Journal* theatre critic Liz Nicholls points out in her review of the Canadian premiere of *Vincent in Brixton* by English playwright Nicholas Wright, "More often than not there's a certain crackpot hilarity attached to portraits of genius artists on-stage or in the movies. They're maladjusted. They brood. They have messy hair. They're intense and tick everyone off. Agony, ecstasy, then wham, they rush wildly to the harpsichord or the easel, and out comes a masterpiece" (E1). Most dramatic representations of Van Gogh are preoccupied with his eccentric behaviour: his self-mutilation and self-destruction, his association with prostitutes and his conflicts with other painters. In effect, these portraits mask the artist, as the playwright Alexander Wedderburn in A. S. Byatt's novel *Still Life* realizes. Wedderburn is frustrated by the limitations of his Van Gogh play, *The Yellow Chair*, because

> [h]e had had trouble finding an appropriate language for the painter's obsession
> with the illuminated material world. He would have been lying if he had recorded
> only the more accessible drama of the painter's electric quarrels with Gauguin in

the Yellow House in Arles, the distant necessary brother who supplied paint and love, the severed ear delivered to the whore in the brothel, the asylum fears. At first he had thought that he could write a plain, exact verse with no figurative language in which a yellow chair was the thing itself, a yellow chair, as a round gold apple was an apple or a sunflower a sunflower.... But it couldn't be done. Language was against him, for a start. (1–2)

Plays that attempt to perform creativity cannot be too literally grounded. Like a portrait painting, they are interpretations of a life—an imaginative construction, not the thing itself.

In *Autobiographics: A Feminist Theory of Women's Self-Representation*, Leigh Gilmore reminds us that "[w]e try to understand reality through our interpretations, through the stories we raise to significance, and through the meaning those stories make in the rest of our lives," and her feminist theory of women's self-representation provides a useful approach to the reading of autobiographical plays (36). Gilmore insists that "[w]hether and when autobiography emerges as an authoritative discourse of reality and identity, and any particular text appears to tell the truth, [this] has less to do with that text's presumed accuracy about what really happened than with its apprehended fit into culturally prevalent discourses of truth and identity" (ix). The artist subject, therefore, may function only as a model for imaginative extemporization, "a potential site of experimentation rather than [a] contractual sign of identity" (42).[1]

Theatrical representations are further complicated when they base their dramatic portraits on an artist's autobiography and pictorial self-portraits—representations of self that are also imaginative constructions. As Gilmore points out, "[a]utobiography provokes fantasies of the real" (16). It has a performative agency. Dramatized biographies of artists are interwoven with portraits of the playwright in these cases: the portrait of the other becomes to some degree a self-portrait. The significance of this "other" life resides in its resonance with that of the playwright—as a transcribed autobiography or a "metaphor of self" (67).

Three recent plays, each representing the life of a painter, focus on the specific challenges I am interested in here. The lives of Vincent Van Gogh and Emily Carr have prompted a range of interpretations—in biographies, novels, films, dances, music, and plays.[2] Many of these works take as their starting point the artists' written records of their lives: Van Gogh's letters to his brother, Theo; Carr's autobiographical stories of her childhood and family, and of her life as a struggling artist in *Growing Pains*, *The Book of Small*, *Klee Wyck*, *The House of All Sorts*, and *Hundreds and Thousands*. In *Vincent in Brixton*, Nicholas Wright imagines a portrait of the artist as a young man, showing how Van Gogh's "artistic genius announces itself at an early age" during a brief tenure in London before he had even recognized his artistic abilities; however, through his portrait of Van Gogh, Wright also conveys his own aesthetic philosophy and point of view (Wright vii). In *Talking to Trees*, Elizabeth Bowering attempts a biographically "accurate" portrait of Emily Carr in middle age that dramatizes her creativity through debate and explanation. In *Song of This Place*, Joy Coghill visualizes Emily Carr in old age as a correlative for her own struggles as an artist, and she externalizes Carr's creative impulses in the form of the animals (mimed by actors) and significant individuals in her life.[3]

During his short life, Van Gogh wrote nearly a thousand highly expressive and confessional letters, mostly to Theo, who supported him financially and psychologically throughout his life. When Theo's widow, Johannes Van Gogh-Bonger, published the first complete edition of Vincent's letters to her husband in 1913, she included in her introduction the hope that the letters would be read "with consideration," and that his dramatic life would not obscure or distort the reception of his paintings (de Leeuw ix). Moreover, in his letters, Van Gogh is sometimes frustrated by the limitations of words, and includes sketches as visual indicators of his response to his environment, thereby supplementing narrative with art. According to the editor of the 1996 selection of his letters, Ronald de Leeuw, in his paintings and letters Van Gogh "aimed at the greatest possible authenticity of form, when the object represented is, as far as style is concerned, in harmony with and at one with the manner of representation" (xi): "The letters convince because they are fashioned by inner compulsion and broach subjects of existential concern to the artist" (xvi). However, the records of artists who knew Van Gogh suggest that it is problematic to take his words too literally. The letters he wrote to Theo while he was in London, for example, are usually carefully phrased so as not to arouse the alarm of his family; the prevalent tone is circumspection. De Leeuw believes that they "constitute an eloquent apologia in which Van Gogh pleads his own cause" (xii).

Vincent in Brixton is a freely drawn portrait of an incipient artist that imagines Van Gogh's response to his London boarding house and extemporizes on a few passages from the letters Vincent had written to Theo between 1873 and 1875, while he worked for an art dealer. In his introduction to the play, Wright also doubts the "truthfulness" of the young Van Gogh's letters and comments wryly on "the well-known tendency of young men writing home to be less than frank about their most formative experiences" (vii). He does not take these early letters, then, as authoritative or even accurate discourses of reality and identity, but as imaginative self-portraits, in which Van Gogh articulates his impressions of life in London, critiquing English artists, reading English novels by George Eliot and Charles Dickens, in which he discovered "plastic qualities just as powerful as, for instance, a drawing by Herkamer, or Fildes, or Israels" (xx), and responding to Shakespeare's plays: "How beautiful Shakespeare is, who else is as mysterious as he is; his language and method are like a brush stroke tumbling with excitement and ecstasy" (xx). The brief references in the letters to personal interactions, however, are highly glossed in Wright's play: he works in the interstices of the artist's autobiography, giving voice to the silences.

Vincent in Brixton is set in a South London boarding house in 1873 and 1876. A sketch of this house on Hackford Road is Van Gogh's earliest English drawing. A naïve, outspoken young Dutchman persuades Ursula Loyer, a reluctant widow who runs a school in her home, to rent him a room while he works for an art dealer in London. Her other boarder, Sam Plowman, an aspiring artist, is conducting a clandestine affair with her daughter, Eugenie, which she is trying to conceal to protect the reputation of her school. The Dutchman, Vincent, impulsively falls in love with the daughter; when rebuffed, he just as impulsively turns to the mother as the object of his desire and a model for his drawings. A visit from his sister, Anna, disrupts this relationship and reminds him of his responsibilities to his family. When he is summoned back to Holland by his father, Vincent temporarily abandons his London connections but returns three years later to pursue what he believes to be his vocation—that of a preacher and teacher among the poor. But his destiny is prefigured by his compulsive drawing of a pair of old boots on the kitchen table, witnessed by Ursula (see figure 8), the woman whose only wish in life has been "to be the cause of something remarkable," which she has tried to fulfill in her relationship with Vincent (Wright 68). The basis for their hypothetical love affair in the play is constructed wholly from an observation in one of Van Gogh's letters to Theo (31 July 1874): "There is much more to love than people generally suppose.... Il n'y a pas de vieille femme!" (*Letters* 7). The last part does not mean there are no old women, only that a woman does not grow old as long as she loves and is loved. Quoting French historian Jules Michelet, Wright's Vincent expands upon the terse comment in Van Gogh's actual letter to Theo to deliver a speech that seduces Ursula into believing his sincerity:

> "This woman has been in my mind for thirty years, so innocent, so honest, so
> intelligent, yet lacking the cunning to see through the stratagems of this world." ...
> "*Il n'y a point de vieille femme, tant qu'elle aime et est aimé.*" "No woman is old, as long
> as she loves and is loved." I love you. I love your age. I love your unhappiness. (37)

However, during the course of the play, Vincent rarely articulates his vision of the world. Instead, descriptions and prefigurations of his future life and art are given to Ursula. She, in effect, functions as a muse, anticipating what he later expresses through his painting. Like Vincent, she finds in the natural world a heightened significance, and it is *she*, not the painter, who says,

> I'd look at things around me, perfectly humdrum things, a patch of snow, or a
> knot in a piece of wood. I'd stare and stare, and every bit of it would have a
> meaning. Heaven knows what. It's odd, looking back on it. The nights were clear,
> not a hint of fog. I've never seen so many stars in London. I'd look up and ... what
> I saw was the way I felt. The sky was so black that there seemed to be no end to it,
> but it was dotted with these brilliant, blazing lights. (36)

Figure 8. Sandra M. Nicholls as Ursula and Martin Happer as Vincent in Nicholas Wright's *Vincent in Brixton* at Theatre Network, Edmonton, 2004. Photograph by Ian Jackson.

Furthermore, her critical responses to his early sketches also anticipate his later work: "Then you told me about the way you'd felt that day ... all that fury, all that anger and confusion ... and I looked at the drawing again and I couldn't see any of that. That was the most important thing that was happening at that moment, and you left it out" (58).

Wright projects Van Gogh's obsessions and predilections through the words of other characters as well. His love of Dickens and Shakespeare, and his conviction that art should have a social significance are articulated by Sam Plowman, the failed artist, who also previses a Van Gogh painting:

> It is important. That man had been robbed of his sense of beauty. Beauty was under his nose, if he only could see it. In his builder's hands and his broken-down boots. I'll tell you a beautiful picture.... It's a night scene. There's a half-dead lamp over a gateway and people in rags, all waiting for their bed for the night. It's cold, they're freezing. You can't see hardly anyone's faces except for a man with a stick and a parcel. He's blind, he's given a scrap of paper to a copper and the copper's reading it out to him. It's a picture of hell, except it's real. People say, oh nobody wants to know about gloomy things, well that's all rubbish. (17)

This "socialist" aesthetic is also an expression of the playwright's values: Wright's reading of Ruskin and William Morris convinced him of the social significance of art. Wright also believes that sexual awakening is essential to artistic awakening, a belief that he explores through the relationship of Vincent and Ursula in a love affair that is purely speculative, but wholly convincing as autobiographical theatre.

Van Gogh's artistic preoccupations are also anticipated in his excitement over seeing a drawing of Dickens's chair at the art dealer's where he works, called *The Empty Chair*: "That is all you notice in the picture. Just the chair. But when you look, you see the character of the man who sat in it "(24). They are also evident in his enthusiasm for gardening behind Ursula's house, his habit of smoking a pipe, and his vivid evocation of the London he experiences on his long walks: "All last week, when I walked to work, there were apple trees in blossom, lilacs, hawthorns, chestnut trees. If you love nature, you can find beauty anywhere, even in a city. This morning I woke at six. I went for a walk on the common. The sky was blue and a lark was singing. I ran to the church as though I was carried by wings, and I sang so joyfully that all the people around me turned and stared" (24). The set for the Theatre Network production of the play in Edmonton also suggested the ways in which Vincent might envision his world in his painting: the angles of the walls, the old boots on a wooden table, the rustic chairs, the starry night backdrop. Ursula's black dress and posture as she sat at the table correcting children's exercise books also suggested Van Gogh's portrait of a woman entitled *L'Arlesienne: Madame Ginoux with Books* (1888). As Liz Nicholls points out in her review of the Canadian premiere, "Like a painting, the play lives in the texture of domestic details" (E5). In her review of the National Theatre production in London, May 2002, Susannah Clapp comments on the oblique way in which the play approaches the life of an artist: "What [Wright] demonstrates is the single-minded passion of the creator, and the casual disregard of anyone who gets in his way." The play functions as an artist's self-portrait—encoding in verbal and visual clues the "soul state" of Van Gogh.

At least seven Canadian playwrights have attempted dramatic portraits of Emily Carr, including Herman Voaden, Don Harron, Joy Coghill, Eileen Whitfield, Alan Richardson, Jovette Marchessault, and Elizabeth Bowering.[4] Voaden exploits the life and works of the artist as a vehicle for his theatrical theories of "symphonic expressionism." Harron constructs the narrative of Carr's life as a Canadian Cinderella story. Whitfield interprets it in terms of social conflict. Richardson and Bowering attempt to show the interconnectedness of artist and environment. Coghill and Marchessault dramatize the fragmented internal life of an artist, and the soul-making/soul-destroying forces that condition this life; their plays also present their own struggles as artists. All of the plays mine Carr's written work for narrative shape and anecdote, voice, and epiphany. Two recent productions in particular attempt to enact "the essence of a painter's life" (Grace 2004, n.p.): Elizabeth Bowering's *Talking to Trees* and Joy Coghill's *Song of This Place*, the first in a more realistic style of portraiture, the second in a more expressionistic style and, for this reason, they are especially germane to my present concerns.

In *Talking to Trees*, which premiered at the Edmonton Fringe Festival in the summer of 2003, Bowering strives for authenticity: she "blends what [she] believes [Carr] would have said with quotes just as [Carr] wrote them."[5] She incorporates passages from Carr's writings, since "she has best expressed all her moods and eccentricities in her very own words" (2003b, n.p.). *The House of All Sorts* also provides the central conflict of the play: "the alienation and isolation which kept her from her art during that period." In her program note for the play, Bowering recounts how she lived with Carr for over a year: she visited the House of All Sorts in Victoria and "retraced her steps from Simcoe St. to Dallas Cliff Road and grew chilly with goose flesh as [she] stood where [Emily] most likely threw her sack of dead puppies over the cliff" (n.p.). After months of reading about her and studying her art, Bowering felt a sense of closeness to Carr. Bowering imagines her protagonist in terms of her own creative process as an artist. She believes that her play is "not about analyzing the art of Emily Carr or the struggles her career endured in relationship to her social conditions ... [but that] *Talking to Trees* provides a glimpse of a woman with art deep in her soul who just happened to become an historical figure" (email). In order to fill in some facts that helped shape her life, Bowering presents "certain tidbits as flashbacks." Because she does not believe that there was any defining moment or epiphany that could put Carr's whole life in perspective, she offers a "blur" of the artist's life. She is interested in "exploring the inner feelings that compel an artist to paint no matter what" and her challenge, as the playwright, "was to layer such emotions underneath the anecdotes of her famous life" (email).

In *Talking to Trees* four actors—three women and one man—play Emily and the multiple characters who inhabit her stories, including her sisters Alice and Lizzie, Carol, the child she befriended, a Native woman, and Mayo Paddon, a rejected suitor. Scene I begins with an interview in which a reporter questions Emily about the way her painting has been influenced by "the new French style," and his reaction to her works is literal and limited, typifying the response of the time: "Wow ... Startling! ... I mean ... quite the riot of colour.... When you painted this did you actually see those blues and greens?" (2). *Talking to Trees* responds to this question, showing how Carr saw her world and struggled against the philistinism of her family (represented by her sisters) and her society. Its approach is primarily explanatory, effected through different means, including direct address, letters, brief reflective monologues, and instruction: "Create! Don't just copy! These days there are cameras for copying! ... See any fool can copy if they put their mind to it. I want you to get the feeling of what you're painting and put that down on the paper" (36). Bowering attempts to realize Carr's creative impetus and passionate response to nature through her love for trees as manifestations of a life force: "I can see the trees ... they'll be all shimmery in halos of sparkling new green and yellow shades. They will be bursting with new growth and I am bursting to get away from here" (27). But like the playwright in Byatt's *Still Life*, Bowering struggles to find an appropriate language for the painter's obsession with the illuminated material world, an objective correlative for the vibrant paintings:

> I will awaken you ... you beautiful tree. Can you feel my paint swirls
> embrace you? Curling, undulating ... writhing.
> The feelings that stir inside me!
> Mmm. Delicious green ... visceral reds.
> Am I hallucinating or can I touch your heart with the tip of my paint brush? (38)

For the mise en scène, Bowering calls for copies of Carr's paintings to be displayed and identified on stage, but, as such, they remain illustrative props with little correlation to the language.

The conclusion of *Talking to Trees* vindicates Carr's struggle and authenticates her as a Canadian icon. A second, more enthusiastic newspaper reporter in the play provides a more positive review than the first: "Exceptional colour! So vigorous! And a very well organized composition. The way the water, hills and sky are harmonized, balances the forms of the totem poles" (51). Even while vindicating Carr's vision, however, Bowering implies through these clichéd phrases that a positive response may be as fatuous as a negative one.

Despite the compelling enactment of the character of Emily by Alison Wells in the premiere production, the play is primarily a biographical synopsis—an explanation of the artist more than a resonant and empathetic realization of her life and art. The attempt at accuracy of representation, based on Carr's writings, is inhibiting. When used literally, her words lose their authenticity. *Klee Wyck*, *The Book of Small*, and *The House of All Sorts* are emotional responses to places and people, not "accurate" autobiographies. Carr's stories constitute what Leigh Gilmore terms "biomythographies." The self, "auto," is renamed "myth" (27).

Coghill's *Song of This Place* is much more self-reflexive in its orientation and construction than is *Talking to Trees*. Coghill interrogates the creative process by splitting the psyche of the protagonist/author into the "self" and the "other" as projections or creations of the self. The protagonist who initiates the quest into the self via the other is a disabled older actor named Frieda, who has written a play about Carr *"as a theatrical vehicle for her old age. It is her way of facing the limitations that begin to menace her"* (8). She searches for the "soul stuff" of Carr by placing the rehearsal of her play in the woods that the artist had inhabited in flesh and spirit. For her, as for Carr, the woods symbolize the Jungian unconscious. The title of the play is taken from Carr's journal, *Hundreds and Thousands*: "I worked well this morning and again before dark and felt things (first ideas) then drowned them nearly dead in paint. I don't know the song of this place. It doesn't quite know its own tune. It starts with a deep full note on the mighty cedars, primeval, immense, full, grand, noble, from roots to tips, and ends up in a pitiful little squeak of nut bushes" (56). Coghill freely adapts several excerpts from Carr's *Hundreds and Thousands* as the means by which Frieda attempts to speak in Carr's voice; her meditation on a fuchsia bush is an example of the transformation of prose autobiography into dramatic monologue:

> Life, even now, carries such exquisite pleasures. Outside my window is a fuchsia bush.... It is scarlet and purple. A tiny, dainty swayed bell. It is as if you could stick out your finger and stroke the joy of life.
>
> As I lie in bed close to the open window there is a constant humming, a soft, fine whir. Hummingbirds are sipping the nectars—the life of my fuchsias—thrusting long beaks into the inexplicable core and essence of her being. But her bells hang like scarlet drops. Their secrets are still inside them, gummed up in a silence that even the tiny loving bird cannot penetrate. (9)

Frieda is accompanied into the woods by a group of young actors for a rehearsal of her play. They manipulate the puppets who play the significant characters in Carr's "autobiography": Emily as a young girl (Small); her sister Alice, a spinster school teacher with inhibited Victorian sensibilities; her Native friend, Sophie, who is in touch with the spirit world; her authoritarian father; her mentally disabled friend, Harold, who is also trying to write a biography of Emily;[6] and the animals which shared her House of All Sorts. These "characters" comprise Emily's inner voices—expressionistic projections of her psyche. The animators or puppeteers are visible and provide the voices, but the puppets, with their white masks, are much more present on the stage; they project the emotions of the characters. According to director Robert More, who introduced this style of Bunraku puppet manipulation to Coghill's play,

> The manipulator's primary job is first and foremost to get out of the way and become an open channel for creative energy. Any diminishment of this energy will result immediately in diminishing the life of the mask. Any tension, any doubt or judgment, hesitation or lack of clarity, will rob the puppet of life. In this sense, the puppet manipulator is truly an embodiment of Emily Carr's own notion of the creative sensibility with its understanding that the first duty of the artist is to maintain clear pathways for the self so that the inner voice may be heard. The manipulator is the living representative of the "space between." He/she is an open channel for thought and a puppet is thought manifested in his/her hands. (n.p.)

In his review of the 1987 production, *Vancouver Courier* critic Craig Spence described the puppets as "float[ing] in white-faced clusters about the stage, bringing to life characters like Small, Carr's childlike alter ego, or Sophie, the wise old Indian woman who was Carr's spiritual mentor. They become more and more real as the play progresse[s] and Carr's world emerge[s] like one of her own paintings on a blank canvas" (16). This effect was successfully replicated in the 2004 production, although in some respects the engaging animation of the puppets took the focus away from the protagonist/playwright, Frieda, and her "subject," Millie (see figure 9).

Although the puppet/characters are in effect enacting Carr's life, Frieda becomes increasingly frustrated over her inability to realize the spiritual life of Carr, and she implores the artist to reveal herself: "Here I am Emily Carr ... where are you?... I am trapped inside you like a spirit in a tree. No way in, no way out, without your blessing. Here in your forest your power is paramount and I am at risk" (17). Millie at first resists Frieda's summons and resents her attempt at enacting her life. She accuses Frieda of "second-hand living" (23), but she is gradually drawn into the autobiographical process and begins to play the part of Emily herself, inhabiting a role which she has lived—her relationship with Alice, and her struggle to survive in Victoria. In effect she provides the biographical material for Frieda's play, which Frieda assumes to be true, only to be told later by Millie that it is a lie, as is any attempt to recreate a life: in the telling, even as autobiography, there is necessarily and inevitably fabrication.[7]

In the second act they go deeper into the forest and deeper into Emily's life. The puppets become life-size actors, but their roles are still extensions of Emily's struggle for self-expression and freedom. The character of young Emily or "Small" tells the story of her youth in excerpts from Carr's autobiographical stories, *The Book of Small*. Small embodies Carr's creative spirit, and her death and rebirth are scripted as signs of the loss and

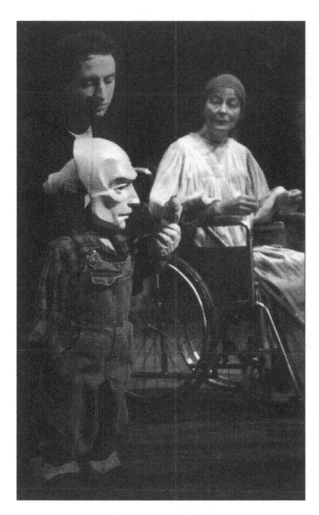

Figure 9. Ryan Beil and Donna White (as Frieda) in *Song of This Place* at the Frederic Wood Theatre, University of British Columbia, Vancouver, 2004. Puppet and mask design by Trish Leeper. Photograph by Tim Matheson.

subsequent rediscovery of Carr's creative impetus. Frieda speaks in the voice of Small as she evokes visions of Emily's youth. She is beginning to see through Emily's eyes:

> My Small was quiet and shy and no one knew what beauty cost her. Even the weight of a small rose would make her breathless. Green things in spring hurt her eyes. She swallowed each dawn and sang it wild across the sky.... And all in silence.... As she grew, birds gathered in her blood and in her breathing. So that she felt herself to be a tree protecting spirits. This went on through motherhood and marriage as if they were stages on the way to being. And then one day this tree that was herself began to fall. It fell so slowly she had time to think, "so this is what it is like to begin to die." (53)

Figure 10. Joy Coghill as Frieda and Joan Orenstein as Millie in the premiere of Coghill's *Song of This Place* at the Vancouver East Cultural Centre, 1987. Photograph by May Henderson.

Finally, a "transfer" takes place *"as MILLIE gives and FRIEDA takes over MILLIE's 'life' and memory"* (56). At this point, Frieda *is* Emily Carr (58). Millie in effect validates Frieda's artistic process (see figure 10)—and the play concludes with a euphoric self-affirmation:

> MILLIE: We are sisters. The vulture trusts us and the eagle. We stroke their feet.
> We leave our legs behind when we fly away into the upturned bowl of the sky. If
> we have wings we do not need legs. (61)

Frieda rises from her wheelchair and joins Millie and the puppets in the *comus*—a celebratory dance and singing of "The Song of This Place":

> Standin' in this swirling forest
> Blue sky rushin' around you
> Hear the song and feel the power
> Rising up inside you (61)

Although a fragmentation of the psyche of the artist is at the centre of the play, *Song of This Place* is very much about self-realization through empathy—between the actor and the painter, between the painter and her world. It is a play that enacts autobiographics.[8] In the original production Coghill played the role of Frieda, with Joan Orenstein as Millie

Carr. In the 2004 production, when Frieda was played by Donna White, opposite Barbara Pollard's Millie, Coghill found it very difficult to be an observer rather than a participant in the play, perhaps because the play is so intensely autobiographical. As Sherrill Grace points out in her program note for the 2004 production:

> *Song of This Place* tells us less about Carr's forests and canvasses than it does about the autobiographical self-as-artist. To reach that autobiographical place is, in the words of Emily Carr, to pull "into visibility what every soul has a right to keep private." In many ways, *Song of This Place* is Joy Coghill's self-portrait as Emily Carr. She has dared to ask if theatre can match painting and if her professional dedication and art (whether as actor or writer) can match Carr's. Her answer is yes, not because this play is better than that painting, but because both arts demand a life of continuous artistic performance and a profound belief in one's art and one's self.

Coghill had long felt a connection with Carr, as a woman artist struggling with incipient old age, with public apathy towards the arts in Canada, and with the frustrations and challenges of a creative life. She believed that, like Carr's painting, "acting at its best is like diving into the sky without a safety net" (quoted in King 10), but when she began to write the play she found Carr to be an intractable subject. While struggling to transform Carr's life into theatre at the Playwright's Colony in Banff in 1984, she claims to have experienced a visitation by the artist in which Carr responded to her despair over the artist's struggle to reach an audience by dismissing Canadian philistines as "silly buggers." Coghill "started having conversations with her, in [her] head, and writing them down, and that became the basis for the play" (2004, n.p.). In its final form, the play became a freely imagined exchange between two women with a shared vision of the relationship between art and life.

Dramatizing autobiography, particularly that of an artist whose life and work have been heavily overlaid by a personal mythology received as "authentic," risks both caricature and hagiography. Portraits of artists on the stage assume life and veracity when they are imbricated with the sensibilities and convictions of the playwright, when they become vehicles for self-expression. Like a self-portrait, any play about an artist is an imaginative expression of a series of possibilities, created as a way of understanding the subject and the self: the playwright *is* the artist.

Notes

1. In her consideration of the possibilities for "performing lives," Susan Bennett shows how Linda Griffiths's interpretation of Canadian poet Gwendolyn MacEwen in *Alien Creature* "takes to task the authority of objective narrativity that once typified biographies ... eschew[ing] the project of showing a single trajectory of 'what really happened' to its protagonist and suggest[ing] a multiplicity of possibilities" (34).

2. Margaret Hollingsworth has written an imagined portrait of Emily Carr in the form of a self-reflexive novel entitled *Be Quiet* (2003). Hollingsworth imagines the lives of Carr and a contemporary Canadian painter named Catherine Van Duren as correspondent: each woman is cast as marginalized by age and behaviour, and each is driven by the desire to engage with the reality of the universe—to express the "areness" of life through art. The mirrored portraits of these two women also reflect the life of Hollingsworth—in terms of her frustrations as a woman artist marginalized in Canadian society. Like Catherine and Emily, she is engaged in the process of "defining identity through art" (408).

3. *Vincent in Brixton* was first produced in the Cottesloe at the National Theatre, London in 2002; *Talking to Trees* was first produced in Edmonton in 2003; and *Song of This Place* was first produced in the Queen Charlotte Islands and Vancouver in 1987 and remounted in the Frederic Wood Theatre at the University of British Columbia in 2004.

4. I have examined the ways in which the first six of these plays attempt to realize the subjectivity of Emily Carr in "Staging a Woman Painter's Life: Six Versions of Emily Carr."

5. All quotations from Bowering's 19 January 2004 email to me are cited as "email."

6. Harold begins to identify his work on Emily Carr as "auto" (11); the word is corrected and/or completed by Frieda as "biography," with the ironic self-reflexive implication that biography is autobiography—as in the case of her own attempt to play the life of Emily Carr.

7. In a discussion during the 2004 UBC workshop "Putting a Life on Stage," playwright Sharon Pollock made the point that even when recalling her life for a biographer, she may be lying—in effect, "playing" her life for an audience.

8. Sherrill Grace explores *Song of This Place* as autobiographics in "From Emily Carr to Joy Coghill ... and Back: Writing the Self in *Song of This Place*."

Works Cited

Bennett, Susan. "Performing Lives: Linda Griffiths and Other Famous Women." In *Performing National Identities: National Perspectives on Contemporary Canadian Theatre*, ed. Sherrill Grace and Albert-Reiner Glaap. Vancouver: Talonbooks, 2003. 25–37.

Bowering, Elizabeth. "Talking to Trees: A Portrait of Emily Carr." Unpublished manuscript. July 2003a.

———. "Program Note." Program, *Talking to Trees: A Portrait of Emily Carr*, Edmonton Fringe Festival, Edmonton, Alberta, August 2003b. n.p.

Byatt, A. S. *Still Life*. London: Penguin, 1985.

Clapp, Susannah. Review of *Vincent in Brixton*, by Nicholas Wright. *The Observer*, 5 May 2002.

Coghill, Joy. *Song of This Place*. Toronto: Playwrights Canada, 2003.

———. "Playwright's Note." Program, *Song of This Place*, Frederic Wood Theatre, Vancouver, B.C., February 2004. n.p.

Gilmore, Leigh. *Autobiographics: A Feminist Theory of Women's Self-Representation*. Ithaca: Cornell University Press, 1994.

Grace, Sherrill. "From Emily Carr to Joy Coghill ... and Back: Writing the Self in *Song of This Place*." *BC Studies* 137 (Spring 2003): 109–30.

———. "Staging Autobiography." Program, *Song of This Place*. Frederic Wood Theatre, Vancouver, B.C., February 2004. n.p.

Hollingsworth, Margaret. *Be Quiet*. Vancouver: Blue Lake Books, 2003.

King, Valerie Hennell. "Joy's Song Is Ambitious." *Playboard*, August 1987, 10.

More, Robert. "Puppet and Mask Manipulation: Inhabiting the 'Space Between.'" Program, *Song of This Place*, Frederic Wood Theatre, Vancouver, B.C., February 2004. n.p.

Nicholls, Liz. "Young Vincent Paints a Glowing Portrait." *Edmonton Journal*, 7 February 2004, E1+.

Nothof, Anne. "Staging a Woman Painter's Life: Six Versions of Emily Carr." *Mosaic* 31, no. 3 (September 1998): 83–109.

Spence, Craig. "Centre Stage." *Vancouver Courier*, 30 September 1987, 16.

Van Gogh, Vincent. *The Letters of Vincent Van Gogh*. Ed. Ronald de Leeuw. Trans. Arnold Pomerans. London: Allen Lane, 1996.

Walker, Stephanie Kirkwood. *The Woman in Particular: Contexts for Biographical Images of Emily Carr*. Waterloo: Wilfred Laurier University Press, 1996.

Wright, Nicholas. *Vincent in Brixton*. London: Nick Hern Books, 2002.

Yeats, W. B. "The Fascination of What's Difficult." In *The Collected Poems of W. B. Yeats*. London: Macmillan, 1956. 91–92.

Auto/Biography and Re/Vision: Betty Lambert's *Under the Skin*

Cynthia Zimmerman

> Playwriting is a sort of quest in itself.... You move through your own subject.
>
> —Timberlake Wertenbaker

I assume the presence of autobiographical input in every created product. Maybe it is merely a trace, "the fingerprint of the source," as playwright Sharon Pollock once said.[1] Or maybe the created product has significant links to the autobiographical that are close-to-home at every point. Between these two lies a huge range of possibilities, for the playwright-artist will use as material whatever comes to mind, whatever is at hand that serves her purpose. There is recyclable material everywhere that can stimulate and inspire: people, incidents, scenes, anecdotes, conversations. Such stimulants to the imagination are not necessarily rooted in her life; maybe they touch it only tangentially. Moreover, the creative process engages not only what can be known but also what can only be imagined. The imagination is not limited by time, place, or direct experience. Nor is it necessarily confined by rational processes. In fact, some artists deliberately court the irrational, the free flight of fancy, in pursuit of that elusive goal, the artistic imaginary.

Nonetheless, whether the art created is "pure" fiction or one of those wonderful hybrids like biography or autobiography (which even more overtly exists at a shifting boundary between the real and the imagined), the artist is in her art. Although the art will have an independent life, she is the author: beginning with an impulse, an idea, a creative spark, she labours creatively, selecting, shaping, editing, and developing until it is ready, this offspring, to be sent out into the world. What emerges is the result of her vision, her judgment and perspicacity, her emphasis, her sense of structure, and her skills as the dramatist able to bring to life what was hitherto only imagined. In this process the writer reveals her own "literary" personality, a personality connected to her biography but not bound by it, not identical to it. As Henry James reminds us, "[T]he deepest quality of a work of art will always be the mind of the producer" (quoted in Drew 224). That mind and that artistic sensibility will weave together particles from numerous sources, both real and imagined. As playwright Sharman Macdonald said, when interviewed about her play *A Winter Guest*: "It sounds as if everything I write is autobiographical and indeed it is, but it also leaps with the imagination. I've never met those two old women [in the play] ... and they were such a gift" (quoted in Stephenson 68). Michael Frayn has said a similar thing about the creation of *Copenhagen*: "The great challenge facing the storyteller and the historian alike is to get inside people's heads, to stand where they stood and see the world as they saw it.... Even when all the external evidence has been mastered, the only way into the protagonists' heads is through the imagination" (4).

The subject of my chapter, Betty Lambert, creates a fictional relationship with her characters in *Under the Skin*. How else could she imagine their thoughts and invent dialogue? To do that requires emotional empathy, even identification with the subject. However, while Lambert begins with an actual historical event, she is not creating conventional autobiography, biography, or docudrama. Instead, with a firm base in the records of the real event, she borrows and bends material to suit her ends. She includes some biographical details connected to the original participants (which I will explore below) but, more importantly, she weaves into the narrative and into the women characters aspects of herself, echoes which have profound connections to her own autobiography. Her characters contain the particular kind of tension Nadine Gordimer says marks the skilled writer: "The tension between standing apart and being fully involved" (4). Ultimately, *Under the Skin* dramatizes a dilemma of urgent importance to Lambert herself. Lambert wrote this play knowing her time might be limited; she had been diagnosed with a fatal illness.

Autobiographics is a discipline interested in the links between the writer and her work, between the creator and the created. It is interested in those correspondences which can illuminate the text. In her book *Autobiographics: A Feminist Theory of Women's Self-Representation*, Leigh Gilmore states that autobiographics asks questions like "Where is the autobiographical? What constitutes its representation?" These are questions which can also be applied to texts not ordinarily seen as autobiographies. To be more precise, Gilmore uses the term "autobiographics" to "describe those elements ... that ... mark a location in a text where self-invention, self-discovery, and self-representation emerge" (42). The privileging of the work as creative fiction remains. Gilmore calls autobiographics a "feminist interpretive strategy" (5), in part because gender is a central part of the analysis. Biographical information is studied, the material circumstances surrounding and perhaps affecting a project are tracked to discover how these influences enter the work, or how they are altered or even omitted entirely. Where are factual connections and where is invention, rearrangement, or realignment? This is done not to unearth mundane details of everyday life, but rather to come upon something more essential: what is she after? What personal issues or prevailing concerns might inhabit this particular creative work? In his biography of Harold Pinter, Michael Billington points out that Pinter experienced a betrayal similar to the one depicted in his well-known play by that name (257–58). What difference does that make to the play? To his craft and to the impact of his work?

In my attempt to address such questions regarding Lambert, my methodology has been influenced not only by Gilmore but also by Porter Abbott. In *Beckett Writing Beckett: The Author in the Autograph*, Abbott talks about a "continual revelation of authorial consciousness at the moment of writing" (3). He says that autobiographical writing is not merely "a mode of recovery or reconstruction or even fictionalizing of the past but a mode of action taken in the moment of writing" (x). One need not look only to the past, to biographical facts or to history. Each work can be seen as part of a "continuous autobiographical project" (22), as an autobiographical investment now, in the moment of writing. To describe this field, which goes beyond traditional autobiography and the story of one's life, he coins the term "autography." When the study of thematics is exhausted, what will remain is "the signature," the "voice" which carries over from one work to another. In Abbott's phrase, one is "reading for the signature" (175). Authors are not only what can be known from their lives but what can be "inferred from their texts" (120), even though we have long been cautioned against this.[2] And with a deeply reflective subject, like Beckett, and I would say like Lambert, the writer's self will inevitably be woven into the work. This, then, is also part of "the autographical character of art" (179). Lambert's *Under the Skin* offers a particularly striking example of this process at work. Her signature is on all of her work, but is especially powerful in this play, the last she wrote.

Betty Lambert was a playwright and English professor at Simon Fraser University in Burnaby, British Columbia, a suburb of Vancouver. She published ten plays (two for children) and had many more produced. She moved into writing adult stage plays in the mid-seventies. Her first, *Sqrieux-de-Dieu* (1975), written for the New Play Centre, was a commercial hit by Vancouver standards in those days. She was already well known for her many plays for CBC radio and television. Of the radio scripts, only five have been published, three of them in an edition by Malcolm Page. She also wrote short stories and one novel, *Crossings*, which was published in 1979 by Pulp Press and later by the American publisher Viking under a new title, *Bring Down the Sun*. Lambert was a prolific writer who created approximately seventy plays for stage, radio, and television (Messenger 163). Even as a young girl she was writing poems and short stories and winning contests. She continued writing until her very last minutes in November 1983. She died when she was fifty years old.

Lambert remains largely unknown, in good measure because so little of her work made it into print. One of the plays she is known for is the chilling drama *Under the Skin*. This play was first produced after her death by Vancouver's New Play Centre at the

Waterfront Theatre in November 1985. Pam Hawthorn, the director, says that the play was initiated by discussions they had had over the telephone, because Lambert was already not well. By the time the first draft arrived, Lambert had been diagnosed with lung cancer.[3] The intended summer workshop never happened; Lambert was too sick. The rapid rewrites, which Lambert was well known for, could not happen either. In fact, after Lambert's death and before production, Hawthorn had consulted with Lambert's daughter and her sister, Dorothy Beavington. Hawthorn expressed concern about the dark tone throughout the play and its unresolved ending.[4] However, the final result, as Hawthorn writes, is that they "played the script as written, with only a few minor cuts taken during rehearsal" (9).

A realistic play set in a recognizable middle-class kitchen, *Under the Skin* takes place in the present. The plot centres on the kidnapping of a young girl, Emma, and the harrowing effects of this on her mother and her mother's friend and neighbour, Renee. The victim remains offstage but her abductor, Renee's husband John, is also an important character. Charismatic with a strong male presence, he has a powerful hold on both of these initially unsuspecting women.

Under the Skin is based on an actual kidnapping which occurred in Port Moody, B.C. The Vancouver papers covered it extensively. It lasted from the 10th of March to its miraculous conclusion on 5 September, 1976, when thirteen-year-old Abby Drover was rescued, after 181 days of hell. Lambert followed the news reports and knew all the details: that the abductor, Donald Hay, was a neighbour who lived only about half a block away; that he had befriended Abby and her two sisters who were new to the area; that the Drover children were good friends with Hay's three stepchildren; and that Hay had even gone with search parties to look for Abby. Behind his house on Barnet Highway, Hay had built a large workshop where he made camper units for pickup trucks. Seven feet below the garage floor, he had built a small concrete room which he later claimed was intended as a bomb shelter. He had equipped it with a bed, sink, stove top, radio, and some provisions. It was there that he kept the little girl. The room was well sound-proofed and camouflaged. Its entrance lay inside an inconspicuous cupboard covered by a piece of plywood with paint tins glued to it. The police came by because Hay was an early suspect, but they found nothing.

Lambert would also have read about how Abby was discovered: Hay's common-law wife, Hilda, called the police saying she believed he had gone out to the garage to commit suicide. When the police came, they found the garage door locked; they broke down the door and still found nothing. They left. But Hilda and her daughter Wendy held back because the door to the cupboard was open and things had been moved aside. When Hilda looked down the shaft she saw Hay's feet, she said, and Wendy called for the police to return. As they re-entered the garage, they saw Hay climbing up the shaft and then they heard a small voice—it was Abby.

Other details came out in the newspapers during the trial (Hay was sentenced in 1977). Hilda knew that Hay had been convicted of attempted rape eighteen years earlier, that he had spent time in prison, and that there had been a more recent assault charge, which was dismissed. But she knew nothing of other elements of his criminal record, and still more allegations arose after all the publicity surrounding the trial.[5] Hilda had attributed his past behaviour to his alcohol abuse. At one point he had spent time in a detoxification centre. In 1974 she had threatened to leave him after an extended drinking binge; that time he had held her and her three children at gunpoint until the police came. He was still on probation as a result of that incident. Hilda and her children also knew about the room under the garage. The little boy thought it had been filled in; Hilda believed Hay used it for better access to the underside of the trucks.

It was also reported that Hay would be away from the site for days at a time, on a binge, that he had been hospitalized for a week after a suicide attempt, and that the family took a holiday in August. This means that for extended periods of time Abby was left without food. Maybe he wanted her to die there. But Abby Drover proved to be a resourceful little girl. The psychologist at the trial believed her religious convictions helped her (she was a Seventh-Day Adventist), and perhaps the combination of her compliance and resistance kept him from taking her life. The details of the investigation, her terrifying ordeal, and the court proceedings were published in 1999 in a book titled *Resurrection* by John Griffiths, a staff reporter for the *Vancouver Province* who was assigned to the story after her rescue.

Barnet Highway is not far from where Lambert was living with her twelve-year-old daughter, Ruth Anne. They would drive there, through the trees, when they went to the beach. What Ruth Drover experienced is every parent's nightmare. Like Drover, Lambert was a single parent. Ruth Anne was her only child. Many of the single-parent concerns the character Maggie expresses were hers: for example, Maggie says Emma misses her dad, and in the play it is Maggie who insisted on the separation (188). Lambert also worried about Ruth Anne's not having a father figure in her life.[6] Moreover, Maggie feels guilty about Emma's being such a trusting child. The day after Abby was found, Lambert wrote in her journal some details of the case and a number of associations: "I am putting this all down because somewhere in this is some clue to myself" (8 September 1976). She was to be haunted by this event for a long time. While writing the play, her empathic connection with the character Maggie's circumstances surely would have been dramatically heightened by her own fears about her inoperable cancer and the unknown dangers facing both herself and her daughter, by that time a teenager. In the play Maggie says, "Sometimes I think her god wants me to curse him and die. But I won't" (190).[7]

What Lambert includes of this horrible story, what she amends and what she imagines provide a wonderful illustration of the creative process at work. Lambert kept the basics of the event, including the 181-day countdown. She begins the play in the spring in order to conclude in the fall, on Halloween. The kidnapped child is offstage throughout, as are all the other children—but we are constantly aware of their absence. Emma and her mother live right next door, instead of half a block away. And the entire play, with the exception of one critical scene in the workshop, takes place in the kitchen of the abductor's wife. In Lambert's play, Renee, the abductor's wife, and Maggie, the mother of the kidnapped girl, are good friends. This is an item of pure invention. Their complex relationship is the focus of the play.

The marked changes from the facts of the case lie in the transformation of the central players. Lambert reveals some of the conflicts she intends to exploit in the character descriptions. Ruth Drover was a bookkeeper, a religious woman, who raised her three daughters alone. In contrast, the fictional Maggie has clear connections to Lambert herself. Maggie, who casually corrects her friend's grammatical errors and makes offhand literary references, is an assistant professor of English at a nearby university. A single mother of one daughter, like Lambert, Maggie is trying to manage on her own, without men.[8] Her name, Maggie Benton, is taken from the name of the student union building, the Maggie Benston Centre, at Simon Fraser University where Lambert was teaching.[9] Lambert's involvement in a serious plagiarism case in the early eighties is alluded to in an argument in scene 4 between Renee and Maggie.[10] However, unlike Drover, Maggie is comfortable financially and, as Lambert writes, *"[c]omes from secure class."* The character Renee Gifford, described as *"too consciously feminine"* and *"[w]racked with self-doubt"* (114), has already lost one husband to a younger woman. Like the real abductor's wife Hilda, according to the newspaper accounts, Renee is in a relatively new common-law marriage. Money is a major concern in the Gifford household and this disparity generates envy. A full-time homemaker and mother of two children from her former marriage, Renee is jealous of Maggie's professional status, her economic security, and her obvious independence.

Donald Hay goes through a complete transformation in his fictional recreation as John. While Hay was considered a good father and husband when he was not drinking (he was a heavy drinker), he was actually a pathetic pedophile afraid of losing his wife. When he was sober, all the neighbours said he was a likeable guy. John Gifford, the villain in *Under the Skin*, has no drinking problem, no impotence issue, and no affable exterior. From the start he is a dark force that comes between the women, openly abusive of his wife and both seductive and challenging with Maggie.[11] He has no feeling for Renee's children, as he tells Maggie, "I never bargained for her brats. She pulled a fast one on me there" (139). In *Under the Skin* it is Renee who is terrified of losing him (134). That is why she puts up with the abuse, graphically presented in the play. However, during the 181 days of the kidnapping, her situation with John worsens and Renee looks more and more haggard until, finally, she finds the courage and the strategy to do him in. This is a clear performance of female empowerment as Renee moves from a "cringing whelp" (148) to a person with an enhanced sense of self. The problem is that the price is enormous—especially for her friend, Maggie.

According to the records, the choice of Abby as victim was accidental; Hay had originally intended to kidnap his stepdaughter, Wendy. In contrast, Lambert gives John explicit motivation that is both banal and grave. John has two specific scores to settle, both directed at Maggie. First, Maggie humiliated him by being right in an argument about mortgage payments. As Renee tells her,

> You started in about how you had this open mortgage and John didn't know what you were talking about. And he said he'd paid off more than half of the house and you said how long had he owned it and he said 10 years and you said if he didn't have an open mortgage that would probably be impossible.... And he went down to check it out and you were right, and he couldn't even get an open mortgage, there weren't any and he said you must have done something fast, no, pulled a fast one to get an open mortgage, and then you came over and he said, Show me, and you did, you showed him.—God he hated you for that. (187)[12]

Second, Emma's religious faith and her naïve trust in the goodness of people infuriate John. As he explains to Renee, "Maggie taught her to trust people, that was her trouble. In a way, the person who teaches her that lesson is a saviour, an educator, yes, an educator, she could be grateful the rest of her life" (179).[13] He is arguing that it is not in the child's best interests that she be allowed to continue to believe that the world is good. To Renee he defends his actions without telling her what he has done. At one point he tells her, "Even Moses said you should rape the young girls. In Numbers. You didn't know that, did you? Oh yes, when they were going against some tribe, he said kill off all the older women, the ones who are dirty already.... But then take the pure girls for yourself" (179) (see Numbers 31:17). At another point he says, "Dostoyevsky once said that only if you could rape a 10-year-old girl could you say you were truly free. Free of all morality" (176). For John this is the archetypal defiance as he aligns himself with the moral educators—Kierkegaard, Heidegger, Jaspers. "[I]f God exists ... it is our duty to deny him," he says. "It's conventional morality that holds us back, Renee" (176). So it is a warped, self-serving, and highly selective set of authoritative lines that John summons as he parades his intellectual superiority. He is well-read, though he turns the texts to his own dark purposes. Disturbingly, Lambert gives John access to biblical authority and provides him with intellectual justification for his abhorrent act.[14] She renders him formidable.

The core of the play for Lambert can be seen in Maggie's response to Renee when Renee says, "You live in a dream world. Things like that happen." Maggie answers, "Not to people like us" (119). But *it did happen* and Lambert constructs her own plausible scenario, a work which screams "women beware of women." In the process she shatters another of Maggie's optimistic feminist notions: "No woman would do that to a child. To another woman" (191).

Reading the newspaper reports after the rescue, Lambert saw that Hilda knew something of Hay's past. Hilda also knew about the room but for some reason had not mentioned it to the police during the search for Abby. Had she forgotten? Repressed it, and then suddenly recalled the secret bunker? Moreover, when the police first went into the garage they saw no opening to the shaft.[15] If he were down there, wouldn't the cupboard door be open and the cover off? Something seems wrong. Lambert might well have thought, "[Hilda] must have known!!" Just before the end of the play, Renee says to Maggie, although Maggie does not pick up the significance at the time, "The thing was, I always knew about the shop, it was in the house description when we got the place, so I always knew" (187). The play circles around this suspicion: Has Renee always known or, more precisely, at what point did she start suspecting it? And most importantly, after Renee had been to the workshop and her suspicions were confirmed (because she saw the false covering), why did she wait two weeks to call the police? We never know Renee's reasons for either delay, but we can surmise. However, lest we think she was motivated by some humane impulse or sudden compassion for Emma or Maggie, in the script Renee prepares herself with an alibi and goes to check out the workshop because Maggie has told her she saw John take a television in there (161). Apparently that is too much for Renee. She and the children have been without a television for weeks. It is at that point, when checking for the television, that she discovers the wooden plywood slab and the jugs glued to it (174). Renee's call to the police two weeks later and what she says closely follow the newspaper accounts.

In Lambert's play Renee's call to the police happens on Halloween. This too resonates with the play's title. As she comes back into the kitchen after answering the front door, still unaware of how much has been hidden, Maggie says, "God, they're so cute. *Walpurgisnacht*. All Saints' Eve. How we make the horrible ordinary. How we transform it, make it comic and cuddly" (185). It is the "[n]ormalization of our deepest terrors" (186).[16] "[*Under the Skin*] is much more than a thriller," Lambert said in an interview; "it shows how we try to ignore what is happening beneath the surface of our lives because it is much more comfortable to deny it."[17]

I have documented the changes to the original story, keeping the focus on the title, *Under the Skin*, which appears in the presence of the underground workshop, in the associations with Halloween, and in the disguise and dissembling among the characters. All of these belie the apparent openness of the relationships. "I decided to do everything from the top of the skin, so to speak," Lambert wrote to her director.[18] Consistent with this intention, her description of the opening set calls for a sunny kitchen on a spring morning and a central set of large sliding glass doors: "*We open on a stage that is only partly revealed. It is the kitchen of the Gifford family.... We see it from the vantage point of the workshop, which is down the hill. We see a patio on stilts, sliding glass doors which lead into the kitchen. A door leads offstage to a hallway*" (115). These sliding glass doors permit the easy, quiet, and sudden entrances and exits of Maggie and, ominously, of John. Throughout the last scene of the play Renee will stare at them repeatedly, looking out "*toward us, through the sliding doors*" (193). It becomes a visual refrain. The patio is on stilts; the workshop, which is down below, is always there but is unseen until Renee visits it in the penultimate scene of the play.

The title is taken from Rudyard Kipling's 1896 poem "The Ladies": "For the Colonel's Lady an' Judy O'Grady / Are sisters under their skins!"[19] Through this title one realizes Lambert's complicated distillation of her theme. Kipling's poem is not about treachery or sisterhood. Rather, it argues the patriarchal notion that essentially all women are alike. This can be read as part of John's understanding of the proper hierarchical alignment between the sexes. Certainly, all three women pay dearly for his having received what, for him, was a castrating, narcissistic injury.[20] Or as he puts it when Renee's sudden appearance in the workshop has him temporarily on the defensive: "I am just like any man. Just like any man. I have my pride, Renee, you can't undermine a man's pride in his manhood, that's what you have done" (176). How Emma pays for this we never know, but we can imagine.[21] When John successfully avenges his injury on Maggie through the abduction of her daughter, Maggie is totally devastated. This portrait of Maggie's heartbreak, of her deep abiding grief, is wrenching to witness. The situation for Renee moves from the sexual "rough and tumble" (179), which she and John presumably have both enjoyed, to increasingly abusive behaviour, two examples of which are shown on stage. At one point, after he "*backhands her casually*" (171), she falls to her knees and cries, "Oh don't oh don't oh don't ... the kids'll hear *again*" (172, emphasis added). Obviously "it wasn't like it is now" (179). Renee will move to a position of strength but only through arduous struggle. As Lambert wrote to her sister, "How do you fight when the enemy has outposts in your own mind?"[22]

Joy Coghill, who knew Lambert and directed a number of her plays, told me in conversation that Lambert's works were all very personal and that Lambert wrote herself into both these women characters.[23] Lambert's title suggests this, too, for Renee and Maggie are "sisters under their skins." *Under the Skin* indicates that one critical thing they share is a strong sexual attraction to John, the macho male. Even though Maggie says to him directly, "I despise your [bully] type," and she hates the way he ridicules his wife, she also openly admits that he "turn[s] [her] on"(144). It is shattering to Maggie when she comes to full awareness that the charismatic male to whom she is drawn is a psychopath and that her friend has been, at least for some time, complicit in an unfathomable horror. These two women must grapple with the fact of their desire for a man who is dangerous to them (see figure 11). Maggie's shock is palpable; the depth of what Renee must deal with is almost unimaginable. Both the apparently independent

Figure 11. David Clarke as John, Maggie Huculak as Maggie, Tanya Jacobs as Renee in Betty Lambert's *Under the Skin* at Theatre Passe Muraille, Toronto, 1989. Courtesy of Archival and Special Collections, University of Guelph Library.

career woman and the submissive housewife who continues in an abusive relationship have come to a stunning revelation. "[T]he rough and tumble," playful at first, covers an extraordinary cruelty which lies "under the skin." The women's journey to terrible knowledge can be interpreted as an example of autobiographical self-representation; Lambert herself "move[s] through her own subject" (Wertenbaker, quoted in Stephenson 140), and it is conceivable that Renee represents her own worst dream. It also fits Abbott's description of a "continual revelation of authorial consciousness at the moment of writing" (3), for the theme of a powerful sexual attraction for a violent man is one that appears in other Lambert writings.[24]

The two women share other more superficial traits. Each feels some genuine connection to the other, although this will be sacrificed, and both engage in competitive and rivalrous strategies. Maggie must deal with a horrible attack from the external world, although she is secure in her sense of self. Renee undergoes an internal journey towards independence in mind and action, borrowing phrases and behaviour from Maggie as she grows. But ultimately, they also share a sense of desperation. Maggie finally settles into an admirable stoicism: "It's not as though I had hope left," she says. "No, it's not as though I have hope left. Not now" (190). Renee, when she tries to defend a student that has enraged Maggie by plagiarizing, reveals that she too feels desperate: "[M]aybe she was desperate," Renee says. "Maybe she couldn't write her essay and got desperate ...

maybe she needs your compassion" (147). Their combined desperation fuels the intensity, the sense of terrible urgency, as the days and months keep passing, driving the play and making it almost intolerably compelling.

In *Under the Skin* Lambert uses the facts of a sensational kidnapping event to spin her own fantasy scenario. She brings unease and suspicion to the audience gradually, skillfully. The result, this forceful play, reveals her preoccupations, her prevailing concerns: women in relationship, their ruthlessness (as Renee acquires power at Maggie's expense), the evil that exists in the world (which may be banal but its consequences are not), and finally, the toughness of the human spirit: the courage we witness in Maggie, the courage that Renee acquires and, of course, the courage of that unseen little girl. Lambert would identify with this given her circumstances, most particularly with Maggie's strength of character.

In the brilliant closing, as Maggie runs out into the dark, her heart pounding, Renee is on the telephone talking to the police just as she is when the play opens. However, the focus has shifted: now Renee is at the centre of the drama. Grim-faced, alone, with a *"dim spot on [her face]*," she says, "Yes, I'll hold on" (194). Renee will be alone to face her future and her demons. It is a miracle that she finds the strength to call.

Lambert closes the play without letting the audience know if Emma is still alive. This ending, which offers the audience neither comfort nor closure, troubled Lambert's director, as I mentioned earlier. It may be that Renee has resolved her major conflicts, as shown in her new-found sense of power, but for Maggie and her daughter the future remains uncertain, harrowing. Clearly this ending was a conscious artistic decision by the playwright. Lambert knew, as does anyone who can recall the newspaper story, that the child was found alive. In fact, Abby Drover lived to marry and have children of her own. In contrast, Maggie Benton has escaped neither panic nor dread. Her night of terror is not over when the curtain closes. Lambert has refused us a morally satisfying conclusion. She has deliberately omitted the consolation that reality offered. She provides no escape from the conviction that terrible things do happen, even to "people like us" (119). We are left with the awareness of how precarious life is; how at any time, without warning, tragedy can break into it. To my mind, this is evidence of a consummate playwright's craft. Lambert brings down the curtain at the most theatrical moment.

I believe that the ending resonates with Lambert's own plight. She too is awaiting her destiny, which she fears is a death sentence. She too "holds on": will a miracle rescue her? Will her daughter be okay without her? As she said in an interview, "I start out from a problem that I'm having. Then I extrapolate that into the characters" (Worthington 59). The result is a play both intensely written and powerfully imagined. Many of the images that haunt *Under the Skin* are rooted in lived experience; that is one reason for their incredible potency. While she was writing this play, something was happening to Lambert too, and it was going on "under the skin."[25]

Notes

1. Keynote lecture, "Putting a Life on Stage" workshop, University of British Columbia, Vancouver, B.C., February 2004.

2. I am referring to New Criticism here—the work of Eliot, Richards, Leavis, and others, who argued that art "existed as a self-enclosed object, mysteriously intact in its own unique being" (Eagleton 47). Treating the work as a "self-sufficient object," as New Criticism does, means severing ties with the author (with his feelings or intentions or unconscious sources), with the reader/audience (and any subjectivity they might bring to the reception of a work of art), and with any social or historical content (48).

3. According to correspondence found in the Simon Fraser University archives, Lambert began writing *Under the Skin* in January 1983; she was diagnosed with cancer in February, submitted the manuscript in July, and died in November 1983.

4. Ruth Lambert, email to author, 10 November 2004.

5. As late as November 1999 Hay was to go on trial for three new charges of sex offences that allegedly occurred between 1970 and 1976 (Griffiths 284).

6. Elizabeth Minnie Lee wed Frank Lambert in 1952. They were divorced in 1962. Ruth Anne was born in 1964. In her journal Lambert notes that she had "denied" Ruth Anne a father (8 September 1976), which may or may not have been literally true.

7. On 9 July 1983, Lambert wrote Joy Coghill to say that she had finished the manuscript and that her mother was in hospital, dying. About her own illness she wrote, "People keep saying I'm a miracle, but what if I 'recur'? Well, I'm a miracle right *now* anyway." The cancer did recur. Betty's mother, Bessie Smyth, died of cancer one week after the death of her daughter.

8. At the time of the Port Moody kidnapping, Lambert was working on a play entitled *Visiting Hour* about three women in a maternity ward who are waiting to give birth. In her journal (8 September 1976), Lambert wrote that the character Brooke "[m]ust be me. Struggling to be, without men." The same could be said of Maggie Benton.

9. Maggie Benston had been a vital and politically active faculty member of Simon Fraser University. She died of cancer in 1991, at the age of fifty-two. Hired by the Department of Chemistry in 1966, she moved into women's studies and computer science. According to the chair of the committee, the student services centre was so named to honour a woman who had played an important role at the university and who "epitomize[d] the interdisciplinary approach to academic inquiry" (*Simon Fraser News*, 19 September 1996). Lambert would certainly have known and admired Benston's forceful independent personality, as a feminist and as a political activist.

10. Personal correspondence with Lambert's former colleague, Malcolm Page (15 November 2004).

11. John is a divisive force both in what he says and how he is depicted (136, 142, 148, 155).

12. John uses the phrase "pulled a fast one" earlier, when he is speaking of how Renee tricked him (139). This is another illustration of how minor grievances can enrage him.

13. This connects to the play's argument about *The Diary of Anne Frank*, Emma's personal bible. John contends that she has misread the last lines of the published text on the subject of Anne's

faith in human goodness (141, 177). Maggie refers several times to Emma's belief, taken from Anne Frank, that everyone has some human good in them. But John insists, and he is correct, that the final lines read, "[I] keep on trying to find a way of becoming what I would so like to be, and what I could be, if ... there weren't any other people living in the world. Yours, Anne" (Frank 283).

14. The biblical reference is to the Old Testament. Balaam, a non-Jewish leader, was plotting to lead Israel into sin. His people, the Midianites, try to undermine Israel's sexual morality (25:1) and so "the people began to play the harlot." The punishment was to wipe out the Midianites. "The young girls" in the King James version is translated as the "female children" in other translations. Those who are to be kept are "children," that is, younger than marriageable age. A gloss by one commentator is that "for yourselves" means "for your use as domestic servants." The word choice in the actual biblical passage is "female children," neither "pure" nor "virgin," and without the sexual reference or the suggestion of sexual pleasure. John interprets the word "take" sexually and even asserts that Moses said "you should rape." Of course, in the classical epics the women and children of the vanquished were treated as booty or war trophies.

15. In *Resurrection*, Hilda is reported as saying that after the police had been to the garage without success, "her daughters had reminded her about the existence in the garage of an underground pit.... 'The girls mentioned the hole,' said Hilda. Noticing that several bottles of gasoline and glue appeared to have been moved aside from one of the cabinets, she had opened the cupboard doors and knelt beside the floor of the cabinet. 'I lifted the board and could see his feet. I thought he was dead, and Wendy called the police again. I left the board off the hole and we waited by the door. That's when you came in and saw him crawling out.' It was all so clear now: the missing potato chips; the bag of apples that Wendy had found in the garage; the hours on end that her husband had been spending out there alone" (Griffiths 143). There does seem to be some important information missing: that is, was Hay able to remove and replace the cover of the shaft from below?

16. Renee will repeatedly call John her "gruffy bear" or "grumpy bear" (130, 137, 140, 148) in an attempt to mollify his anger. Since this usually occurs in Maggie's presence, Renee may also be trying to minimize the significance and seriousness of his moodiness to her friend.

17. "Betty's Story: A Polished Diamond," *Simon Fraser Week*, 21 July 1983, 2.

18. Covering letter to Pam Hawthorn which accompanied the draft submission, 9 July 1983. Playwrights Theatre Centre Archives.

19. Lambert indicated the source for her title in a letter to Pam Hawthorn (3 January l983): "I have begun the play, called *Under the Skin* (the Colonel's lady and Rosie O'Grady are sisters).... " Playwrights Theatre Centre Archives.

20. In her article, "The Culture of Abuse," Ann Wilson uses this play, as well as two others, to illustrate "the victimization of women." She argues that "the sexual abuse of children is not an isolated evil but the horrifyingly logical effect of ideologies which shape our understanding of gender and sexuality" (161).

21. The actual victim, Abby Drover, was sexually abused repeatedly by her captor.

22. Lambert quoted by Dorothy Beavington, "Betty Lambert, 1933–1983." 8 August 1985. Special Collections, Simon Fraser University.

23. Joy Coghill, personal interview with author, 2 August 2004. Rosalind Kerr's article on Lambert's *Jennie's Story* mentions how that play began from a personal experience, a story about the tragedy of a young wife on a neighbouring farm that Lambert's mother frightened her with when she was young.

24. A volatile and perhaps sadistic sexual relationship is also central to Lambert's novel *Crossings*, her radio play *Grasshopper Hill*, and her early short story "The Pony."

25. I would like to thank my research assistant, Carolyn Henry, who tracked down a lot of this source material. I would also like to thank Ruth Lambert and Dorothy Beavington for their open dialogue with me, and the archivists at Special Collections, WAC Bennett Library, Simon Fraser University, who proved so helpful.

Works Cited

Abbott, H. Porter. *Beckett Writing Beckett: The Author in the Autograph*. Ithaca: Cornell University Press, 1996.

"Betty's Story: A Polished Diamond." *Simon Fraser Week* 26, no. 11 (21 July 1983): 2.

Billington, Michael. *The Life and Work of Harold Pinter*. London: Faber & Faber, 1996.

Drew, Elizabeth. *The Novel: A Modern Guide to Fifteen English Masterpieces*. New York: Dell, 1963.

Eagleton, Terry. *Literary Theory: An Introduction*. Oxford: Basil Blackwell, 1983.

Frank, Anne. *Anne Frank: The Diary of a Young Girl*. Trans. B. M. Mooyaart. New York: Doubleday, 1952.

Frayn, Michael. "From the Postscript to *Copenhagen*." Program, *Copenhagen*, Winter Garden Theatre, Toronto, Ont., January–February 2004, 3.

Gilmore, Leigh. *Autobiographics: A Feminist Theory of Women's Self-Representation*. Ithaca: Cornell University Press, 1994.

Gordimer, Nadine. Introduction to *Selected Stories*. London: Bloomsbury, 2000.

Griffiths, John. *Resurrection: The Kidnapping of Abby Drover*. Toronto: Insomniac Press, 1999.

Hawthorn, Pamela. Introduction to *Jennie's Story and Under the Skin*, by Betty Lambert. Toronto: Playwrights Canada, 1987. 7–9.

Lambert, Betty. *Crossings*. Vancouver: Pulp Press, 1979.

———. *Three Radio Plays*, ed. Malcolm Page. *West Coast Review* 19, no. 3 (January 1985).

———. *Jennie's Story and Under the Skin*. Toronto: Playwrights Canada, 1987.

Kerr, Rosalind. "'Swallowing the Lie' in Betty Lambert's *Jennie's Story*." *Modern Drama* 47, no. 1 (Spring 2004): 98–113.

Messenger, Ann. "Betty Lambert." In *Dictionary of Literary Biography*. Vol. 60. *Canadian Writers Since 1960*, 2nd ser., ed. W. H. New. New York: Bruccoli Clark, 1987. 161–64.

Stephenson, Heidi and Natasha Langridge. *Rage and Reason: Women Playwrights on Playwriting.* London: Methuen, 1997.

Worthington, Bonnie. "Battling Aristotle: A Conversation with Betty Lambert." *A Room of One's Own* 8, no. 2 (1983): 54–66.

Wilson, Ann. "The Culture of Abuse in *Under the Skin; This is for You, Anna* and *Lion in the Streets.*" In *Contemporary Issues in Canadian Drama,* ed. Per Brask. Winnipeg: Blizzard, 1995. 160–70.

A Ship of Fools in the Feminine: Six Characters in Search of Self

Louise Forsyth

What is it with the persistent use of I in this text?
—Nicole Brossard, *The Aerial Letter*

Qui suis-je moi qui n'ai jamais été? (Who am I, I who have never been?)
—Denise Boucher, *Les fées ont soif*

La nef des sorcières was published and first staged in 1976 at the Théâtre du Nouveau Monde during the week of International Women's Day. It was also performed in translation as *A Clash of Symbols* at the Firehall Theatre in Toronto in 1978.[1] This was a heady time for a rebellious and passionately engaged generation of feminist writers, artists, actors, and activists in Québec, whose generation rejected, often violently, the cultural traditions and legal structures that had deprived women of educational opportunities, narrowly circumscribed their sexuality, and imposed insignificant supporting roles on the professional lives of most of them. The moment was propitious for women's confrontational voices to be heard and for new notions *au féminin*[2] of women's place in society, of their sexuality, theatricality, identity, agency, and language to be developed. In such an effervescent climate, *La nef des sorcières*—a ship of witches, hysterical fools, or madwomen—was received with both enthusiasm and controversy. Critical response from journalists and university scholars to *La nef* was, in the main, sneering and dismissive, despite packed houses and an extension of the run.[3] It seems that at the time the notion of ordinary women staging their own lives was widely viewed as nonsensical. The play has since been recognized generally, although not unproblematically, as marking a determining moment in Québec theatre and feminist history.

Although *La nef* did not present itself as autobiographical theatre and has not, as far as I know, been studied as such, I intend to show that its dramatic characteristics derive from foundational assumptions about autobiography, that is, assumptions regarding a self who comes to voice in order to represent some part of a real life. In order to stage one's own story and to use the pronoun "I" in doing so, on the assumption that readers and spectators will recognize the person speaking as a unique individual, that person must have some basis for believing in the reality of her own identity. The dramatic conflict of *La nef* is both internal and external, between two conflicting voices inside each character and between the character and the audience, addressed directly at several moments in the play.

The starting point for the characters in *La nef*, which rang compellingly true in Québec in the 1970s, was the awful realization that they did not know who they were, how they could represent themselves, where to find their place on society's many stages, or how to undertake their life's journey. Their "I" rang hollow; they were out of touch with their own bodies. Their distressing situation is captured in the epigraph at the beginning of this paper, taken from Denise Boucher's question that launches *Les fées ont soif*: "Who am I, I who have never been?" The characters of *La nef* affirmed throughout the play that, since they collectively felt they had little ontological status, by speaking in their own voice, showing their bodies, and performing their memories and desires, they were doing the magical and alchemical work they had to do in order to bring themselves into existence as autonomous human beings. This strategy was necessary to open the path to the narrative coherence that underlies even the most fragmented of personal stories. The writers and actors of *La nef* drew particular attention to individuals engaged in self-reflection and creative acts using verbal and non-verbal languages. They were doing what Leigh Gilmore (1996) studied so cogently two decades later, calling the approach *autobiographics*. They were producing *autography*, which has been described by Jeanne Perreault as "the process by which feminist writers redefine the subjective Self. This writing the 'body' frees feminists from the constraints of history, economics, class, and race, laying claim to a fundamental concept of wholeness outside the patriarchy" (n.p.). The simple sentence, "I am speaking," echoes through the monologues of *La nef* like a *leitmotif* underlining the women's astonishment and pleasure at finding themselves in a place that gives them permission to speak for themselves.[4]

Using words to speak for oneself in order to "redefine the subjective Self" and so lay "claim to a fundamental concept of wholeness" was a primary characteristic of Québec writing *au féminin* in the 1970s, particularly in poetry and works of fiction. *La nef*, being a play created on this autographical principle, was unique at the time. The dramatic text it most resembles is Eve Ensler's *The Vagina Monologues*. These two plays are a composite of monologues constructed from words uttered by several different women speaking about intimate experiences not previously discussed. Both combine elements of theatre and performance art in that they are on the edge between fictional and real space. In their frank language and their display of women's bodies and corporeal functions, they boldly draw attention to arbitrary taboos imposed on women's behaviour and speech, and they gaily break these taboos. The underlying postulate of both plays is that women will be in a position to represent themselves in a satisfying autobiographical way only when they feel no fear about taking their experiences out of the closet and talking about them. Through their theatrical performance the characters write, speak, and act themselves into a tentative reality, ready to set out on their personal journey.

The preparation of *La nef* as published script and theatrical event involved a year of intense activity, during which time writers, actors, and a designer met regularly to write, rehearse, design, and stage the play. The project produced tense moments as they collectively confronted the challenge of acknowledging the stories they had to tell about themselves. Hélène Roy's full-length video documentary "Une nef ... et ses sorcières" is an invaluable source of information on the emergence of the play as autography and autobiography. The documentary contains precious clips from the show and footage of rehearsals and round table discussions. The viewer is able to hear the women's voices and feel their compelling and intense personal engagement in the process. They were surprised to find themselves thinking, saying, and doing things for the first time. Occasionally such a revelation was exhilarating; more often it produced denial, fear, and a daunting sense of vulnerability, particularly when the revelation brought to light contradictions between a new image of self and now-problematic established patterns in daily lives and work.

Actor and playwright Louisette Dussault, then at the beginning of an eminent career, captures in her essay "Itinéraire pour une moman" this daunting recognition of self and personal agency produced by participation in *La nef* and Boucher's *Les fées ont soif*:

> J'ai toujours eu l'impression de jouer derrière des écrans jusqu'au moment où il y a eu *La Nef des sorcières* et *Les Fées ont soif*: ... Ces expériences-là ont été déterminantes pour moi, très douloureuses aussi, parce que les personnages dans ce qu'ils charriaient me confrontaient profondément dans ce que j'étais, à l'idée que je me faisais de moi-même. (22, 24)
> (I have always had the impression that I was acting behind screens until the moment when there was *La Nef des sorcières* and *Les Fées ont soif*: ... Those experiences were decisive for me, very painful as well, because what the characters were conveying forced me in a profound way to take a look at what I was, at the idea of me I was constructing for myself.)

La nef is composed of seven monologues written by seven different women. In each monologue the character performs a typical moment in the life of a woman whom social discourse has cast in the role of a feminine type and whose subjective sense of individuality has been thereby eclipsed: the Mad Actress, the Menopausal Woman, the spinster Garment Worker, the Girl (with slippage in identity among the Daughter, the party Girl, the call Girl, and the good-time Girl who loves to shop and is obsessed with her appearance), the Lesbian (two monologues, both played by Pol Pelletier), and the

Writer. Two of these were played by their authors, while five were played by actors who collaborated throughout the year with the authors in workshops and rehearsals.

Members of the *La nef* team initially felt they had no personal stories to tell that would capture the imagination of an audience. The occasional mention in the play of childhood or family memories serves only to underline ironically the narrow banality of most girls' and women's lives and the unremarkable uniformity of women's experiences. Also, since many girls and women in Québec had limited access to public space, activities and opportunities, usually under the pretext of providing some kind of protection for them, they had few unique experiences of their own to perform on stage. Like Agnès in Molière's *L'école des femmes*, the script against which they undertook their journey of self-discovery—they and the women after whom they might model themselves, such as their mothers, friends, or fellow-workers—seemed equally imprisoned in invisibility behind fictitious masks.

In order to stage lives that were theatrically interesting, the creators of *La nef* moved in the direction of performance art, as it was just coming to be practised in the 1970s. Jeannie Forte describes the performance artist as not playing a role written for her by others, but rather performing autobiographically, speaking and writing for herself, affirming the reality of her material and corporeal presence, making her subversive, satirical points using non-canonical acting strategies, and undermining the symbolic structure of dominant representational systems, whose arbitrariness and contingency she is exposing and challenging: "As a deconstructive strategy, women's performance art is a discourse of the objectified other" (252). Viewing *La nef* through the prism of women's performance art, as we know it today and as it has been theorized by Forte and others, provides insight into the extraordinary originality of *La nef* and the radically subversive quality of its approach to autobiography: "Women's performance art has particular disruptive potential because it poses an actual woman as a speaking subject, throwing that position into process, into doubt, opposing the traditional conception of the single, unified (male) subject" (254).

At the beginning of each monologue of *La nef*, light comes up on the character that will perform it. Costumes, make-up, and props provide immediate information on the easily recognizable feminine role that the character has played up to this point in her life and career. The dramatic conflict of the monologue is established when the actor/character takes a step back in order to look at the image of herself, recognizes the alienated identity that stereotypes have imposed on her, affirms the reality of unspoken experiences, and seeks, often with anger and defiance, ways to get on with her life beyond the debilitating impact of powerful fictions and illusions. By standing back in this way and taking enough distance to analyse the way they are most often seen, the characters are rendered three-dimensional, intimately engaged with their own personal lives as both experiencing subjects and objective observers capable of lucid reflection. There is slippage, dialogue, and dramatic conflict between masks and faces. This theme of self-reflection and the doubling of the perspective on actors and the characters they play was highlighted throughout *La nef* by the image of mirrors which was used frequently by the characters and was represented in Marcelle Ferron's stark design that seemed to have been built on light and mirrors.

The monologues are recognizably autobiographical to varying degrees. There are numerous indications in the texts that show how real individuals have dramatized some part of their own personal stories through the creation of fictitious dramatic figures. For example, in the opening monologue, "A Mad Actress," the *persona* of writer, actor, and director Luce Guilbeault recalls experiences that would be those of Guilbeault in her theatrical career. In her final two lines she speaks to herself using the name "Luce" (55). Since Guilbeault played the role herself, its autobiographical dimension would have been obvious to all members of the audience. The text indicates that the name is to be changed to that of other actors playing the role. Similarly, in the final monologue of *La nef*, the *persona* of writer Nicole Brossard takes positions that are very close to those Brossard was assuming in her writing in the mid-1970s, and she evokes memories of the recent birth of "Julie," the name of Brossard's daughter born in the mid-1970s.

In "A Mad Actress" Guilbeault stages her frustration as a skilled theatre professional in almost never having come across a theatrical role she could get her teeth into. For years she has had to suppress her own emotions, the feelings of her body, and her thinking capacity in order to squeeze herself into narrow and banal female characters. The Mad Actress arrives on stage costumed, coiffed, made up, and ready with her lines to play the archetypal feminine role of Agnès in Molière's *L'école des femmes*. Almost immediately, she has a memory lapse so complete that she cannot play her role. The show cannot go on; even the stage space itself appears to become dark, empty, and insignificant: the players are without a script. The Actress sees herself alone on stage with nothing to say or do; in fact, without her lines she herself is nothing: "Au secours, je ne suis plus rien" (17) ("Help, I've become nothing"). She is shocked as she recognizes the brainwashing she has undergone: "Je crois ce que je dis parce que je le dis par coeur. / Bam, bam, bam dans la tête, les mots / Avec le grand marteau pénis" (17) ("I believe what I say because I say it by heart. / Bang, bang, bang. The words were hammered into my head with a big penis hammer") (3). This makes her think of society's many formulae regarding girls and women, whether in relationships or on the public stage: "Sois belle et tais-toi / Femme" (18) ("Be beautiful and be silent, / Woman") (3). The radical break with the role of pretty, nubile virgin is signalled performatively by her ripping off her wig, casting aside all props, undoing the stays of her costume, lifting her skirts and "squat[ting] in a pissing position" (3), all the better to present visually Guilbeault's own corporeal reality. Similar moments in later monologues when gestures are made or costumes are ripped off to signal an absolute refusal to play stereotypical roles occur when the Menopausal Woman Françoise Berd cries out, when Dussault as the presumably beautiful Girl shows her real and imperfect, unadorned naked body, and when the Lesbian played by Pol Pelletier tears off the wig she is wearing to bare a defiantly shaved head.

The empty theatre space produced by the Mad Actress's memory loss makes possible these violent performances when actors/characters display their refusal of inauthentic identities. The memory loss produces a void on stage; cleared of the canonical play, the stage space remains open and ready for the performance that the women of *La nef*, each in her space on stage, will create one after the other. Without her costume and with only an old piece of fur to wrap around her for warmth, the Mad Actress withdraws at the end of the first part of her monologue to the dressing room set up for her on stage. No longer playing Agnès but still a player inside the fictitious frame of *La nef*, the Actress (representing and played by Guilbeault, but not to be seen as the real Guilbeault on stage) will be a silent spectator of the monologues that follow. She is the intradiegetic feminist spectator of this play emerging into theatrical space from the folds of silence. She awaits the representation of women's life stories from which a new kind of theatre might be made. Her silent gaze follows all the other characters in turn as they construct fragmentary outlines of a coherent and autonomous self. She remains on stage even during intermission. When she resumes her monologue at the beginning of the second act, she recounts a number of personal memories, apparently autobiographical, that tell of Luce's attempts to exist as an independent being in a family that stifled her every initiative in the name of protective love, thereby threatening her with death. Her voice in the second part of her monologue, during which she envisages herself, like Agnès, on a balcony—on the edge—underlines the theme of women's tentative sense of self and existence: "J'existe, je n'existe plus" (52) ("I exist, I no longer exist").

Guilbeault wished to draw the audience into the reality which autobiography implies. She was not only staging her own life, but theirs as well, insofar as representation systems in a sexist society provide them with a reassuring basis for making sense of their lives and the world. She has the Actress she is playing breach the fourth wall and speak directly to spectators, using the second person pronoun. She reminds them that she is looking at them in their deluded belief that they are looking at her real face and her real body:

> Je vous regarde. / Vous regardez mon visage.... Mon visage? / Non.... Vous regardez mon corps. / Mon corps?... Non, un corps déguisé, corseté, creusé à la taille, allongé ou ramassé suivant l'emploi. (19)
> (I am looking at you. / You are looking at my face.... My face? / No ... You are looking at my body. / My body?... No, a body that's disguised, corseted, hollowed out, stretched or padded depending on how it's to be used.)

The Menopausal Woman of the following monologue, "The Change of Life," written by Marthe Blackburn and played by Françoise Berd, begins by announcing that to celebrate her fifty-fifth birthday she is stepping out of the silence and perceived dryness with which older women are commonly associated in order to share her rich archival knowledge, reclaim her gendered body, and emerge as a full human being in her own right: "Je sors du monde du silence ... J'ai des archives dans ma tête. / Ma bouche n'est plus sèche / Je parle. Je peux parler ... J'ai mon corps de femme rempli de mémoire" (21–22) ("I have left the age of silence behind / ... I am carrying archives in my head. / My mouth is no longer dry. / I [am speaking]. I can speak ... my woman's body is heavy with memory") (6). Like the Actress, she realizes that she has been playing a role written for her by others who enjoy power and privilege. She recalls the trite yet hurtful words used by ecclesiastical, medical, and psychiatric experts to relegate her to a shadowy identity. The audience hears the offstage voice of the doctor, who describes all the maladies to which he is sure her flawed body is prone; that of the psychiatrist, whose disgust at her sexualised body is overwhelming; and that of "the man" who ridicules her intention to speak out, saying she is capable of speaking nothing but insignificant lies. The Menopausal Woman screams her refusal of the role of shame imposed on her by this dominant discourse and angrily denounces the lies that have been used, often through violent means, to keep her in her place.

The matronly figure of Françoise Berd made the words of the character in the "Change of Life" resonate with autobiographical authenticity. Refusing the received image of the ugly and feeble older woman who has nothing more to say or do, as well as the abusive use made throughout society of the stereotype of woman's love as it is encountered in traditions of religion, art, literature, and pornography, and as it has been used as a pretext to exclude real women from full participation in society, she proclaims loudly the enduring power of her own desires, her pride in her woman's blood, her sense of dignity in her woman's body, her determination, repeatedly expressed, to speak in her own voice, and her conviction (deliberately making a grammatical error to highlight the fact that *human being* exists only in the masculine in French) that she can bring herself into being as a total human being by thus speaking out: "**LES TEMPS SONT VENUS.** / La femme oubliée, retirée, muette, méditative, **APPARAÎT**. / Elle parle. Elle est solide ... Je suis **UNE** être humaine.... Je parle (29)" ("**THE TIME HAS COME.** / The forgotten woman, the retiring, silent and reflective woman, / **APPEARS**. / She [is speaking]. She is solid ... I am a HU WO HUman WOman.... And I am speaking") (11).

The Menopausal Woman realizes that up to now her sense of self has been constructed entirely out of the lies she has been living for fifty-five years. Blackburn and Berd are positioning themselves differently and outside the box of these lies through the autographical affirmation, "I am speaking." At the same time she acknowledges the strata and labyrinths of lies she must traverse in search of self.

The stereotypical feminine role dramatized in the third monologue of *La nef*, "The Sample," written by France Théoret and played by Michèle Craig, illustrates the life experiences of an unmarried garment worker who has dedicated all her time, energies, and resources to supporting younger members of her family and who consequently enjoys only a tenuous sense of self, with little sense of self-respect, personal entitlement, or a satisfying place in society. Thematically and structurally, then, this monologue resonates with all the other texts in *La nef*, but is the Garment Worker an autobiographical representation? France Théoret implicitly agreed during an interview with Patricia Smart that all her writing is autobiographical: "La voix qui parle dans vos écrits est toujours autobiographique" (11) ("The voice speaking in your writing is always autobiographical"). Despite this affirmation, I can find no explicit indications of autobiography in "The Sample," but perhaps such a truth claim is beside the point because *in performance* the "Je" of this Garment Worker is *heard* by us as confession.

The *loose woman* of Odette Gagnon's monologue, "The Date," played by Louisette Dussault, rebels against the words and images used in normal cultural practice to control women's sexuality: the beauty myth, established patterns of femininity and masculinity, social rituals, the sex trade, and shopping. Such practices have put in place what Pelletier calls in "Marcelle II" the "jeu social de la séduction" (69) ("social game of seduction") (32).

The monologue begins with the Girl chanting as part of the ritual of getting ready to go out on Saturday night, as she has participated in it for many years. Immediately though, the Girl, like the Actress and the woman going through "The Change," has a complete lapse in her ability to play the expected role in the appearance industry ritual, which has consumed all her time, efforts, and resources until now. She announces that she is alone on this Saturday night, that she is expecting no one, that for the first time this situation does not frighten her, and that she does not need anyone with her to feel "worth" something:

> À soir, sam'di ... J'attends pas d'téléphone, j'attends pas d'visite, y a personne qui s'en vient me r'joindre ou qui s'en vient m'chercher ... à soir on va dire, que chus toute à moi! Pour la première fois, j'pense ben, ça m'fait pas peur. (41)
> (Tonight, Saturday night ... I'm not expecting any calls, no visitors, nobody's on his way over, nobody's coming to get me ... you might say I'm all mine. I think this is the first time it hasn't scared me.) (17)

The rest of the monologue is her bitter reflection on the way she was seduced by the quick rewards of allowing her body to be appropriated by others' desires.

The character says that she learned very early that girls and women depend on men for support. She learned to "prostitute" herself in order to obtain nice things, whether in the parish hall, the family, or the work place. She immediately understood that other girls and women were rivals for men's favours and advancement in society. Following the rhythms and logic of her girl's socialization into a sexist society, the early transition to soft prostitution seemed to come naturally: "J'avais 17 ans quand chus rentrée dans l'monde des gars officiellement" (43–44) ("I was 17 when I let guys into my life officially") (18). At this stage in her life when she was entirely possessed by the gaze of any man she might encounter and who might pamper her, the mirror was not for self-reflection but for narcissistic preoccupation with appearance:

> T'arranger pour, ça c'est quequ'chose ... ça coûte de l'argent.... C'est une *job* à plein temps, à vie. Vient un moment donné où tu peux pus mettre le nez dehors sans passer par la chambre de bain pis l'miroir, sans t'arranger pour. (45)
> (Fixing yourself up, it's quite a job ... And it all costs money. Fixing yourself up, there's no end to it once you start. It's a full-time lifetime *job*. The time comes when you can't set foot out the door without stopping in the bathroom to check in the mirror. Without fixing yourself up.) (19)

Plays on words used by this *loose* woman produce association and slippage from prostitution to shopping, revealing their inescapable connection in the socialization of women to be beautiful, charming, and seductive, and so to sell themselves and their bodies: "Faire la rue—faire le trottoir / faire les vitrines—les magasins / c'est deux manières de s'mettre en vente / d'être su l'marché/deux manières de s'prostituer" (46–47) ("Making your rounds on the sidewalks—streetwalking / making your rounds in the stores—window shopping / it's just two different ways of putting yourself / on the market, up for sale. / Two kinds of prostitution") (20). As was shown earlier, Dussault came increasingly to recognize the autobiographical dimension of the role, its relevance as a representation of her own personal and professional experiences, the ways in which the requirement that she please was causing her to deny her own thoughts and feelings. She discusses in "Une nef ... et ses sorcières" the shock of discovery in feeling intimately in her body the internalized messages of the beauty myth. She sees herself staging her own life as she performs along the continuum of obsession with appearance and of selling oneself in the economy of the sexist gaze, whether in the form of prostitution, shopping, or popularity as a performer. As a result, Dussault has the character rip off her robe in order to contemplate the reality of her physical body. At the same time she realizes, like the Menopausal Woman in "The Change," that she has been seduced by cheap and illusory promises of love and romance.

The Girl's choice of words and syntax can be described, unlike the language in any of the other monologues, as *joual*, the language of Montreal streets and factories that was being used autographically elsewhere in the Québec theatre at the time to redefine Québec's collective sense of self and identity. *Joual* in the theatre defiantly represents authentic orality in pronunciation, broken syntax, dropped or added letters and words, and an elementary vocabulary. This is the Girl's medium, as can be heard, for example, in her discussion of her sexual experiences: "y a ben des fois, si ç'avait été just' de moi, j'm'en serais passée ... P't'être ben qu'oui, p't'être ben qu'non, ça va dépendre" (48)

("[L]ots of times, if it had been up to me, I wouldn't have bothered ... Maybe this time ... maybe not ... it will depend") (21). The words she uses to name parts of her body and their functioning during sexual acts would have been seen at the time as shocking, vulgar slang. This linguistic authenticity echoes the frank display of her naked body. The Girl's autographical use of *joual* inscribes both her, as a fictional character, and Dussault, as the actor blatantly performing the character while foregrounding her own body, in the reality of a specific and revolutionary moment in Québec history.

Pol Pelletier performed both monologues written for the Lesbian, "Marcelle," one written by herself and the other by Marie-Claire Blais. Unlike all the other characters in *La nef*, Blais's Marcelle does not begin by foregrounding the stereotypes that are standing in the way of her getting on with her life as she wants to live it. Instead, she reveals the loneliness, unhappiness, guilt, and frustration she feels in being unable to prevent herself from being a control freak in her relations with other women. Rather than critiquing society, she blames herself for being insensitive, too independent, unwilling, or unable to listen to others she loves. It is the only monologue that departs from the structural template introduced in "The Mad Actress," that of a character playing simultaneously in two registers between the stereotype and surging desire, between subjectivity and lucid objectivity. As well, the text contains no signs that point to it as autobiography.

Guilbeault states in the Roy documentary that Blais's representation of a lesbian did not resonate with Pelletier, who then wrote "Marcelle II" as an immediate follow-up to "Marcelle." It was Pelletier's objective to perform the taboo subject of lesbianism on the public stage, to move completely out of the guilt that commonly surrounds lesbianism, and to celebrate with pride, amorously and passionately, the emotional and physical experience of women loving women. Blais's "Marcelle," thus transformed into the first part of a diptych, works as a performance of the problem, much as the Mad Actress coming on stage, costumed to play the role of Agnès in *L'école des femmes*, shows through dramatic ostension the dangerous fictions of the roles she has been called to play. The Actress has had to rip off the costume in order to clear herself and the stage for the play, *La nef*, that is coming into being. Similarly, Pelletier violently rips off the wig she has been wearing as Marcelle to bare the naked head beneath. Pelletier's act of shaving her head and the role itself were audacious in the extreme in the 1970s. The autobiographical dimension of "Marcelle II" is evident in this act and also in part because Pelletier has self-identified theatrically as lesbian,[5] in part because of the personal and poetic nature of the monologue: "Ce corps de femme allongé sur son flanc, moi en face / allongée sur mon flanc à moi, la sensation d'une / peau de femme tout le long de ma peau à moi, les jambs" (69) ("Her woman's body lying on her side, and me facing her / lying on my side, the sensation of a / woman's skin touching mine ... legs") (32), and in part because Roy's video provides incontrovertible evidence of the intensity of Pelletier's personal engagement, in both anger and ecstasy, with the character she wrote and performed. The monologue is a richly poetic and extremely bold personal celebration of *jouissance* in lesbian experience.

Marcelle II poses a question of radical ontological doubt similar to those posed by Brossard and Boucher in the citations given at the beginning of this text: "Où suis-je moi?" (68) ("Where am I, myself?"). Marcelle II is well aware that she can only respond to the question autographically. She is where she writes and performs herself into being, in a never-ending creative process of personal and collective selfhood. This process, like *La nef* itself, promises to allow her to speak of the desires that drive her and to emerge into visible reality on public fora. Autography promises to transform her psychic and social space from the indistinct walls of silent anonymity into a mountainous, vociferous place:

> Je veux parler du désir. De mes désirs ... le désir, l'envie de prendre, d'agir, d'aller au devant de, l'élan, l'instinct de puissance, le besoin de se manifester ... Bientôt les miettes seront cent, seront mille, les miettes apparaîtront au grand jour, elles se coaguleront, se solidifieront, deviendront ... une montagne avec une voix (68, 70, 71) (I want to talk about desire. About my desires ... desire, yearning to grab, to act, to move in front of, thrust, instinct for power, need to show myself ... Soon there will be a hundred fragments, thousands, the fragments will emerge into broad daylight, they will come together, will solidify, will become a mountain ... with a voice.) (32, 33)

In the final, angry, and aggressive monologue of *La nef*, "L'écrivain," written by Nicole Brossard and played by Michèle Magny, in which the character explicitly assumes her identity as a lunatic and hysterical woman, a witch, the autographical theme of spoken and written language that redefines subjectivity through the speaking "I" is central. Read in the light of Brossard's career as a radical feminist writer of poetry, novels, and essays, this monologue, along with the preface to the play which she co-authored with Théoret, has the status of an autobiographical credo in dramatic mode. The Writer insistently draws attention to and illustrates the sexism of French grammar, using the mute *e* as a symbol of the silence surrounding most experiences that are uniquely feminine. At the time, her very role of *l'écrivain* had been conceived and so could be written only in the masculine.

Several of the preceding monologues address the theme of love, which, in all its many forms, has been socially constructed in close conjunction to femininity. In *La nef* love is consistently shown to be, in reality, a minefield for girls and women seeking a sense of self and control of their own sexed bodies. Therefore, using the same template as that of the other monologues whereby the character begins by rejecting stereotypical roles that deceive and constrain, the Writer begins her scene by reflecting objectively, in the third person, on the semiotic, ontological, and epistemological meaning of creativity, specifically here the act of writing. She proclaims firmly that she is not writing love poems, but is rather, as Ensler has done in *The Vagina Monologues*, changing the order of words and so producing images of women's sexual organs, normally left unspoken because of arbitrary taboos:

> Une femme appuie savamment sur son crayon. /Mais elle n'écrit pas de poème d'amour. / Elle dessine des ventres plats. Des vulves totales. / Elle change l'ordre des mots.... Une peau ... Pleine de signes anciens et de mots nouveaux. (73)
> (A woman presses knowledgeably on her pencil / But she is not writing a love poem. / She is drawing flat bellies. Whole vulvas. /She is changing the order of words.... Skin ... Covered with ancient signs and new words.)

These new words will be plays on words and neologisms in order to name that which has not yet been spoken. They will also be modifications of existing words and syntax to combat systemic sexism in language usage.

Starting in the darkness of the night, the Writer opens herself to the glimmers provided by the new words that she needs in order to undertake her autographical project, heeding the call of *ancient signs*. In this monologue, dominated by the first person singular pronoun in which all personal pronouns abound and in which sentence fragments without subjects stand as testimony to absent personal subjects, the Writer announces her need to encounter herself in a place apart from the fictions that threaten to predetermine who she is: "Cette nuit, je me rencontre ... Où et comment suis-je en train de me déplacer?... Entre le fictif et le réel. À quelle fiction me donner / Quand de toute manière celle-ci me précède toujours?" (73) ("Tonight I am going to encounter myself ... Where and how am I in the process of displacing myself?... Between the fictional and the real. Give myself to which fiction? / When in any case fiction always precedes me?").

She continues with her exploration of what it means to her to speak out at this moment on stage. Expressing her own desires, showing her body, staging the birthing experience, and using ostension to perform her physical presence in public space are dramatic acts constituting a necessary prelude to the autobiographical affirmation of selfhood. Without these acts, society is likely to continue to consider the account of her real experiences as uninteresting and fanciful drivel. She uses the second person plural pronoun to address spectators directly and to invite them to share intimately in her reflection on where she is and what she is doing. Together they can undertake a search for new words, heed the messages of *ancient signs* and so create new realities; a spoken and tactile pact between them would be rich with political significance:

> Je parle pour me donner une voix d'accès.... Je parle. Je parle. Je parle en blanc dans le noir d'une salle.... Je parle dans la perspective d'un pacte politique avec d'autres/femmes. Touchez-moi. La vie privée est politique. (74)
> (I am speaking to forge a path through silence.... I am speaking. I am speaking. I am speaking in white in the darkness of a hall.... I am speaking in the perspective of a political pact with others/women. Touch me. The personal is political.)

Recalling the example of the Mad Actress who has brought *L'école des femmes* to an abrupt end, the Writer also declares her intention to make a mess of the patriarchal show and so cease to be a victim of it: "Je gâche le spectacle que les impuissants cherchent à s'offrir à mes dépens" (75) ("I am making a mess of the show that the impotent want to give themselves at my expense").

In claiming full access to language and so recognizing the importance of enjoying the agency necessary to stage one's own story, the Writer has acquired a taste for autobiography:

> Je n'ai jamais aimé parler de moi. Comme si j'avais toujours eu l'impression qu'il n'y avait rien de spécial à raconter sur ma vie privée. Et pourtant c'est celle-là qui compte. Comment on naît, comment on joue, comment on jouit, comment on souffre, comment on meurt. (77)
>
> (I have never liked to speak about myself. As if I had always had the feeling that there was nothing special to tell about my private life. When really that's all that matters. How you are born, how you play, how you know passion, how you suffer, how you die.)

The monologue evokes personal memories that undoubtedly arise out of Brossard's past, and these memories resonate with the stories already staged by the other characters. In a sense, autography has facilitated autobiography.

The six characters of *La nef* are not in search of themselves as isolated, exemplary individuals, as the autobiographical pact used to imply (see Lejeune). The very multiplicity of their monologues in one theatrical event shows the intermingling of their suppressed selves and stories in a common endeavour to pursue their journey on the ship of mad women. Language, spoken, written, and gestural, is their performance strategy for the construction of self. By their collective presence on stage, they affirm their solidarity and the commonality of many of their experiences. In each case, their sense of self remains fragmentary, fluid, and mobile, caught between realities lived and fictions imagined. They have been able to ground their search for a sense of self in their willingness to overcome fear and ridicule, their determination to show their physical realities, and their ability to speak out on the public stage, articulately and poetically, using the first person pronoun, knowing, like the Writer, that until one has recognition that the events of one's life count, no other initiative can be undertaken.

The basis for a shared autobiographical initiative in the theatre three decades ago is remarkably modern in *La nef des sorcières*, in that the monologues do not rest on the presumed metaphorical resemblance of author and character. The authors seem to have anticipated the postmodern view that assumptions regarding a coherent and stable identity of self are illusory. Instead, the authors have given their characters the tools needed to analyse themselves and their place in the world as works in process. Moreover, their constructions of self and memory emerge in incomplete, juxtaposed, metonymic fragments, and this preference for metonymy over metaphor as a satisfactory trope for creating autobiography in the case of members of socially marginalized groups is important. As Gilmore reminds us in *The Limits of Autobiography*, "insofar as autobiography represents the real, it does so through metonymy, that is, the claims of contiguity where the person who writes extends the self in the writing, and puts her in another place" (101). And as members of a socially marginalized group, the six women on this Québecois ship of fools found themselves by finding each other (and us) in a real social place of performance.

Notes

1. All references to *La nef des sorcières* are to the 1976 edition and are indicated by page numbers. Where an English translation follows without a second page reference, the translations are mine. Where a page number does follow the English, it refers to Linda Gaboriau's 1979 translation, *A Clash of Symbols*.

2. The first written usage I have found of the now common expression *au feminin* is by Suzanne Lamy in *d'elles* (56–67).

3. Lorraine Camerlain and Pierre Vallières were two of the very few critics at the time who reviewed *La nef des sorcières* as a serious artistic creation. Jane Moss's analysis of it is probing, as is Lori Saint-Martin's introduction to the second edition.

4. Linda Gaboriau has translated "Je parle" as "I speak." In every citation of this expression, I have replaced "I speak" with "I am speaking," since I believe that this verb form better expresses the progressive and mobile nature of the process in which the characters are engaged.

5. See, for example, her autobiographical play *Joie*.

Works Cited

Blackburn, Marthe, Marie-Claire Blais, Nicole Brossard, Odette Gagnon, Luce Guilbeault, Pol Pelletier, and France Théoret. *La nef des sorcières*. Montreal: Éditions Quinze, 1976.

———. *A Clash of Symbols*. Trans. Linda Gaboriau. Toronto: Coach House, 1979.

Boucher, Denise. *Les fées ont soif.* Montreal: Les Éditions Intermède, 1978.

Brossard, Nicole. *The Aerial Letter*. Trans. Marlene Wildeman. Toronto: The Women's Press, 1988.

Camerlain, Lorraine. "La nef des sorcières." *Cahiers de théâtre Jeu* 16, no. 3 (1980): 216–17.

Dussault, Louisette. "Itinéraire pour une moman." In *Moman*. Montreal: Boréal Express, 1981. 9–38.

Ensler, Eve. *The Vagina Monologues*. New York: Villard, 1998.

Forte, Jeannie. "Women's Performance Art: Feminism and Post-Modernism." In *Performing Feminisms*, ed. Sue-Ellen Case. Baltimore: Johns Hopkins University Press, 1990. 251–69.

Gilmore, Leigh. *Autobiographics: A Feminist Theory of Women's Self-Representation*. Ithaca: Cornell University Press, 1994.

———. *The Limits of Autobiography, Trauma and Testimony*. Ithaca: Cornell University Press, 2001.

Lamy, Suzanne. *d'elles*. Montréal: L'Hexagone, 1979.

Lejeune, Philippe. *Le pacte autobiographique*. Nouvelle édition augmentée. Paris: Éditions du Seuil, 1996.

Moss, Jane. "Women's Theater in Québec." In *Traditionalism, Nationalism, and Feminism: Women Writers of Québec*, ed. Paula Gilbert Lewis. Westport, Conn. and London: Greenwood Press, 1985. 241–59.

Pelletier, Pol. *Joie*. Montreal: Les Éditions du Remue-ménage, 1995.

Perrault, Jeanne. *Writing Selves: Contemporary Feminist Autography*. Minneapolis: University of Minnesota Press, 1995.

Roy, Hélène. "Une nef ... et ses sorcières." 53 min. Quebec City: Vidéo femmes, 1977. Videocassette.

Saint-Martin, Lori. Introduction to *La nef des sorcières*, by Marthe Blackburn, Marie-Claire Blais, Nicole Brossard, Odette Gagnon, Luce Guilbeault, Pol Pelletier, and France Théoret. 2nd ed. Montreal: L'Hexagone, 1992. 21–41.

Smart, Patricia. "Entrevue avec France Théoret." *Voix et Images* 40 (Fall 1988): 11–23.

Vallières, Pierre. "'La Nef des sorcières' met un point final à l'ère braillarde des 'belles-soeurs.'" *Le Jour*, 12 mars 1976, 24.

PART THREE

Theatre Lives: From Autobiography to Biography

Autobiography, Gender, and Theatre Histories: Spectrums of Reading British Actresses' Autobiographies from the 1920s and 1930s

Maggie B. Gale

From the perspective of the *autobiographical I*, it seems appropriate to begin this chapter from my own subject position as a female theatre historian. As a postgraduate, I concentrated on British women playwrights of the early and mid-twentieth century, a focus that took me away from feminist readings prohibited by the then contemporary closed definitions of feminist theatres; these did not allow for an analysis of a huge body of work situated in the realist *prison house* tradition—to be a feminist playwright one was obliged to be experimental in form, to undermine consciously and deliberately the patriarchal hegemony.

But many women playwrights writing for the British theatres of the early and mid-twentieth century were working inside a commercial industry notoriously antagonistic toward the experimental. They were also writing in the aftermath of the Great War and, perhaps more importantly, in the aftermath of the social and cultural upheaval caused by women's struggle for the vote. Many of the plays I analysed during this period of research tuned in to the *feminist* issues of the day, a dispersed feminism which some would say had been watered down and no longer embodied the overt political thrust by which it had once been identified. Inter-war British women playwrights such as Clemence Dane, G. B. Stern, Gordon Daviot, and Aimee Stuart created dominant and powerful female characters as well as narratives and plots centred around the issues which influenced the lived experiences of women of the day: motherhood and work, women's role in the economy, gender roles within relationships, women's contribution to national histories, and so on. Many of these women playwrights were household names, and their repeated successes and continuing presence and popularity caused great angst amongst the critics of the day, critics who consistently expressed the fear that the legitimate theatre (perceived as a male preserve) was being overrun with women playwrights and female audiences. Inter-war women playwrights provide a link between the feminist playwrights of the Edwardian period, the new women playwrights of the 1950s, and those of the "second wave" feminist movement from the 1970s onwards. Their work provides a link in a chain but a glitch for a feminist system of analysis because they were not necessarily driven by an overt and self-consciously *political* agenda, although many may well have been *politicized*. But this was not the only reason they had been written out of theatre history. Theatre historians generally have failed to reassess the period in which these playwrights happen to have been active because of a lack of interest in the commercial theatre system of the time. Feminist historians had assumed their absence—the period has not been well documented—and when feminist historians *were* aware of their presence, the seeming lack of overt feminist content in their work called for a rethinking of the ways in which feminist theatre histories of the time were being constructed (see Gale 1996, 2000a, and 2000c).

All historians *construct* history; those who are more honest point not only to the ways and means by which they construct those histories but also to the agendas at play in the formulating and operating of methodologies. As a researcher, I had a totally biased starting point—I was interested in work made by women. As a historian, however, there were limitations to the materials I could bring to bear on constructing any history. My evidence came from play texts, critical works, journalism, contemporary histories of the commercial theatre of the time, and sociological and historical sources on women's transitional cultural position. There were very few occasions on which the playwrights in question wrote about their own work or even their own lives. Their absence from history, despite their once high-profile position, was in part caused by a lack of academic re-evaluation of this moment in British theatre history despite the fact that literary modernist studies was heralding this period as one of important cultural shifts. There was also, however, a level of unconscious or unintentional collusion on the part of the women playwrights themselves—they did not write about their own work, they did not engage with their own public importance, and so they largely disappeared from history. Women of the time experienced a new level of profile in the public sphere but for the majority of the population, even in the 1920s and 1930s, an ordinary woman's place was still in the home. Thus, in the case of women playwrights of the era, there was a certain amount of social prohibition around the idea of women and work and public success— even in the world of theatre.

In opposition to the majority of women playwrights, actresses of the period often wrote autobiographies, and it was to these I turned after a long period of trawling through libraries and archives for play texts once printed, never reprinted. Actresses had a very different relation to the processes of play production and to the workings of the commercial theatre. They were dominant in the celebrity culture, still developing during the early years of the twentieth century. Actresses were at the forestage, directly in the public eye; they somehow managed to sustain a certain amount of immunity to a public critique of women's roles—being an actress was just about socially acceptable during this period as compared to being a woman playwright; the theatre industry and the critics still perceived playwriting as a male profession, whereas the position of actresses had moved on since the late Victorian period. A study of actresses presented new areas of contention: questions about representations of the female and femininity, issues around the body on stage, celebrity culture and popular perceptions of women's roles. Ironically, many of the women playwrights whose work I had examined, such as Clemence Dane, Dodie Smith and Joan Temple, among others, began their professional careers as actresses; it was the idea of professionalism and career trajectories which drew me both to commercially successful women playwrights and, in particular, to actresses' autobiographies. If the commercially successful women playwrights—backstage, working in private, often isolated from the communal activity of *making* theatre (although many, such as Dane and Smith, often participated in the production process)—appeared to have had no autobiographical sense of their own position as professionals, did the actresses of the day have anything more to offer in terms of acknowledging their own active participation in *making history*? Thus, I came to autobiography and the autobiographic looking for evidence, with all the problems that such materials bring with them.

The "I" That Has Disappeared

The autobiographic text is inherently problematic for any historian, whatever their focus. Texts which are autobiographic in nature can often be found outside the boundaries of actual published autobiography and, as is the case with autobiography, such texts consistently raise questions about authenticity. The autobiographic is not in and of itself history, but a hybrid form which mixes fiction, fantasy, and self-delusion with fact, memoir, and the subject's retelling or narrativizing of a selection of lived experiences. Sometimes such autobiographic texts appear to be written by the subject in such a way that they themselves might even disappear. Such is the case with Clemence Dane, one of the most prolific British women playwrights, whose work was produced from the early 1920s to the early 1960s in the British theatre (see Gale 2000b). Dane, infamous for her novel *The Regiment of Women* (1917), wrote no autobiography; the nearest she came to doing so was *London Has a Garden* (1965), a history of the interface between the geography and architecture of Covent Garden in London, and the theatrical culture which thrived around it. Here, there is remarkably little about Dane herself—she talks a great deal about her flat in Tavistock Street and about attending a variety of rehearsals, but not of her own work. Dane left journalistic writings alongside her plays, novels, and literary/cultural criticism, but appeared to want to keep the details of her private life in a state which was not configured for public consumption. This was in part because of her problematic relation to the public's knowledge or lack of knowledge of her lesbianism, but also because she was more interested in *being* an artist than in *writing* about being one.

In an effort to reconstruct a kind of biographic presence for Dane, I came across all kinds of strange contradictions about her personality and her work. She was a great friend of Noël Coward, for example, someone from whom Coward sought advice and criticism. In the majority of biographies of Coward, however, Dane is recreated as an oddity, an eccentric—much like the character of Madame Arcati in Coward's *Blithe Spirit* for which she was supposedly the inspiration. Yet when one trawls through Coward's *own* autobiography and letters, and works his text *against* the biographical texts, Dane is clearly configured as a strong influence, someone critical of Coward's lesser work and poor career decisions. She was someone with whom Coward identified as an artist (she was also a journalist, novelist, Oscar-winning film writer, sculptor and painter). Dane's own scattered autobiographic writing lays traps for the historian, so the most available way of removing her from her own obscurity is to evaluate her work—perhaps she did not realize that being a woman writing successfully for the theatre and cultural industries of the early and mid-twentieth century did not *actually* qualify her for historical inclusion. There is now an archive of her film scripts, which she left in trust to the actor Marius Goring, so someone can begin filling in the gaps about her oeuvre, but her "identity," who she was, whom she loved or cared for, how she felt about the way the public viewed her or her work will take longer to re-construct; the pieces of the puzzle are still buried in time and so the puzzle cannot yet be put together.

Going in search of Dane, as a theatre historian, opened up further questions about women and their *absence* or *presence* in histories of theatre. How could one trace the trajectory of a woman's career in theatre when the cultural dynamics of the era in which that career happened meant that either this career was presented as flawed or dilettantist? Dane, for example, was often accused of being a "oncer" because she had only one or two plays that ran for a year or more, regardless of the fact that, of course, very few playwrights could claim such an achievement. The fact that the woman herself appeared *not* to want her career examined in terms of her own life, and may deliberately have hidden relevant clues, is also a problem. We can construct an objective sense of a career trajectory, but it is more fruitful to do so in relation to an investigation about how the subject projected herself onto the world.

Self-Confessed Professional "I's"

Looking at actresses' autobiographies provided some answers to the question of how women theatre workers themselves wrote about their own careers, whether they in fact recognized or anticipated the mechanisms by which their work might or might not become integrated into histories of British theatre; whether they had a historical consciousness about themselves as women, working in a field dominated by men, in which the importance of their work might be sidelined. The actress who provided a starting point for such an investigation was Lena Ashwell (see Gale 2004). Ashwell rose to fame through her roles in such productions as *Mrs. Dane's Defence* (1900), *Leah Kleshna* (1905), and Cicely Hamilton's *Diana of Dobson's* (1908); she was also a theatre manager, producer, and social activist, working from the late nineteenth century through to the middle of the twentieth. A number of people have written about Ashwell, mostly in the context of her work with the suffragist Actresses Franchise League, her work organizing and producing concerts for the troops during the First World War, and her extraordinary accomplishments at the Century Theatre in London's Notting Hill and in the London Boroughs during the 1920s. Here, she devoted almost ten years of her life to producing theatre outside of the West End and outside of traditional theatre spaces, often to audiences who previously had little access to drama (see Leask, Dymkowski, and Hirshfield). But few have looked at the way she wrote about *herself* and her own achievements as a professional theatre artist. Of her four books, three without doubt could be seen as autobiographic, *Modern Troubadours* (1922), *The Stage* (1929), and *Myself a Player* (1936), although only one was marketed as autobiography in a publishing economy which was open to, and at times appeared to thrive on, autobiographies of theatre people. Ashwell left scrapbooks full of reviews and articles about her productions, now hidden away in the storerooms of the Theatre Museum and at the British Imperial War Museum in London; there are also letters in the British Museum and in the archives at Rochester and Austin in the United States. These letters are often archived by virtue of her relationship to other artists like Shaw or Granville Barker, with whom she worked. Thus, unusually for an actress/manager of her generation, she left, by actresses' standards, a substantial trail of autobiographical and other evidence about her work and to some extent her life. Ashwell was conscious that what she wrote *herself* about her own career might have an impact on the ways the historian would reconstruct her career: her autobiography contains acknowledgement of her anticipated reader/audience, whom she saw as "the 'daws" (jackdaws) who might peck through the pieces of evidence she had left, and of the need for self-analysis rather than too much celebrity gossip. But turning to theories of reading autobiography can create problems for a historian wanting to reconstruct a sense of the relationship between who Ashwell was and what she achieved. It isn't that the evidence does not exist, but rather that so many of the theories of reading the autobiographic don't allow for the easy flow between reading, interpretation, historical placement, and auto/biography. Theories of autobiography are often predicated on their reading as literary texts, whereas for the historian, autobiography can offer a great deal more as social/historical documentation which relates directly to the construction of individual experience.

Autobiography and the Theatre Historian

Thomas Postlewait has written of the problematics of autobiography as "evidence" of the caution we should take as historians in terms of reading autobiographies as evidence of "true" experience, although he rightly acknowledges their useful qualities: "Autobiographies ... constitute major repositories of information for the writing of histories about theatre productions and practices, the organizational structure of theatre companies, business methods, theatrical touring, the development of national theatres (and of theatre within each nation) ... the spread and success of entertainment" (157). He suggests that we should be aware of autobiographies' relation to one another, their relation to generic types and their contextual dynamics. Yet he is also careful to point out that autobiographies provide "extended networks of information.... In their various modes, autobiographies are records of consciousness. So just like all human documents, they are registers of experience and reflections that the historian interrogates, selects from, and uses as evidence" (159–60). For Postlewait, we as theatre historians tend to use autobiographies rather unquestioningly as historical documents and he cautions us to be more scientific in our approaches to such textual evidence as they provide. The danger here is that in the effort to be *scientific* in our approach to autobiography as a *form*, by defining generic types and patterns, we may end up creating false groupings or simply miss out on the individual worth of particular examples. As well as being aware of similarities in approach, style, and effect, we have to celebrate difference. Just as the women playwrights whose work I have assessed cannot easily fit into a *feminist* framework, we need to look at autobiography on a sample-by-sample basis. So much of women's theatre work is already grouped into easily containable categories, which strangely, never manage to bleed into readily accessible general theatre histories. Equally, of the generic types proposed by Postlewait, only a few fit the women's autobiographies which I have come across. There are certain key identifiable characteristics across a number of examples which I have looked at, but the problem with grouping is that it can undermine the detail of individual difference.

Investigations of autobiography and the autobiographic are also made problematic by the nature of the historian's processes of interrogation. If one is trying to find ways of formulating a history of women working in theatre, it is difficult not to let that enthusiasm and sense of excitement prevail when one comes across an autobiography, which provides another small and awkwardly shaped piece of the puzzle. Thus, when Postlewait mentions Constance Collier, it is in her capacity as a Gaiety Girl, one of those late Victorian beauties paraded on stage in George Edwardes's fashion extravaganzas. He describes Collier's autobiographical depiction of her childhood as Dickensian, and almost accuses her of being coy in the manner in which she describes the giving of gifts to the Gaiety Girls by male admirers, who probably wanted sexual favours as opposed to the social company and celebrity status Collier says the girls provided. That Collier, a skilled raconteur, chose to use a readily available style to tell the tale of her early years is interesting. She came from a world not dissimilar to that which fascinated Dickens. Her mother, who had been a child performer in the music halls, travelled around from one theatrical engagement to another and brought her daughter along with her. Her father, it would seem, provided little if any household income, so when Collier's mother could find no work, there was no money for food and shelter. Collier chose a Dickensian style of writing to depict what was seemingly a Dickensian lifestyle: she would have known that readers could thus make the necessary social connection. Her theatrical career took her from one social class to another, for Collier was far more than *just* a Gaiety Girl, who might typically have married into the aristocracy; in her autobiography she constructs herself as an emerging artist, in tune with Postlewait's identification of autobiographies which take the *künstlerroman* formula (see figures 12 and 13).

Ironically, Postlewait's selection of information from Collier's autobiography fits in with a ready-made argument about the ways in which autobiographies by late Victorian actresses fail to confront the level of sexual exchange which we might assume was present in their professional lives. In this way he questions the authority of the text. And much autobiographical theory does the same. But what levels of authority can we as

Figure 12. Constance Collier, "At the 'Gaiety,'" from *Harlequinade* by Constance Collier. London: John Lane and The Bodley Head, 1929. 54.

Figure 13. Constance Collier as Cleopatra, from *Harlequinade* by Constance Collier. London: John Lane and The Bodley Head, 1929. 186.

historians allow ourselves to give to texts written by women at points in history where women's relationship to the public sphere is problematized through the fact of gender? We can authenticate facts but not feelings, impressions, or expressions of experience. Postlewait may be suggesting that these actresses and women theatre workers such as Ashwell, Collier, and so on could never write *truth* because of the social-historical and gendered context of their work: this to some extent plays into the patriarchal social myths about women's innate inability to be truthful. Or perhaps, like Gilmore, Postlewait is merely pointing to the fact that autobiography "provokes fantasies of the real. Its burden is not only to represent gender, genre and identity in any particular lives and imagined configuration, but to posit a ground from which that configuration is thought to emerge" (Gilmore 16).

I am not suggesting that autobiography or the autobiographic will give historians *all* they need to proceed, but rather, that we should not undervalue the significance of these individual and collective works in and of themselves, as well as in relation to one another. Equally, as historians we need to be aware of our own agendas and our own social-historical contexts as readers. As Mary Jean Corbett so rightly states,

> critics of autobiography ... have ... neglected to consider the historical embeddedness of their own notions about self and have assumed that subjectivity is always and everywhere the same.... [W]omen's autobiographies have been undervalued because they do not fit generic terms derived solely from masculine experiences.... This tactic has been to reinforce the notion that texts worth reading are few and far between, even as certain texts have been brought to the forefront. (4–6)

The question of levels of authority predominates in theories of autobiography but my frequent problem with actresses' autobiographies is not so much their authoritative status as the seeming absence of the evidence I have initially sought. There is a kind of autism at work here—and I mean autism in the most general of senses. Just as autism is a generic term which describes a spectrum of so-called behavioural and communicative disorders, so too am I suggesting that the reading of many of the autobiographies written by actresses whose careers crossed over from the late Victorian period into the middle of the twentieth century involves a collaborative/interpretative approach spanning our own expectations, the expectations of the original readers, the intentions of the author, and an understanding of the cultural context from which the writing derived. Is what they wrote so shaped by a social prohibition from writing private "truth," or might we read the chosen form of communication in a number of ways? My experience with autism is that what we often perceive as problems with communication may not actually be problems at all, but simply different and unrecognizable systems for communication which we may not understand. Autistic children do not use language in the same ways we do, but that does not mean that they are not communicating.

This link between the actresses' life stories and autistic communication may come across as spurious, but it is proposed as a metaphor. I am suggesting that when we read actresses' autobiographies we have to engage a number of reading mechanisms at any one time. Thus, we might read autobiography just as we read performance: we look at the event and the context in which that event is embedded professionally, developmentally, aesthetically, technically, and temporally; we read performance vertically and horizontally, in the moment and after the event. Actresses often write about their work in a particular production as an organic whole. They might write a little about the events of their engagement—how they got the role, a rehearsal or period of rehearsals, and a first night. Or they may describe their work on the production in terms of a whole series of performances. As historians, we often look for the highlights—the key performance, the details of technique, and so on. As performers, they might be writing about a particular role twenty years after the experience of playing it, probably without the help of journal entries and with the underlying agenda of wanting to discredit poor reviews or heighten the significance of good ones, or the significance of playing in a production with another performer whose fame has now outstripped their own. Actresses' autobiographies, just as any other's, involve a process of narrative-driven self-creation with reference points to events that might tap into potential contemporary readers' horizons of experience and expectation. Thus, as some theories of autobiography suggest, it is a performative genre and we should perhaps more consciously engage a spectrum of reading influenced by performance. For Smith and Watson, "[a]utobiographical narratives, then, do not affirm a 'true self' or a coherent and stable identity. They are performative, situated addresses that invite their readers' collaboration in producing specific meaning for the 'life'" (11).

Just as reading performance is a collaborative act, so too is reading autobiography. Lena Ashwell, for example, actually writes very little about her work in the Actresses Franchise League (AFL), and yet revisioned histories of this organization have brought Ashwell's name into the still emerging cultural field of women and theatre history. She was a pro-active suffragist, part of the AFL, a radical organization set up to champion women theatre professionals as well as to support the struggle for female franchise. Yet what Ashwell does write about the AFL is embedded in a wider concern about the role of theatre in society in general and the specific inequalities which relate to women's position within the profession; the autobiography was written during a period of feminism when the suffragettes had become a part of recent history. Ashwell, thus, integrates the specifics of her work with the AFL into writing on theatre and community and on the role of the artist as social activist. As a historian I wanted to find out in detail about her work in the AFL, but as the author she wanted me to look beyond this to her involvement with the suffrage movement in the context of a whole matrix of beliefs and practices by which she operated during her career. Ultimately, what *she* wants me, the reader, to see is actually far more historiographically productive than what I might originally have been looking for. As Jacky Bratton has recently suggested, "the medium of print is subject to all sorts of interventions and mediations; its witness to its own times and its transmission of the history of the stage must be read as part of the hegemonic process...." She goes on to propose that we "read this auto/biographical material as far as possible in its own terms, accepting the picture it paints as the intended activity of its authors, male as well as female. They are intent upon projecting an image of the world in which they are actors, those who do, not objects; they deflect us from themselves even as they describe who they are" (99–101).

A significant number of autobiographic works by actresses was published in the 1920s and 1930s when women's work in theatre has often been seen as ephemeral, inconsequential, commercialized, insignificant, intrusive, superficial or simply unworthy of history, both by theatre critics contemporary to the era and by more recent theatre historians. It is interesting that many of these are published at a time when women really were becoming more visible as professionals in the public sphere, when working women were supposedly swamping the job market and were, therefore, prohibited from working in certain fields once married and so on. These autobiographies may or may not have shared features, but it is important to resist the temptation to group such writings into types before we look at what they are and how they work.

Having said this, there are some generic traits that characterize what many of these autobiographies are *not*. Few autobiographies written by actresses during the late nineteenth and early twentieth centuries fit neatly into Postlewait's proposed twelve generic types, as I have already said. But it could be said that even fewer contain clearly demarcated areas where ideas on the processes or techniques of practice are discussed. Such elements are often integrated into the texts, interwoven with anecdote or more factualized information about, for example, work on specific productions or rehearsals or even critical reception. There does appear to be a gender-differentiated relationship, within the autobiographical work of actresses of this era, to the *writing out* of ideas about technique or methodology. Equally, there is often a reticence in talking about personal relationships in detail, as Postlewait suggests. Although here I should point out that while discussions of professional or familial relationships are often prevalent, the personal relationships one would normally associate with the private sphere are often framed in terms of the professional. For a number of the actresses I have focussed on, the hours, days and months of a working life bleed into their lived experience within the private sphere; Collier writes about the sheer length of rehearsals building up to performances in Beerbohm Tree's productions, for example. To be an actress in a competitive market may have meant that few relationships existed outside of the public or work realm—not to say that sexual relations didn't exist, but rather, that marriage outside of the industry often meant giving up work. In turn, to write about a professional career in theatre once you were removed from the industry by way of marriage may not have been socially acceptable or viable in terms of the market for theatrical autobiography. Thus, some actresses of the period write little about the *actual* industry once they are removed from it by marriage—here the detailing of professional relationships is often outweighed by the depiction of social ones. Instead, they often write about social engagements and friendships more than their actual work experience.

Self-Confessed Professionals II: From the Gaiety to Beyond

The market for autobiography may in fact have influenced the production of such publications more than we realize. Two sets of autobiographic writing that I want to look at briefly here were clearly produced for a perceived market by women who had some of their early professional experiences as Gaiety Girls in George Edwardes's spectacular stage events, which largely celebrated fashionable and arguably risqué theatrically constructed femininity during the late nineteenth and early twentieth centuries. Ruby Miller originally went to work for Edwardes when she was underage; when found out, she was told to return at the appropriate age. She re-started her career by working with Beerbohm Tree, then returned to work in musical comedy under Edwardes. The title of her second autobiography, *Champagne from My Slipper*, published in 1962, is a reference to a duke who admired her so much that he used her shoe as a receptacle for his champagne, then bought her numerous expensive replacement pairs. The book pays tribute to her days as a Gaiety Girl, with detailed anecdotes on productions such as *A Little Bit of Fluff* in 1916 and *What a Catch!* in 1918. Here, writing at the end of her career, Miller is very careful to lay out and detail the progression of that career from understudy and walk on in Tree's productions, to musical comedy star, to *vamp* in numerous silent movies made in both Britain and the United States, to screenwriter, and so on. She carries on working, to some extent on the periphery of the theatre, and still has some celebrity status at the time of her death in 1976. Miller's writing is entertaining but lacking in any real self-analysis. Her approach, in her early seventies, is nostalgic and romanticized, although the memories of her professional experiences as she constructs them may be verifiable by comparing her descriptions of her career with more factual historiographic materials. However, her earlier autobiography, written after the sudden death of her husband Max Darewski, *Believe It or Not!*, published in 1933 under the name "Mme. Max Darewski" (Ruby Miller), consists of page after page of only fleeting details about her career but a great deal about her celebrity lifestyle. It also includes painful descriptions of her close relationship with her father and her fateful liaison with Darewski, a pianist and composer with whom she had fallen in love but refused to marry, because of their career commitments, until the late 1920s.

The foundation of *Believe It or Not!* is two-fold: an actress, relatively new to the art of writing, who makes an easy transition from stage to film work, but not from silent films to talkies, and a woman who is suffering from the most appalling experience of grief after the early and shocking death of her new husband. The text itself consists of stream-of-consciousness writing which, when not about her father or the life and achievements of her dead husband or his family, focusses mostly on superficial details of productions, travelling, and her connections with other celebrities. Chapters often end with a confession of tiredness but with the promise to keep an appropriate level of concentration in the following chapter: "My spirit is very willing to continue, but my hand is tired so.... " (165). *Believe It or Not!* slowly moves to its end with more and more focus on Miller's belief in her own psychic powers, her chance meetings with others who share her "gift," and finally on her ability to communicate with her dead husband. Miller was not so unusual for an artistic woman of her era in terms of her belief in the "spiritual" dimension—many actresses refer to the failings of a materialist lifestyle. But the whole narrative builds towards the dénouement when she informs the reader that, in fact, her husband's creative spirit is able to live on through her. Such discussions of life beyond materialism are often textually placed in direct relation to the aftermath of the First World War, which in turn, could be seen to have transformed the nature of *memory* in aspects of cultural production during the 1920s and 1930s, and this has an impact on a number of actresses' autobiographies of the era. However, the construction of the text of Miller's first autobiography is so radically different from the second, where there is little if any real mention of her psychic phase in her early forties, that it appears to have been written by a different woman, although many of the same stories are re-told.

Jacky Bratton's statement about theatrical anecdotes is relevant here. According to Bratton, "Theatrical anecdotes told by their subject tend to be both self-exposing and self-protecting, in that while they may reveal weakness or personal faults, they simultaneously ward off criticism by making that weakness into an amusing story to disarm the listener, and fulfil the contract between the entertainer and the audience" (103). Miller very much saw herself as an entertainer, and she obviously had a significant following for whom she saw herself writing. As she writes, she often appears to be appealing to her readers as well as assuming certain knowledge of her celebrity persona on their part. By the point at which she writes Autobiography II (*Champagne from My Slipper*), the contract between "the entertainer and the audience" is different. Although the targeted reader may have been of her own generation and thus could tune in to her nostalgic demeanour, she is also conscious of the need to provide more contextual material, which often comes down to providing a temporal context. Autobiography I (*Believe It or Not!*) jumps around in time and Miller rarely gives dates of events. Autobiography II, on the other hand, is more consciously chronological. Autobiography I was written whilst Miller was experiencing the process of grieving, but still had a great deal of celebrity currency, and this is reflected in the style of writing. Autobiography II was written towards the end of a long career that had crossed media from stage to screen to literature, back to theatre and radio and so on. At this point she clearly wished to place herself more definitely inside a history of popular theatre culture. Here, whatever our investments as theatre historians, it is clear that to a large extent form follows function; it is not only age that makes Miller use a different style but the need to position herself more forcefully within the development of the industry. The authorial agenda is different at different points in a career.

Lastly, I want to return to another Gaiety Girl, Constance Collier, born in 1878, whose career in theatre stretched from the late nineteenth century to the 1950s. Collier was a striking beauty whose mother had performed as a child and an adult on the musical hall and provincial circuits into the late nineteenth century. Collier's professional debut was also with the Gaiety Girls; she then went on to work with Beerbohm Tree as his leading lady; as a co-author with Ivor Novello in film; as one of Somerset Maugham's leading ladies; and as a librettist, director, and producer in the United States with roles late in life in such films as *Stage Door* (1937) and *Rope* (1948). She was also, late in her career, a much sought after voice coach in Hollywood. Her autobiography, *Harlequinade: The Story of My Life*, was published in 1929 and, as a consequence, much of her later career as director/producer and voice coach is not described from a subject position. Compared to Miller's autobiography, there is an enormous amount of humour and detail in Collier's writing. She has the added advantages of being a very competent writer and storyteller and of having the ability to self-reflect. Her class origins were much more lowly than Miller's and perhaps, as a result of this, she self-consciously depicts her career chronologically and developmentally in professional terms: she writes largely from the subject position of the performer, self-consciously framing her narrative in terms of her *professional experience* as an actress.

Miller's depiction of her early career is framed by nostalgic romanticism: "I am now living in the sixth reign since my birth and still declare, from my heart, that for me the Edwardian era was nearest to perfection.... when Edward VII was King of England; when George Edwardes was King of Musical Comedy; and when Gaiety Girls were the toast of two continents" (186). In contrast, Collier, who had very different class origins and very strong memories of the hand-to-mouth existence provided by life on provincial touring circuits—although pleased to have been given a career break by Edwardes—has, later in life, few illusions about the career option of being a Gaiety Girl. She knew that being picked by Edwardes to appear in his lavish productions provided a fleeting professional opportunity, where the illusion of success was fuelled by parties, flowers, borrowed dresses and accessories from the marketing-conscious fashion houses of the day, and gifts from the stage-door johnnies. *Harlequinade* is much more of a *künstlerroman*, a detailing of the growth of an aesthetic and artistic sensibility, than Miller's writing. So Collier is happy to point out: "Had I been plain I should not have been engaged—the girls were not chosen so much for their ability to act and sing and dance as they are nowadays.... We only had to stand about in those days, and nobody worried about voice" (50).

Collier does not autobiographically frame her career so much in terms of her innate talent having been discovered; she does not play into this aspect of celebrity autobiography. Rather, her descriptions of long days spent in rehearsal and study at the British Museum with the playwright/poet Stephen Phillips reveal an actress with no formal education, concerned with learning her trade, learning technique, and critiquing practice. Her descriptions of rehearsals with Tree are invaluable to the theatre historian, as are her descriptions of her involvement in early film-making. As she looks back on a career almost ended by severe illness, Collier moves away from description and anecdote towards a more reflective and analytical authorial voice. So, for example, in her preface, which appears to have been written as the autobiographic project began, she praises her readers as fans who have "given her a place in the sun" and saved her from "poverty and obscurity," but by the end of the book she is openly annoyed by a request for an autograph which disrupts her concentration and process of self-reflection whilst writing on the deck of a ship returning to England. This level of reflection invites the reader, in this case a theatre historian, to credit the text with a belief in its authority if not its authenticity. It is a great shame that Collier wrote about her career only until the late 1920s. Her work in the United States from the 1930s through the 1950s has to be reconstructed and evaluated without the aid of her own autobiographic texts.

The autobiographies of these two actresses, who both once worked as Gaiety Girls and so shared a similar entry into the theatre industry, offer a great deal to the theatre historian. Both contain elements of the autobiographic of which the theatre historian should arguably be cautious. Yet we need to take into account the fact that, at certain points in theatre history, the writing of an autobiography was one of the few activities by which an actress might take the opportunity to find authorial expression for her professional experiences. The fact that, as in Lena Ashwell's case, we might not find what we are looking for and thus have our agenda re-shaped or our analysis re-directed, or, as in Ruby Miller's, we might be disappointed by the disorganization and literary impoverishment of what we read, is not really relevant. If we read these autobiographies in a multi-layered, intertextual fashion, taking into account their social-historical context, their gender specificity, their place amongst and in relation to other historiographical materials, their textual dynamics, and so on, all in relation to the possible identity of their original readership in relation to our own identity and agenda as readers, then we can find them of great use as well as pleasure.

I am attracted to autobiography in the way that others are attracted to detective novels, and I wonder if there is in fact a similar process going on in the reading of each. *Doing* theatre history is a little like detective work, especially when you are interested in work made by women. We work with autobiography because it is endlessly fascinating as a form; we work with it because we like it. And as Georges Gusdorf proposes, maybe, sometimes,

> [o]ne must choose a side and give up the pretence of objectivity, abandoning a sort of false scientific attitude that would judge a work by the precision of its detail.... [I]n autobiography the truth of facts is subordinate to the truth of the man (*sic*), for it is first of all the man who is in question.... The significance of autobiography should therefore be sought beyond truth and falsity, as those are conceived by simple common sense. (quoted in Marcus 160)

Works Cited

Ashwell, Lena. *Modern Troubadours*. London and Copenhagen: Gyldendal, 1922.

———. *The Stage*. London: Geoffrey Bles, 1929.

———. *Myself a Player*. London: Michael Joseph, 1936a.

———. *Reflections on Shakespeare*. London: Hutchinson, 1936b.

Bratton, Jacky. *New Readings in Theatre History*. Cambridge: Cambridge University Press, 2003.

Collier, Constance. *Harlequinade: The Story of My Life*. London: John Lane and the Bodley Head, 1929.

Corbett, Mary Jean. *Representing Femininity: Middle-Class Subjectivity in Victorian and Edwardian Women's Autobiographies*. New York: Oxford University Press, 1992.

Dane, Clemence. *London Has a Garden*. London: Michael Joseph, 1965.

———. *The Regiment of Women*. 1917. Reprint, London: Virago,1995.

Darewski, Mme. Max (Ruby Miller). *Believe It or Not!*. London: John Long, 1933.

Dymkowski, Chris. "Lena Ashwell and Her Players: Popular Performers on Extraordinary Stages." In *Extraordinary Actors: Essays on Popular Performers*, ed. Jane Milling and Martin Banham. Exeter: Exeter University Press, 2003. 120–34.

Gale, Maggie B. *West End Women: Women on the London Stage, 1918–1962*. London: Routledge, 1996.

———. "Errant Nymphs." In *British Theatre Between the Wars, 1918–1939*, ed. Clive Barker and Maggie B. Gale. Cambridge: Cambridge University Press, 2000a. 113–34.

———. "From Fame to Obscurity: In Search of Clemence Dane." In *Women, Theatre and Performance: New Histories, New Historiographies*, ed. Maggie B. Gale and Viv Gardner. Manchester: Manchester University Press, 2000b. 121–41.

———. "Women Playwrights of the 1920s and 1930s." In *The Cambridge Companion to Modern British Women Playwrights*, ed. Elaine Aston and Janelle Reinelt. Cambridge: Cambridge University Press, 2000c. 23–37.

———. "Lena Ashwell and Autobiographical Negotiations of the Professional Self." In *Autobiography and Identity: Women, Theatre and Performance*, ed. Maggie B. Gale and Viv Gardner. Manchester: Manchester University Press, 2004. 99–125.

Gilmore, Leigh. *Autobiographics: A Feminist Theory of Women's Self-Representation*. Ithaca: Cornell University Press, 1994.

Gusdorf, George. "Conditions et Limites de l'autobiographie." 1956. Reprinted in *Autobiography: Essays Theoretical and Critical*, ed. James Olney. Princeton: Princeton University Press, 1980. 28–48.

Hirshfield, Claire. "The Suffragist as Playwright in Edwardian England." *Frontiers* 9, no. 2 (1987): 1–6.

———. "The Actress As Social Activist: The Case of Lena Ashwell." In *Politics, Gender and the Arts: Women, the Arts and Society*, ed. Ronald Dotterer and Susan Bowers. London and Toronto: Susquehanna University Press, 1992. 73–86.

———. "The Woman's Theatre in England: 1913–1918." *Theatre History Studies* 15 (1995): 123–37.

Leask, Margaret. "Lena Ashwell, 1869–1957: Actress, Patriot and Pioneer." Ph.D. thesis, University of Sydney, 2000.

Marcus, Laura. *Autobiographical Discourses: Theory, Criticism and Practice*. Manchester: Manchester University Press, 1994.

Miller, Ruby. *Champagne from My Slipper*. London: Herbert Jenkins, 1962.

Postlewait, Thomas. "Theatre Autobiographies: Some Preliminary Concerns for the Historian." *Assaph C* 16 (2000): 157–72.

Smith, Sidonie, and Julia Watson, eds. *Interfaces: Women, Autobiography, Image, Performance*. Ann Arbor: University of Michigan Press, 2002.

Untold Stories: [Re]Searching for Canadian Actresses' Lives

Paula Sperdakos

I have been engaged in the search for the theatre lives of Canadian women performers for almost twenty years now. Tracing the careers of these actresses is an exciting adventure, full of delightful and often unexpected discoveries, an equal measure of disappointment and frustration, and an abiding awareness of loss.[1] Most recently I have begun work on what I hope will be a book about six actresses in whom I have been interested for several years: Elizabeth Jane Phillips, Charlotte Nickinson Morrison, Ida Van Cortland, Catherine Proctor, Margaret Bannerman, and Judith Evelyn. Few nowadays will be familiar with their names, in spite of the considerable degree of celebrity they enjoyed during their careers, all of which were notable ones. Something they all have in common, apart from their Canadian roots or links, is that for the most part they have been lost to history, forgotten, even—or perhaps especially—by Canadians. The reason for this is to be found in what is to me the most significant common aspect of their stories: that to a greater or lesser degree they had to leave home in order to train for and pursue their careers.

It was my research for what became a biography of one of Canada's foremost theatrical pioneers, Dora Mavor Moore, which set me on the scholarly path I am following to this day (Sperdakos 1995). Those interested in the theatre in this country may be aware that the Toronto theatre awards—colloquially known as the Doras—are named in her honour, but for the most part only Canadian theatre scholars are likely to know why: through her creation (with her son, Mavor Moore) of the New Play Society in 1946, when there was no home-grown professional theatre in English-speaking Canada, Dora Mavor Moore was instrumental in the professionalizing of the theatre in Toronto, and by extension of the Canadian theatre as a whole, in the crucial twenty-five-year period following the Second World War. In fact, though, Dora was fifty-eight years old in 1946, and she had been teaching, producing, and directing in the amateur and educational theatre in Canada for four decades, laying the groundwork for the professional theatre along with other intrepid teacher-directors like her, many of them women.[2] But as of the mid-1980s, when I began to research her story, no major study had been made of this remarkable woman's life and accomplishments. I was soon to discover that such neglect of our theatrical figures is an all-too-common phenomenon in Canada.

One of the aspects of Dora's story I found particularly intriguing was that her earliest theatrical ambition had been to become an actor, and had the circumstances of her life worked out differently than they did, it is quite likely that her achievements would have been lost to Canada. In 1912, when she decided to pursue an acting career, there were simply not enough opportunities available to her at home. Virtually all professional theatre was imported from elsewhere, so "Canadian" theatre meant theatre performed for Canadian audiences, but not usually performed by Canadians. As a result, like so many aspiring actors before (and after) her, Dora had to leave home, going first to London to train at the Academy of Dramatic Art (thereby being the first Canadian to attend what later became RADA), and then appearing on Broadway, touring the Northeastern United States, and performing at the Old Vic in London. Fortunately for Canada, though, she chose to return home after the First World War, and dedicated her life's work to the Canadian theatre. Many of our other expatriate theatre artists never returned home, however, unless occasionally as part of touring companies; their creative accomplishments benefited the theatre elsewhere, and were lost to our own.

Pondering the implications of the Canadian cultural diaspora, or "talent drain," particularly as it related to those of our actresses whose careers had taken place entirely or in part during the pre-professional period of Canadian theatre, became something of an *idée fixe* in my scholarly work. Whereas it seemed unproductive to speculate too much on what might have been if the conditions of our theatre's development had been different and the scattering had not had to take place; and if, throughout the nineteenth century and well into the twentieth, more of our theatre people had been able to stay here and contribute their creativity to a dynamic theatre as Dora Mavor Moore did, I determined that something positive I could do with my *idée fixe* was at the very least to go in search of these actresses, to find out where they went and what happened to them.

In 1998, I decided to draw together as many of the names as I could find of nineteenth- and early twentieth-century Canadian-born or -raised female performers who were trained, and whose careers were conducted, entirely or for the most part, in either the United States or Britain, or in relentless cross-border touring. I presented my findings in a paper to the Association for Canadian Theatre Research conference in Ottawa, where I was gratified but also faintly unsettled by the surprised response to my "roll call" of names. The actresses discussed or mentioned in the paper were Elizabeth Jane Phillips (1830–1904), Charlotte Nickinson Morrison (1832–1910), Clara Morris (1847–1925), Ida Van Cortland (1854–1924), Margaret Mather (1859–1898), Louise Beaudet (1861–1948), May Irwin (1862–1938), Annie Russell (1864–1936), Viola Allen (1867–1948), Julia Arthur (1869–1950), Marie Dressler (1869–1934), Rose Stahl (1870–1955), Roselle Knott (1870–1948), Lena Ashwell (1872–1957), Maude Eburne (1875–1960), Margaret Anglin

(1876–1958), Eva Tanguay (1878–1947), Christie MacDonald (1878–1962), Mae Edwards (1878–1947), Lucile Watson (1879–1962), Catherine Proctor (1879–1967), Maud Allan (1883–1956), Alice Yorke (1886–1938), Dora Mavor Moore (1888–1979), Mary Pickford (1892–1979), Nella Jefferis (d. 1944), Beatrice Lillie (1894–1989), Martha Allan (1895–1942), Margaret Bannerman (1896–1976), Eleanor Stuart (1900–1977), and Judith Evelyn (1913–1967). I was struck by the number of my colleagues who remarked that they had had no idea there were so many expatriate Canadian actresses with such distinguished careers and were taken aback to learn that actresses they had assumed to be American or British—Dressler, "America's Sweetheart" Pickford, Irwin, Lillie—were actually Canadian. What was particularly significant to me, though, was their rather shame-faced acknowledgement that they had never heard of most of these performers. I realized then that, as a result of their having been obliged to leave home, these actresses had in a sense gone missing from our Canadian consciousness; since what is absent is soon forgotten, far too many of their remarkable stories had been lost to us. I resolved to start telling at least some of the untold stories that have been lost, forgotten or absorbed into the theatrical fabric elsewhere. However, I soon realized what a daunting undertaking this would be, because the problems associated with the loss of our theatre artists have made the research adventure an unusually challenging one.

To begin with, as a direct consequence of the enforced scattering of our actors well into the twentieth century, we Canadians have lagged well behind our counterparts in the United States and Britain not only in the effort to define a tradition of acting in this country, but also, as I first discovered when researching the life of Dora Mavor Moore, in the project of recovering and documenting the careers and, to the extent that we can, the lives of most of our theatrical figures, but particularly of our actors, and even more particularly of our actresses. Furthermore, the absence of our performers has meant that only a few of them—the "stars"—have been considered important enough to warrant having their stories told by Canadians. Consequently, I am one of very few Canadian theatre historians presently engaged in this kind of theatrical archeology, trying to recover, or as it sometimes seems, exhume, the record of work by Canadian actresses— wherever it took place—before we were in a position to develop our own professional theatre community in this country.

There are no Canadian equivalents to works such as *A History of American Acting* (Wilson 1966) or *That Despicable Race: A History of the British Acting Tradition* (Forbes 1980). We do have a few biographies of Canadian actors who may have been born or have worked elsewhere but who spent most of their careers in Canada, such as William Hutt (Garebian 1988), Mervyn "Butch" Blake (Ashley 1999), Don Harron (Harron 1988), and John Drainie (Drainie 1988)—the last two written by the actors' daughters—and, within the past fifteen years, the memoirs of such actor-directors as Gordon Pinsent (1992), Mavor Moore (1994), Tony van Bridge (1995), Leslie Yeo (1998), Al Waxman (1999), Fred

Euringer (2000), and Vernon Chapman (2001) have been published. Among the even fewer actresses' memoirs are those of Claire Drainie Taylor (1998), Nonnie Griffin (2002) and Amelia Hall (1989). Edited by Diane Mew, Hall's memoirs were published posthumously, and unfortunately they end in 1953 with her appearance as the first Canadian actor to speak on the stage of the Stratford Festival Theatre.[3]

Some work, in the form of biographies and journal articles, has been done by Canadians on the stories of some of our more famous expatriate women performers, such as Margaret Anglin (LeVay 1989), Marie Dressler (Lee 1997), Mary Pickford (Whitfield 1997), and Julia Arthur (Salter 1984). However, we have woefully few studies which attempt to trace and define a tradition of Canadian women's participation in the theatre, whether at home or abroad; by comparison particularly with the United States, where such titles as *Women in American Theatre* (Chinoy 1987); *American Actress: Perspective on the Nineteenth Century* (Johnson 1984); *Forgotten Leading Ladies of the American Theatre* (Turner 1990); *Women in the American Theatre: Actresses and Audiences, 1790–1870* (Dudden 1994); and *Nineteenth-Century American Women Theatre Managers* (Curry 1994) reflect the broader interest in the subject of women's work in all theatrical fields; but also in comparison to Britain, with such works as *Actresses As Working Women: Their Social Identity in Victorian Culture* (Davis 1991) and *The First English Actresses: Women and Drama, 1660–1700* (Howe 1993), and several books that concern themselves with female playwrights as well as other women theatre practitioners, including actresses, such as *Innocent Flowers: Women in the Edwardian Theatre* (Holledge 1981) and *West End Women: Women and the London Stage, 1918–1962* (Gale 1996).

Nevertheless, although my search for lost stories has sent me into somewhat uncharted territory, my task would be even more daunting than it is without the pioneering work, often in M.A. and Ph.D. theses, of such Canadian theatre historians as Patrick O'Neill, James Aikens, Mary Shortt, Kathleen Fraser, Mary M. Brown, Robert B. Scott, David Gardner, Ann Saddlemyer, and Richard Plant.[4]

The most fundamental difficulty in tracing the lives of *my* six actresses relates to the inescapable reality that much of who they were is unrecoverable; that indeed only traces remain, in the form, for the most part, of secondary documents: programs, photographs, newspaper reviews, interviews and articles. Furthermore, chronological inaccuracies and false leads complicate this kind of work immeasurably; anecdotes can be unreliable, and people's memories of their own lives, much less of the lives of others, are notoriously faulty. Documents disappear, are lost, misplaced, or destroyed, and the process of interpreting those that remain is fraught with problems.

Nevertheless, enough documentation of certain kinds is available, if widely scattered, to have made it possible for me to assemble extensive chronologies for most of their careers; gaining access to their inner lives has proved far more problematic, however. It is particularly the lack of autobiographical testimony that makes these so shadowy.

It has become something of an axiom of the life writing practice that the subject chooses the biographer rather than the other way around, and although the idea for the book on which I'm presently working began to take shape during the summer of 2003, I realize now that in a gathering process that remains somewhat inexplicable even to me, I had been creating for years a mental short-list of intriguing stories that were clamouring for my attention. In each case, I was drawn by the mysterious and puzzling aspects of these performers' lives and careers.

For example, I had first encountered Ottawa-born Catherine Proctor's name while researching Dora Mavor Moore's story in 1986, in a reference to a visit made to her in New York by Dora, then an aspiring actress, in 1912, when Proctor was a featured player on Broadway (see figure 14). I came across her name next when Dora invited her long-time friend Proctor to star in the Mazo de la Roche play *The Mistress of Jalna* in Toronto as part of the New Play Society's 1953–54 season. Further research revealed that Proctor had had a successful, almost seventy-year acting career, working with such prominent Broadway producers and directors as Charles Frohman and David Belasco, and such celebrated actors as Annie Russell, Maude Adams, Laurette Taylor, Lynn Fontanne, and George M. Cohan. I wondered why so little seemed to be known about Proctor in Canada: was it simply because the majority of her credits had been gained in the United States? I filed away her name for future study.

Following my "discovery" of Proctor, Judith Evelyn was suggested to me as another actress worthy of study by Professor Ronald Bryden of the University of Toronto's Graduate Centre for the Study of Drama. My cursory survey of Evelyn's career at that time revealed another remarkable story, also sadly unknown. Born Evelyn Mae Morris in Seneca, South Dakota, in 1913, Judith Evelyn grew up and began her work in the theatre in Canada. Hers was a truly impressive career on radio and television, in films (she is best known as Miss Lonelyhearts in Alfred Hitchcock's *Rear Window*), and on stage, where she was acclaimed for her many stage portraits of "abnormal women," the first of which was the tortured Mrs. Manningham in *Angel Street*, with Vincent Price (see figure 15), which she played on Broadway for over a thousand performances in the early 1940s. Again, as I had for Proctor, I determined to research her story further at the first opportunity.

Added to my mental short-list were other actresses whose activities had received at least some scholarly attention, but whose inner lives remained mysterious to me because of perturbing gaps in the record of what seemed to be known about them. Thanks to Murray D. Edwards's book *A Stage in Our Past: English-Language Theatre in Eastern Canada from the 1790s to 1914*, I had been aware for some time of Ida Van Cortland (see figure 16), born Emily Ellen Buckley in Manchester, England, who had spent most of her career touring the United States and Canada as the leading lady of the Taverner Company, which she managed with her husband and stage partner, Albert Taverner.

Figure 14. Catherine Proctor, ca. 1907, as Hermia in Annie Russell's production of *A Midsummer Night's Dream*. From *The Stage*.

Figure 15. Postcard of Judith Evelyn and Vincent Price in *Angel Street*, ca. 1942.

Figure 16. Ida Van Cortland as Galatea in *Pygmalion and Galatea* by W. S. Gilbert, ca. 1888. Taverner collection, Toronto Reference Library. Reproduced courtesy of the Toronto Public Library.

However, I remember being puzzled by Edwards's relatively uninterrogated account of the decision of Van Cortland, apparently "once ... an idol in countless Canadian towns," suddenly to leave the theatre after twenty years in the profession and, separating from her husband, to take a job as sales manager of insurance with the Independent Order of Foresters in Michigan. Further, I found it difficult to understand Edwards's acceptance of the suggestion that "to the end she was serenely happy to know that she had 'sacrificed metropolitan success for the wee bit of domestic life accorded to [her] by a life on the road'" (55–6). It seemed to me that what was missing from this picture was the illumination of Van Cortland's inner life in a way that would help explain, among other things, what it would have meant to a successful woman performer of the nineteenth century suddenly to give up her life's work. The clues were intriguing, the details elusive. I wanted to know more.

Another mysterious figure about whom I knew only a few tantalizing facts was Elizabeth Jane Phillips. I first became aware of Mrs. E. J. Phillips, as she was known professionally for most of her long career, through Mary Shortt's entry about her in the

Oxford Companion to Canadian Theatre, when I was doing the research for a paper entitled "Women in the Canadian Theatre," which I ultimately delivered at the Association for Canadian Theatre History's conference at Queen's University in 1991. I was particularly intrigued by Shortt's observation that Phillips (see figure 17) had acted with the Hamilton Amateur Theatrical Society at the Royal Lyceum Theatre in Toronto in 1849, "when women amateurs were almost unknown" (415), before going on to become a member of former garrison-actor-turned-professional John Nickinson's (1808–1864) Royal Lyceum Company from 1852 until 1858 and, thereafter, sustaining an acting career in the United States that lasted until her last theatrical appearance forty years later, in 1898. It seemed to me that E. J. Phillips had to be one of the earliest Canadian-born actresses to have such a career, yet hers was another essentially untold story.

I wondered what it must have been like for a young woman who did not come from a theatrical family, as most actresses did during the first half of the nineteenth century, to go on the stage, albeit at an amateur level, and also when she decided to make the transition to the profession, further setting herself apart from the norm for women by spending the first six years of her career in straitlaced Toronto, where there was considerable anti-theatrical prejudice, particularly with regard to actors and actresses. I found it interesting, too, that the leading lady of the Royal Lyceum Company, John Nickinson's eldest daughter Charlotte, also Canadian-born, was almost the same age as Elizabeth Jane Phillips. Charlotte, another figure who had long intrigued me, was already a theatre veteran by 1852, having been on the American stage with her father since the age of fourteen, so her life experience would have been very different from Phillips's, but I tried to imagine what sort of a relationship they might have had working side by side for so many years, their different status in the company—with Charlotte a star, and Elizabeth Jane a supporting player—notwithstanding: was it possible that the two young women might have been friends?

In delivering my 1991 paper, I mentioned my curiosity about Elizabeth Jane Phillips, and I speculated on what it must have been like for women to feel isolated from other women because of what they did to make a living or express themselves. I suggested that some of them dealt with this situation by being models of Victorian rectitude and decency themselves, and referred to Charlotte Nickinson Morrison, who it seemed to me was able—as a result of her worthy efforts at the Grand Opera House as likely Canada's first actress-manager, but also because of her impeccable reputation—to remove at least a little of the stigma that was associated with the theatre in 1870s Toronto. At this point I was unaware that Charlotte's story was for the most part one of the best kept secrets of Canadian theatre history.

When the session concluded, I was approached by Patrick O'Neill, a professor at Mount St. Vincent University in Halifax, who is one of Canada's most indefatigable researchers and theatre historians; he suggested that one of the main reasons Charlotte

Figure 17. Elizabeth Jane Phillips, ca. 1894, from *The Marie Burroughs Art Portfolio of Stage Celebrities*, part 2. Chicago: A. N. Marquis, 1894.

Morrison had become a model of propriety was to counteract the scandal in which her father, John Nickinson, had been involved in 1858, when Elizabeth Jane Phillips had given birth to a son by Nickinson, after which she and Nickinson had left Toronto. This bombshell made me all the more fascinated by Phillips's story; I determined to research her career further some day as well.

Accordingly, as of 2003 my short list of actresses whose stories I had definitely decided to include in my book consisted of Catherine Proctor, Judith Evelyn, Ida Van Cortland, and Charlotte Nickinson Morrison. But although I very much wanted to include E. J. Phillips, I was concerned about whether I would be able to discover enough about her to warrant dedicating a whole chapter to her. Would she have to be merely a supporting character in Charlotte's story?

What happened next is a classic example of the wild roller coaster ride endemic to this kind of recovery project. I decided to "Google" Phillips on the Internet, little expecting to find very much more about her out there in cyberspace. What I did find first was an expired site which alluded to letters between Phillips and John Nickinson: the idea that there was evidence of their relationship still in existence made my researcher's heart beat very fast indeed. My next discovery was a wonderfully detailed and impeccably researched web site dedicated to the life and times of Elizabeth Jane Phillips, the curator of which was Phillips's (and Nickinson's) great-great-granddaughter, Mary Glen Chitty, of Boston, Massachusetts. Furthermore, in a psychic confluence so timely as to be positively spooky, on the very day of my discovery, as I attempted to frame an email to Mary telling her how much I wanted to include E.J. Phillips in my project, she emailed me to say that she had just found online my article entitled "Canada's Daughters, America's Sweethearts: The Careers of Canadian 'Footlight Favorites' in the United States," in which I mentioned Phillips.[5]

Mary was delighted to learn of my interest in telling her great-great-grandmother's story in print. Since then, I have travelled to Boston to visit with Mary, who has graciously allowed me access to the treasure trove of Phillips-and-Nickinson-related papers, photographs, and theatrical memorabilia she possesses, including a medal of the Peninsular War (deemed to have belonged to Nickinson's father), Masonic paraphernalia (Nickinson was a prominent Mason), an extraordinary quilt made by Phillips from scraps of her worn-out costumes, and, most remarkably, the thousand or more letters that were written by Phillips between 1883 and 1902, mostly to her son, Albert Nickinson (1864–1948), while she lived the precarious and peripatetic life of a stock company actress of the late nineteenth century.[6]

The saga of dis/recovery of a number of Phillips-and-Nickinson-related "relics" (as the family referred to them), including the letters, is a marvelously complicated and lengthy one, but well worth the telling, because from my point of view the fact that these letters still exist, added to the way that they were found and gathered together, epitomizes the capricious arbitrariness of this kind of biographical research.

Albert Nickinson, EJP and John Nickinson's son, met and married Mary Penelope (nicknamed Neppie) Macardell in Middletown, New York in 1889. They had one child, Edward "Ted" Phillips Nickinson (1890–1948), who settled in Pensacola, Florida; he and his wife, Em Turner Merritt, had three children: Mary Elizabeth (Chitty), Edward Phillips, Jr., and Em Turner (Kuhl), Mary Glen Chitty's mother. Albert and Neppie moved to Pensacola in the 1920s to be with their son and his family. However, Neppie returned to Middletown annually to visit her family, and when the last of her unmarried sisters died in the 1950s, Arthur Chitty, the husband of Neppie's granddaughter, Mary Elizabeth, went to Middletown and sent a number of boxes of family papers and several trunks to Sewanee, Tennessee, where he worked for the University of the South as a fundraiser and historiographer. These boxes and trunks would appear to have contained most (though not all) of the EJP-related memorabilia in the possession of this branch of the family. (The Dolman family, descendents of EJP and John Nickinson's daughter Christine Harriet [Hattie] [1860–1946], also has EJP-related memorabilia, including two more of her quilts.) The letters, stored in a styrofoam ice chest in the attic in Sewanee, Tennessee might have stayed there indefinitely, had Chitty not decided to go looking for them in 1991, when she was there on a visit. To this day she cannot recall what prompted the search, but she does remember that having found the letters in the ice chest, she became fascinated. She enlisted her mother to begin transcribing the letters, while Mary edited them; this mammoth process occupied both women throughout the 1990s. At one point, another trunk full of letters, papers, artifacts, and photographs turned up in a garage in Pensacola, and then a few more letters surfaced in 1999.

There is a somewhat similar story related to the recovery of the Ida Van Cortland-Albert Taverner papers, now housed at the Toronto Reference Library.[7] According to an unpublished paper about the couple by Ann Stuart, the contents of the Collection had been found by their children, Percy Algernon Taverner and Ida Clare Taverner McLeish, in their father's abandoned summer cottage after his death in 1929.

For every such story of lucky documentary recovery, however, there is an equivalent story suggesting documentary loss. For example, theatre historian Mary Shortt actually made contact with Charlotte Nickinson Morrison's grandson, Edward Brown, in Toronto during the early 1970s, but, as she wrote in a 1980 letter to John Nickinson's great-granddaughter, Mary Elizabeth Nickinson Chitty, Shortt was disappointed to find "that he seemed to take so little interest in his Nickinson forebears. [He] died about seven or eight years ago, and whatever papers he had (all too few, I fear, as his mother, Charlotte's daughter, had a mania for getting rid of old things!) went to relatives in the [United] States."[8] It is so tantalizing to speculate about what happened to even these few papers, and what posterity might have learned about Charlotte had her descendents, like Phillips's, made the effort not only to preserve them, however casually, but also to archive them on the Internet, where researchers and historians could access them.

Although the Internet can certainly be more bane than boon to the inexperienced researcher, it has played a vitally important role in my research, and several of my most serendipitous discoveries have been made on it. Not only is it doubtful that without it I could have considered including Elizabeth Jane Phillips in my study, but the Internet also played a pivotal role in my decision to include Margaret Bannerman (born Margaret Le Grand in Toronto), another actress who had interested me for some time, but about whom I knew little more information than what was said about her in a few references in *Later Stages: Essays in Ontario Theatre from the First World War to the 1970s* (Saddlemyer 64, 160, 164, 178): without the Internet I simply would not have realized the extent of her career.

I was amazed when I first Googled her, and the search phrase "Margaret Bannerman" produced close to three hundred results. Admittedly, most of these results related to the sixteenth-century Margaret Bannerman of Scotland, His Royal Highness Prince William's eleven times great-grandmother (and, in fact, the nine times great-grandmother of Camilla Parker-Bowles), but a significant number of these results related to *my* Margaret Bannerman and, I was surprised to find, several involved images of her. My search for the story behind the most spectacular of these images typifies the jigsaw-puzzle nature of this kind of biographical research. The original print of the image, which is now among the holdings of the Royal Photographic Society, Bath, shows Bannerman in profile. It was taken in 1925, when she was at the height of her obviously considerable and much celebrated beauty and a major star in the firmament of London's West End. Two years earlier, I subsequently learned, she had scored a striking success in the leading role of Lady George Grayston in the British premiere of Somerset Maugham's satirical play *Our Betters*.[9] Largely on the strength of her brilliant performance, which became the talk of the town, *Our Betters* had an unusually long run of 548 performances.

When I discovered that I could buy copies of this almost eighty-year-old photograph in postcard form on the Internet, at www.pomegranate.com, a publisher of books, calendars, and cards based in Petaluma, California, I was mystified. I found it hard to reconcile this with the impression I had received that Margaret Bannerman was someone who had been lost to history, her career essentially forgotten. One small piece of the puzzle fell into place when I determined that this particular 1925 photograph is so readily available today because of the fame of the photographer, Dorothy Wilding (1893–1976), a contemporary of Bannerman's, who had by the late 1920s become one of the foremost society portrait photographers in London.[10]

Wilding's star was rising when she took this particular photograph, and several others, of Margaret Bannerman. Conversely, however, although Bannerman's career as a constantly employed actor continued for another four decades, both in Britain and later in the United States, she was never again able to find a role in which she could repeat her success in *Our Betters*. How ironic that her short-lived stardom should have made her image so easy to find (see figure 18), while her life, as opposed to the course of her career, should seem so elusive by comparison.

This discovery highlighted for me one useful strategy in this kind of research: what might be called "tracing by connection or association," by means of which we can access aspects of the stories of our subjects by examining the lives of more celebrated performers with whom they were associated, either in their work contacts or their personal relationships. Random mentions of lesser known performers are occasionally to be found in the autobiographies by and biographies about more celebrated ones: these can be invaluable clues for filling in the blanks in the untold stories.

I thought that I had discovered all I was likely to about this photograph, until an item for sale on eBay in late March of 2005 supplied me with another piece of the puzzle. It was a program of a 1925 Globe Theatre production of a play entitled *Beginner's Luck* (by Fred Jackson) in which Bannerman played the leading role of Lady Mariott, on the cover of which was the Dorothy Wilding photograph. It would appear that the lessee of the

Figure 18. Postcard of Margaret Bannerman, "A Popular Picture Player," ca. 1920, from the series *Cinema Stars*.

Globe Theatre, Anthony Prinsep, who was soon to become Margaret Bannerman's second husband, must have commissioned the portrait photograph in order to capitalize on Bannerman's *Our Betters* fame. Unfortunately, *Beginner's Luck* was not particularly successful, and sadly, this photograph, and the many others that regularly turn up for sale on eBay, tell us only how famous Margaret Bannerman once was.

Staged photographs of the kind that Wilding took of Bannerman may have their limitations as evidence of inner lives, but at least they do tell us something (however elusive) about the subject's public mask. With one striking exception, I have been fortunate in being able to see—and even purchase—several images of each of my actresses, and in the cases of Proctor, Bannerman, and Evelyn, to view actual film and television performances. Something of an exception is, ironically, Charlotte Nickinson Morrison. There seem to be only two photographs of her in existence: one theatrical and the other domestic; she is alone in neither of them. In the first much reproduced photograph she and her father, John Nickinson, appear in character as Melanie and Havresack in Dion Boucicault's play *Napoleon's Old Guard*, roles they had been identified with for many years (the original is in the Harvard Theatre Collection), and in the other, she appears with her husband, Daniel Morrison, after her retirement—as she then thought forever—from the stage (see figure 19). It's disappointing and intriguing at the same time that someone who spent so many years of her life in the public eye would have left so little in the way of photographic evidence behind her. Would it be far-fetched to speculate that if most of her later career had been spent in the United States instead of Canada, this would not have been the case? The examples of her contemporary, Elizabeth Jane Phillips, as well as of her sisters, Virginia (Mrs. Owen) Marlowe and Isabella (Mrs. Charles) Walcot, all three of whom did spend most of their careers in the United States, and of whom many photographs exist, suggest otherwise.

Although as performers my six subjects all led far more public lives than other women of their time, the fact that they were for most of their careers working actresses rather than stars means that as long as they were associated with theatrical centres, such as New York, London, and, in Canada, Toronto and Montreal, their activities can be traced. However, the farther they went away from these centres, on the tours that were inevitably part of an actor's professional life during the nineteenth and early twentieth centuries, the more difficult the task of following them becomes. However, for all that these actresses' stories have gaps in them, periods when they are on tour or stretches when they are "at liberty" and seem to drop out of sight, the public nature of their work places them at the centre of historical events. Occasionally their memories of the experiences of these events are recoverable; more often they are not.

Judith Evelyn, for example, was aboard the *S.S. Athenia*, returning to Canada from Britain, when it became the first passenger liner to be torpedoed at the outset of World War II; she and her travelling companion, Andrew Allan (of CBC fame) narrowly escaped

Figure 19. Charlotte Nickinson Morrison and family, ca. 1868. Notman & Fraser, "Photographers to the Queen," Toronto. Photograph courtesy of Mary Shortt.

death; hundreds of others, including Allan's father, did not. For some time afterwards, Evelyn was inundated with requests, mainly from the press, to give interviews about the tragedy, which she did, until, having been forced to relive the ordeal each time she spoke of it, she announced that she no longer wished to discuss the experience.

Elizabeth Jane Phillips was performing at Pike's Opera House in Cincinnati with Junius Brutus Booth, Jr. on 14 April 1865, the night when Booth's brother John Wilkes Booth, also an actor, assassinated Abraham Lincoln in Ford's Theatre in Washington. This much is fact; however, I have been unable to verify whether Phillips's great-great-grandson's assertion on his web site that "the acting company had to leave town under the protection of a covered wagon to protect their lives" is true or not. Certainly EJP does not seem to have performed again in Cincinnati; in fact there is no trace of her after this infamous night until some time in 1866, when she resurfaced as a member of Ben DeBar's company in St. Louis. If she did leave Cincinnati, where she had been living since 1863, questions remain as to where she went, how she lived, and how she supported her children, John Nickinson having died by this time. In any case, we can only imagine the shock and dismay that must have been felt by the Pike's Opera House company of which Phillips was a member, because her memories of the night she played a minor role in the American tragedy of Lincoln's assassination, if they were ever recorded, have been lost.

Just as there is no lack of documented *real-life* drama in some of these stories, there is no end of mystery in others. For example, there is intriguing evidence to suggest that Ida Van Cortland was the only member of her family to survive the Great Chicago Fire in 1871, when she was still called Emily Ellen Buckley. However, since Van Cortland may have fundamentally reinvented herself when she came to Toronto in the 1870s with a child to whose father there is no extant evidence that she was married, taking her glamorous new name and joining Mrs. Morrison's Grand Opera House stock company, it is possible that this is an example of self-mythologizing in order to erase an unwanted past. Or, it could be true, but how can we ever be sure? Even her son's biographer, John L. Cranmer-Byng,[11] was unable to corroborate the statement made in *Saturday Night* in 1944 that "Taverner's is the tale of a lad who didn't have either breaks or chances, finding them for himself, making himself into something. He was born in Guelph, sixty-nine years ago, the son of two school teachers. His mother had been a child in school in Chicago at the time of the fire, lost her home and entire family in the disaster but had stayed on at her school and eventually taught there" (Cox 2).

As I mentioned earlier, the most significant problem I have encountered in the search for these actresses' lives is the absence of autobiographical testimony. I could wish that my six had been as forthcoming about their personal lives, and their thoughts and ideas about the acting profession, as the prolific Canadian-born Clara Morris was with her three books of memoirs—*Life on the Stage: My Personal Experiences and Recollections*

(1901), *Stage Confidences: Talks About Players and Play Acting* (1902), and *The Life of a Star* (1906)—and her many articles on acting contributed to various magazines. Unfortunately, however, none of them left behind much in the way of autobiographical writing. Or, if they did, it has vanished. Perhaps if they had, their memoirs would be as much a part of theatre history as Morris's are now. Both Phillips and Van Cortland did write short memory pieces toward the end of their lives: the former for her family and the latter for a formal address delivered at least three times to such Ottawa groups as the Women's University Club and the Drama League ("Address given about 1918," Taverner Collection, Box 8). Phillips's account is welcome for what it does say, but equally frustrating because of what it leaves out, glosses over, or even gets completely wrong; and Van Cortland's, though quite delightful, is in many instances rather strangely impersonal, at least in terms of offering insight into her feelings about her life, as opposed to her work. Perhaps it is not surprising that she should only once mention her husband Albert, from whom she had been estranged for many years when she delivered her address.

On 26 August 1961, Ralph Hicklin of the *Globe and Mail* reported that Catherine Proctor was engaged in writing her memoirs ("Grand Lady of Stage Pens Memoirs"). However, it would appear that anything she may have written has been lost. Judith Evelyn's mother kept scrapbooks of her daughter's theatrical accomplishments, which she donated to the Toronto Reference Library when Evelyn died in 1967. But what happened to Evelyn's personal papers? Only a few letters that she wrote to her mentor and friend, Nancy Pyper, which are also to be found at the Toronto Reference Library (Nancy Pyper Collection, Envelope 23), allow us to hear her private voice.

Yet another example of personal papers and, therefore, possible autobiographical documents lost, gone astray, or destroyed involves Margaret Bannerman. At the time of her death in hospital in 1976, she had been living for some years in the Actors' Fund Home in Englewood, New Jersey. It occurred to me to contact the home, now called the Lillian Booth Actors' Home of the Actors' Fund of America, to ask if they had any kind of an archive dedicated to their former residents. I reasoned—or fantasized, perhaps—that since these were mainly performers, there might be some under-utilized treasure trove of personal documents and scrapbooks to be found there. Sadly, my emails and letters have gone unanswered. Although I will persist in my attempts to make contact, it seems likely that Margaret Bannerman's possessions have been lost to history as completely as has her voice.

In the absence of personal testimony, then, what strategies remain to the biographer to aid in the search for these life stories? Regardless of the events in each of these actresses' individual lives, it is clear that their chosen profession had a major effect on the way those lives played out, so we must ask what impact their private lives had on their work, and vice versa. Were their careers interrupted by marriage, child-raising, their own illnesses or those of family members, the necessity to follow their spouse, or marriage breakdown? How many of them had to cut themselves off from marriage and children, if they wanted a life in the theatre, and how did such a decision affect them and their work? What was it like for those actresses who did marry and have children? An actor could leave his wife and children at home and go on tour, but what of the actress? What would be the effect on a woman, out of necessity, to be without her children for extended periods of time?

Of my six subjects, only the elder three—Phillips, Morrison, Van Cortland—had children, whether within or outside of wedlock. Of the other three, only Bannerman married: twice, unhappily. Proctor and Evelyn both said more than once that they felt the actor's life was not conducive to marriage: they were wedded to their careers. Hardships and tragedies occurred in the lives of all these women: early widowhood and the death of children (Phillips and Morrison); marriage breakdown (Van Cortland and Bannerman); poverty (Bannerman); illness (Evelyn); professional uncertainty and disappointments and the loneliness of endless touring (all six). Charlotte Nickinson had to give up her career when she married Daniel Morrison, only to return to it when he died, in order to support herself and her children. The exigencies of touring forced the other five actresses into a state of fundamental homelessness, perpetually on the move from one town to another, one hotel to another.

As the teller of their stories, obliged to fill in the blanks created by lack of evidence, one of my most essential strategies must be to speculate on how they would have felt about such life experiences: to go on an "emotional journey" with them, as, in fact, the actress does with her characters. The challenges to the speculative or reconstructive mode are most likely to come in the secrets and the deliberately buried aspects of their lives: these have to be creatively imagined, and, I suspect, written with the understanding that a certain degree of "fictionality" may—inevitably—be involved.

I am going to enjoy writing the following scene immensely, speculative though some of it may be. It is the 22nd of April, 1858, Charlotte Nickinson's wedding day. On the previous evening, Charlotte has given what she thinks is her last performance as an actor, and has officially retired from the stage at the urging of her husband-to-be, journalist Daniel Morrison. Who's at the wedding? No doubt her father, actor-manager John Nickinson; probably the shadow figure of her mother, Mary Ann Talbot, almost completely lost to history; perhaps Charlotte's actress sisters, her actor brothers-in-law, and her sometime-actor brother, John Jr. Are any members of John Nickinson's stock company there? Perhaps, though certainly one company member is very unlikely to be there: Elizabeth Jane Phillips, who nine days later will give birth to her first child by John Nickinson, with whom she has been involved for six years. Soon, both John and Elizabeth Jane will move to the United States, where it will be assumed that they are married. However, when John dies suddenly in 1864, in Cincinnati, and his obituaries make reference to his second wife, Elizabeth Jane, his son John, Jr. will write to the various newspapers and make it quite clear that his parents were never divorced.

As I engage in the kind of scholarly sleuthing that this project of mine demands, it often feels to me as if a large, highly detailed picture has been torn into innumerable tiny pieces and scattered. The pieces are everywhere, and each one tells a story, or part of a story, but unless as many of them as possible can be gathered together, the whole story will never emerge from the picture. As the teller of what is inevitably my version of these actresses' life narratives, I know that the *truth* of their lives is elusive, perhaps unrecoverable. But by engaging in a process of creative empathy for them and their experiences as women, both in their lives and in the theatre, I can perhaps reveal some of what is or has been hidden and give at least a little substance to their shadows. I have come to feel deep admiration and affection for each of my six actresses, regarding myself as their advocate, so I see this task as my obligation and my privilege.

Notes

1. This chapter is dedicated to Professor Ronald Bryden (1927–2004), with love and gratitude.

2. Dorothy Maud Somerset in British Columbia, Elizabeth Sterling Haynes and Betty Mitchell in Alberta, Mary Ellen Burgess in Saskatchewan, Nancy Pyper in Manitoba, Josephine Barrington and Dorothy Massey Goulding in Toronto, Martha Allan in Montreal, and others founded drama leagues, directed Little Theatre groups, taught drama privately and in conservatories, schools, and extension departments, contributed to the Dominion Drama Festival, and brought theatre to places where there had never been any before.

3. For a relatively complete list of books about Canadian performing artists, see Gardner 2001.

4. See, for examples, O'Neill, Aikens, Shortt 1977, Fraser, Brown, Scott, and Gardner 1997.

5. This is the expanded version of the paper I delivered to the Association for Canadian Theatre Research in 1998. For the purposes of the article, I decided to limit my focus to performers born during the nineteenth century.

6. There are also indeed a (regrettably) few letters from John Nickinson to Elizabeth Jane Phillips, written for the most part in 1859.

7. We have the redoubtable Heather McCallum, for many years the director of the Theatre Department at the Toronto Reference Library, to thank for much of the library's extraordinary theatre collection.

8. Letter, dated 14 January 1980, from Mary Shortt to Mary Elizabeth Nickinson Chitty. This letter is now in the possession of Mary Glen Chitty, M. E. N. Chitty's niece.

9. The world premiere of *Our Betters* took place in New York in 1917.

10. Wilding's clientele included entertainment notables such as Maurice Chevalier and Noël Coward, and she was the first woman photographer invited to photograph the coronation of a British king, George VI, in 1937. After the death of George VI in 1952, Wilding was called upon to photograph the new queen; her portrait of Elizabeth II was used on British stamps until 1967.

11. See Cranmer-Byng. Percy A. Taverner was Ida Van Cortland's son and Albert Tavernier's stepson. He took his stepfather's real surname.

Works Cited

Aikens, J. R. "The Rival Operas: Toronto Theatre, 1874–84". Ph.D. thesis, 2v., University of Toronto, 1975.

Ashley, Audrey M. *With Love from Butch: A Stratford Actor.* New Brunswick: AB Collector, 1999.

Brown, Mary M. "Entertainers of the Road." In *Early Stages: Theatre in Ontario, 1800–1914,* ed. Ann Saddlemyer. Toronto: University of Toronto Press, 1990. 123–65.

Chapman, Vernon. *"Who's in the Goose Tonight?": An Anecdotal History of Canadian Theatre*. Toronto: ECW, 2001.

Chinoy, Helen Krich and Linda Walsh Jenkins, eds. *Women in American Theatre*. Rev. ed. New York: Theatre Communications Group, 1987.

Chitty, Mary Glen. "Life and Times of Actress EJ Phillips." http://home.comcast.net/˜m.chitty/index.html

Cox, Corolyn. "Name in the News: Famous Canadian Ornithologist Gave Up Back-stage for Birds." *Saturday Night* 4 (November 1944): 2.

Cranmer-Byng, John L. *A Life with Birds: Percy A. Taverner, Canadian Ornithologist, 1875–1947*. Special Issue of *The Canadian Field-Naturalist* 110, no. 1 (January–March 1996): 4.

Curry, Jane Kathleen. *Nineteenth-Century American Women Theatre Managers*. Connecticut: Greenwood, 1994.

Davis, Tracy C. *Actresses As Working Women: Their Social Identity in Victorian Culture*. London and New York: Routledge, 1991.

Drainie, Bronwyn. *Living the Part: John Drainie and the Dilemma of Canadian Stardom*. Toronto: Macmillan, 1988.

Dudden, Faye E. *Women in the American Theatre: Actresses and Audiences 1790–1870*. New Haven and London: Yale University Press, 1994.

Edwards, Murray D. *A Stage in Our Past: English-Language Theatre in Eastern Canada from the 1790s to 1914*. Toronto: University of Toronto Press, 1968.

Euringer, Fred. *A Fly on the Curtain*. Canada: Oberon, 2000.

Fraser, Kathleen D. J. "Theatrical Touring in Late Nineteenth-Century Canada: Ida Van Cortland and the Taverner Company 1877–1896." Ph.D. thesis, University of Western Ontario, 1985.

Forbes, Bryan. *That Despicable Race: A History of the British Acting Tradition*. London: Elm Tree, 1980.

Gale, Maggie. *West End Women: Women and the London Stage 1918–1962*. London and New York: Routledge, 1996.

Gardner, David. "Variety." In *Later Stages: Essays in Ontario Theatre from the First World War to the 1970s*, ed. Ann Saddlemyer and Richard Plant. Toronto: University of Toronto Press, 1997. 121–223.

———. "A Checklist of Books by and about Canadian Artists in the Performing Arts." *Theatre Research in Canada* 22, no. 1 (Spring 2001): 72–91.

———. "Checklist Addendum 2003: Additions to the 2002 Checklist." *Theatre Research in Canada* 23, nos. 1–2 (2002): 130–38.

Garebian, Keith. *William Hutt: A Theatre Portrait*. Oakville, Ont.: Mosaic, 1988.

Griffin, Nonnie. *Showbiz and Other Addictions*. Oakville, Ont.: Mosaic, 2002.

Hall, Amelia. *Life Before Stratford: The Memoirs of Amelia Hall*. Toronto: Dundurn, 1989.

Harron, Martha. *Don Harron: A Parent Contradiction*. Toronto: Collins, 1988.

Hicklin, Ralph. "Grand Lady of Stage Pens Memoirs." *Globe and Mail*, 26 August 1961, 15.

Holledge, Julie. *Innocent Flowers: Women in the Edwardian Theatre*. London: Virago, 1981.

Howe, Elizabeth. *The First English Actresses: Women and Drama, 1660–1700*. Cambridge and New York: Cambridge University Press, 1993.

Johnson, Claudia D. *American Actress: Perspective on the Nineteenth Century*. Chicago: Nelson-Hall, 1984.

Lee, Betty. *Marie Dressler: The Unlikeliest Star*. Lexington: University Press of Kentucky, 1997.

LeVay, John. *Margaret Anglin: A Stage Life*. Toronto: Simon & Pierre, 1989.

Moore, Mavor. *Reinventing Myself*. Toronto: Stoddart, 1994.

Nancy Pyper Collection, Performing Arts Centre, Toronto Reference Library.

O'Neill, Patrick B. A. "A History of Theatrical Activity in Toronto, Canada: From Its Beginnings to 1858." Ph.D. thesis, 2v., Louisiana State University, 1973.

Pinsent, Gordon. *By the Way*. Toronto: Stoddart, 1992.

Saddlemyer, Ann, ed. *Early Stages: Theatre in Ontario, 1800–1914*. Toronto: University of Toronto Press, 1990.

Seymour Jr., Charles. "Theatre in His Blood." http://www.cloche-dor-productions.com/overview.htm

Salter, Denis. "The Acting Career of Julia Arthur." *Theatre History in Canada* 5, no. 1 (Spring 1984): 1–35.

Scott, Robert B. "Professional Performers and Companies." In *Later Stages: Essays in Ontario Theatre from the First World War to the 1970s*, ed. Ann Saddlemyer and Richard Plant. Toronto: University of Toronto Press, 1997. 13–120.

Shortt, Mary. "From *Douglas* to *The Black Crook*: A History of Toronto Theatre 1809–1874." Master's thesis, University of Toronto, 1977.

———. "Phillips, Elizabeth Jane." In *The Oxford Companion to Canadian Theatre*, ed. Eugene Benson and L. W. Conolly. Toronto: Oxford University Press, 1989.

Sperdakos, Paula. *Dora Mavor Moore: Pioneer of the Canadian Theatre*. Toronto: ECW, 1995.

———. "Canada's Daughters, America's Sweethearts: The Careers of Canadian 'Footlight\Favorites' in the United States." *Theatre Research in Canada* 20, no. 2 (Fall 1999): 131–58.

Stuart, Ann. "The Taverners: A Preliminary Study." 1975–76. Taverner Collection. Performing Arts Centre, Toronto Reference Library, box 8.

Taverner Collection. Performing Arts Centre, Toronto Reference Library.

Taylor, Claire Drainie. *The Surprise of My Life*. Waterloo: Wilfred Laurier University Press, 1998.

Turner, Mary M. *Forgotten Leading Ladies of the American Theatre: Lives of Eight Female Players, Playwrights, Directors, Managers, and Activists of the Eighteenth, Nineteenth, and Early Twentieth Centuries*. Jefferson, N.C.: McFarland, 1990.

van Bridge, Tony. *Also in the Cast: The Memoirs of Tony van Bridge*. Oakville, Ont.: Mosaic, 1995.

Waxman, Al. *That's What I Am*. Toronto: Malcolm Lester, 1999.

Whitfield, Eileen. *Pickford: The Woman Who Made Hollywood*. Toronto: Macfarlane Walter & Ross, 1997.

Wilson, Garff B. *A History of American Acting*. Bloomington and London: Indiana University Press, 1966.

Yeo, Leslie. *A Thousand and One First Nights*. Oakville, Ont.: Mosaic, 1998.

Totem Theatre: AutoBiography of a Company

Denis Johnston

A research obsession of mine has been to try to understand how theatre movements, careers, and companies get started. This obsession has led to my writing one book of theatre history, *Up the Mainstream: The Rise of Toronto's Alternative Theatres* (1991), and editing two books of theatrical autobiography, *Also in the Cast* by Tony van Bridge (1995) and *A Thousand and One First Nights* by Leslie Yeo (1998). After spending some years with this kind of material, I feel that some useful generalizations can be applied to the theme of "Theatre and AutoBiography." One is that theatre history is inseparable from AutoBiography: theatre movements and companies are invariably started by people driven by an ambition to work in the theatre, and what these people do is inseparable from who they are. Another is that the early years of any theatre company are poorly documented, so that the only way of getting at questions of genesis is through oral history, either by interviewing the participants oneself or by using interviews done by others. Inevitably, the recorded history that results has embedded in it, to a degree that is difficult to measure, the opinions and agendas (hidden or otherwise) of the interviewer, the interviewee, and the writer who finally tells the story. Some historians will be better than others at imagining and allowing for points of view that may have gone unrecorded, or at combining and reconciling oral sources with whatever documentary evidence can be found. But most often, a choice must be made, not between having some history or a better one, but between having a flawed history or none at all.

A generational model can be applied to the growth of indigenous professional theatre in Canada since the Second World War. Tracing it backward, one can see gay and feminist theatres of the 1980s breaking off from alternative theatres of the 1970s, which in turn were a reaction to the regional theatre network created primarily in the 1960s. The regional theatres in their turn were built largely on a foundation of highly organized community theatres which dated back to the Dominion Drama Festival of the post-war and inter-war periods. Bridging these two stages, in the 1940s and 1950s, were a few important companies which had professional aspirations but lacked the kind of official support later provided by the Canada Council (founded in 1957) and some provincial counterparts. Among these companies were the Canadian Repertory Theatre in Ottawa, the New Play Society in Toronto, the Actors Guild in Winnipeg, MAC-14 in Calgary, and, in Vancouver, such groups as Theatre Under the Stars (TUTS), Everyman Theatre, and Totem Theatre. Of these, Totem Theatre, which operated from 1951 to 1954, seems to me the clearest antecedent to the Canadian regional theatres that followed. When the Vancouver Playhouse opened in 1962 and a resident regional company was founded the next year, Totem's style—its team management structure, its promotion of local talent, its determination to be considered professional—would have been fresh in the minds of the people involved.

My interest in Totem Theatre started with a peripheral involvement in an oral history project launched in the late 1970s by Peter Mannering (1925–2000), founding artistic director of Bastion Theatre in Victoria. Originally from Vancouver, Mannering was anxious to write a book about the theatre scene in which he had grown up. He received a grant which enabled him to embark on an ambitious program of audiotaping dozens of oral history interviews with people he had known and worked with in the 1950s and to have these tapes transcribed; the results are deposited in the Provincial Archives of British Columbia. But forming these recollections into a book proved to be a more complex chore than he had anticipated, and no publications resulted from his work.

When I listened to these tapes, a decade or more after they were made, the conversations seemed to be conducted in some kind of code: if you already knew the people and events, perhaps the story would be clear, but it wasn't to me. Among the many people he had interviewed were the three principals of Totem Theatre: Thor Arngrim, Stuart Baker, and Norma Macmillan. Baker had died in the interim, but Mannering put me in touch with Arngrim and Macmillan, who were then living in California. I asked them to critique a short article I had already written on Totem, which had been published in 1989 in a newsletter of Vancouver's regional theatre, the Playhouse Theatre Company. The sources I used for this article were a number of loose newspaper and magazine articles in the clipping files of the Vancouver Public Library, plus a performance calendar I compiled from newspapers on microfilm, supplemented by a few quotes from Mannering's audiotapes. In October 1992, when Arngrim and Macmillan came to Vancouver for an extended visit, I was able to interview them myself, taping about six hours of conversations in three meetings. I was also able to add to my store of documentary evidence copies of articles from their own scrapbooks. The story that emerged—and which is told here—is largely their story: the auto/biography of a theatre company.

The story of Totem Theatre is best understood in four distinct periods, corresponding to the four venues in which it played. The first period was the summer of 1951, when Arngrim and Baker founded the company to play weekly summer stock in a public park in West Vancouver, a suburb of Vancouver. The second began that fall, when they moved the company from weekly stock to (most often) tri-weekly, mounting their productions in a rented hall in downtown Vancouver. There they operated for two more years, in the winter and summer, and bragged of being the only year-round professional theatre in Canada: these were the halcyon days of Totem Theatre, a period through which it found an audience and made a lasting impact on the cultural scene of the growing post-war city. The company might have lasted there for much longer had it not been for problems with the venue: the building's owner was reluctant to extend Totem's lease, while at the same time the city's fire regulations were becoming more modern and more stringent. Instead of choosing to cease operations, however, the Totem trio moved to another venue in another town: a former vaudeville house in Victoria where, beginning in August 1953, increased expenses forced them back into weekly and then bi-weekly stock. Finally, at the invitation of another venerable but rather down-at-heels playhouse, Totem moved back to Vancouver for one last summer of weekly stock, playing a larger arena stage at the Georgia Auditorium. At the end of August 1954, the company's founders folded it and left for Toronto, where opportunities were greater for careers in the theatre.

The founders of Totem Theatre, Thor Arngrim and Stuart Baker, had both cut their theatrical teeth in Vancouver's post-war cultural environment, and although their backgrounds were very different, they soon became fast friends and skilled collaborators. Arngrim was born Thorhallur Arngrimson in 1928 and raised in an Icelandic community in Mozart, Saskatchewan, where his adoptive parents farmed wheat and livestock.[1] Though the one-room school he attended had only eight students, it put on Christmas concerts and other entertainments in which he played leading parts, both on stage and behind the scenes. In addition, his parents regularly took him to see touring productions in Regina and annual pageants staged by the local Icelandic community. When Arngrim was fourteen the family moved to Campbell River, a town on the east coast of Vancouver Island and, since Arngrim had no desire to continue his education into high school, the next year he began working at a series of jobs to which he had no particular commitment: operating a signal whistle at a logging camp, assisting surveyors on a new hydroelectric project, delivering groceries by car to rural residents. In 1945, knowing that Campbell River offered no life that suited him, he moved, with his parents' blessing, to Vancouver, where he boarded with family friends.

In Vancouver too, Arngrim held a series of jobs—selling stove parts for one department store, decorating windows in another, finally achieving some financial success selling magazines door to door. But in Vancouver the jobs mattered little, for he had found his calling: the theatre. He bought tickets to every play, every symphony concert, every performance that he could possibly attend. He carried a spear with a touring opera company, and began going to auditions at the city's most important theatre company of the time, the Vancouver Little Theatre Association (VLTA). In 1947, through people he had met at the VLTA, Arngrim obtained an unpaid position as a bit player and assistant stage manager for a new theatre company, the Island Theatre Summer Stock Company, based on Bowen Island, a few miles northwest of Vancouver. The company travelled by boat to other islands that had summer residents, performing mainly there and in Gibsons Landing, Horseshoe Bay, and West Vancouver. While the circumstances of this company were modest, its personnel included some of Vancouver's best actors, such as Sam Payne and Dorothy Davies, and the experience marked the beginning of Arngrim's rigorous education in what was soon to become Canadian professional theatre.[2]

Stuart Baker was born in Sydney, Australia in 1924.[3] After his father died less than two years later, Baker's mother moved with her baby back to her original home in Kent, England. (For much of his career Baker acted under the name Stuart Kent, the name derived from his boyhood home.)[4] In 1940, along with hundreds of other English children, Baker was sent overseas to be out of the way of German air raids, in his case to live with relatives in Vancouver. While still in high school he began haunting radio studios, hoping to be cast in juvenile parts, and he appeared regularly on local broadcasts. At age eighteen Baker joined the Canadian Army, and on his release two years later he chose to return to Vancouver—it had become his home. He began finding radio work again at the CBC and auditioning for roles at the VLTA, and in both places he met many of the people he was eventually to employ at Totem. One of them, for example, was Juan Root, an American actor and a familiar voice on local radio, who had been artistic director of Arngrim's Island Theatre Summer Stock Company experience while Baker was still in the armed forces. Another was Phoebe Smith, a *grande dame* of Vancouver's thriving amateur theatre, whom Arngrim and Baker were later to describe as their "stage mother." She called them "the boys."

Baker met Arngrim at an audition at the VLTA in 1948—in fact, when they met, the returning veteran Baker felt sorry for the teenage neophyte, until he realized that Arngrim was the better-known actor there![5] They both acted in a University of British Columbia Summer School production of *Antigone* in 1949;[6] and on the basis of their performances, both were invited to join Sydney Risk's Everyman Theatre the following season. While Everyman was styled a professional company, its actors did not receive a salary—they might get one dollar per show for carfare and other expenses—and they were expected to contribute to the mounting of shows as well as to appear in them as needed. Baker was no good with a hammer and saw, but he could write and so he started doing publicity. When he joined forces with Arngrim, who had experience as a salesman, they made a potent publicity team for Everyman, and soon they began earning money as freelance publicists for other local theatre projects and companies.

The Vancouver theatre scene in the 1940s had several *grandes dames*, as was the case in many other Canadian cities.[7] These were mature women who ploughed their considerable talent and energy into what might be called Canadian pre-professional theatre: men were always in shorter supply in amateur theatre, especially during the war years, and few other fields welcomed creative leadership from women and tolerated eccentricity as the theatre did. There seem to have been more such women in Vancouver than in other cities, perhaps because there was such a multiplicity of theatre companies, none of which held clear dominance in the city's arts scene. At Theatre Under the Stars, there was choreographer Aida Broadbent. At UBC, there was director Dorothy Somerset. At the VLTA were directors such as Phoebe Smith and Yvonne Firkins. There were also private drama coaches such as Elsie Graham and Dede Rutherford who would produce shows, generally one per year, with their students. Of course, men too were involved in similar pursuits and held similar positions of leadership; Sydney Risk is a prominent example. But in a society dominated by male executives in virtually all walks of life, gender appears to have been no barrier to advancement in Canadian pre-professional theatre of the 1930s, '40s, and '50s.

The initiative of one of these women led directly to Arngrim and Baker's founding of Totem Theatre. "The boys" recall that Yvonne Firkins occasionally started new companies that would survive for a show or two and then dissolve, usually through personality conflicts.[8] She also taught drama classes in a studio space at 1644 West Broadway, and there, in October 1950, she mounted an arena-style production of Moss Hart's *Light up the Sky*, featuring an impressive cast of actors mainly from CBC Radio. By the time it opened, Firkins's new company, dubbed the Vancouver Stage Society, was already disintegrating into factions, but the show was successful nonetheless.[9] Baker was acting in it, and some cast members asked him to investigate the feasibility of remounting it without Firkins—since Baker was a publicist, he had more experience with budgets than most of them. In turn he got Arngrim involved, and they began to consider starting their own company in the coming summer: if it survived, then they could look at continuing into a winter season.[10]

One of the first decisions they made was that bills would be paid before the artists saw any money. Their experience told them that actors, designers, and directors wanted, more than anything else, opportunities to act, design, and direct. Arngrim and Baker also knew that many suppliers of *ad hoc* theatre companies had been stuck with unpaid bills and that, if their company was to have a longer life, they would need to establish some fiscal credibility. This new enterprise would continue only if they could break even on their initial summer operation, and they were determined to do so. For start-up funds they approached a family friend of the Arngrimsons', a retired Saskatchewan farmer named Valdi Grimson, who gave Arngrim and Baker an interest-free loan of six thousand dollars, on the understanding that if the company proved viable, Grimson would be repaid from weekly box-office receipts.[11] They planned a summer season of plays and began the process of securing performance rights. They dubbed their company Totem Theatre, in hopes of appealing to a summertime tourist trade. Then they went looking for a place to perform.

Arngrim and Baker first looked at existing performance spaces, but quickly determined that they didn't have enough money to rent them. Then they looked at creating a makeshift space in a major hotel such as the Hotel Georgia or the Hotel Vancouver, but found that the managements were not interested. They even looked at vacant retail spaces in the new Park Royal Shopping Centre, just across the Lions Gate Bridge in West Vancouver. At the suggestion of Larry McCance, a freelance stage technician long associated with outdoor productions at Theatre Under the Stars, they also looked at an outdoor site: Ambleside Park, west of Park Royal, where four years earlier Arngrim had worked on an outdoor stage with the Island Theatre Summer Stock Company. They approached the Parks Board of West Vancouver, which owned and managed the park, and obtained permission to put on plays there. The Board did not ask for any rent; it felt that such an operation would be good for the community. Arngrim and Baker negotiated with a building supplies firm to give them the lumber on credit, again on the understanding that the bills would be paid from weekly box-office receipts. They had a proscenium stage built with a roof over it, along with the necessary wing-space, an adjoining building for dressing rooms and storage, and a tall board fence to enclose the audience and to make sure that people had to pay to see the show.[12] They rented folding chairs to put on the lawn, and they set up a rudimentary sound reinforcement system—perhaps a couple of microphones concealed in the proscenium arch, linked to a public address system along both sides of the seating area. They recruited a very impressive company, including some of Vancouver's top actors and directors. They hired stage technicians, had sets designed and built, started rehearsals, took out advertisements, and on 2 July 1951, they opened Totem Theatre with a new production of *Light up the Sky*. Baker was twenty-six years old; Arngrim was twenty-two (see figure 20).[13]

The financial tone of the operation was set in their first week of performance. Vancouver has a notoriously rainy climate, and as showers continued through one afternoon, Baker got ready to refund customers' ticket money. Arngrim, however, came up with a creative solution. "We're going to have the first drive-in live theatre," he announced, and set the backstage and front-of-house staff to removing all the chairs in the seating area and some of the wooden walls around it. As cars arrived, they were directed to park in front of the stage to watch the show: no ticket refunds were required. To hear the dialogue, audience members had to lean out of their car windows into the rain, and they applauded by tooting their horns. By the end of the summer, Totem had produced seven plays in eight weeks: after *Light up the Sky* came *Hay Fever, Personal Appearance, Harvey, Charley's Aunt, Room Service,* and *Born Yesterday.* Attendance was

Figure 20. Fledgling producers Thor Arngrim and Stuart Baker watch the skies anxiously, in the kind of photo they often staged to get free publicity in the local papers. The date circled on the calendar is that of the first-ever opening for Totem Theatre, West Vancouver, July 1951. Stuart Baker Collection, University Archives, University of Victoria.

good to begin with and improved as the summer progressed: both *Harvey* and *Charley's Aunt* enjoyed half-week extensions, and *Born Yesterday* could have run longer if the park had been available for an extra week. Part of this last production's success may have been due to a publicity stunt that Arngrim and Baker staged. They entered a float in the high-profile parade that opened Vancouver's annual Pacific National Exhibition. For the float they had a large stork built of *papier-maché*, holding in its beak an oversized diaper in which reclined the star of *Born Yesterday*, the attractive Lillian Carlson, dressed only in a swimsuit and a borrowed fur coat. This was one of many photo opportunities featuring attractive actresses—"leg art" it was sometimes called—that garnered Totem Theatre a lot of extra newspaper coverage. Now their own publicists, Arngrim and Baker could sense a good story, and the young women posing did not seem to mind.

While they did not pay their actors a weekly salary, Arngrim and Baker established artists' payment on a "unit" system that they had learned from working with Sydney Risk at Everyman Theatre. Participation in a production earned so many "units," with leading roles earning more units than smaller parts or walk-ons. At the end of the season, payment amounts would be determined by dividing the available money by the total number of units. At one point in mid-summer, the two producers were nearly ousted in a kind of palace coup. Following an afternoon rehearsal, they were summoned to a meeting with their actors, who had begun to suspect that there was money available that they had a right to receive. But after looking at the financial obligations that would have to be assumed if they took over the company, the actors abandoned their demands and went to get ready for the evening show. At the end of the summer, the company's bills all got paid as did the artists, and Baker and Arngrim began looking for a winter home to follow up on the success of their first summer season.

The space they settled on was a hall owned by the Electrical Workers Union on the corner of Dunsmuir and Beatty streets in downtown Vancouver. At the corner of the three-storey building, a door from the street led up a flight of stairs to a meeting hall, and up another flight to some offices and music studios. The main door on Dunsmuir Street led to the building's foyer and a coffee-shop,[14] and a door on Beatty Street led to the Press Club, which occupied most of the ground floor below the meeting hall's lobby and auditorium. For Totem, the Press Club turned out to be a very important neighbour. It was a private club where members, generally print and radio journalists, could buy a drink if they chose. At the time, there were very few public places in Vancouver where a person could buy a drink; but Arngrim and Baker negotiated with the Press Club to grant temporary memberships to Totem subscribers. It was a happy situation all round: audience members could buy refreshments before or after the show, the Club's bar revenues increased, and the bar's presence was a major attraction to potential audience members, especially men. The arrangement also made local journalists, whether or not their beats included entertainment, more aware of the presence of Totem Theatre. But due to the stringent attitudes at the time regarding liquor licensing, this feature was never mentioned in any advertisements, reviews, or news reports about the company.

The new Totem Theatre had an excellent location, right downtown and directly across the street from the interurban bus station—a great convenience for audience members who lived in the suburbs. But it was just a hall, not a playhouse. When Arngrim and Baker climbed the stairs from Dunsmuir and Beatty, they found an open area that could serve as a lobby and, beyond a wall with two doorways through it, a bare rectangular meeting hall. Their solution was to install a modified arena stage, which they used mainly as a thrust stage with seating on three sides of the playing area. They had seen arena stages once on a trip to Seattle and once for Yvonne Firkins's production of *Light up the Sky*, but their choice here was less an aesthetic decision than a practical one: this was the only configuration that would allow sufficient audience seating. Local designer Derek Mann, who had designed Totem's summer productions at Ambleside Park, now designed its new stage and auditorium at III Dunsmuir Street. Several levels of platforms were built to raise the seats, with other platforms for the main playing area. As they got used to the space, Totem's designers found they could create very effective scenery using scrims and directional lighting. A single dressing room was built in a back corner of the hall, a rudimentary box office was set up at the back of the lobby, and a large blue neon sign with a Totem motif was ordered and attached to the corner of the building. Seating capacity was about 370, and the lease arrangement included a small administrative office on the top floor.

As Arngrim and Baker began planning for their first winter season, they looked more closely at people whom they wanted to include among their core personnel. First was their "stage mother" Phoebe Smith, who had directed half their summer offerings at Ambleside Park and who would direct their fall opener, the American comedy *Biography* by S. N. Behrman. Next, despite some reservations from Smith, they asked Ian Dobbie to join as technical director. At that time the resident director of the VLTA, Dobbie was a rare combination of actor, director, designer, and technician; he had learned lighting while working for a film company in pre-war Germany, and the Totem partners believed his lighting and his sense of unified production values were well beyond anything else they had ever seen. As it turned out, the thrust configuration proved especially well-suited to his sculptural style of lighting. Though Dobbie had a reputation for being difficult, Arngrim and Baker found him easy to work with if they treated him with the same brusque (though often tongue-in-cheek) professionalism with which he treated other people. "Is nothing sacred?" he would gasp; "No, nothing," would be the reply, and they would all get on with the job. Besides lighting virtually every show Totem produced at its Dunsmuir Street location, Dobbie excelled in leading roles there in productions that included *No Exit*, *Private Lives*, *Present Laughter* (which he also directed), and *Nina*. He also played strong supporting roles in several others (including *Summer and Smoke*), and he directed more Totem productions than anyone else during the company's two years on Dunsmuir Street. His fifteen productions there included particular successes with *The Glass Menagerie, Rope, A Streetcar Named Desire, The Man Who Came to Dinner*, and *Peg o' My Heart*. "He had a habit of washing himself up—self-destructing," Arngrim recalls, "but we prevented people from self-destructing because we couldn't afford to let them! It wasn't like the Little Theatre [that had other people who could carry on]."

The actors they asked to join their company included some of the best talent around. Though still very young, Arngrim and Baker had a lot of theatrical experience in Vancouver, and they had noticed that many actors remained identified with only one company: for example, their directors at Ambleside Park were Dorothy Davies and Phoebe Smith from the VLTA and Juan Root and Frank Vyvyan from CBC; their actors included familiar faces from both, plus TUTS and Everyman regulars such as Doris Buckingham and Peter Mannering, and even a maverick actor-manager in Frank Lambrett-Smith. With the TUTS summer season over, three TUTS regulars—E. V. Young, James Johnston, and Betty Phillips—joined Totem's first cast on Dunsmuir Street. (Phillips, a young musical-theatre star appearing in one of her first non-musical roles, went on to become one of Vancouver's favourite "straight" actors.) Also in the cast were actors from Totem's summer productions who were eager to return, such as Dorothy Davies, Babs Hitchman, and Wally Marsh. Because the capacity of their auditorium downtown was much less than at Ambleside, Arngrim and Baker planned on opening a new show every two or three weeks; weekly stock would have created a crushing workload to sustain over a whole winter and would not have allowed audience numbers to build for potential hit shows.

Biography opened at the new Totem Theatre on 20 November 1951, to good reviews and generally good houses. The producers followed this with equally successful productions of a delicate wartime romance (*The Voice of the Turtle*), an existentialist problem play (*No Exit*), and a bittersweet modern classic (*The Glass Menagerie*). When there were shows they did not like, such as a holiday double-bill of *The Red Velvet Goat* and *The Romance of the Willow Pattern*, they closed them more quickly and brought in the next production a bit sooner. The management style of Arngrim and Baker evolved as the company did. Except for written material, which Baker wrote and Arngrim edited, there was no division of responsibility, nor did they make time to devise any. They "spun in shorthand," Arngrim recalls, and coped with daily decision-making in a spirit of adventure and improvisation. Of the two, Arngrim was considered the tougher businessman; but while Baker had a reputation for being facile and amusing, underneath it all his partners found him very solid and serious, and very dependable in a crisis.

Early in that first season, the core of the company expanded to include Norma Macmillan. The daughter of a prominent local physician, Macmillan had begun performing as a child singer but soon discovered she preferred acting. By her early twenties she was writing plays and touring them to community halls and social clubs in Vancouver and environs. Her first breakthrough to a wider public was playing Sybil Chase in the VLTA's 1947 production of *Private Lives*, and she became a fixture in shows there. She recalls telling another young actor, Jack Droy, just before Totem's first summer season was announced, that there was not enough action in Vancouver and that she planned to go to California. Droy had similar plans, he said, and when they met each other backstage working in Ambleside Park, they would tease each other by asking, "How was California?" Macmillan played in *Charley's Aunt* that summer alongside Droy, Baker, and Dave Broadfoot, who later became a legend in Canadian comedy. When Totem moved into their Dunsmuir Street office, Macmillan moved in too, because she could type and Arngrim and Baker desperately needed the help. By the time she came to charm audiences in *The Glass Menagerie* and *Present Laughter*, Macmillan was already a fixture in the office, and the producing duo had become a trio. She was imbued with the same spirit of adventure as Arngrim and Baker, and she picked up their shorthand style very quickly—she remembers laughing a lot while working in the office. Arngrim says that, at that time, he knew of only three actors in Vancouver whose mere presence in a show would sell tickets: Dorothy Davies, Sam Payne, and Norma Macmillan.

By early 1948, Vancouver audiences were warming to the variety and quality of productions that Totem continued to offer. A string of successes with modern classics began with *No Exit*, Jean-Paul Sartre's heavily ironic drama set in an anteroom in Hell. The cast included Ian Dobbie, in his first onstage appearance at Totem, opposite Dorothy Davies. This production, directed by CBC and TUTS veteran James Johnston, challenged and intrigued audiences: this was material that no one else in Vancouver was doing. After a short run of *East Lynne* came *The Glass Menagerie*, another challenge to the audience and another success at the box office. Directed by Dobbie, the *Menagerie* cast featured Macmillan as Laura and two actors from New Westminster, Verlie Cooter and Bruno Gerussi, as her mother and brother. Cooter was well known in the Lower Mainland, one of those women who acted, directed, produced, and taught; Gerussi was a virtual unknown at the time, but he later played leads at the Stratford Festival and became a household name in Canada through the long-running TV series *The Beachcombers*. Next at Totem came *Private Lives*, always an audience favourite, directed by Phoebe Smith and again starring Davies and Dobbie, whose caustic wit gave him a good feeling for Coward. He was tall, suave, and very English both on stage and off: "Canada's Rex Harrison," says Macmillan.

In March came successful productions of *Rope* and *Come Back Little Sheba*. Both did good business, Arngrim recalls, but all were outdistanced by *A Streetcar Named Desire*, which opened in early April. An excellent cast featured Gerussi as Stanley and local actor Murial Ontkean as Blanche (see figure 21).[15] Gerussi in particular was a sensation, and

Figure 21. Bruno Gerussi as Stanley (third from left) with the cast of *A Streetcar Named Desire* at Totem Theatre's arena stage in Vancouver, April 1952. Personal collection of Thor Arngrim. Photograph by Eric Skipsey.

the material once again challenged (and perhaps titillated!) Vancouver theatre-goers, as the run was extended by a week to cope with eager audiences. Two of Arngrim's favourite stories come out of this production. The famous film of *Streetcar* was then playing at Vancouver's flagship cinema, the Orpheum, and when the Orpheum's long-time manager Ivan Ackery heard that the same show was being performed live, he threatened legal action to close down Totem's production. He believed that one of Totem's staff—perhaps Murial Ontkean, who worked at the Orpheum as an usher—had pirated the dialogue by copying it down from the movie! Once Arngrim and Baker had explained to him that *Streetcar* had been a play before it was a film, and that Totem had secured the first Canadian rights for all of Tennessee Williams's stage plays, the matter was quickly resolved.[16] The second incident came a few years after Totem had closed, when Gerussi had become a fixture with the Stratford Festival, playing Romeo opposite American star Julie Harris's Juliet. An interviewer asked Gerussi if he had had any diffculty adjusting to Stratford's revolutionary thrust stage and was dumbfounded by the actor's reply that, no, it was similar to the one on which he had learned back home in Vancouver.

A key addition at this time was the husband-and-wife design team of Charles Stegeman and Françoise André. The way that they became part of Totem was typical of the inclusiveness with which the company operated. During rehearsals for *Streetcar*, Totem received a call from the Community Arts Council of Vancouver. At the Arts

Council office was a young couple, visual artists from Belgium, new in town, who were penniless and needed work. Could Totem do something for them? Perhaps the call was prompted by Totem's habit of displaying the work of local artists in their lobby. In any case, Arngrim told the caller that Totem had no extra money to hire visual artists, but he'd be happy to meet them and see their work. He was impressed with their portfolios, and they loved the little theatre and offered to help out. They slept in the theatre the first night; the Totem managers brought them some food and a bottle of scotch, and soon found them a place to live. The Stegemans began painting sets right away, often in the middle of the night. They worked very well with Dobbie, and as the company prospered, Arngrim and Baker were able to give them a little more money. The Stegemans painted most of Totem's sets for the next two years, before making names for themselves as visual artists.[17]

The modern classics continued with Dobbie's productions of *Present Laughter* in May and *The Man Who Came to Dinner* in June, before the company turned mainly to British potboilers for the summer. Totem also changed the runs from three weeks to two for the summer, with one exception: Dobbie's production of *Pygmalion*, though a lesser one by Totem's standards, was held over for an extra week. (It is worth remembering that, even before *My Fair Lady* had appeared, *Pygmalion* was the world's favourite Shaw play.) While the local audience may have been smaller in the summer—there was TUTS to compete with, not to mention Vancouver's glorious summertime weather—the numbers were swelled by tourists who, at the time, would have had fewer options for evening entertainment than they have today. Arngrim and Baker always made sure that cab drivers and desk clerks knew about the work at Totem, and gave them free tickets whenever there were seats available.

Beginning in June 1952, Totem's advertising trumpeted a new feature at their arena theatre: air conditioning. In fact, this was an advance in creative thinking rather than in technology. When Totem rented the hall, it had a rudimentary ventilation system: there was a large paddlewheel-shaped fan in the attic, which blew air into ductwork leading to a wall grille at the back of the seating area two floors below. Arngrim and Baker arranged for an ice company to install a large tray in front of the attic fan and to deliver a block of ice every afternoon before a show. Air conditioning was a very important marketing feature for summer audiences, especially visitors from the United States, and the fan blowing over the ice did indeed cool the air that flowed into the auditorium. This rather unorthodox cooling system led to two accidents, however. One evening the pipe that drained the melted ice must have become clogged, for when Arngrim went to investigate the sound of trickling water, he discovered a small waterfall cascading down the stairs toward the lobby entrance. The second accident was signalled by a deafening crash one afternoon that startled the people in Totem's office on the top floor. Rushing down the hall, they found that the large block of ice had apparently not been set securely into the tray. It had fallen off the tray and through the attic floor; and beyond the dust billowing out of a music studio, they could see the ice now embedded in a grand piano. In an ironic twist, the piano was on loan from TUTS, Totem's main summertime competitor. The music student, now in hysterics, was there taking her first lesson, and never returned for her second.

Totem's second winter season began with *Peg o' My Heart*, an American classic that became one of Norma Macmillan's most memorable stage roles (see figure 22). The story of a plucky Irish girl who overcomes her origins, it exerted a powerful effect on anyone who was an underdog, or who cheered for the underdog: Arngrim recalls that Harry Musikansky, a Jewish man who sold program advertising for Totem and most other theatres in Vancouver, came every night to see the show and, to Arngrim's chagrin, led the applause at the end of every scene. After *Peg* came a more recent American classic, *Summer and Smoke*, Totem's third Tennessee Williams play in 1952. While productions later that autumn may not have lived up to these two artistically, audiences remained loyal and the mood of the company was buoyant. Arngrim and Baker continued to work at getting press coverage that went beyond the entertainment pages: to publicize a rather fatuous English comedy called *Tony Draws a Horse*, for example, they arranged for a press photo of a real horse sitting in the front row of their audience! They managed this by persuading an exotic dancer, who was appearing at the nearby Cave Supper Club under the name Lady Godiva, to bring her performing partner to Totem one evening just before curtain time. The audience roared in disbelief as the horse took its seat and the flash-bulb

Figure 22. Thor Arngrim and Norma Macmillan in *The Moon Is Blue*, Totem Theatre, Victoria, November 1953. Personal collection of Thor Arngrim. Photograph by Eric Skipsey.

went off. Arngrim remembers that Lady Godiva herself, wearing a long blonde wig and a flesh-coloured body-stocking, looked rather perplexed by the proceedings.

For the 1952 Christmas season, Totem again tried to mount a holiday show, and again it was unsuccessful. This was a recent script called *Mother Goose*, in the style of a traditional English pantomime, written by the famous Canadian comedy team of Johnny Wayne and Frank Shuster along with actor Eric Christmas. Versions of the script had been produced for three Christmases in a row in Toronto and Montreal, so it seemed a well-established property. But the Totem producers ran into trouble by departing from their usual methods of production. They rented a larger venue for this production, the Georgia Auditorium at Georgia and Denman streets. The extra rent, elaborate sets and costumes, and the union orchestra combined to send production expenses far over budget. In addition, Arngrim and Baker ignored the authors' advice to do as many matinees as possible so that parents would bring their children for a holiday treat. Despite a strong cast of mostly TUTS performers, *Mother Goose* lost a good deal of money. In fact, if the producers had not been doing so well on their plays on Dunsmuir Street, this one failure might have spelled the end for Totem Theatre.

The new year saw a renewal of Totem's mix of potboilers and modern classics. Among the most memorable productions were *No Time for Comedy* and *The Little Foxes*, both featuring Arngrim and Macmillan in the cast, and a sentimental comedy set in Quebec called *The Happy Time*. The producers didn't care much for this old-fashioned play, but the audiences did, and like *Streetcar* it was held over for a fourth week. Next came *Dark of the Moon* by Howard Richardson and William Berney, a durable 1940s drama set in rural America, depicting the mythic and ill-fated union between a witch boy and a beautiful local girl named Barbara Allen. The play contains a powerful scene, made the more harrowing by Totem's intimate auditorium, of a Christian revival meeting which culminates in a rape committed by Barbara's ex-suitor, urged on by Preacher Haggler and his flock, to release Barbara from the witch's power. Two incidents from this production stick in the minds of everyone associated with it. One was a publicity photo of a young female witch that showed rather a lot of thigh—so much so that the actress's irate mother phoned Totem and threatened to sue the company, though on what grounds she did not make clear. The second arose from a special Sunday matinee for which the entire house was sold to a local synagogue, which had booked the play because two young men from its congregation were in the cast. But as the play's Christian rhetoric began to heat up, one of the synagogue's leaders stood and called out to all the other audience members to leave the auditorium immediately. Peter Mannering as Preacher Haggler was positioned to deliver his fundamentalist exhortations upstage to the crowd, and when he was finally able to turn around, he found that most of the audience had left!

Meanwhile that winter, at another theatre downtown, a historic theatre controversy had been raging around Everyman's production of another modern American play,

Tobacco Road. Set in an impoverished and somewhat decadent rural America, the play originally opened in New York in 1933 and ran for over seven years, becoming one of Broadway's longest-running non-musicals. This was not the old Everyman Theatre, but a new incarnation: Sydney Risk had gone into partnership with night-club owner Izzy Walters to produce a season of classic plays using American stars supported by local talent. (These were not what one would call "A-list" stars: the new Everyman opened in September 1952 with *Macbeth*, starring the American actor Dean Goodman opposite Dorothy Davies; other imported stars that season included Zasu Pitts, Joe E. Brown, and Lon Chaney Jr.) For this season, Everyman moved from its small Main Street studio into an old vaudeville theatre, the State, and renamed it the Avon to give it a higher tone. Doing mostly classics in mostly two-week runs, the new Everyman had a season-long struggle at the box office and found the cost of the American imports difficult to recoup. *Tobacco Road* featured an ensemble cast made up entirely of local actors. The police department received complaints of immoral doings on stage that would be considered tame nowadays—a man urinating with his back to the audience, an unmarried couple in bed offstage—but in Vancouver in the early 1950s such goings-on could have shocked some members of the audience. The play opened on 7 January 1953, and nine nights later the police raided a performance and arrested all the cast, along with director Davies and producer Risk.[18] Eventually seven participants were convicted of staging an indecent performance. Risk's partners saw the controversy as an opportunity to make some of their money back, but Risk himself—whose personal style was always very gentlemanly—withdrew Everyman's name from the operation, and that was the end of his company. Wanting to make some box-office hay out of the production's notoriety, Izzy Walters asked Baker and Arngrim to produce a touring version of this production, but as they felt the issue was dead and the play was dated, they declined the offer.

In the context of importing stars to boost the box office, it is interesting to note the different kind of star system promoted by Totem Theatre. The advertising and house programs for all their productions, right from the beginning in Ambleside Park, prominently featured the names of the leading actors. They featured the actors' names, says Baker, because they really didn't have anything else to sell. Now that Totem had lasted into a second winter season, and staged some thirty-five productions in their two locations, they were starting to see the results of a self-fulfilling prophecy: the public was beginning to perceive these local actors as stars in their own right. Eavesdropping in the lobby at intermissions, Arngrim and Baker found that some of their audience actually thought Totem's stars must be from Toronto or the United States—how else could they be stars? The inability of Canadians to develop and market their own stars, says Arngrim, who was later to spend over thirty years in show business in the United States, is the biggest difference between the entertainment industries in the two countries.

The only time that Totem used a real international star was in the production that followed *Dark of the Moon* in April 1953: the French comedy *Nina*, starring Austrian actress Elfi Koenig. This connection began when a local bank manager, whom Arngrim and Baker knew as a regular audience member, phoned their office one day to say he had a client, a wealthy Montreal industrialist, who wanted his wife to appear at Totem. The Totem producers weren't interested—they had seen expatriate Europeans starring occasionally at TUTS, and while some of them were very good, others could not come up to the high standards that local theatre was setting. The banker persisted, and after several attempts he finally persuaded Arngrim to accept an all-expense-paid trip to Montreal to see a show in which Koenig was currently appearing. The industrialist, Louis Levin, had financed this production of *Nina* in Montreal, and wanted Arngrim to advise him on whether he should finance a transfer to Broadway.[19]

This was the kind of money that Arngrim had never seen. A limousine picked him up at the airport and took him to a suite at Montreal's Ritz Hotel, where he found liquor and flowers but no people or itinerary. Eventually came a hand-written note from Levin, instructing him that a car would arrive to take him to the theatre. It was a large old playhouse, and a very well-heeled audience. The sets, props, and costumes were impressive, but when the actors started talking, Arngrim realized that they were American and that their style did not suit the continental flavour of the play. After about ten minutes, Elfi Koenig made her entrance. "She lit up the stage," recalls Arngrim. "She was petite and vivacious and the audience loved her. It was like listening to Sam Payne: I don't know what she's saying, but I don't care!"

After the show Arngrim gave his verdict to Levin. "She's terrific," he said, "but you can't take this show to Broadway. You don't want to expose her to that." The industrialist thanked him, and then asked if Arngrim would please do the play at Totem Theatre— Levin would pay all the expenses—and Arngrim agreed. The next day, before he was taken back to the airport, Arngrim received a phone call from Koenig, who added her thanks—she also felt that a Broadway transfer would have been unwise. Back in Vancouver, Arngrim and Baker arranged for Peter Mannering to direct *Nina* and assembled a supporting cast of Totem regulars: Ian Dobbie, Jack Droy, and Jerry Stovin.[20] They all found Koenig to be a polished professional, gracious to work with, and her performances in Totem's small space displayed her genuine star quality.

During that second winter season, the Totem team came to realize that their days at Dunsmuir Street were numbered. The Electrical Workers Union was reluctant to renew Totem's lease because it now wanted the hall for its own purposes. More importantly, however, pressure was being exerted by the Vancouver Fire Department regarding upgrades now required for fire safety in places of public assembly. Totem's hall, in a wood-frame building with inadequate safety features, was regularly being used by up to four hundred people per night, and the electrical wiring—especially considering the demands of theatrical lighting—was not up to new standards. Under the leadership of local department-store heir David Spencer, a building fund for Totem was established and a committee was looking at other potential locations, but Arngrim was not optimistic.[21] Indeed, every space the committee investigated would have also required extensive upgrades for fire safety, and the costs of such upgrades were far beyond the funds being raised. Only a few years after this, many Canadian cities were pouring public and corporate money into city-owned performance buildings—the O'Keefe Centre in Toronto (1960), the two Jubilee Auditoriums in Alberta (1957), the Queen Elizabeth Theatre in Vancouver (1959)—but this idea had not permeated the public consciousness in 1953. Arngrim was ready to close the company, but Macmillan and Baker persuaded him to try another tack: to move it to the York Theatre in nearby Victoria.

What was then called the York Theatre, now the McPherson Playhouse, had been built in 1914 by vaudeville impresario Alexander Pantages, as one link in his extensive chain of vaudeville houses, mostly in the western United States and in Canada.[22] By 1953 Victoria's Pantages Theatre was owned by Thomas Shanks McPherson, a Victoria real-estate dealer whose name is now memorialized not only in that theatre but also in the McPherson Library at the University of Victoria. Arngrim had two occasions to visit the Victoria theatre in 1953: first when Macmillan was invited to reprise her star turn in *Peg o' My Heart* for the York Theatre's current tenants, a local stock company run by actor-manager Ian Thorne,[23] in a production that opened in February which Arngrim travelled to see; and three months later when he participated in a theatre conference held in conjunction with the finals of the Dominion Drama Festival, which were presented that year in Victoria.[24] When Thorne's company collapsed amid debt and dissension, McPherson was left with an empty theatre, and he offered it to Totem for about the same monthly rent that they had been paying for their hall in Vancouver.

The move to Victoria was a desperate one and involved increased expenses. While they found some actors in Victoria for smaller parts, essentially Arngrim and Baker had to bring a core company with them, which meant keeping more people on weekly retainers than was their practice in Vancouver. Moving to a larger playhouse (the York Theatre sat about eight hundred) meant buying a new front curtain, buying more lights, and building larger sets, especially since it had a proscenium rather than a thrust stage. To try to meet these increased expenses, and with a smaller audience population on which to draw, Totem returned to weekly stock for the first time since Ambleside Park, opening a new production every Monday night. The York's name was changed to Totem, and the neon marquee was brought from Vancouver and mounted outside their new home. Totem's first production in Victoria, the non-musical version of *Gigi* (a transfer of the final production from Dunsmuir Street) opened on 14 August 1953, to a black-tie audience that included the province's Lieutenant-Governor. In October they abandoned the grind of weekly stock and moved to two-week runs.[25]

Despite strong support from the daily newspapers and from a few dedicated patrons, the community did not support Totem in the audience numbers required. (Arngrim considered the Victoria audience rather parochial, in fact, as they preferred English potboilers to more cutting-edge drama such as *Antigone*, *The Glass Menagerie*, or *No Exit*.) At this time there was no financial support for professional theatre from any level of government: more galling still was a 17 percent entertainment tax on ticket sales levied by the Province of British Columbia that, incredibly, throughout Totem's existence, was collected by a government functionary every evening after the show began. In the new year, the producers told the company that they could no longer afford to pay weekly salaries, and the actors stayed anyway. In February, Arngrim suffered a nervous collapse and was hospitalized for over a week. He attributes the collapse to the strain of trying to make something work in which he had had no faith from the beginning. "'No' is a wonderful word," he says, and his hospital stay helped him to understand that he should have refused to take part in the move to Victoria.

The company limped through another half-dozen shows in Victoria before closing operations there. A noteworthy production that spring was a play that Norma Macmillan had written and produced in her pre-Totem days. Entitled *A Crowded Affair*, this new version opened in late March and featured a Victoria setting. Two months later, during the run of Totem's last production in Victoria, *A Crowded Affair* had a very successful one-night stand at Vancouver's Georgia Auditorium, where Totem had played *Mother Goose* more than a year earlier. The success of *A Crowded Affair* prompted the Auditorium's manager, Derek Inman, to invite Totem back for a summer season in 1954. Again Arngrim did not want to make this move—he thought it was time to fold the company— but Baker and Macmillan were anxious to keep it going. They produced nine shows in weekly stock there, from late June to late August, and then closed the company. Three days after their last performance at the Georgia Auditorium, Arngrim and Macmillan were married, with Baker as their best man, and all three left for Toronto to pursue careers in show business. As they were leaving, Sam Payne pushed some money into Arngrim's hand and said, "One day, you will help someone else."[26]

The Arngrim family all made good careers for themselves in show business. They moved from Toronto to New York in 1956 and then to California in 1965, where Arngrim helped to manage his own family's careers plus those of such stars as Beatrice Lillie and Liberace.[27] Macmillan, with her light and malleable voice, played children's roles in radio in Toronto, New York, and Los Angeles. One of her voices became familiar to millions as Casper the Friendly Ghost, another as the claymation hero Gumby, still another as Caroline Kennedy in the comedy album *The First Family*. As a child, their son Stefan (b. 1955) played television leads in soap operas and on the series *Land of the Giants*, and continues to work today as an actor and screenwriter. Their daughter Alison (b. 1962) became perhaps the most hated teenager in America as little Nellie Oleson on *Little House on the Prairie*,[28] and while still in her teens embarked on a second career as a standup comic. Baker gave up theatre for a time, working as an editor at the National Film Board, but later returned to acting, mainly in Ontario and British Columbia. He died of cancer in June 1986 in Victoria. In 1993 Arngrim and Macmillan retired to Vancouver, after an absence of almost forty years, and Macmillan died of a heart attack there in 2001.

For anyone interested in theatre history, the fragile nature of our collective memory is appalling. If Arngrim and Baker had not been publicists, most of their memorabilia would be long gone. The Vancouver Public Library once had virtually a complete run of Totem programs, but they seem to have vanished. I left Vancouver a few months after taping my interviews with Arngrim and Macmillan, and since then I have returned only for short visits: by the time I listened to the tapes eleven years later, Macmillan had died and Arngrim had suffered a stroke. But during his recuperation he and I met several times, with me prodding to resolve inconsistencies and fill in gaps in the Totem story, him straining to bring back memories more than half a century old. "Do you know that or are you guessing," I sometimes ask, and I think he usually tells me the truth.

Thor and I have had many hours of conversation that never made it onto any of the tapes, and somewhere among them he told me my favourite story about Totem. Perhaps it is my favourite because it seems to say something about the nature of memory—or perhaps it just strikes me as funny. During the company's last summer in Vancouver, Baker directed *The Man Who Came to Dinner*, Kaufman and Hart's classic comedy about an egocentric radio personality named Sheridan Whiteside. At the time of Totem's production, a circus was in town, and Arngrim hit on the idea of hiring an elephant and his trainer to make a cameo appearance in the play, entering down an aisle as one of Whiteside's unlikely Christmas gifts from his wacky Hollywood friends. The trainer wanted to stay and do some tricks with the elephant, but Arngrim's theatrical sense told him that the joke would be ruined by this, that it worked only as a throw-away gag. The trainer was obviously disappointed, so Arngrim mollified him by engaging the elephant to perform some tricks outside the theatre at Georgia and Denman. There was a marketing bonus to be gleaned here: this intersection was a terminus for a free shuttle offered to people going to Stanley Park to see the current TUTS musical, and Arngrim happily noted that some of them, drawn at first by the elephant, came inside instead to see *The Man Who Came to Dinner*.

But when they folded the company two months later, "the boys" left town without ever paying for the services of the performing elephant. And Arngrim's two children, literally born into show business and now in middle age, never tire of telling their father that one day the elephant is bound to reappear and demand his money: "After all, Dad, an elephant never forgets" [29] (see figure 23).

Figure 23. Arngrim and Baker with Suzie the elephant in front of the Georgia
Auditorium, Vancouver, July 1954. Stuart Baker Collection, University Archives,
University of Victoria. Photograph by Eric Skipsey.

Notes

1. Arngrim and Macmillan's recollections are taken mainly from a series of personal interviews I conducted with them in October 1992, most of which are audiotaped but not yet deposited in any public collection, and from a number of follow-up interviews with Arngrim in 2004 and 2005.

2. There were other apprentices engaged for this company, in an American summer-stock tradition by which apprentices pay for the privilege of working in the theatre. Most were from the United States, where this was a common practice, but Arngrim as a local boy and a known commodity did not have to pay to join the company. As he recalls, the other apprentices, aghast at the rustic living conditions, fled after their first night there but never got their money back.

3. Unless otherwise cited, Baker's recollections are taken from audiotaped interviews by Peter Mannering dated 16 June 1979 and 29 August 1979, held in the aural history collection of the Provincial Archives of British Columbia. His theatrical memorabilia resides in the University Archives, University of Victoria Libraries, while his birth and death dates are taken from an obituary in the *Victoria Times-Colonist*, 2 July 1986.

4. Actors Equity has a longstanding rule that no new member can use the same name that another member is already using, a rule which required Baker to adopt a stage name when he joined Equity.

5. The recollections of Arngrim and Baker on this point confirm an earlier report by Thelma Root; see Root.

6. This production was directed by Robert Gill, the long-time artistic director of Hart House Theatre in the University of Toronto, who came to UBC that summer as a guest director.

7. For instance, annual theatre awards in Vancouver, Edmonton, Calgary and Toronto are named after important women pioneers in those cities' theatrical life: respectively, Jessie Richardson, Elizabeth Sterling Haynes, Betty Mitchell, and Dora Mavor Moore.

8. One of Firkins's start-up companies, which she began in 1958, survived to become Vancouver's largest theatre company today: the Arts Club.

9. In an end-of-year retrospective, one columnist described the production as "a bright fast moving comedy which because of its arena style setting and star-studded cast has not been equaled this year"; see Daly.

10. Arngrim and Baker's taped recollections differ on this point. Arngrim recalls that the success of their summer season prompted them to try a winter one, while Baker recalls that their plan all along was to use that first summer season as a launching pad for the following winter.

11. Arngrim's recollection on this point confirms an earlier report by Audre Cecil; see Cecil.

12. There are perhaps a thousand photographs of Totem Theatre in the Stuart Baker Collection, University Archives, University of Victoria. In some of them are pictured the productions, personnel, and seating area at Ambleside Park.

13. Press reports of the time list Baker's age as twenty-four, but this is at odds with his obituary. Other papers in the Stuart Baker Collection, notably an information form he filled out for the Canadian Theatre Centre in the 1960s, suggest that he was not always consistent when stating his age.

14. The coffee shop had a theatrical flavour, too. It was operated by Suzanne Sysak, sister of the famous Canadian pop singer and TV host Juliette—"our pet Juliette"—who starred in a phenomenally popular CBC-TV variety show in the 1950s and '60s. Sysak was a well-known singer in her own right, locally at least; professionally both sisters used only their first names.

15. Murial Ontkean's husband Leonard Ontkean was also part of the extended family of Totem Theatre: he was house manager for most of their productions in Victoria and Vancouver, and acted in several productions as well. Programs sometimes list their surnames as "Von Keane." Their son Michael Ontkean, born in Vancouver in 1946, has had a productive career in American movies and TV; he is best known for playing the lead role in *Twin Peaks*, David Lynch's groundbreaking TV series of the 1990s.

16. See Ackery, who does not mention this incident.

17. Charles Stegeman (b. 1924) and his wife Françoise André (b. 1926) were very active in the Vancouver arts scene for the ensuing ten years, and there are several articles about them in the clipping files of the Fine Arts Department, Vancouver Public Library. One article describes how they managed to paint sets for Totem Theatre in its 1953–54 season on Vancouver Island, while maintaining a gruelling pace of classes and commissions on the mainland: see McGrath.

18. This summary of the *Tobacco Road* controversy is taken mainly from the local press coverage, which was extensive. See Hoffman.

19. In our interviews, Arngrim could not remember the surname of Elfi Koenig's businessman-husband. But an article and play advertisement in the *Montreal Star* (28 February 1953, 29) ties Levin and Koenig together, along with KoolVent (Levin's aluminum-awning business) and their theatre company which was dubbed the Canadian Players. This Montreal-based company evidently had nothing to do with the more famous touring company of the same name, which was started in Stratford the next year by Tom Patterson and Douglas Campbell.

20. Stovin later had a long career in movies and television, appearing in such films as *Lolita* and *The Pink Panther Strikes Again*, and in TV series such as *The Pallisers*.

21. Despite the committee's efforts, and despite fundraising appeals following most performances, by the time Totem left Dunsmuir Street in August 1953 only $7,000 had been raised of the building fund's $160,000 goal, as cited in an undated newspaper clipping in Arngrim's personal collection.

22. For a summary of Pantages's career, see Saloutos.

23. Both Ian Thorne and Stuart Baker later acted with the Shaw Festival in Ontario. Thorne appeared in all three of the Shaw's productions in 1963, and Baker (as Stuart Kent) appeared in four productions in 1974 and 1975: see Johnston and German.

24. Arngrim's participation is confirmed in "Theatre Conference Parley On," *Victoria Daily Colonist*, 5 May 1953.

25. In their residency in Victoria, which lasted nine months, most of Totem's productions (sixteen of twenty-one) were of plays they had previously mounted in Vancouver. The next summer at the Georgia Auditorium, by contrast, only four of Totem's nine productions were remounts.

26. This was evidently a habit of Sam Payne's: Peter Mannering, who founded Victoria's Bastion Theatre in 1963, recalls (in his interview with Arngrim and Baker held in the Provincial Archives of British Columbia) that when the opportunity arose to provide this fledgling company with its

first permanent home, a disused church on Chambers Street, Payne gave him $150 to cover the first month's rent.

27. Arngrim's post-Totem career is summarized in an interview with B. V. Arnason.

28. A recent retrospective article described "the brilliantly scary Alison Arngrim [whose] Nellie Oleson was motiveless malignancy in petticoats, an expression of every little girl's darkest fantasies" (Nussbaum 35).

29. I would like to acknowledge the encouragement and guidance of Sherrill Grace and Jerry Wasserman, as well as the financial support of the Social Sciences and Humanities Research Council which supported me with a Canada Research Fellowship during the period when my original research for this article was done. Without all their help, the story of Totem Theatre might never have been told.

Works Cited

Ackery, Ivan. *Fifty Years on Theatre Row*. North Vancouver: Hancock House, 1980.

Arngrim, Thor. "Former Campbell River Resident on Way to Fame and Fortune." Interview by B. V. Arnason. *Campbell River Courier*, 28 June 1967.

Cecil, Audre. "Where the Audience Gets into the Act." *Mayfair*, September 1953.

Daly, Paddy. "Happenings in the World of Drama." *Vancouver Sun*, 30 December 1950, 8.

Hoffman, James. "Sydney Risk and the Everyman Theatre," *BC Studies* 76 (Winter 1987–88): 33–57.

Johnston, Denis W. *Up the Mainstream: The Rise of Toronto's Alternative Theatres*. Toronto: University of Toronto Press, 1991.

———, ed. *Also in the Cast: The Memoirs of Tony van Bridge*. With a foreword by Christopher Newton. Oakville, Ont.: Mosaic, 1995.

———, and German, Jean, eds. *Shaw Festival Production Record, 1962–1999*, 3rd ed. Oakville, Ont.: Mosaic; Niagara-on-the-Lake, Ont.: Academy of the Shaw Festival, 2000.

McGrath, Helen. "City Abounding with Talent European Artists Maintain." *Vancouver Herald*, 9 February 1956, 11.

Nussbaum, Emily. "A Not-So-Little Nightmare on the Prairie," *New York Times*, 14 December 2003, 35.

Root, Thelma. "Top Men on a Totem." *Vancouver Sun*, 21 June 1952, 18.

Saloutos, Theodore. "Alexander Pantages, Theater Magnate of the West." *Pacific Northwest Quarterly* 57, no. 4 (October 1966): 137–47.

Yeo, Leslie. *A Thousand and One First Nights*. Ed. Denis Johnston. Oakville, Ont.: Mosaic, 1998.

David Mamet: Life Without an Archive

Ira Nadel

Where should a biographer, especially of a playwright, begin? In the case of David Mamet, dramatist, essayist, novelist, screenwriter, and director—and my current biographical subject—there are plenty of public but few private sources and no visible archive. Three related areas, however, present themselves: publications, people, and performances. Mamet's published works are plentiful and contain numerous statements about his theatrical practice. From play-texts to novels, from screenplays to essays, these works record Mamet's ideas and theories of acting, directing, and writing. In *On Directing Film*, for example, he offers this Hemingwayesque guide on the art of elimination: "[A] good writer gets better only by learning to cut, to remove the ornamental, the descriptive and especially the deeply felt and meaningful. What remains? The story remains" (xv). In much of Mamet's non-fiction, one uncovers not just his aesthetic of reduction but the shaping features of his cultural memory and writing practices.

In other sources, like *On Acting* by Sanford Meisner, the founder of the Neighborhood Playhouse in New York, and one of Mamet's most influential teachers, presents the origin of Mamet's directorial style and dialogue. Through his emphasis on directness, clarity, and precision, Meisner taught Mamet the importance of action; as Meisner endlessly repeated, "the foundation of acting is the reality of doing" (16). Mamet's determination to translate desire "into clean action, into action capable of communicating itself to the audience" is a consequence of the Meisner method and a crucial element of his theatre celebrated and repeated in his essays (Mamet 1986, 20). But not only in the essays. In *American Buffalo*, Danny Dubrow tells Bobby, "action counts. (*Pause*) Action talks and bullshit walks" (3–4). Although for Mamet, acting "is living truthfully under the imaginary circumstances of a play," action is what measures an actor's and character's strength (quoted in Bruder 8).

Autobiographies by others provide additional details about Mamet's professional life, conveying, for example, what it is like to work with him. The movie executive Mike Medavoy recounts his completing Mamet's first movie deal (*House of Games*), done in "eleven words of low-level Mamet speak," while the producer Art Linson narrates the comic details of accompanying Mamet to pitch a new movie before a studio executive. The short but painful ordeal is not unlike the moment when Joe Gilles visits the producer Sheldrake in Billy Wilder's film *Sunset Boulevard* to pitch his story—in sixty seconds (Medavoy 169; Linson 29–31). The argument in *Speed-the-Plow* between Bobby Gould and Charlie Fox over which script to "green light" reflects the arbitrary decisions of many studio executives outlined by Mamet in his essay "Producers," from his collection *Jafsie and John Henry* (69).

Interviews are another major source of information, although almost every interviewer notes a certain impenetrability when referring to Mamet's taciturn and often obscurantist manner. "One doesn't talk with David Mamet. One jockeys for position," a journalist reported (Kane 2001, 3). Avoiding, rather than challenging, the questioner, Mamet prefers curt if incomplete statements. Asked about his working habits and productivity, he answered, "Well, that's what I do. That's all I do" (quoted in Kane 2001, 192). He withholds as much as he reveals, but occasionally there are enigmatic gems: "You can be taught to act, but you can't be made to act" (31); "I have always been interested in the continuum that starts with charm and ends with psychopathy" (127). Limited biographical details sometimes seep out, so that one learns that he was a child actor or that television was an influence on writing his first hit, *Sexual Perversity in Chicago* (196, 28). But his interviews have limited usefulness because his statements are made to startle rather than reveal. They assist but only in a minor fashion, becoming essentially "a series of tactical evasions" (226).

Mamet's plays are also sources for life details, although the works are only modestly autobiographical. Plays like *The Old Neighborhood* (about Jewish life in Chicago) or the earlier *Lakeboat, Cryptogram, American Buffalo*, and *Glengarry Glen Ross* reflect aspects of Mamet's personal past. *Lakeboat*, originally staged in 1970 at Marlboro College, incorporated his summer work on the ore carriers of the Great Lakes. *Cryptogram*, situated in a Jewish home where the father has abandoned the mother, evokes a world of suspicion and betrayal directly known by the playwright from his own home (Kane 1999, 187, 348 n. 4). A poker group Mamet played with in Chicago is one source for *American Buffalo* and it was there, he occasionally mentioned, that he went to a nearby prison to teach: hence his nickname "Teach" and that of the character in the play. *Glengarry* originated from a 1970 summer job in a real-estate office on the North Side of Chicago.

But the biographer seeking the private Mamet is stymied, although infrequent moments in his published essays and reminiscences of life in Chicago and Vermont provide snapshots of his personal life. In these, he frequently recounts the painful, intimate dynamic of his family, such as his disappointment when he was ordered home for Thanksgiving from college, thinking that his father would at last honour a promise to give him a car and finding that he would receive only a pocket watch; or the more devastating incident when his stepfather threw his sister against a wall, cracking a vertebra in her neck; or the occasion when Mamet pitched a rake at his sister, splitting her lip. The mother's reaction to the children's code of silence at the dinner table meant that the sister ate her meal with blood from her lip gushing onto her food, which she had to eat. Only at the end of the meal, with napkin after napkin drenched red, did the parents take the girl to the hospital for stitches (1992a, 31–40, 9–11). The intensity and friction in the family clearly penetrated Mamet's sense of drama and dialogue, shaping a distinct psychology. "Nobody with a happy life," he declared, "[ever] went into showbiz" (1992b, n.p.).

Actors, directors, managers, producers, and others who have worked with Mamet form a crucial, live archive. William H. Macy, whom I interviewed in New York on the set of *American Buffalo*, was an important guide—from his undergraduate days at Goddard College as a student of Mamet's to their formation of an acting school in Chicago, to workshops at New York University and at the Atlantic Theatre in Manhattan. An interview with one of Mamet's English professors at Goddard, who made a rare campus visit the day I was there, was as valuable as the waitress at the River Run Café in tiny Plainfield, Vermont, who regaled me with stories of Mamet's visits and his role in formulating the *River Run Cookbook*, which contains Mamet's recipe for burnt toast: after you "burn the toast / Apologize to and dismiss firemen" (59). Mamet's foreword to the book is equally enlightening, as he describes his early and lasting attachment to Vermont, recently expanded in *South of the Northeast Kingdom*, his Jeffersonian account of life in the state and what it has taught him.

Performances of Mamet's plays recorded in reviews, commentaries, and even videos provide another source of information and insight. His directing further expresses his evolving sense of dramatic purpose through the treatment of character and action, while repeating his constant absorption with moral vision and ethical choice. Through his comic and corrosive world, centring first on men as in *Sexual Perversity in Chicago* and *Glengarry Glen Ross*, and more recently shifting to women as in the all-female cast of *Boston Marriage*, Mamet exposes the hypocrisy and secrecy of how we live. Evaluating his language patterns, as well as the dramatic structures in his plays, takes us further into the centre of his vision, although Mamet has provided another source for understanding the obsessions of his life—his spirituality.

For the past two decades, Mamet has renewed his identity with Judaism, confirmed in one of his latest works, *Five Cities of Refuge*, written with Rabbi Lawrence Kushner. The book is a dialogue between the two on forty-seven passages from the Torah. His recent essay on names (see Mamet 2004b) and the published account of his first visit to Israel (see Mamet 2002) similarly explore the spiritual significance of his ethical and religious rediscovery of Judaism. It also helps that his current rabbi in Los Angeles is an ex-Marine and shares with Mamet a macho approach to religion and life that Mamet has not only promoted through his love of guns and knives, but extended to a failed attempt to set up a clothing company that specialized in outdoor clothes for men. In fact, that combination of the spiritual and military outlines many situations in Mamet's work, especially in films like *Homicide* and *Spartan*.

At this stage of his life—Mamet was fifty-eight in 2004—he is still in combat, a kind of Rambo with a typewriter who has battled to gain the respect of actors, audiences, and even Hollywood. Yet the two phases, uniting in a militant spirituality, are strangely in concert. It is not surprising, then, to learn that Mamet's latest play to be performed, which opened at the Magic Theatre in San Francisco in late February 2004, deals with this very theme. The work is *Faustus*, an odd re-working of Marlowe and Goethe, showing at first a supremely confident hero. The play begins on the day Faustus completes his *magnum opus*, a numerical explanation of the universe slowly coming undone as he realizes he does not have the answers for either history or the order of the stars and may have "borrowed" the final formula from his son. At one moment, Faustus believes he has discovered "the secret engine of the world, regret," but in the next, he realizes this is false (37). The work is a deeply ironic examination of those who believe history or science answers all questions. History, like the Torah, may be interpreted and reinterpreted but never completed, according to Mamet (Kushner and Mamet 172).

Skeptical of history, Mamet impedes the recovery of his own past; hence his distrust of archives and their value. Tradition and ritual he can accept, and his understanding of the Jewish past as inherited practice passed on through custom and ceremony is premised on these values—but not in archival terms because archives are rigid and untrustworthy interpreters of the past that imply completion and fixity. By contrast, ritual and myth sustain openness to interpretation, event, and meaning. Archives have little or no validity for Mamet because history is essentially not information but imagination, which is always incomplete. History for Mamet is a story, a memoir, a reminiscence, as he makes clear in his 1992 essay "Seventy-First and Jeffery," on his Chicago youth, and in the 1997 *The Old Neighborhood*, a set of three plays, one of which he calls *The Disappearance of the Jews*. History is telling, not experiencing. According to Mamet, the past is in a constant state of decay; therefore, it can only be renewed imaginatively through art (1986, 111). To the young, Mamet writes, history seems to be either "(1) Yesterday [or] (2) The dinosaurs," but, as we age, "history falls in upon itself" and even implodes (1999a, 4). But the reason Mamet resists fact, certainly biographical fact, is not only because it seems manufactured and fixed which life, as he understands it, never is, but because it has betrayed him. His past has been one of frustration and anger caused by the bitter divorce of his parents when he was ten. Family life was, in the words of his sister, "an emotional hurricane," as they lived in a home that expunged all tradition. "Nothing old in the house. No color in the house," Mamet has said (quoted in Lahr 73). History is either to be hidden or invented but never relived.

The Disappearance of the Jews, part of *The Old Neighborhood* trilogy, elaborates this view of history. Bobby Gould revisits his pal Joey Lewis and begins to ask about past friends and events. But Joey has little time for reminiscence, preferring to seek a grander return, to Europe and life in a shtetl. He imagines himself flourishing spiritually and physically there, living with a purpose instead of enduring his job in a restaurant and his marriage to a woman he does not desire. He also senses the danger of modern America and the possible sudden rise of anti-Semitism and pogroms his father has warned him about. Bobby, similarly disconnected, also has fears but of lesser intensity. He has left his wife but instead of imagining a spiritual past, he wants to return to the early days of Hollywood when Jews ruled the industry. His absent moral centre means he is incapable of any more substantial return; he can only seek the life of the old neighbourhood. The two characters silently acknowledge that you cannot relive the past but approach their conclusions differently. Bobby still hopes it is possible to return, and is eager to re-meet Deeny, one of his old girlfriends, in the final lines of the play. Joey seeks to flee to a more distant past, one focussing on the origin of the Jews. The two characters evoke the two lives of David Mamet, one non-introspective and all bravado and action (Bobby), the other restless and introspective, seeking something to live for, suggested by a spiritual loss (Joey).

In *True and False: Heresy and Common Sense for the Actor*, Mamet writes that "there is no character. There are only lines upon a page" (8), prefaced by his 1981 remark that "you don't create a character; you describe what he does" (quoted in Kane 2001, 40). The same could be said about his paradoxical idea of history: there is no history, only texts without references—but there are also ceremonies, rituals of the past that have meaning which Joey, in *The Disappearance of the Jews*, understands (1998b, 139). Consequently, while archives are invalid, biography valueless, and the past no more than a misread gathering of incomplete materials that lead to nostalgia, history marked by ceremony still has meaning. "Drama is basically about lies," he has stated, but it nevertheless must be performed (quoted in Schvey 63).

For Mamet, the attempt to stabilize a life in biography is fundamentally false because the past is no more than a memory or reconstruction. Biography misrepresents experience which is more complex and changeable than it can convey. Biography cannot know or accurately record the past, turning it, instead, into a fiction. In many instances it invents the past, constructing unnecessary emphases or interpretations of moments that to the subject seem, and remain, unimportant. Yet narrative, detail, and the desire to interpret turn such moments into decisive events in the biographer's gaze, even if the subject dismisses them. Mamet knows that the past and history are always questionable and presents them in his work as allusive and inventive. His early but unpublished play *Marranos* (1975) explores the very uncertainty and danger of identity as the past entraps the characters who are living fraudulent lives. The play dramatizes how a Portuguese Jewish family, about to flee the Inquisition, discovers that their clouded Jewish past imperils their survival. The past, reconstructed by others, becomes a new and dangerous reality.

Works like *A Life in the Theatre*, in which an older actor reminisces with a younger one; *Lone Canoe*, which deals with nineteenth-century explorers; or *Edmond*, a satire on contemporary social history in which the hero jettisons a middle-class existence for the disastrous and nightmare underworld of the city, collectively show the insecurity and instability of the past. This view unites with Mamet's belief that "[he has] always felt like an outsider," expressing his marginalization from history, as well as culture, while masking a deeply felt need to belong (1986, 73). To be "cut-off from one's identity is a terrible, terrible thing," he later commented (quoted in Kane 2001, 183). Consequently, he dramatizes in his work a Jewish identity that was denied him largely because his parents strenuously fought for acceptance and success in an America which discouraged any religious or ethnic identity.

Stories, not facts, contain the truth for Mamet—and they survive partly because they cover up the past. His own "facts," beginning with a placid middle-class childhood on the South Side of Chicago, became distorted as his life was torn apart by bitter family disputes and his parents' divorce when he was ten. These wrenching events cannot be forgotten but, for Mamet, it is better to hide them and interpret the past as a con, or a false account, in order to survive. Reality does not need to be acknowledged. This attitude is clear in *The Shawl*, in which a phony clairvoyant tricks a troubled young woman out of a fee over the matter of a contested will which he reinterprets. History is again untrustworthy, rarely to be valued even in its totemic presentation, as a knife in *The Cryptogram* shows when it turns out to have a meaning vastly different than first thought: rather than symbolizing a pact with the past, it is a sign of betrayal. While Mamet's origins, especially those of his family with its Polish/Russian beginnings, remain important to him, he distrusts the seeming orderliness, impersonality, and supposed security of history. "I never want my stuff in an archive," he told a critic, yet that does not (paradoxically) prevent him from presenting characters who seek to find or even collect signs of the past, even if they do not understand their significance.[1] As he once remarked, "most of us tend to surround ourselves with tchotchkes [unnecessary things], so we can actually be sure we have a past ... or a life" (quoted in Lahr 1997, 82).

Mamet has made it clear, however, that the exploration of his own past is not welcomed because it is painful and easily misread. Biographers or archivists would only distort, alter, or over-interpret the material; furthermore, "no one else would protect it as well" as himself, he has stated, expressing his wish to control his story because he was unable to control his early life.[2] Exerting influence over its telling and material existence is crucial for him, a test of his authority, which naturally makes it difficult for a biographer, especially one who feels compelled to document the past to understand the present. Mamet's ironic desire to deny or at least hide the past has likely originated from his parents' determination to forget their European heritage: they enthusiastically dedicated themselves to "the materialist values of American society. At home everything was defined negatively," Mamet has said, "let's stop being poor, let's stop being Russian, let's stop being Jews" (1986, 90). His poem "Song of the Jew" enlarges this theme of disenfranchisement:

> I write in complacency,
> In the hypocrite love of life-as-it-appears.
> With a mind no ancient law has filled with bliss,
>
> . . . .
>
> An outcast, self-banished from the tribe
> I elect and administer by bribe.
>
> (1999b, 30)

Such an abandonment likely shaped his own skepticism about history at the same time as it reinforced his need for it. But Mamet also recognizes the power of the dramatic over the factual: no account is ever neutral or disinterested; and it is the fictional that gives value to writing (see Mamet 1998a, 31). The playwright Joe Orton warned in *Loot* that "anything is legal with a corpse" (261), a thought that Mamet finds fearful. Biographers, he understands, can do anything with their subjects, hence his need to keep many things to himself.

Archives, however, are relatively new. For centuries the collection of papers, records, and documents was more accidental than planned. The National Archive of France came into existence only in 1798, that of Canada in 1872, that of Germany in 1919, that of the United States in 1934. The move to house private as well as public records importantly redefined archives, paradoxically creating forbidden archives, records, and documents restricted from public view. The politics of the archive, however, leads to an important question, one with practical implications for a biographer: is it possible to write a life without an archive? Can we understand an artist, poet, composer, or dramatist without the supplement of letters, manuscripts, notes, autobiographical journals, or even bank books? Mamet challenges this supposition.

The life of a theatrical figure is doubly challenging, especially if one tries to present the inner, creative world of the subject. Theatrical biography might, itself, be thought of as a faux form—not because evidence is so often fragmentary and dispersed but because the subjects are themselves invented. In the world of illusions, they—the actors, playwrights, even producers—exist as illusions even in their own eyes: "Don't you see? We're *actors*— we're the opposite of people!" exclaims the Player to Rosencrantz and Guildenstern in Stoppard's play (83). The attempt to document a theatrical life is fundamentally ironic, since it narrates performance with the actor cast as a performer of his own story. But biography tries to stabilize this temporal if not ephemeral world where reviews and interviews provide the only (limited) record. Consequently, theatrical lives often focus on process, the making of an actor rather than the acting in an individual production (see, for example, Croall). A world that lives through performance, imagination, and playwriting is notoriously difficult to pin down.

Alexander Games's effort to write the biography of the British playwright Alan Bennett, author of *Forty Years On, The Madness of George III*, and *Talking Heads*, is one such example. Games found Bennett singularly uncooperative, while many close to Bennett refused to speak to him, so many at one point that he was convinced that he received refusals from more people than he had written to. But a sudden breakthrough occurred when he pursued Bennett's one-time girlfriend who owned a café in North Yorkshire. She suggested that she might effect an introduction, although the result was farce: seated early one Sunday morning in the back garden of the café, Games unexpectedly spied Bennett in his adjacent garden. A quick glance at the intrusive Games, however, sent Bennett racing inside, out the front door and into his car. "He was getting away," Games writes. He rushed through the café and into the street, boldly stepping in front of Bennett's idling automobile. In a shrill if not desperate voice, he shouted, "I'm not trying to be difficult!" The playwright paid no attention to the pleading biographer and gunned the engine, speeding at the obstructing pedestrian with remarkable precision. Games leapt out of the way but not before he imagined a fictitious headline: "Attacked by Subject, Biographer Dives for Cover." After recovering in the bushes, he offered a quick good-bye to the café owner and a short apologetic note to the escaped Bennett, and glumly took the train back to London (291).

In Stoppard's *The Invention of Love*, Oscar Wilde declares that "biography is the mesh through which our real life escapes" (96). Earlier, in Stoppard's *Indian Ink*, the sister of the poet Flora Crewe tells the comic biographer, Eldon C. Pike, that "biography is the worst possible excuse for getting people wrong" (5). As Stoppard envisions it, biography is the reshuffling of remembered inaccuracies, especially apt for the lives of theatrical figures. Built on reputation and myth, theatrical lives are deftly constructed; as the spy Guy Burgess remarks in Bennett's play *An Englishman Abroad*, "If I wore a mask, it was to be exactly what I seemed" (quoted in Games 2). The public image of an actor or playwright appears to determine the construction of her or his private life: "If you're a star, you should behave like one. I always have," Noël Coward once asserted (quoted in Fisher 1). The performance of personality is a prerequisite for a theatrical subject. "I am a performer who needs an audience, not a writer who likes writing for its own sake," Kenneth Tynan admitted in his diary three years before his death (383).

Biography may, itself, be closer to a dramatic text than its frequently cited contemporary model, the novel. Like a play, a biography possesses a setting and a cast of characters in a temporal structure defined by individual scenes and events, often arranged into acts. Drama and biography have clear beginnings and usually definite endings. Unlike fiction, with its multiple characters, digressive actions, confusing points of view and multiple narrative styles, drama and biography often concentrate on a single story and emphasize the consequence of actions. Contradiction, if not conflict, is often at the heart of both narratives. Furthermore, the biographer, like the playwright, seeks the well-told, or well-made, life, imposing order even when it does not exist. Events become actions in biography as they do in a play, transforming incidents into telling moments that without structure remain contingent and diffuse.

One example is Geoffrey Wansell's 1995 life of the British playwright Terence Rattigan, which opens with five scenes beginning in 1951 and ending in 1977 in a London hospital room. John Lahr's 1978 biography of Joe Orton follows an Aristotelian dramatic structure, moving in stages to its tragic end: Orton's murder by his lover Kenneth Halliwell described in the opening paragraph. The biography itself becomes the dramatic text which, as we read through its five chapters, we increasingly recognize as a five-act tragedy.

Supplementing the reliance on dramatic structure, a biography, to seem credible, must also rely on an archive—to corroborate, confirm, or possibly contradict the stories, tales, and adventures of the subject. But archives are themselves incomplete and conceal as much as they reveal, frequently omitting the very personal details that provide the fabric of a life: the breakups, personal crises, and financial worries, what Balzac labelled "the reverse of the tapestry" (quoted in Edel 4). In an archive, everything seems public but the truth remains private. Archives are mixed blessings: on the one hand they provide privileged access, on the other they are an excuse for "glacial procrastination" (Toobin 31). Biographies that are archive-centred frequently become compendia that substitute detail for the story of a life and often grow to immense proportions.

But the absence of an archive should not prevent the writing of a life, although a life without an archive must be careful in its assertions and clear in its intentions. As it veers between invention and history, it must choose between consciously indicating its originality or focussing on the available record, self-consciously telling the reader exactly where the evidence stops and invention begins. The technique should be as transparent as its reliance on art as a key to the understanding of the life, a form of biography that relies on texts as an invisible archive of the subject. Such work uses these creative texts as a form of personal history. How Mamet's plays, novels, and non-fiction reflect his life is another statement of this approach. But a life of David Mamet should also incorporate his times, from the sexual revolution of the sixties and seventies to the political correctness of the eighties. The absence of a documentary archive, a repository of items, should not prevent a reading of plays, books, and films as forms of cultural exchange between the artist and his age. Such exchanges mark moments of transformation which, as Virginia Woolf noted, are the very core of life writing. Biography, she wrote, should be "the record of the things that change rather than of the things that happen" (184). Texts are no more than clues to a life.

But the absence of an archive should not allow a biographer licence to tell the story of his subject untruthfully. On the contrary, he or she should strive to make it more accurate, although not at the cost of imaginative truth. Wilde in Stoppard's *The Invention of Love* understands this clearly. When A. E. Housman tells Wilde that an event he cites in one of his poems is true because he found the details in *The Evening Standard*, Wilde ironically responds, "Oh, thank goodness! That explains why I never believed a word of it."

> Housman: But it's all true.
>
> Wilde: On the contrary, it's only fact. Truth is quite another thing and is the work of the imagination.

Wilde then elaborates, "I was said to have walked down Piccadilly with a lily in my hand. There was no need. To do it is nothing, to be said to have done it is everything. It is the truth about me" (95–96). But pursuing a life without an archive still obligates the biographer to make the truth visible and its expression concrete. Such a dialogue with the past, as Mamet might say, is where the action is.

Notes

1. Leslie Kane, telephone interview by author, 29 July 2004.

2. Quoted by Kane in telephone interview, 29 July 2004.

Works Cited

Bruder, Melissa, et al. *A Practical Handbook for the Actor*. With an introduction by David Mamet. New York: Vintage, 1986.

Croall, Jonathan. *Gielgud: A Theatrical Life*. London: Metheun, 2000.

Edel, Leon. *The Age of the Archive*. Wesleyan, Conn.: Center for Advanced Studies, Wesleyan University Press, 1966.

Fisher, Clive. *Noel Coward*. London: Weidenfeld & Nicolson, 1992.

Games, Alexander. *Backing into the Limelight: The Biography of Alan Bennett*. London: Headline, 2001.

Kane, Leslie. *Weasels and Wisemen: Ethics and Ethnicity in the Work of David Mamet*. New York: Palgrave, 1999.

———, ed. *David Mamet in Conversation*. Ann Arbor: University of Michigan Press, 2001.

Kushner, Lawrence, and David Mamet. *Five Cities of Refuge: Weekly Reflections on Genesis, Exodus, Leviticus, Numbers, and Deuteronomy*. New York: Schocken Books, 2003.

Lahr, John. *Prick up Your Ears: The Biography of Joe Orton*. London: Penguin, 1978.

———. "Fortress Mamet." *The New Yorker*, 17 November 1997, 70–82.

Lee, Hermione. *Virginia Woolf*. London: Chatto & Windus, 1996.

Linson, Art. *What Just Happened?: Bitter Hollywood Tales from the Front Line*. New York: Bloomsbury, 2002.

Mamet, David. *American Buffalo*. New York: Grove Press, 1977.

———. *Writing in Restaurants*. New York: Viking, 1986.

———. "David Mamet, Interview." *Time Out*, November 1986. In *File on Mamet*, by Nesta Jones and Steve Dykes. London: Methuen, 1991a.

———. *On Directing Film*. New York: Penguin, 1991b.

———. *The Cabin: Reminiscence and Diversions*. New York: Turtle Bay, 1992a.

———. Interview by Alan Dershowitz, Cambridge, Mass., 1992b. Rpt. Mamet Info.Page. www.home.comcast.net/-jason-charnick/mamet-museum/dershowitz.html (2004).

———. "Seventy-First and Jeffery." In *The Cabin: Reminiscence and Diversions*. New York: Turtle Bay, 1992c. 125–28.

———. *3 Uses of the Knife: On the Nature and Purpose of Drama*. New York: Columbia University Press, 1998a.

———. *The Disappearance of the Jews*. In *The Old Neighbourhood*. New York: Samuel French, 1998b.

———. *Jafsie and John Henry*. New York: Free Press, 1999a.

———. "Song of the Jew." In *The Chinaman*. Woodstock, New York: Overlook, 1999b. 30.

———. *True and False: Heresy and Common Sense for the Actor*. 1997; New York: Vintage, 1999c.

———. Introduction to *River Run Cookbook*, by Jimmy and Maya Kennedy. New York: Harper Collins, 2001.

———. "'If I forget thee, Jerusalem,' The Power of Blunt Nostalgia." *Forward*, 27 December 2002.

———. "Faustus." Unpublished typescript, February 2004a.

———. "Secret Names." *Three Penny Review* 96 (2004b): n.p.

Medavoy, Mike. *You're Only As Good As Your Next One*. New York: Pocket Books, 2002.

Meisner, Sanford, and Dennis Longwell. *On Acting*. With an introduction by Sydney Pollack. New York: Vintage, 1987.

Orton, Joe. *Loot*. In *The Complete Plays*. With an introduction by John Lahr. New York: Grove Weidenfeld, 1990.

Schvey, Henry C. "Celebrating the Capacity for Self Knowledge." In *David Mamet in Conversation*, ed. Leslie Kane. Ann Arbor: University of Michigan Press, 2001. 60–71.

Stoppard, Tom. *Rosencrantz and Guildenstern Are Dead*. New York: Grove, 1967.

———. *Indian Ink*. London: Faber & Faber, 1995.

———. *The Invention of Love*. 2nd ed. London: Faber & Faber, 1997.

Toobin, Jeffrey. "A Not So Brief Recess." *The New Yorker*. 5 January 2004, 28–29.

Tynan, Kenneth. *The Diaries of Kenneth Tynan*. Ed. John Lahr. London: Bloomsbury, 2001.

Wansell, Geoffrey. *Terence Rattigan: A Biography*. London: Fourth Estate, 1995.

Woolf, Virginia. "Stopford Brooke." In *The Essays of Virginia Woolf*, vol. 2, 1912–1918, ed. Andrew McNeillie. London: Hogarth Press, 1987. 183–88.

Behind the Scenes: Irish Theatre, Irish Lives, and the Task of the Biographer

Ann Saddlemyer

Some twenty miles south of Florence lies a small Tuscan village largely unmarked by the surrounding development, despite its proximity to the major autostrada between Rome and Milan. Bordered at one end by a hospital and the other by an impressive cemetery, birth and death encompass the village life in between, where in the church square, as in centuries past, mothers and grandmothers keep a watchful eye on their children while contemplating the present and forecasting the future. Surprised by the magnificence of the mausoleum, truly a temple celebrating death, some months ago my companion and I wandered through the marble hallways. Turning a corner, I discovered to my astonishment two memorial plaques commemorating Signor Michele Esposito and his wife Natalia Klebnikoff.[1] How had this become the final resting place of two people whose biographies settled them firmly within the Irish cultural setting of John Millington Synge, James Joyce, Lady Gregory, W. B. Yeats, and Samuel Beckett? And what has my discovery in Antella to do with my subject (no relation, incidentally, to the athletic Canadian Esposito brothers)? Perhaps even more than the critic, the biographer stores away apparently unrelated facts, minute details, and chance encounters in an effort to connect the dots between performance and intention, experience and recollection, fact and fiction. Frequently the subjects themselves offer through their unedited correspondence (the more unbuttoned the better) clues to a hidden, or at least submerged, truth. But in the interpretation of these offhand remarks, the line inevitably blurs between biography and autobiography, the tale and the teller, the event and its interpretation.

As for Antella, it all began with music, the first love of Shaw, Synge, and Joyce, all three of whom knew the pianist/composer Michele Esposito.[2] He was already professor of pianoforte at the Royal Irish Academy of Music when Synge studied there; as composer of various works on Irish themes, including the cantata "Deirdre" (a theme later used by both Synge and Yeats), his work was of interest even to the notoriously tone-deaf Willy Yeats; as participant in numerous Dublin concerts and musical soirées he shared the stage with the young tenor Joyce, whose voice he praised; Shaw would have approved his introduction of Wagner to a wide audience as founding conductor of the Dublin Orchestral Society; Augusta Gregory doubtless attended his public concerts; and Beckett was particularly impressed by his edition of nineteen sonatas of Domenico Scarlatti. So significant was Signor Esposito's role in the cultural life of Dublin that Trinity College gave him an honorary degree in 1905, and he was awarded the title "Commendatore" in 1922.

The entire Esposito family was involved in the arts (and also, it seems, with the Irish Republican Army). Madame Esposito translated Synge's *Riders to the Sea* into both French and Russian and assisted the fledgling Irish theatre movement as a costumes mistress. Their daughter Vera (acting under the name of "Emma Vernon") was an early member of the Abbey Theatre company, earning special praise for the role of Mary Doul in Synge's *The Well of the Saints*. Ironically, she is remembered not for her considerable acting ability but as the anonymous young lady who stumbled over a drunken James Joyce collapsed in the theatre doorway; as she stepped daintily around him, Joyce lurched up to accuse her of being a prostitute. And the entire family had a later connection with Beckett: the Italian music teacher in *Embers* was probably modelled after the Commendatore; his daughter Bianca, whose name appears in *Krapp's Last Tape*, was Beckett's tutor in Italian; and Vera and her brother Mario were companions during his first visit to Florence.

But it was Synge who knew the Esposito family best, and was frequently invited into their home in Ranelagh. It may well have been Michele who encouraged him to write an opera on "Eileen Aroon" and would certainly have been interested in his early compositions. (Synge, born in the same year as Emily Carr, won awards for both counterpoint and harmony from the Academy, while at the same time receiving only a pass degree from Trinity College where his lowest mark was in English literature.) When he finally decided against a professional career in music and turned to writing plays, Synge continued to show a concern with form, harmony, and rhythm in his work. *Riders to the Sea*, with its incessant mingling of sea, wind, and grief, is nearly a tone poem (adapted to operatic form by Vaughan Williams without altering a line), and all his later plays develop contrapuntal themes in an artificial language echoing the natural rhythm and pattern of Irish. He even, like Yeats, experimented with codifying the human voice, annotating his prose like a musical score, and marking the margins of his drafts with instructions like "crescendo," "diminuendo," "current."[3] Yet unlike his fellow Directors at the Abbey Theatre, which celebrated its centenary in 2004, Synge rarely spoke in public, while Yeats was never silent about himself and his plans. It is almost entirely through Synge's letters that we learn of the man and the intentions behind his plays.

Listen, for example, to his defence of *The Playboy of the Western World*: "[T]he romantic note and a Rabelaisian note are working to a climax through a great part of the play, and

... the Rabelaisian note, the 'gross' note, if you will, must have its climax no matter who may be shocked" (Saddlemyer *Letters* 2: 47). And when an actor dared to criticize *The Well of the Saints* as being unrealistic, he shot back: "[W]hat I write of Irish country life I know to be true and I most emphatically will not change a syllable of it because A. B. or C. may think they know better than I do.... I am *quite ready* to avoid hurting people's feelings needlessly, but I will not falsify what I believe to be true for anybody" (Saddlemyer *Letters* 1: 91). Not surprisingly, his letters to his fiancée, the actor Molly Allgood, reveal most about his attitude to his audience. His private assessment of the riot over *The Playboy* was cavalier: "I feel like old Maura [of *Riders to the Sea*] today—it's four fine plays I have though it was a hard birth I had to everyone of them and they coming to the world." But then he added, "It is better any day to have the row we had last night, than to have your play fizzling out in half-hearted applause. Now we'll be talked about. We're an event in the history of the Irish stage" (1: 285).

Synge's letters to Molly were where I first learned of his friendship with the Espositos: "I am not going to *John Bull*['s *Other Island*, produced by William Poel] or the Abbey today, I haven't been quite so well this week," he wrote. "I do not feel the slightest inclination to go and see Shaw—I'd rather keep my money for Esposito's concert tomorrow and hear something that is really stirring and fine and beautiful" (2: 84). Synge had earlier been instrumental in the Abbey's rejection of that very play by Shaw even though it had been written for the newly established theatre; yet his attitude towards the extreme Irish nationalists who complained about his own work is very similar to Shaw's in *John Bull's Other Island*, where the Irishman Larry Doyle scornfully dismisses his English partner Broadbent's romanticism: "An Irishman's heart is nothing but his imagination.... An Irishman's imagination never lets him alone, never convinces him, never satisfies him; but it makes him that he can't face reality nor deal with it nor handle it nor conquer it: he can only sneer at them that do.... When people talk about the Celtic race, I feel as if I could burn down London" (16).

Shaw later offered his own explanation for the Abbey's reluctance to produce *John Bull's Other Island*: "It was uncongenial to the whole spirit of the neo-Gaelic movement, which is bent on creating a new Ireland after its own ideal, whereas my play is a very uncompromising presentment of the real old Ireland" (1907b, v). Synge's argument with a friend who had objected to the sexual frankness of *The Shadow of the Glen* is not so very different:

> On the French stage the sex-element of life is given without the other balancing elements; on the Irish stage the people you agree with want the other elements without sex. I restored the sex-element to its natural place, and the people were so surprised they saw the sex only.... When I deny Ireland's peculiar sanctity, I do so as compared with other potato-fed, thinly populated lands of same latitude, and I do not know that there is anything blessed in anaemia.

He then adds a comment that could have come right out of one of Shaw's prefaces: "I think the Law-Maker and the Law-Breaker are both needful in society" (Saddlemyer *Letters* 1: 74, 76n).

Had Synge been more sympathetic, he might have appreciated how much else the two playwrights had in common, for Shaw too based his plays on musical, frequently operatic, forms, layering his voices in choric structure and, like Synge, depending upon the rhythm of the soundscape. Shaw was not entirely joking when he reminded us that his play should be rehearsed as Italian opera,[4] and a flurry of correspondence advised actors on how to perform their roles. It is clear from their letters and detailed stage directions that neither Shaw nor Synge really trusted the actor: both punctuate for sound and rhythm as much as for sense. Both require strong acting: Shaw wrote to his good friend Lady Gregory, who was directing *The Shewing-up of Blanco Posnet* (produced by the Abbey because it was banned in England), "[T]he actor of Blanco ... must rise to the occasion, and get that new speech in. And he must not funk it, as the Playboy people funked when they first played in London. The speech, as now written, will carry any audience if it is rammed down their throats with conviction and energy" (Shaw 1972, 2: 861). Such letters, especially the unbuttoned ones, can be revealing for other production values. When deciding details of Christy Mahon's racing costume for the famous scene in *The Playboy*, Synge wrote to his good friend Jack Yeats, the artist brother of W. B. Yeats, with whom he enjoyed visits to the Queen's Theatre, Dublin's home of Irish melodramas. What would a west of Ireland jockey wear? A long-time aficionado of races on the strand, Jack replied with not one but three suggested costumes. When news of the *Playboy* riots reached England, Jack sent him another pair of drawings, wondering what Synge's next play would be like: "Will it be as mild as milk?" (a man with a bird perched on his arm, surrounded by women), "or will it be?" (a group of men throwing a man over a cliff) (Arnold 147). Unfortunately, Synge died before he could produce any more *Playboy*s.

Because a drunken priest appears in Synge's *The Tinker's Wedding*, that play was considered too dangerous for Dublin until fifty years after his death. When Yeats saw the premiere in London (produced by Herbert Beerbohm Tree), he walked out after the first act, angrily writing to Augusta Gregory,

> a most disgraceful performance, every poetical and literary quality sacrificed to continuous emphasis and restlessness.... This emphatic delivery and movement— which is the essence of the English idea of romantic acting—evidently fits nothing but plays written in short sentences without music or suggestion.... [T]he opening dialogue, Synge meant to be quiet, with the heaviness of roads in it.
> (Yeats 1955, 538)

Silence and stillness, punctuated by movement only when necessary, became hallmarks of the Irish players' acting style, encouraging the audience to lean in and listen. "It was certainly a day of triumph when the first act of *The Well of the Saints* held its audience," Yeats would later write, "though the two chief persons sat side by side under a stone cross from start to finish" (1961, 528). Yeats himself, in an image more familiar to readers of Beckett, once contemplated rehearsing the performers in barrels so they could not move until he pushed them about with a stick—he didn't trust actors either.

Such examples of playwrights' reactions could be multiplied many times over in their private papers. Obviously letters of this kind are a helpful index to theatre business. They can also be one of the biographer's most useful tools—although we must constantly be aware of the author's own posturing for his readership of one (or more). I would like to move on to a more singular example of auto/biographical scribbling, thirty years later. This time we travel from Dublin to London, to a cultural context beyond music yet with its own rhythms, and ostensibly to a different biographical subject and a quite unusual correspondence between two extraordinary partners.

In 1917 William Butler Yeats married a young English art student half his age, but already adept as an astrologer, a student of the occult.[5] Like him, she was a member of the Order of the Golden Dawn, dedicated to the study of the interrelationship of the spiritual and material worlds—they had frequently encountered each other at séances—knowledgeable in music, and familiar with contemporary literature in five languages. Through his marriage to this singularly brilliant woman, Yeats not only became a much better educated man, he would soon rejoice in his own domestic Sibyl. For as most people who are familiar with Yeats's story know, his marriage was somewhat hasty—even though he and Georgie Hyde-Lee had been family friends and fellow occultists for seven years—following sharply on the heels of his rejection by his early love Maud Gonne and his later love, Maud's daughter Iseult. Within days of the wedding Yeats began to doubt whether he had done the right thing—had he not, in his desire to have a settled life, perhaps damaged three lives? As her husband became more and more distressed while trying not to show it, Georgie (or George, as she preferred to be called) realized that something dramatic would have to be done to save her marriage. And so, as they sat miserably in their honeymoon hotel in Ashdown Forest, she took up a pencil and initiated what would become a complex correspondence with a goodly number of non-corporeal personalities.

Intending only to provide a harmless and temporary distraction, George Yeats truly believed that she was seized by a power beyond her control. "To her utter amazement," as Yeats later described it in *A Vision*, "her hand acted as if 'seized by a superior power.' The loosely held pencil scribbled out fragments of sentences on a subject of which she was ignorant" (1962, 8). Automatic writing, now used by psychologists and clinical practitioners although there is still little scientific study of the phenomenon, is produced without control of the conscious self who may be at some level of trance or hypnosis. The handwriting is usually abnormal, may even be mirror-writing or upside-down, and usually the pencil trails from one word to another; not surprisingly for an artist, George's also included many drawings and diagrams. Yeats, who had devoted much of his life to studies of magic and all methods of making contact with the world beyond, was immediately transfixed. No easy believer, he had for years questioned all forms of such communication, making such a nuisance of himself at séances by demanding proof that even Madame Blavatsky had taken him aside and advised him to go pursue his researches elsewhere. But now, he had unwittingly married his very own medium. His indigestion suddenly cleared up, he ceased to lament those wasted years, and in great excitement began to prepare questions for the "Instructors" (nineteen in all) who wrote through his entranced wife's hand.

Judging by the various levels of awareness in the script it is clear that George was one of those rare people who could self-hypnotize, helped considerably by her early studies in the Order of the Golden Dawn. The experiment went on for three years, sometimes two sessions a day, piling up more than 5000 manuscript pages and 782 index cards, which they then pored over, discussed, and researched—even living in Oxford for three years so they could have access to the Bodleian Library. Each day they prepared further questions for the spirit guides, several of whom were principals, creating a vast dialogue with its own elements of comedy, passion, and insight. George's automatic script devoted considerable time to the relationship between the spiritual and the material world, inner and outer nature, process and concept. Philosophically, the Yeatses explored and developed the concept of a balanced relationship between creativity and sexuality— leading to what they called "Unity of Being." More openly, much deliberation on the phases of personality led to their attempting to place historical figures and their own friends and acquaintances in different categories. As an unsuspecting guest departed, one would murmur to the other, "a 19, don't you think?" After a number of years the automatic writing was followed by "dreamspeaking," which the Instructors felt would be easier on the busy housewife, especially once the demands of children began to interfere with intense concentration. In this process Yeats hypnotized his wife, her answers to his questions apparently emanating from somewhere above her head. Sometimes the experiment ended in farce, as when one crusty Control objected to their cat's presence, grumbling, "Washing, washing, more washing & swallowing all the dirt."

It is difficult not to become embroiled in an analysis of where the automatic script and the ensuing unique "pillow talk" came from. Even Northrop Frye admitted, "Not having any explanation of my own to offer of this account, I propose to accept [Yeats's] at its face value" (13). But whatever you choose to call the extraordinary phenomenon that began in October 1917, the prose, poetry, and drama that followed are ample evidence of a remarkable partnership and literary collaboration. For George's script not only made for a successful marriage, it provided imagery and prose texts for some of the poems, and scenarios for plays. As Yeats wrote in a verse fragment: "Where got I that truth? / Out of a medium's mouth, / Out of nothing it came" (1952a, 241).

Out of that experience and based on the philosophical system he and his wife developed arose Yeats's book *A Vision*, their joint attempt to comprehend and apprehend reality—time, space, history, personality, psychology—within a much larger and more universal framework than one lifespan or one nation's history or even the world as we know it. For the Yeatses, reality could not be pinned down by age or place: there is far more than we can see or touch or even imagine; within us are many lives, within space there are many places. Once finding the right keys, they believed we should be able to push past the veil of our senses to greater understanding, to the pool of universal memory and spirit, the *Spiritus Mundi* of Yeats's famous poem "The Second Coming." A holy book for students of the "New Age," *A Vision* was for many years an obstacle for those scholars who preferred to look at the poetry and drama only. As W. H. Auden later remarked about "all that occult," "How on earth, we wonder, could a man of Yeats's gifts take such nonsense seriously?... Mediums, spells, the Mysterious Orient—*how embarrassing*" (188–89). But Yeats throughout his life insisted that in order to understand his writing, it was necessary to come to terms with what he called his "Magic." And *A Vision*, full of diagrams drawn by his artist wife, and charts and schemes for personality and history, was the barest of outlines for that larger understanding.

George objected to having her part in this strange partnership made public, for Yeats was an inveterate, irrepressible storyteller and gossip; not for nothing did she dub him "William Tell." So the playwright fell back on fictionalizing their biography—in his essays, poetry, and also his drama. Much of George's early automatic script was taken up with Yeats questioning why he had devoted so many years to a barren obsession with Maud Gonne; gradually, however, the script weaned him away from autobiographical introspection and into other more productive areas. His Cuchulain play *The Only Jealousy of Emer* was not only developed with the advice of George's Instructors but makes use of the characters and his relationship with all three women involved in his life at the time of his marriage. Once the outline of *The Only Jealousy of Emer* was settled, other topics were suggested, and the plots of at least two more completed plays were discussed by the metaphysical dramaturges—the Noh drama *Calvary* and the kyogen-like *The Cat and the Moon*. But the philosophical system that surfaced in George's automatic script runs like a thread through all Yeats's later work and marks his incessant revisions. *The Resurrection* and *The Death of Cuchulain* depend upon the cyclical theory of *A Vision*, while *The Words Upon the Window-Pane*, a play his wife urged him to write, is as I know from my own direct research a strikingly realistic portrayal of a séance.

Much of her automatic script reflects George Yeats's dialectic frame of mind, the inclusivity of her studies and exploratory instincts, her natural empathy. Yet the automatic writing she produced cannot be dismissed as a symptom of multiple personality syndrome, one of the current catch-all interpretations for unexplainable schizophrenic behaviour; for like a stage manager moving the various ghostly characters about, part of her mind was always in control. And a streak of common sense surfaces in the extensive passages offering domestic and even sexual advice—in a sense, private memos to her husband. No wonder she always rejected scholars' pleas to examine the magic notebooks with the curt refusal, "That's too personal."

Obviously, George was a subversive woman, determined that although her husband's story would be told, hers should not be. She buried everything she could, even landmark events, deep down without markers, where not even her family might follow. So why did I write her biography? I didn't want to; it never occurred to me when I knew her as a young graduate student that I ever would. I never took notes of our meetings—although I soon learned that I had to write myself into her story. Twenty years after her death her children, realizing that scholarship was encroaching and they could no longer honour her need for privacy, talked me into it, insisting that they would not read anything until it was published. I stalled, offering various weak excuses, and even after I agreed I often wished I had not taken it on. And it took so long that I was embarrassed to meet colleagues who inevitably asked, "How's the work on George going?"

However, as I began that long laborious process of digging, trying to get behind the smokescreen she had deliberately set up, unravelling the many different versions of the stories she told serious scholars, she took over my life. George was a masterly, mischievous storyteller, shaping the version of events depending on her audience. She also charmed others into respecting her silence—Richard Ellmann, who probably knew her best, reluctantly agreed that there was a book to be written—but, he added, a very *small* book. (Better I suppose than his advice to Brenda Maddox that Nora Joyce's life was not worth writing about at all.) Others were equally protective—reluctant to talk about the automatic writing, did not want to believe it existed, and refused to discuss the alcoholism that dogged her later years. But I knew I *had* to tell the whole story if I were to tell it at all, for the very reason that she had been such a subversive character. But George was certainly no help. A friend suggested I repair to an upper room, pencil in hand, and do some automatic writing myself; but I was afraid that recognizable, bold large handwriting would appear commanding me to STOP THIS AT ONCE! And by then, of course, I couldn't; I had to find, in Joy Coghill's words, George's "Song," or in Sharon Pollock's, "the essence of a life."

Throughout their married life George was an active critic of, and sometimes a participant in, Yeats's experiments in the theatre, which occasionally prompted complaints of interference from sensitive stage managers and directors. Early on, her husband consulted the ghostly Instructors as to whether his artist-wife might become the Abbey Theatre's much needed stage designer: "I think of asking medium to help with plays etc." But the moving finger quickly responded, "She cant do anything till this is done." The theatre would not have a permanent designer until young Tanya Moiseiwitsch was hired almost twenty years later. George's interests did, however, go beyond the playscripts themselves. She was a keen judge of acting and design, to such an extent that Willy again tried to lure her into practice. On visiting Cambridge to see Terence Gray's production of Yeats's *The Player Queen* in 1927, he wrote excitedly, "I think you must go to this theatre & study it. It is apparently the one centre of scenic & lighting experiment now in England." Again she had to squash her impulsive husband. George did assist with the occasional production—she recalled wearing roller skates to help paint the backdrop for Yeats's dance play *Fighting the Waves*—and she always took special note of costuming and decor for both the Abbey Theatre and the Dublin Drama League, in which she was actively involved as Honorary Secretary and unofficial dramaturge. She wrote at least two plays, but like the novel she also embarked on, they have disappeared. I sometimes wonder whether they might not have been produced under a pseudonym, for Dublin always suspected her hand behind plays produced anonymously, and she was a great friend of playwright Lennox Robinson, who wrote and directed for both the Abbey and the Dublin Drama League.

When Yeats was away she also became his ears and eyes on the Irish social and political scene. She had refused to put pen to paper until after their marriage when the automatic writing began; in a very real way that script was the beginning of their correspondence, for it is almost entirely in dialogue form. Later, whenever they were apart, they corresponded regularly. His letters, sometimes as many as three a day, faithfully report on all his activities: whom he met, what he was reading and writing, even the clothes he bought. Hers (he always claimed she was "much the best letter writer" he knew) relay all the news of Dublin and Ireland, discuss the political situation at home and abroad, remind him of appointments, comment on their friends' and her own activities, report on the development and activities of their two children—and criticize the productions of both the Abbey Theatre and its rival the Gate. During the last two years of Lady Gregory's life, when Yeats spent much time at Coole, the letters take on even more urgency, for George, as she explained to a friend, had to keep "all Willy's irons hot" during his absence. With both founders away and Synge long dead, this meant keeping an even closer eye on the Abbey Theatre, sometimes even casting and costuming the actors for her husband's plays.

As time passed, however, another member of the family assisted as stage watchdog, when Anne Yeats, at a very early age, was selected by Tanya Moiseiwitsch to be her assistant. In 1938 the Abbey Theatre held an international festival and Yeats, always loyal, offered his powerful one-act poetic tragedy *Purgatory* to artistic director Hugh Hunt. His daughter, who had already won praise for her fresh design of his plays *On Baile's Strand* and *The Resurrection*, was given the task of designing that first production. The dramatically intense and ironic *Purgatory* is very much of its time, questioning whether pollution can be purified by violence; the play ends with the Old Man's anguished "Twice a murderer and all for nothing." It is also a ghost play emphasizing the destruction of a great ancestral house, the role of personal responsibility for the suffering of others, and the inability of both the living and the dead to foresee the consequences of action. And perhaps more than any other play it reflects the cyclical philosophy developed by the Yeatses' automatic script: that each soul, in order to free itself of life, must wind back through past actions, reliving the very passions that shackle it. It is no accident that the action in *Purgatory* takes place by moonlight: "The moonlight falls upon the path, / The shadow of a cloud upon the house, / And that's symbolical" (1952a, 681). Lunar symbolism with all its astrological implications—as opposed to the movement of the sun—had been strongly emphasized in George's automatic script; in fact their placement of time, history, and personality depended upon the twenty-eight phases of the moon (her good friend Ezra Pound thought Yeats particularly "queer in his head about 'moon'").[6] Later, George would instruct one reader that "the Moon is commonly supposed to symbolize imagination and according to some old Cabalist writers it is the cause of heretical opinion, and the moon is also symbolically 'old' whereas the 'Sun' is young."[7] Clearly Yeats's stage directions, embedded in the poetry ("Study that house"; "Study that tree"; "Look at the window"), were to be attended to closely.

But the playwright was in England during rehearsals for this first production, and director Hugh Hunt longed to include in his set more than the simple bare tree and backcloth stipulated in the script. George reported the controversy to Willy in a barrage of daily letters: "Anne and Hunt had a long session regarding setting for 'Purgatory,' and Sean Barlow [long-time stage carpenter] was given design. To Anne's amazement two mornings later she found Sean had not only built the tree (which is to be solid) but also made the back-cloth." In her next letter came the warning: "Hunt is threatening to have a MOON in the backcloth of 'Purgatory.' Anne is refusing. If she does not win, she is going to say that she does not wish to have her name on the programme as designer of the setting. He talks of having a round hole (stage left) covered with gauze and lit from the back. I told Anne to say that you did not want a moon, only moonlight." This may have been when Hunt was heard to mutter as he, Tanya, and Anne worked on the set, "Father says.... Father says." But although none of them could be certain it was Yeats's last play for the Abbey (he died a few months later), Hunt was as aware as Anne that the production was historically as well as aesthetically significant. From all accounts Anne won the design battle. But Hunt continued to call up George with various questions, all again faithfully relayed to Willy: "He asks if, as 'Purgatory' comes between three other plays, it should be introduced by music, or 'percussion' or drums. I said that as far as I knew you did not want any of these things; that you wanted a bald production, no noises off, the whole to be concentrated on the two characters OLD MAN and BOY, and the appearance of the woman at the lit window of the burnt out house." She then repeated her main concern: "I told him that Anne had told me that he had an idea of a moon in the backcloth, lit; and that I thought you wanted an indication of moonlight but NO

MOON." The playwright was not entirely intransigent. Hunt asked "if he could cut the line about 'I will cut a stick out of that tree' and if you would give him a line instead, as the OLD MAN would probably have a stick in his hand. I agreed, but gave him your address.... Please reply to him by return!!!" (Saddlemyer 2002, 552). Yeats obligingly replaced the line with "Stop; sit there upon that stone" (Siegel 160).

The production itself and his daughter's designs were praised. But much to Yeats's delight—for he always loved a good battle—*Purgatory* raised considerable debate during the festival, apparently instigated by an American priest who took exception not only to the play's theme but to Yeats's curtain speech. "My Purgatory made no end of a fuss," he wrote with pleasure to a friend in England. "An American Jesuit priest demanded information as to what exactly I meant by God when one of my characters said 'the Mercy of God' in the play. Nobody would tell him as his aim was clearly to confound a heretic with scholastic philosophy & start a row." But then he added, "My speech is misreported. I said: 'I have put nothing into the play because it seemed picturesque; I have put there my own conviction about this world and the next.'"[8] That conviction, encouraged by George's automatic script and studies, has worked through his poetry and into the popular mind—especially as evoked in his poem "The Second Coming," which was quoted almost daily after the events of 9/11.

Inevitably, biography of all kinds and genres has much to do with the "Other." Because details are selected by a particular personality, it also reflects the "Omitted." For although selectivity becomes a further charge on the biographer, personal bias is a perpetual danger. Let me illustrate with another travel adventure. Several years ago we were taken to a Tibetan monastery in Northern India, where carpets were made and sold. My companion, struck by the remote, silent, hooded monk overseeing the factory, asked permission to take a photograph; he graciously complied, but threw back his hood to reveal an ordinary balding head and a brilliant, toothy smile, a generous insistence on self and community which bore little resemblance to the ascetic hooded image of the Other she sought to capture on film. That incident represents, in brief crudity, part of the biographer's conundrum: whose story are we intent on telling, and why? For the biographer is always an Outsider, frequently an unwelcome visitor attempting to get past the smokescreen we all deliberately set up, never able to achieve that much vaunted (and I believe impossible and restricting) quality: Objectivity. Can we really find "truth" (whatever that may be) in our research and our reading? Take the researcher's first tool, fact finding. What makes us think we can trust the institutional records and events—parish registers, rate books, legal proceedings, property records, family Bibles, histories both personal and public—and all the other paraphernalia biographers tend to rely on—letters, memos, photographs, memories, diaries, published memoirs, interviews, conversations, and other "substantiated hearsay," to say nothing of the created works themselves? George Yeats's birthday was always celebrated on perhaps the wrong day;

or did she remake that as well as her name? Is it ever possible to make a coherent narrative out of the haphazard assemblage of materials uncovered or discovered, frequently unintentionally, on the way to something else?

Biography is an exceedingly personal adventure, a voyage of discovery as much into one's self as one's subject. It must always verge on the autobiographical. Which leads to another danger, what Phyllis Grosskurth has described as "the attempt to appropriate the personality of another," even if, as in autobiography, that self bears some physical and emotional resemblance to the author (D14). As Virginia Woolf said, when she turns to an author, she is always making up the story behind the story, and as to the writer's life, she will "make him up a little differently at every reading" (quoted in Heilbrun 4).

But even with these caveats, it is not surprising that we can often find in their correspondence and private papers the personal vision and various interpretations of the playwright, suggestions for casting, staging, and performance, expectations of and for the stage—the entire corpus of theatre business—especially in those letters blotted by urgency and hastily mailed without careful thought. They can also provide an intriguing timeline of influence through the years.

Let me conclude with one last example from correspondence. In 1956 actor Cyril Cusack was engaged in another Dublin Theatre Festival, this time to celebrate the centenary of the birth of Shaw. He wrote to the ex-Dubliner who would become the third Nobel Laureate in the history of Irish theatre (to date; Seamus Heaney makes four laureates). Would Mr. Beckett kindly write a few words to embellish the program? As was his custom, Beckett politely refused. But his reply, not quite so brief and noncommittal as usual, neatly traces his own dramatic lineage from Yeats and Synge to O'Casey:

> I wouldn't suggest that G. B. S. is not a great playwright, whatever that is when it's at home.
>   What I would do is give the whole unupsettable apple cart for a sup of the Hawk's Well, or the Saints', or a whiff of Juno, to go no further.[9]

Oh yes, a closing note concerning the Espositos' final resting place: both had returned to Italy the year before Michele's death. A few weeks after my visit to Antella I learned at one of those accidental dinner conversations in Dublin that there had been at one time a College of Music in the village. Perhaps not such a coincidence—but that is the beginning of another kind of journey.

Notes

1. Michele Esposito (1855–1929) and Natalia Klebnikoff Esposito (1857–1944).

2. Scattered biographical information about the Esposito family can be found in Ellmann, Knowlson, O'Connor, Starkie, Saddlemyer 1983–84, and the Contemporary Music Centre Ireland at http://www.cmc.ie/composers/index.cfm.

3. See the appendixes to Synge.

4. See Laurence 12.

5. Material on the Yeatses' marriage and occult activities and their correspondence with each other are drawn from Saddlemyer 2002, especially chapters 6–12. I am indebted to Michael B. Yeats for permission to quote from their unpublished letters.

6. Ezra Pound to John Quinn, quoted in Saddlemyer 2002.

7. Letter from George Yeats to Frank O'Connor, 25 June 1941, in Special Collections, Boston University.

8. Letters by W. B. Yeats to Edith Shackleton Heald and Dorothy Wellesley. As quoted in Saddlemyer 2002, 552.

9 Samuel Beckett to Cyril Cusack from Paris, 1 June 1956, quoted in the program of *Androcles and the Lion* performed at the Gaiety Theatre, Dublin, 2–7 July 1956 in honour of the centenary of the birth of George Bernard Shaw. I am grateful to Dr. Lois Overbeck, General Editor of the forthcoming correspondence of Samuel Beckett, for confirming this reading.

Works Cited

Arnold, Bruce. *Jack Yeats*. New Haven and London: Yale University Press, 1998.

Auden, W. H. "Yeats as an Example." *The Kenyon Review* 10, no. 2 (Spring 1948): 187–95.

Ellmann, Richard. *James Joyce*. New York: Oxford University Press, 1959.

Frye, Northrop. "The Rising of the Moon: A Study of 'A Vision.'" In *An Honoured Guest: New Essays on W. B. Yeats*, ed. Denis Donoghue and J. R. Mulryne. London: Edward Arnold, 1965. 8–33.

Grosskurth, Phyllis. "Biographer Relives Narcissism of Youth." *Globe and Mail*, 21 June 1997, D14.

Heilbrun, Carolyn. "A Life of Heroism." *Women's Review of Books* 14, no. 9 (June 1997): 4.

Knowlson, James. *Damned to Fame: The Life of Samuel Beckett*. London: Bloomsbury, 1996.

Laurence, Dan H., ed. *Shaw's Music: The Complete Musical Criticism in Three Volumes*. Vol. 1, 1876–1890. The Bodley Head Bernard Shaw Series. London: Max Reinhardt, 1981.

O'Connor, Ulick. *Oliver St John Gogarty: A Poet and His Times*. London: Jonathon Cape, 1964.

Saddlemyer, Ann, ed. *The Collected Letters of John Millington Synge*. 2 vols. Oxford: Clarendon Press, 1983–84.

———. *Becoming George: The Life of Mrs. W. B. Yeats*. Oxford: Oxford University Press, 2002.

Shaw, George Bernard. *John Bull's Other Island*. In *John Bull's Other Island and Major Barbara*. London: Constable, 1907a. 3–116.

———. "Preface for Politicians." In *John Bull's Other Island and Major Barbara*. London: Constable, 1907b. v–lix.

———. *Collected Letters 1898–1910*. Ed. Dan H. Laurence. Vol. 2 of 4 vols. London: Max Reinhardt, 1972.

Siegel, Sandra F. *Purgatory: Manuscript Materials Including the Author's Final Text by W. B. Yeats*. Ithaca: Cornell University Press, 1986.

Starkie, Enid. *A Lady's Child*. London: Faber & Faber, 1941.

Synge, J. M. *Plays, Books One and Two*. Vols. 3–4, ed. Ann Saddlemyer. *Collected Works of J. M. Synge*, ed. Robin Skelton. 4 vols. London: Oxford University Press, 1968.

Yeats, W. B. *The Collected Plays*. London: Macmillan, 1952a.

———. *The Collected Poems*. London: Macmillan, 1952b.

———. *The Letters of W. B. Yeats*. Ed. Allan Wade. New York: Macmillan, 1955.

———. "An Introduction for My Plays." 1937. Reprinted in *Essays and Introductions*. London: Macmillan, 1961. 527–30.

———. *A Vision*. London: Macmillan, 1962.

Sharon Pollock's *Doc* and the Biographer's Dilemma

Sherrill Grace

> *Doc* is very close to me. It is not "my" story nor the story of my family. There is a lot of my father in Ev, my mother in Bob, and me in Catherine, but Ev is not my father, Bob my mother, nor Catherine me. They are extensions of real people and through telling their story, my personal journey of discovery is hopefully made large enough to communicate itself to you.[*]
>
> —Sharon Pollock

I

Doc is possibly Sharon Pollock's most important play. Jerry Wasserman has called it "her *ur*-play, the archetypal drama Pollock has played out in many different forms over the course of her stage career" (67). Since Wasserman made this comment in 1987, Pollock has gone on to write several more major plays that explore the kind of archetypal drama she gave us in *Doc*: *Moving Pictures* stages the multiple selves and changing life story of early actor/filmmaker Nell Shipman (see Pollock performing Shipman, figure 24); *End Dream* recreates the probable events of an actual unsolved murder from the perspective of the dying victim; and *Angel's Trumpet* replays a pivotal scene from the tragic lives of Zelda and F. Scott Fitzgerald. In short, Pollock's archetypal drama, as Wasserman calls it, is a drama about profoundly personal life stories—the biography and autobiography of actual people—that illustrate what happens when an individual is caught in the vise of interpersonal, cultural, and political agendas. And I could easily reflect back from 1984 and *Doc* to say that Pollock's earlier plays, like *Blood Relations* (1980), *One Tiger to a Hill*

---

[*] This comment is from the "Playwright's Notes" in the program for the November 1984 National Arts Centre of Canada production of *Doc*. An earlier version of this chapter appeared in a 2004 *Festschrift* in honour of Albert-Reiner Glaap, edited by Michael Heinze and Elke Müller-Schneck. I have revised that discussion to expand on the biographical context of the play in the light of my continuing research for Pollock's biography.

(1980), or *Walsh* (1973), demonstrate clear signs of Pollock's interest in this intersection of the private/public, personal/political, and in the role of autobiography and biography in grounding her plays.

But my focus here is not on Pollock's *oeuvre*. I want to look closely at *Doc*, this "*ur*-play" that has received remarkably scant academic attention since its premiere and publication (see Belliveau, Bessai, Kerr, and Wasserman), and I want to consider, through *Doc*, some of the challenges I face as Pollock's biographer. As many review titles make clear, theatre reviewers have stressed the autobiographical subject of this play, sometimes criticizing Pollock for *using* her own family and story (see Czarnecki, Knowles, and Macpherson). However, the mining of life story is scarcely new in twentieth-century North American theatre; indeed, theatre reviewers have often railed against playwrights for washing their dirty linen in public or for failing to *create* imagined characters. Other familiar examples of the kind of auto/biographical theatre that Pollock provides in *Doc* would include Eugene O'Neill's *Long Day's Journey into Night*, Tennessee Williams's *The Glass Menagerie*, and perhaps most notoriously Arthur Miller's *After the Fall*. In their reviews of the 1964 premiere of *After the Fall*, the New York critics were savage: Kenneth Tynan chastised Miller for indulging in "self-flagellating narration" and Robert Brustein found the play tedious, superficial, shameless, and "a confessional autobiography of embarrassing explicitness" (quoted in Gottfried 370). By comparison with these comments, Pollock and *Doc* have fared well. But then times have changed since the 1960s and in Canada, at least, auto/biographical plays have become familiar and popular.[1] Those modernist strictures on the personal that banished the portrait and the human body from painting and the author from his or her own storytelling (think of Joyce in *Ulysses*, absent like God, paring his fingernails, or Lowry, that most autobiographical of the great modern English novelists, dispersing his identity across several characters in *Under the Volcano*) have given way to what is being examined in this book as the auto/biographical impulse—the staging of one's own story in relation to the stories of others' lives. Poststructuralist claims about the death of the author notwithstanding, the author is back and striding across contemporary stages with great vitality. Canadian playwrights who have created auto/biographical plays include Guillermo Verdecchia, R. H. Thomson, Linda Griffiths, David French, and Lorena Gale, as well as major figures like Sharon Pollock and Michel Tremblay, and in the case of Pollock and Tremblay we have masterpieces of the form in *Doc* and *The Real World?*

These two plays would reward a close comparative study for what they demonstrate about the complexities and challenges of writing AutoBiography for the theatre because in each play the pivotal character is a writer who revisits the trauma of growing up in a severely dysfunctional family. For Pollock the revisiting is represented as an actual return, years later, to her father's home where, prompted by an unopened letter, the old man and his estranged daughter remember their dead wife and mother—a woman driven to alcoholism and suicide—and their own younger selves who enact the terrible pain of the past in a fluid memory play framed by the present reunion. For Tremblay, the revisiting is represented as a play-within-a-play (or a doubled play) as the grown son confronts his mother, who is outraged when she reads the play he has written about the family, and his father, who has betrayed each member of this family and yet remains violently self-righteous and controlling to the end. *The Real World?* premiered in 1987, so it is possible that Tremblay was thinking of *Doc* when he decided to tackle this deeply personal subject, but despite their striking similarities in subject, approach, and themes (especially themes of guilt, trauma, betrayal, and the status of *truth*), it is the differences that linger in my mind as thought-provoking and interesting.[2] One of the most significant of these differences occurs in the closing moments when someone burns an important and unread document: in *Doc* that document is the still unopened letter with which the play begins, a letter addressed to Doc (Dr. Everett Chalmers) by his own mother before she committed suicide; in *The Real World?* the document is the only copy of Claude's, the son's, play manuscript, which exposes his father's behaviour. In Pollock's play the act of burning the letter seems to symbolize the shared knowledge and understanding reached by this elderly father and his daughter, who have relived the tragic past, in a sense laid the ghosts to rest, and, thus, do not need to read the letter; in Tremblay's, the father's vicious destruction of his son's work has been circumvented by the very play we have just watched, but no understanding has been reached between the two men, or, for that matter, between the son and his mother. Each of these powerful auto/biographical plays leaves its audience (and readers) stunned by the destruction buried in the bosom of families, amazed by the creativity that can be nurtured by such trauma, and troubled by the ambiguity that permeates both works.

And it is for this last reason—ambiguity—that I mention *The Real World?* together with *Doc* because it is the richness of ambiguity that finally makes these plays so comparable and so rewarding, not merely for their authors, who have (one hopes) come to terms with personal trauma by writing them, but for anyone who sees or reads them, and most certainly for the biographer who must decide how to use such powerful material. In the final analysis, *Doc* and *The Real World?*, like *The Glass Menagerie*, offer wider lessons in what it is to be human, to be part of a family, to take responsibility for our own and others' lives, to accept guilt but to carry on, and, ultimately, to love. And both plays ask big questions *through* the vehicle of AutoBiography: What is the truth and who has access to it? Has a writer the ethical right to portray his or her family's story in a public work of art, or is such a creative act simply a further betrayal? How does memory function to create—or *invent*—the past, and to what degree is memory the reliable connective tissue of identity? And, finally, how far can the biographer trust the life story created by the writer of such plays? But *Doc* is my subject here and I want to focus on how *Doc* made its way from Pollock's life story to a complex and moving

auto/biographical play. *Doc* is representative of what can be done by a great artist—
Tremblay, Miller, Williams, O'Neill, and others—who grapples with the facts of life to
wrestle them into fiction.

II

Doc is a memory play, but it is a memory play with a difference because the memories
are divided between the two main characters in the present action—the father, Ev, "an
elderly man in his seventies," and his daughter, Catherine, who is "in her mid-thirties"
(v). Catherine has come back to visit her father after a long absence, in part because he is
about to have a hospital named after him, in part because he has recently survived a heart
attack, and in part because, as she says in reply to his skeptical questioning, "I came
home to see you" (13). This scene of home-coming takes place in what Pollock describes
as the "now" (v) of the play. It serves as a temporal anchor for the wrenching drama that
is about to unfold, and the stage instructions are precise about the way the action must
move from present to past as the remembered characters appear: "the physical blocking
must accommodate" the immediacy and fluidity of shifts in time; the actors must not
"hold" for these shifts; the design should not be literal; and the characters are usually
kept on stage throughout the performance (v–vii). As the play opens, the stage is dark
and we hear the murmuring of voices. As the lights come up, we distinguish Ev, the old
man sitting beside a trunk with an unopened letter in his hand; then others appear in the
light—Bob (Ev's wife, Eloise, who calls herself Bob), Oscar (Ev's friend, a fellow physician
and a loyal supporter of Bob's)—as the sounds of young Katie's skipping and singing
gain in clarity and volume. Catherine enters with her overnight bag and immediately
joins in with Katie, her childhood self. At this early point in the play, it seems as if the old
Ev is the rememberer who is conjuring up his wife, friend, and young daughter as he sits
by the trunk holding his unopened letter. He even seems to have called up his grown
daughter, who, as soon as he acknowledges her arrival, will begin to challenge him in the
present to answer her questions about the past.

They are a lot alike, this father and daughter, so their relationship is fraught with
accusation, guilt for the past, and an inability to communicate or demonstrate the love
they feel for one another; they are both workaholics who have to win, unlike the dead
wife and mother who was an alcoholic and a suicide, and thus, in Catherine's eyes, a
loser. Possibly because of these similarities, they share not only their unexpressed grief
but also feelings of considerable guilt for the fate of Bob, who, as she increasingly
dominates the remembered past that constitutes so much of this play, pleads for
understanding, appreciation, and attention from her husband and child. As the past is
re-enacted, we watch Ev refuse to acknowledge either Bob's need for his attention and
love or her desire to work at her profession of nursing, and we observe young Katie as

she grows to loathe and reject this mother who is always drunk, always firing the maids, always spending time with Oscar, and always—as Katie sees it—having excuses made for her behaviour. One of the worst confrontations of this memory narrative occurs when Katie strikes Bob, knocking her to the floor, and the child repeatedly rejects any suggestion that she is like her mother—or like the grandmother who killed herself—thereby denying a large part of her own identity along with any ability to love this mother who embarrasses and neglects her.

The structure of *Doc* is complex and subtle. It requires consummate acting and set design because at no time should we feel the temporal gears grinding as the action glides smoothly between now and then, between Catherine's return to visit her elderly father and the painful scenes from the past. Moreover, this past is much more than one moment, and the many moments that are remembered and enacted do not recur chronologically or in a neat linear progression. Memory and emotion do not work in such a straightforward manner. Instead the characters move by stages into the very core of their pain until they reveal not only the causes of Bob's suffering, which in turn so traumatizes her daughter, but also the consequences of living in such an abusive context. But if there is no tidy temporal progression to the memories, there is a development in this play as Katie and Catherine gradually meet and merge. Through reliving the past and remembering her younger self, the adult woman learns many things: most importantly, she learns to forgive herself for hating her mother and, in a key passage, she accepts the crucial truth that she is very much like her mother and her grandmother:

> KATIE: I wonder ... do you know what I wonder? I wonder, did she take the pills to sleep like she sometimes does, or did she ...
>
> CATHERINE: It was
>
> KATIE: An accident? ... Sometimes I look ...
>
> CATHERINE: ... in the mirror, I look in the mirror ...
>
> KATIE: ... and I see Mummy and I see ...
>
> CATHERINE: ... Gramma, and Mummy and me ...
>
> KATIE: ... I don't want to be like them. (108)

And in some ways, of course, Katie/Catherine is not "like them"; she is a survivor. But in this scene, it is the similarities that are significant. When Catherine recognizes her maternal lineage in the mirror, the split between child and adult is healed, and this unification of multiple selves is acknowledged in a poignant moment before the memory play's end when Katie, refusing to cry over her mother's terrible death and suspecting she was an unwanted child, turns to Catherine, who tells her(self), "You can cry, Katie, it's all right to cry" (121). To consolidate the acceptance, understanding, and self-forgiveness that have been won through the ordeal of memory, Katie asks, "Would you want to have me?" and Catherine answers immediately, "Yes, yes I would" (121).

There are other lessons learned in the course of *Doc* and other acts of forgiveness that must be undertaken before Ev and Catherine can carry on. In the closing moments of the play, back in the present, Ev continues to hold the unopened letter from his mother, the letter that Bob insists will explain his role in his mother's suicide. Catherine, who takes the letter from her father, asks him if she should open it, and then she strikes a match as if to burn it. But he tells her that he knows what it says and says she can go ahead and burn the letter. Together, this is exactly what they do. Clearly, these two have reached a degree of mutual forgiveness and understanding, possibly even of complicity. On the one hand, it seems that Catherine and Ev are agreeing to reject the past represented by this letter and that Catherine, in particular, is siding with her father against her maternal ancestors. However, I have come to feel that this rapprochement between father and daughter is finally possible because they have faced the worst ghosts from their shared past, allowed those ghosts to speak, to accuse, to plead, to judge, and, as the survivors in the present, they are able to accept what they cannot change and to assuage their guilt for the past. This, at least, is how I see Catherine, who strikes me as learning far more than Ev does through what amounts to her dialogue with the dead. Not only has she come back to face her living father and the past (an act of considerable courage), she has given centre stage in the memory play to the lost, tragic figure of Bob, and she has remembered that mother with a passion and a compassion that belies Katie's frustration and anger. Where the child thought she hated, the adult woman realizes that she feels great pity for a beautiful, talented, and ambitious woman who was trapped and crushed by patriarchal conventions. If she is not like this woman, it is because this woman showed her what it would cost to submit to a father's will.

But what has all this to do with Sharon Pollock's *life*? And how did this play start? The play itself began with an undated draft, probably from the early 1980s, called, even in its first iteration, *Doc*. But the story began with Pollock's birth in 1936, as Mary Sharon Chalmers, in Fredericton, New Brunswick, the first child in the marriage of Everett Chalmers, a charismatic physician, politician, and raconteur, and Eloise Roberts, a beautiful and gracious trained nurse, the only member of her large New Brunswick family to receive such an education. There were two children born to this couple, Sharon and her younger brother Peter, but the marriage was less than happy. To this day, Doc Chalmers is remembered in the small city of Fredericton as a controversial character—a dedicated and skilled medical doctor, a leading conservative politician, a drinker, a loud swearer, and an arrogant, self-assured, handsome man.[3] He was immensely admired by many and thoroughly disliked by others. Eloise Chalmers, who was known as Bob, apparently tried to be a proper doctor's wife according to the social codes of the day, but she was also deeply unfulfilled, frustrated, and never able (in fact, not allowed) to return to her own profession once her children were born. She became an alcoholic, was sent away to Montreal or New England on several occasions for treatment, attempted suicide more than once, and finally succeeded in killing herself in 1954 when Sharon was eighteen and Peter sixteen. Those who remember her speak of her with affection and sympathy. The Chalmers house itself was a large, gracious, white clapboard home on spacious grounds (it is still an impressive home) with room for a live-in maid, a back stairs connecting the kitchen area with the second floor, and a formal entrance and main staircase at the front. Despite the decorous façade, it would seem that most of Fredericton, a typical small town community, thought they knew what was going on inside the Chalmers home, and they had views about the rights and wrongs of those goings-on.

When Eloise died on 12 May 1954 after several days of acute suffering in hospital and less than a month after her daughter's eighteenth birthday, Pollock was away at a private school in Quebec. She was called home, and she has often commented in interviews that she was terribly embarrassed by the funeral and had little sympathy for her mother, despite Eloise's painful death from mercury-based poisoning.[4] In 1980, at about the time she was beginning to contemplate writing a play like *Doc*, she recalled disliking her mother intensely as someone who was in "full-blown, self-indulgent disintegration," but she also admitted that over time she had come to "understand [her] mother better" and to "see now what a difficult position she was in" (quoted in Hofsess 44, 48). Whether she blamed her mother or her father or both for the trauma of her childhood, she would never again settle permanently in Fredericton and she left the place as soon as she could. But there is no doubt that the place and the family shaped her, in part by forcing her to chart her own path and to make a success of her life. That she would decide to write forthrightly about her parents and the pain of growing up in that home roughly thirty years after the events portrayed illustrates the lasting impact that family past had on her subsequent life. When she finally began to tell her story, and that of her parents', she was already an accomplished playwright with the necessary experience and craft to transform autobiography and biography into art. Nevertheless, a glance at the early drafts of the play reveals a great deal about the process of transformation that the play underwent because Pollock began with a script that was far more specifically, narrowly personal than the final text we know and much less enriched by the ambiguity, nuance, and compassion of the polished play.

There are at least three drafts of *Doc* with the Sharon Pollock Papers at the University of Calgary, but the first of these has the most to tell us about where Pollock began and how far she would travel to create the play. In this typescript, the woman who returns to visit her elderly father is called "Sharon" and her younger self, aged fifteen, whose first name is "Mary" (ts 92A), is called "Sharnee," Pollock's actual childhood nickname. The younger brother, who does not appear in any version of the play, is called "Peter," but otherwise the characters' names will remain the same: Doc is Ev, Bob is Eloise, his wife, and the fellow doctor and family friend is Oscar. The play and memory play—for the doubled memory play structure is there from the beginning (although the role of the adult daughter is less developed)—take place in a "large" house with "gables, bay windows, oddly-shaped rooms" and an "exterior made of clapboard"(i).[5] The action is set in "the maid's room ... at the rear of the kitchen" (i), and, after a careful description of the layout of this house, these stage instructions specify that "the maid's room is a forgotten room in the house" where "no one enters" (ii). It is used for storage and contains a "number of items" that "belonged to one person" who "has been dead for a number of years" (ii). And then, as if to mitigate the realism of this description, Pollock comments, "[T]he room is a gateway to the past. This room explodes the clock and the calendar. Although I speak [and surely this "I" is none other than the playwright herself] of the reality of the house, I am not sure that this room is a real room" (ii).

At this stage, *Doc* is still a comparatively literal replaying of Sharon Chalmers's life and of the memories that haunt that gracious home on tree-lined, quiet Grey Street in Fredericton, where such tragedy took place in the 1950s. There most certainly was a maid's room near the kitchen, and the Chalmers family had a loyal housekeeper who was devoted to Eloise Roberts. It is also *true* (that is, a matter of factual description corroborated by others) that after Dr. Chalmers had remarried in 1956 many of Eloise's things remained in the house, although the bedroom where she was found after taking the poison was not used to store her personal effects. In short, Bob did remain present in that house long after her death. Moreover, the character Oscar is based on the man who was a close family friend and medical colleague of Pollock's father; what the playwright does not reveal (and as a child would not have grasped) is that this man was well known to be gay and, therefore, his devotion to Eloise was no threat to the Chalmers' marriage.

Even at this early draft stage, the letter device is already in place and it will be burned at the end; the memory play is there from the opening, and the adult Sharon will enter to interrupt her father's memories of his child's and wife's voices; and many of the key details in the final play occur in this draft, such as Sharnee's hatred of her mother, whom she will knock to the floor, or the photograph of Bob feeding a piglet from a baby's bottle (the actual photograph still exists), and, of course, Bob's death. The differences, however, are crucial, and they are far more extensive than mere name changes or cuts to the description of the house/set. Many aspects of the draft reveal how literally Pollock was drawing on her own life and memories and, thus, provide a benchmark for assessing the artistic transformation of the script. For example, at this stage, the structurally crucial memory play is both more linear and much more tied to Ev and Sharnee than to Sharon, who enters late in the first act and never achieves a real bond *through memory* with her Sharnee self or with Bob. Even more important, the ending is controlled by Sharon, and Ev seems less certain about whether or not to open his mother's letter. In the final play, Ev does not debate what may or may not be in the letter but simply states, "I know what's in it" (125), and he is holding the letter when he tells his daughter to "[b]urn the goddam thing" (126). In the draft, Sharon has the letter and sets fire to it before the pair leave the room together. At this early stage there is less complicity between the two—or less sense of complex sharing and forgiveness—and Doc, though still a powerful presence, seems less dominant, and hence less of a threat. But above all, much less understanding is achieved by the adult daughter, who plays a relatively minor and more mechanical role than the later Catherine will.

III

In the first draft of *Doc*, Sharnee is a brat for whom it is difficult to feel much sympathy: she hates everyone—Bob, Peter, Oscar, God—except her father; she is especially nasty to Bob and believes there is a simple "truth" about her mother. When her father explains that Bob is "sick," she retorts, "Tell Peter that. He wants to believe that. I want *the* truth" (ts 10, emphasis added). Katie will want the same thing, of course, but in the final play we see much more of Catherine and more of Katie *through* Catherine. The result is a more complex, multifaceted set of truths and a greater compassion for the child and the mother. What began as a desperate rejection of everything associated with the mother changes into an acceptance of the mother's crucial role—for good and bad—in the adult woman's life, and Pollock even goes so far as to suggest that young Katie has herself attempted suicide, that she is so much like her mother that, in the rhetoric of this household, she too is "accident-prone" (58). In the context of the play, the factual truth of this attempt is beside the point; we do not need to know whether or not the young Mary Sharon Chalmers really tried to slit her wrists to be able to appreciate her creation of a child's confusion, grief, and self-hating rage.

On this subject of truth, an autobiographical play confronts the same challenges as do all forms of autobiography and biography. The facts, while important, are never enough, and they are rarely clear-cut. Truth is always ambiguous, fractured and dispersed across the perspectives of all contributors to the life story, and no one's life story is ever only their own. By shifting our perspective away from the child and distributing the story more equally between the two rememberers (Ev and Catherine), by carefully complicating the interpretation of events, and by allowing a profound sympathy to emerge between Katie and Catherine and within Katie/Catherine for Bob, Pollock has put this interrelated set of life stories to work for herself and for us. She has also addressed other major questions that autobiographers and biographers must face. She has dramatized the process of memory to show us how fluid, unreliable, and yet important it is. In performance we can watch that process unfold, shift, and double back on itself and discover a mirror, in that dramatization, for our own memory plays. Moreover, she has demonstrated how we all rely on memory to know who we are, to realize how we can change (and be changed) because of the interrelatedness of lives, and to appreciate how those whose life stories inform ours might see *us* or feel about *our* acts.

Speaking of this play, Pollock has said that "it's taken as long as I've lived to confront my personal history, to embrace the many and complex feelings that examination generated, and *Doc* is the result" (1990, n.p.). The emphasis here, I feel, is on the word "embrace," and this is one of the main points on which *Doc* differs from Tremblay's *The Real World?* Although both plays address the key dilemma of ethics in life writing, Tremblay insists that it is his/Claude's right to tell the family story because it is his story too, and the play we see is the play his father burns in manuscript, thus giving the playwright the final word. Pollock reaches the same conclusion about her right to tell, but in her story there are as many winners as possible and no one gets the final word about the past. The truth of that unopened letter remains in the realm of conjecture, forever hidden, because it cannot be nailed down, asserted, even were it to be read. That letter, after all, was another written story, created from one perspective, and in Pollock's version of imagined autobiography everyone's story matters and they are all different. By deciding to burn that letter, the artist asks us to imagine what it says, to imagine what we might do in a similar position, and to understand why reading (or not reading) the letter does not matter. The factual truths of autobiography can be misleading; the truths of imagination and art can bring wisdom.

For *this* biographer, however, that letter has become something of an obsession. I confess that it haunted me many years ago when I saw my first production of *Doc* and that it has troubled me ever since. How, I have always wondered, could one *not* read such a letter, assuming it really did exist? Why would these people agree to burn it, assuming they really did? In my current role as Pollock's biographer (and as a former editor of Malcolm Lowry's *real* letters), that letter in *Doc* taunts, tantalizes, and tempts me. It *taunts* me because I doubt that I shall ever know absolutely whether or not it existed and, if it did, what it had to say. It *tantalizes* me because it is always possible that it did exist and still does somewhere: on the one hand, many boxes of Everett Chalmers's papers have survived (including letters) and they remain with the family; on the other hand, I have to admit, the letter (lost, found, read, unread) is a familiar narrative and theatrical device, used to great dramatic effect by generations of novelists, playwrights, and filmmakers. And it *tempts* me in a host of more or less ethical ways! If we are to believe Henry James (*The Aspern Papers*), A. S. Byatt (*Possession*), Tom Stoppard (*Arcadia*), or Carol Shields (*Swann*), biographers are easily tempted by letters and will commit any number of sins, venial and deadly, to lay their hands on such documents. But, of course, it is not the letter itself that tempts me or even the *idea* of the letter: Sharon Pollock is the tempter—Pollock the mature and canny artist, and Sharon Chalmers, the girl growing up on that Fredericton street, with that troubled family, in that gracious (yet haunted) house. It is Sharon Pollock who puts the question: did her paternal grandmother, Mary Branch Chalmers (for whom *Mary* Sharon Chalmers was named), commit suicide by walking out on the old railway bridge to meet the local train on 5 August 1940? All the newspapers tell me is that her death, falling from the bridge that to this day spans the Saint John River, was an "accidental drowning." If she did kill herself, and some people believe emphatically that she did, was her son Everett in some way to blame, and if she did choose to end her life in such a violent manner at the age of sixty (scarcely an *old* age even in 1940), can her reasons (if known) provide some form of warning or lesson for other women in the family, especially for the young granddaughter called Mary whose own mother would also take her life? It is not, finally, the letter that is so important. It is what that letter might, or might not, confirm about the grandmother's death that is potentially significant for Pollock's biography (or, at least, for my growing conception of the life story).

Surely this is one of those classic dilemmas faced by all biographers, and autobiographers for that matter, because by signing the auto/biographical pact we hope to gain insight into the meanings and motivations of our lives. We want to believe that some event, some moment, some *thing* (very possibly a letter, given how much faith we place in the written word) will reveal all. But if I listen carefully to *Doc* (that is, to Pollock's art) instead of to Pollock herself (or to others I have interviewed), I will be cautious about trusting any documentary temptations. That letter, real or apocryphal, is after all only a letter, one more version in the always receding, proliferating, accumulating process of living and (to borrow Paul John Eakin's phrase) of turning our lives into stories. If I can accept that process, which Pollock accepts and stages, and put my trust in the truth of art, then my dilemma will be a delicious one and my challenge will be not to nail down the facts (did she or didn't she, to paraphrase that provocative line in Pollock's *Blood Relations*), but to capture the dilemma itself in all its complexities, nuances, and shifts, faithfully, for you.

Notes

1. I have discussed this phenomenon in my introduction to a new collection of long monologues by Canadian women playwrights, *A Voice of Her Own*, and I have probed the theory informing autobiographical plays in "Performing the Auto/biographical Pact."

2. Tremblay's *Le vrai monde?* (translated as *The Real World?*), premiered in 1987 at Montreal's Théâtre du Rideau Vert; its first production in English was at the Tarragon Theatre in Toronto in 1988 under the direction of Bill Glassco. *Doc* premiered at Theatre Calgary in April 1984, under the direction of Guy Sprung, with Pollock's youngest daughter, Amanda Pollock, as Katie. The play then underwent extensive rewriting for its September 1984 production at Toronto Free Theatre, again under Sprung's direction. It was published by Playwrights Canada Press in 1984, the year it won the Governor General's Award for Drama. All my references are to this publication. *Doc* has received numerous productions. Among the most important are its November 1984 production at the National Arts Centre directed by Guy Sprung with sets by Terry Gunvordahl, starring Clare Coulter as Catherine, Michael Hogan as Ev, and Kate Trotter as Bob, and its March 1986 production for Theatre New Brunswick, directed by Pollock, under the title "Family Trappings." Everett Chalmers attended this home-town production (and other productions), and despite the name change it was obvious to all who attended that the play was about him and his family. Reactions from the Fredericton audience were mixed on the choice of subject: some people with whom I have spoken were appalled at a daughter's portrait of her father and family; others believed the portrait to be both accurate and acceptable. Every Frederictonian I have interviewed was profoundly moved by the play. The play was translated into French by Francine Pominville and performed by Québec City's Théâtre de la Commune in February 1988, under the direction of Denise Gagnon. This production postdates Tremblay's *The Real World?* but he could well have seen *Doc* in Toronto or Ottawa while he was working on his play.

3. My observations on Pollock's family are drawn from interviews with Pollock, her family, and Fredericton acquaintances. There are many more specific parallels between the play and the real lives of individuals than I can discuss here, but this wider context will be fully explored in my biography of Pollock, *Making Theatre: A Life of Sharon Pollock*.

4. Stories vary about what poison Eloise Chalmers took, but her death certificate notes toxemia and kidney failure as contributing causes. It is generally believed that she ingested some form of household poison, possibly a type of silver polish, consumed in a sandwich. She was found in her bedroom and rushed to hospital, but she could not be saved; she lingered in great pain for three days. Her husband was profoundly distressed and her son devastated by the loss, but Sharon Pollock's reaction seems to have been internalized and complicated in ways that would take another thirty years to work through.

5. All quotations from unpublished material are from the typescript (54.6.4) of *Doc* marked, in Pollock's hand, as "first draft" and held in the Pollock Collection housed in Special Collections at the University of Calgary. This is a 185-page typescript of the complete play.

Works Cited

Belliveau, George. "Daddy on Trial: Sharon Pollock's New Brunswick Plays." *Theatre Research in Canada* 22, no. 2 (2001): 161–72.

Bessai, Diane. "Sharon Pollock's Women: A Study in Dramatic Process." In *A Mazing Space*, ed. Shirley Neuman and Smaro Kamboureli. Edmonton: NeWest Press, 1986. 126–36.

Czarnecki, Mark. "Ghosts in a Family Attic." *Maclean's* 97 (23 April 1984): 52.

Eakin, Paul John. *How Our Lives Become Stories: Making Selves*. Ithaca: Cornell University Press, 1999.

Gottfried, Martin. *Arthur Miller: His Life and Art*. Cambridge, Mass.: Da Capo, 2003.

Grace, Sherrill. "Voicing Women's Experience: An Introduction." In *Voice of Her Own: Long Monologues by Kirsten Thomson, Linda Carson, Lorena Gale, Linda Griffiths, and Sharon Pollock*, ed. Sherrill Grace and Angela Rebeiro. Toronto: Playwrights Canada, 2004. iii–viii.

———. "Performing the Auto/biographical Pact: Towards a Theory of Identity and Performance." In *Tracing the Autobiographical*, ed. Marlene Kadar, Linda Warley, Jeanne Perreault, and Susanna Egan. Waterloo: Wilfrid Laurier University Press, 2005. 65–79.

Heinze, Michael and Elke Müller-Schneck, eds. *Canadian, Literary and Didactic Mosaic: Essays in Honour of Albert-Reiner Glaap*. Trier: WVT, 2004.

Hofsess, John. "Families." *Homemaker's Magazine* 15, no. 2 (1980): 41–60.

Kerr, Rosalind. "Borderline Crossings in Sharon Pollock's Out-Law Genres: *Blood Relations* and *Doc*." *Theatre Research in Canada* 17, no. 2 (1996): 200–15.

Knowles, Richard Paul. "Sharon Pollock: Personal Frictions." *Atlantic Provinces Book Review* 14 (February–March 1987): 19.

Macpherson, Margaret. "Family's dark secrets on stage." *SEE Magazine* (Edmonton), 11–17 November, 1999, 27.

Pollock, Sharon. *Walsh*. Vancouver: Talonbooks, 1973.

———. *Doc*. Unpublished typescript, first draft (n.d.). Sharon Pollock Papers (54.3.26). University of Calgary, Alberta.

———. *Doc*. Toronto: Playwrights Canada, 1984a.

———. "Playwright's Notes." Program, *Doc*, National Arts Centre, Ottawa, Ont., November 1984b.

———. "The Playwright." Program, *Doc*, The Vancouver Playhouse, Vancouver, B.C., March 1990.

———. *Blood Relations and Other Plays*. Edmonton: NeWest Press, 2002. Includes: *One Tiger to a Hill, Generations*.

———. *Sharon Pollock: Three Plays*. Toronto: Playwrights Canada, 2003. Includes: *Moving Pictures, End Dream, Angel's Trumpet*.

Tremblay, Michel. *The Real World?* Trans. John Van Burek and Bill Glassco. Vancouver: Talonbooks, 1988.

Wasserman, Jerry. "Drama." *University of Toronto Quarterly* 57, no. 1 (1987): 62–74.

———. "Daddy's Girls: Father-Daughter Incest and Canadian Plays by Women." *Essays in Theatre* 14, no. 1 (1995): 25–36.

PART FOUR

Creating AutoBiography on Stage

Writing and Performing Lives: Ten Playwrights Speak

Jerry Wasserman

Academic work on theatre always gets most exciting when the traditional gaps between theory and practice, classroom and stage are bridged. At the "Putting a Life on Stage" workshop in February 2004 that launched the compilation of this book, the buzz was usually loudest when the eight playwrights in attendance—most of whom are also actors who have performed their auto/biographical subjects as well as written them—were discussing or reading their own work, or responding directly to the academic papers. They read and spoke in various combinations on panels ranging from "Reading and Performing the Female Artist" to "Community and AutoBiography," with Sharon Pollock additionally discussing her auto/biographical writings in a keynote address. By the end of the weekend it had become clear that these dramatists could talk about their A/B work with elegance, rigour, and intelligence; that there were wide variations and many commonalities in their approaches; and that it might be most valuable for this book to attempt to capture their insights in a semi-systematic fashion. Invitees Guillermo Verdecchia and Tomson Highway, unable to attend the workshop, graciously agreed to be included in the subsequent email exchanges that resulted in the virtual roundtable below.

Following the workshop (with the exception of Pollock, whose keynote address is reproduced here), I asked each of the playwrights six basic questions about their work:

1) What is your process for writing these plays? For example, do you begin with monologues? Do you do any kind of research?

2) How, if at all, does writing about "real" people differ for you from playwriting about fictitious characters?

3) How, if at all, do you draw on your actor's processes in the creation of A/B characters?

4) How much of yourself goes into these characters? How does performing a character yourself affect your writing of him or her?

5) How does your sense of audience factor into the creation of these plays?

6) How much obligation, if any, do you feel to recreate the "truth" of the original character or story? Do you believe there is such a thing as historical truth? What, if any, are the ethical issues?

Sometimes I asked variations depending on the circumstances. For instance, Tomson Highway does not perform his own characters in *The Rez Sisters*, *Dry Lips Oughta Move to Kapuskasing*, or subsequent plays, so I omitted that question. For Highway, Andrew Moodie, and Marie Clements, many of whose plays are biographies of a community to which they themselves belong, I asked in question 2 whether any of their characters were based on real people that their audience might recognize, and for Moodie and Clements whether it mattered that the plays were set explicitly in the cities in which they live (Toronto and Vancouver). I also asked Highway why, given that his novel *Kiss of the Fur Queen* is explicitly autobiographical, his plays were not. For eight of the playwrights these exchanges took place via email. Only Joy Coghill, at her request, spoke to me in person. Our discussion was a little more extensive and wide-ranging but the questions were essentially the same.

Little was systematic and nothing scientific about the choice of playwrights we invited to participate. All ten are Canadian, write in English, and have created notable work with auto/biographical subject matter. Geographically, Toronto and Vancouver are heavily over-represented. Lorena Gale is originally from Montreal, and both her explicitly autobiographical play, *Je me souviens*, and her historically based *Angélique* concern her home province. But otherwise Quebec has been neglected. The Maritimes are represented only as Sharon Pollock's birthplace (and the setting of her play *Doc*), though Pollock has lived in Calgary most of her life and considers herself Albertan. Ethnically, they are a fairly diverse group with two First Nations writers, two African-Canadians, an Argentinian-Canadian and five Anglo-Canadians. All are well-established in their field. The first plays by Pollock and Linda Griffiths date from the 1970s. The others began writing in the 1980s or 1990s. All have performed professionally, Coghill since the 1940s, Pollock since the 1960s. Most have also directed and many have run theatre companies. All are thoughtful and articulate.

Each writer's statement reveals a distinctive process and a unique voice but some common denominators quickly become apparent. One is the primary importance of narrative and storytelling, superceding any simple notion of the playwright as auto/biographer. "It is impossible to write or portray a Life. It can only be lived," says Pollock. "However, we can and do see external bits and bites of a life critically, as a story." Andrew Moodie says, "If you want history, turn to the historian. If you want a story ... turn to the playwright." Verdecchia talks of realizing "that my autobiography was simply a metaphor, a narrative ... " R. H. Thomson is even more succinct: "We are only the story that we tell." These sentiments are shared by Coghill and Gale, too, even as they insist that "all writing is autobiographical." The subject provides the auto/biographical raw material; the playwright transforms it into narrative art.

But that doesn't mean the process lacks rigour. Sally Clark, Gale, Coghill, Thomson, and Verdecchia all insist on their extensive, detailed, sometimes exhaustive research. "You suck in everything that you can about the person," says Griffiths, "you stuff yourself like a prize goose." Not surprisingly, the writers who are also actors frequently describe in visceral terms the process of internalizing or coming to inhabit their subject. "On a blood level the street research was already in me," Marie Clements says of her preparation for writing *The Unnatural and Accidental Women*. As a child, she knew the Skid Row streets walked by the murdered women whom she memorializes in her play. She "understood on a profound level" how little separated her from them. Tomson Highway is virtually alone in denying that he does any research at all: "fact does not interest me near as much as fantasy." Yet even he acknowledges beginning with real people he knows intimately, such as his mother and aunts in the case of *The Rez Sisters*, then embroidering them "until they are absolutely ridiculous, or mythical, in proportion."

One of the richest, most complex topics mined in these statements involves the nexus where auto/biographical subject, writer, and actor overlap. The literal physicality and embodiment involved in the process of creating and portraying these characters introduces a dimension of performativity lacking in other kinds of auto/biographical writing. Griffiths quotes director Paul Thompson as saying, "There are some things the actor knows that the writer doesn't." In that sense an actor/writer like Griffiths has an advantage over non-actors: "When I feel the writing is getting dead, or too 'writerly,' as opposed to coming from the gut, that's when I go into a room, get someone to watch, and start talking/improvising." Similarly, Thomson describes how, in performing *The Lost Boys*, he transcended the script he had written, which transcribed the letters of his uncles who had fought in the Great War: "I sensed that by speaking their words night after night we shared intimacies that lay beyond their words. There can be a cadence to language that only an actor comprehends. They are now my brothers." Yet for some, the writing and acting selves may pull in different directions. Coghill describes a point when the writer and researcher in her has to move aside for the performer: "when you must shed all your responsibilities and terrors, all the talk and opinion, and commit yourself to the moment ... it is only you and that audience creating theatre." Gale's internal actor is unsparingly critical of her playwriting self: "If I let my actor take over, I could never write."

The question of ethics, truth, and responsibility elicits perhaps the most interesting and diverse responses. All these artists feel a strong responsibility: some to their biographical subjects—"the responsibility I feel to the people I have shared a room with," in Clements's words—some to "the truth" or "the integrity of the work," to "art" or "the theatre." But these categories are slippery; they blur and frequently overlap. Pollock and Griffiths call their work "theft," then justify it. Gale doesn't see "any ethical issues at all" because "[a]ll is fair fodder for the creative mill." Moodie agrees that "the only responsibility an artist has is to create a work of art. Period." Verdecchia insists on the importance of acknowledging "historical truth" yet feels no obligation to its "literal, 'surface' details." But in the end, I think, all would agree with Clements that some kind of ultimate accounting comes into play, some kind of karma, "because in the end you are made accountable personally, ethically, artistically, and professionally. You know what it cost them, and what it cost you, and after all that you better be able to stand."

The statements that appear below are the playwrights' own words, edited by me for clarity and sometimes brevity, but without changing their meaning or intention. A bibliography of the primary playtexts cited in the statements is appended at the end of this section. Brief biographies of the playwrights are included, with those of the other contributors, at the end of this book.

Playwright: Parasite or Symbiont

Sharon Pollock

Whenever I sit down to draw my thoughts together for an address like this, or something similar, an image comes to me. It's from *The Exorcist*. The priest is sitting by the bedside of the physically transformed and possessed child. The priest asks, "Who are you?" A deep frightening voice answers, "I am legion."

Well, I am legion. I am many competing thoughts and voices, and No Theories. One of my thoughts is that I may have imagined this scene from *The Exorcist*, combining something I saw with something I read with something I dreamt. It doesn't matter.

I am legion. My head is full of voices. I open my mouth and speak. Before the sentence, phrase, or word is out, internally I'm hearing three or four conflicting statements: "That can't be right"; "True today, what about tomorrow?"; "What a load of crap." And "Oh, shut up!" I don't know if everyone carries within them this simultaneous broadcast. It's not something I miss knowing.

Those multitudinous voices are not characters demanding I spew them on a page. I'm just engaged in an internal and eternal questioning of *what is*, *what isn't*, and *why* in the increasingly complex world around me and within me. I know it's impossible to find out *what is*, *what isn't*, and *why* but that in no way diminishes my desire or need to continue the search, which is not confined to my life in the theatre. The voices within do motivate my work in the theatre, although they don't appear in my plays. They are silent when I sit down to write. They are useful critics of the work once words are on the page or realized in performance.

In this dialogue with myself, and in conversation with you, I'm trying to figure some things out, although tomorrow I may disagree with this morning's conclusions.

When I consider what I do, I wonder about my relationship, if any, with those historical individuals who often provide the catalyst for a play, and whose lives I mine in writing the play. There's a fair number: Major James Walsh in *Walsh*; Hopkinson in *The Komagata Maru Incident*; Lizzie Borden in *Blood Relations*; Mr. Big of *Whiskey Six Cadenza*; Prince Albert Victor ("Eddy") in *Saucy Jack*; Janet Smith in *End Dream*; Nell Shipman in *Moving Pictures*; Scott and Zelda Fitzgerald in *Angel's Trumpet*; Sarah Moore Grimpke in *The Making of Warriors*; Mary Steinhauser and Andy Bruce from the BC penitentiary mutate

Figure 24. Sharon Pollock as Shipman from the opening scene of her 1999 play *Moving Pictures*, directed by Heather Inglis at the Timms Centre for the Performing Arts, Edmonton, 2004. Photograph by Ed Ellis.

into Dede Walker and Tommy Paul in *One Tiger to a Hill*. And my son-in-law's family seeded the Nurlins in *Generations*.

Is my relationship of an intimate and respectful nature, mutually beneficial, as in my creating a viable stage play while at the same time offering for public consumption a historical figure in as objective and compelling a dramatization as possible?

Or do I simply pry from the life what is of value to me and consign the rest to the slagheap?

The former would dictate adherence to factual evidence; the latter makes no such demands. The former appears symbiotic to me; the latter, let's face it, seems exploitive and parasitical. In my opinion, the former would lead to the creation of biography, the latter wouldn't.

I think of biography as an attempt to capture the essence of a life and personality and to place it in context in as interesting a way as possible, after learning as much as possible about the subject through reading, research, and interviews. One would not invent characters interacting with the subject or create situations, conflicts, or gatherings for which there was no factual evidence. The biographer's analysis of the life would not depend on such invention, and any conjecture about the life would be supported by an explanation of the reasoning behind it.

If I had a desire to create biography it would imply my acceptance of my role as the means whereby the life story of another would be told as honestly and truthfully as possible and any subjective roots of my analysis of the life would be acknowledged in some way.

It's possible I may find out over the next several days that this is not biography. However, that's how I think of it today.

It is impossible to write or portray a Life. It can only be lived: this happens ... and then that happens ... and then what comes after ... happens. An audio tape running or a camera recording a master shot every moment from birth—a beginning, if that's what it is—to death and the end, if that's what it is, could only record the external. All the spoken words made concrete on a page, apart from creating a very large volume and necessitating the death of many trees, would not be the Life.

However, we can and do see external bits and bites of a life critically, as a story. We see the drama inherent in them. We can be moved to make something from them. But in the creation of anything from something (or nothing), criteria emerge that govern choice and reflect the nature of the creator as well as certain principles of form or structure relating to the object being created: *this belongs, this doesn't; this is better here than there; I don't know why but this is right and that is not.* Thus, in attempting to encapsulate, capture, document, or display in some way the essence of the life through portions of the life as recalled or recorded, selected material from the life is molded to fit the aesthetics of the container, be it literary non-fiction, documentary film, a poem, or a play. That molding will also reflect to varying degrees the subjectivity of the creator.

Biography founded on that symbiotic relationship I described is not well served by the container of theatre. Time and space, the play script, the performance, the production elements, and multiple layers of interpretation transform biography into an ephemeral performance subject to further change with the vagaries of casting, a new director, or a bad house. While dramatized historical figures and events on stage may engender strong impressions of authenticity among audiences, this only speaks of the potency of live performance, not of biographical or historical reliability.

It has never been my intention to create biography, docudrama, or documentary in putting a life on stage. I think of biography as an aspect of my research, a means to some other end in which the life and times provide bits or chunks of raw material.

I can reveal James Kenneth Stephen as a murderer, have William Hopkinson embrace the Sikh religion at the moment of his death, turn Walsh into a drunk in the Yukon. Historically, none of this is true. I can have people meet that never met and people die that never lived. I can compress time, manipulate facts, attribute motivations, and create dramatic action for which there is no biographical evidence. And I do.

I could say the plays are more truthful to the meaning of these lives than biography could ever be. That might or might not be true.

I will say that I am attracted to those lives that resonate, sometimes in unlikely or surprising ways, with mine. I sense in certain aspects of their lives and times a lens through which to see more clearly significant issues of my life and times. Focussing that lens involves creation, imagination, and invention.

I am no more comfortable with autobiography in my work than I am with biography. My feelings about *Doc* illustrate why.

I can't deny that the play draws heavily on my personal history. It manipulates certain landmark events in my mother's and father's lives, omits some, and invents others. I don't bother changing anyone's name, except for the two characters who, it is assumed, play versions of me. I gave them the name of the play's first director's child, Catherine and Katie.

No one was more surprised than I was when "autobiographical" came up, or when the media asked how my father would react to seeing himself on stage. I hadn't given it a moment's thought. I didn't think he was going to appear on stage. While watching one production, I wondered why the actor playing Catherine wore glasses like mine, dressed as I often was, and sported my hairstyle. "That's not Catherine," I thought. "That's an imitation of me."

I found it odd and interesting that in later years my father, whose mind and memory were razor sharp, spoke of events in the play as if they had actually happened, when in fact I knew they had not. Our family life became what I had written and not what he had lived.

This did not convince me that I had written autobiography; it convinced me of the power of theatre.

Bob, Ev, and Oscar are not imitations or illustrations of real people who bear the same names and lived through a version of some of the events in the play. None of the characters are theatrical clones of Bob, Ev, Oscar, or Sharon. They are creations, not tracings, and they are created for a purpose. When the playwright (who I acknowledge is me) mixes together those characters, dialogue, story, structure, content, and form, she has created a recipe for performance. The separate ingredients cannot be isolated or identified with anything other than that for which they were created, which is the play that has its own imperative. The play is like a cake made up of eggs, butter, flour, a bit of vanilla. Show me any of these once the cake is baked. You may draw assumptions about the real-life people as easily as you may draw the egg in its shell from out of the cake.

Doc is baked.

In mining my personal history, in putting the lives of the created characters Ev, Bob, Catherine, and Oscar on stage, I searched myself and the real people for pieces of our lives that served the play. You could say I was looking for human generalities made specific. I did not intend to share any part of my family history or to introduce my mother, father, and Uncle Oscar to an audience.

But then again, I don't believe the playwright's intention matters. If all that is realized in the creation of a play is the playwright's conscious intention, the play is pretty thin. I'm not sure if you can have an unconscious intention but actually it may be the most important thing you can achieve in the play—your unconscious intentions.

Subconscious intention, well, it might have been my subconscious intention to write an autobiographical work for the stage. It might have been necessary for me to think of it as other than that in order to write it. But even supposing that were so, I believe the transformative nature of theatre makes it an impossible place to create biography or autobiography.

There is that shadow of autobiography. I believe playwrights do reveal, encode, and embed aspects of themselves, whether they intend to or not, in the lives they put on stage. But surely there is a yardstick for embedding which determines the validity of its interpretation as autobiography as opposed to being defined as simply style, as in a *Griffiths play*; a *Murrell play*. You could ask whose life is it anyway, the historical figure's, the character's, or the playwright's? I believe the only life on stage is that of the play. Any other life is merely a component or aspect of that one vital, multi-layered entity, the play in performance.

I confess I don't like the thought of aspects of my life submerged or emerging in my plays. Even when that autobiographical smudge contributes something to the play, I feel as if the playwright should have asked me. (You see I differentiate between "the playwright" and "me.") That makes me wonder what would happen were I to bump into Major Walsh, Scott Fitzgerald, or Janet Smith on the street. Fortunately they're dead, but is there an ethical dimension to my cutting and pasting their lives to make a better dramatic point or play? I believe acknowledging and not pussyfooting around my theft and manipulation of their lives meets my ethical obligation to them. My primary ethical obligation (if one can prioritize ethics) is to the integrity of the work.

I realize a psychological profile emerges. It's clear I have a problem with authority, with conforming to society's, often to my family's, and on occasion to my profession's expectations. It's true my characters are similarly afflicted. It may be my interest in self, my need to find a rational explanation for my own actions, that triggers this thematic strain in characters and plot. They mirror parts of me. But I'm reluctant to believe that this possible evidence of a subconscious desire to make sense of myself constitutes autobiography. I prefer to think of it as nothing more than motivating my initial interest and attraction to certain historical figures and events.

But that legion of voices challenges my reluctance. I'm forced to note the playwright's (or my) avoidance of principal female characters in the early work. Lizzie is the first full-blown woman. It wasn't that I chose not to write women in principal roles. It was that I could not. I'm a great believer in not judging my characters' actions or motivations. The audience will do that. I could not write women until I could move beyond judging myself and other women. And it was necessary for me to come to a place in my life where I could see myself and my female characters as action figures—active in their world which overlays or underlies the male's world.

As well I must confront *Getting It Straight*. I know that Eme, spelled E-M-E, the only character in that particular play, is ME when spoken. I know that that play is far more autobiographical than *Doc*. Eme is me and I think I knew it as I was writing it.

As well I note that in my work male characters are revealed and developed in action and interaction with others, while the female characters often are revealed and developed in action or interaction with themselves. Helen/Nell/Shipman; Miss Lizzie/Actress; Eme with her crowded inner world; Catherine/Katie. I must begin to consider whether the female playwright, me, is revealing and developing her own character by her interaction with herself, her plays being that self. I can't tell you how much I hate that idea.

Another thing that disturbs me greatly—I generally hate plays about art or artists or any characters that work in ad agencies, art galleries, publishing houses, or theatres. But then what do I do? I write a play about Nell Shipman, actress, director, and producer of silent films in *Moving Pictures*. As if that isn't bad enough I continue on to write *Angel's Trumpet* about Scott and Zelda Fitzgerald. In *Doc* I at least concealed in Ev my questioning of the ultimate value of what I do. I don't know who might have noticed the character's lines at or near the end of the play when he attempts to weigh the lives he has saved against the loss of one life. He demands of Oscar, "Was it worth it? You tell me! Was it worth it?" Oscar doesn't answer. And yesterday, in Linda Griffiths's wonderful reading of a scene from *Moving Pictures*, Shipman asks Nell, "Was it worth it?" *Doc* leaves the question hanging. *Moving Pictures* attempts to answer that question, even if the answer is that the question is irrelevant. One has no choice. The work is something that must be done.

But the closer the work comes to me and the more clearly it is self-reflective, the more I suspect the worth of doing it.

I read some place that I had "matured" or was "a mature playwright." That made me think of the decay and rot that quickly follows *mature* in the life of the banana. And someone once said something along the lines of "decadence triumphs when it is promoted as an agent of progress." These words resonate for me in a political and societal sense, as well as in relation to the plays I create.

All of this brings me to a certain conclusion. I've determined that I am a parasite. The more autobiography emerges in the work and the more biography is manipulated in text, the more parasitical I am revealed to be. I try not to think of that as a value judgment. Although my relationship to historical figures and my use of them is parasitical, I still believe the relationship of my work to the society to which I offer it is symbiotic.

I Am a Thief ... Not Necessarily Honourable Either

Linda Griffiths

I've never written a biographical play. *The Duchess* was once listed as a "bio play" and I was insulted. The real people are springboards into an intersection between reality and the imagination. Maybe there's no such thing as a biography, even in book form. The good ones always involve a transgression, a crossing of the line, conjecture on the mystery of the person's life. I don't know how to describe what I do. All I know is that I have written more plays inspired by real people than any other Canadian playwright, so something must be going on. The plays inspired by (admittedly) real people are *Maggie & Pierre, Jessica, The Duchess*, and *Alien Creature: A Visitation from Gwendolyn MacEwen*. Other kinds of plays are *O.D. on Paradise, The Darling Family, A Game of Inches, Brother Andre's Heart*, and *Chronic*.

You suck in everything you can about the person, you stuff yourself like a prize goose. The limit is how much time, money, how long you can wait. You talk to people, you read, you ingest. Talking to people is hard. You have to call them up, you have to make human contact. Sometimes they have nothing to say you can use, but maybe you've gotten a whiff of them, a bit of cellular detritus—something of that person is clinging to people they knew. As you're going, you're writing notes, little phrases, thoughts, bits and pieces. Contradiction: sometimes you just intuitively *know*, and need to do less research than at other times. Then comes the expiration. It's like a purge. By that time you and the person have merged, your adolescence twisted through Margaret Trudeau's, your relationship to ambition coming through Wallis Simpson, your need for a spiritual life merging with Maria Campbell's. Then there's synchronicity. An ex-lover of Gwendolyn MacEwen gets drunk and does an impression of MacEwen's mother at a party. Once you start fixating on the subject, synchronicities abound. *Jessica* was another weird twist, acting out the person it's (sort of) about, while they're in the same room. In that highly unusual case, with the "subject" in the room where the play is being created, you will always transgress. Whatever the subject thinks they have to give, it will always be more, it will always hurt. The person is always more than whatever you imagine at first. The real-life clues give you the opportunity to go deeper, if you dare. You also have to ingest the time they lived in, the world they created inside and outside themselves.

Figure 25. Linda Griffiths as Pierre Trudeau in *Maggie & Pierre* by Linda Griffiths with Paul Thompson, at the Royal Alexandra Theatre, Toronto, 1982. Photograph by James Gilmore, courtesy of Linda Griffiths.

For the real people plays, so far, I improvise and "paper-write" in combination. If you improvise, someone has to watch. When I'm improvising I think I mostly begin with monologues; but when you're working on your feet, it doesn't feel like "monologue," it feels like talking to someone or some thing. When I'm paper-writing, unless it's a one-person show, I begin with scenes to make sure the dynamic between characters is hot. *Maggie & Pierre* began with scenes between the characters. Whether you're at a computer or not, it helps to feel the person in your body, to imagine them deep inside you and to look at the world with their eyes.

When you're writing real people, you're always afraid. Maybe that's a good thing, maybe it raises the bar. If they're alive, or even if they're not, you're afraid of what they'll think, of what their friends and family will think—sometimes you're afraid of getting sued. The real person becomes your lie detector, and even though you may have fun at their expense, you're responsible to them. If I were to do a play about Hitler, I would be responsible to Hitler, even though I hate him. This relationship with the real person as judge isn't there with the fictitious characters, or rather, it becomes more real as the fictitious characters become more real. Ultimately, characters have to be three-dimensional, and the more flesh they have on them, the more you can feel them breathing over your shoulder. The advantage with real people is that they begin as flesh and blood. Because of my training as an actor with [Theatre Passe Muraille's] Paul Thompson (in collective creations), I find writing about real people expands, instead of limits, my imagination. Of course this involves transgression. The truth is, most writers base their characters on someone real. That's where you get the great line "they're a conglomerate." Of course, made-up characters can be as compelling as characters inspired by real people, and the joy of making up someone who transcends literal experience is very special. I hope I can say I've experienced both. I feel like the real people/made-up people question brings out the ambidextrous in me. I try to be able to use both hands to create.

Yet real life is extraordinary. So often writers say they deliberately didn't use much of a real person or real story, and I always think, "Why didn't you?"

Paul Thompson's collective creations get you outside of yourself and what you already know. You also make up things based on tiny clues: a conversation in a bar or in a field or in their house. Many writers do this, but to call that person their real name as opposed to a "conglomerate" is to bring it out in the open—and to create danger. How will that person or their friends or family, they themselves respond? When I can place a real character, even someone I meet on the street, in my body, then somehow things start to fly. I try to teach some of this in my Visceral Playwriting class.

I hate talking about process because my process is so complicated, and it's different for each play: I do a dance among "mostly," "sometimes," and "always." I don't always ultimately perform the parts/plays myself, but I mostly do at the beginning stages, like with *Jessica* and *O.D. on Paradise*. All this is changing as I write this. I wasn't in *Chronic*, I wasn't in *Brother Andre's Heart*, I won't be in *The Odd Women*. The actor is giving way to the writer because it's getting too hard to do both, or because the process is changing. So what I "always do" is always different.

My experience and training as an actor with Paul Thompson is fundamental to my process. I began as an actor, and I began writing by improvising—which is on-your-feet writing. Because Thompson's improv work involves using real models, my work began not as "biography" but as *imitation*. This process began because, at one time, there were no Canadian characters on any stage in this country, and so to find them we had to use real models. In *The Farm Show*, the people who were being imitated were called by their real names. It was part of the celebration that was going on—a self-celebration of the people of this land. This then evolved into using real people and then their stories in plays, as with *Maggie & Pierre*. Michael Healey's *The Drawer Boy* [based in part on *The Farm Show*] has an interesting take on the ethics of this. To some it's stealing, to others it's the creation of mythology. The idea of biography is a literary model. What we were doing in the collective creations was physically and vocally creating characters for the theatre. A visceral, not a literary process. I think this is why collective creations are so misunderstood in academic circles.

In terms of my work so far there's mostly been some improvising, sometimes a lot, like with *Alien Creature* (75 percent improvised), sometimes a little, like with *Chronic* (20 percent improvised), and sometimes there's none, like with *O.D. on Paradise* and *The Darling Family*. There's usually, but not always, a lengthy rewriting stage after the improv—many, many drafts to incorporate the on-your-feet work. For the play I'm working on now, *The Odd Women*, so far there's been no improvising. When I feel the writing is getting dead, or too writerly as opposed to coming from the gut, that's when I go into a room, get someone to watch, and start talking/improvising. Sometimes other people help me do that. *The Duchess* had a two-week improv session with Thompson directing and six actors, bless their hearts. *Jessica* also had an initial process like this. I was one of the actors. At a later stage of *Jessica*, I improvised all six of the characters that had been created with Thompson and Maria Campbell feeding in. I don't know anyone else who does this. It's cumbersome, this improvising. You need a space, people have to be paid, someone has to watch. It's just another version of the writer pacing up and down talking to themselves, except real acting is accessed and with it another kind of unconscious knowledge. Paul Thompson once said to me, "There are some things the actor knows that the writer doesn't." In one way I have an ordinary process: I sit down and write at a computer. But when the writer doesn't know something, sometimes the actor within me does. I mostly try to access both.

You're creating *Maggie & Pierre* and you know people hate Trudeau at that moment. You sort of do as well. When the relationship between the real people and the audience is hot, as it was in that play, you dance with it. People think Trudeau is cold, so you get him on his knees praying. I knew that would challenge perceived understanding but it was also a reasonable leap to make. It's an awareness that can fuel the heat, the sense of danger and challenge, not an awareness that censors. We knew also that people thought Maggie a flake so we showed the flake and then turned it around. All theatre tries to surprise, but in this case the audience shared in the moment very personally because they had arrived with preconceptions. It's so much fun, so alive, to play with these. Also, in performance it was different to play Trudeau in Montreal than in Calgary. The writing didn't change but the relationship to the audience had to remain alive.

With *Alien Creature* I assumed the audience would know nothing, and that was its own challenge. I didn't want to be stuck giving biographical information; there was already a book about Gwendolyn MacEwen (*Shadowmaker* by Rosemary Sullivan). In this play I came completely from character. This woman spoke in a certain way because she was a poet. No one had to know her poetry. Some people would know that the "stinky man" was Milton Acorn but you didn't have to. I also had a stinky man in my life. MacEwen and I merged at many points. I used pieces of her real poetry to ground the work but they didn't ultimately have to be there. They're in the play as homage and that is between her and me. In *Alien Creature* I felt the connection between us was so strong, I took the chance that the audience would feel it.

With *The Duchess*, the audience that came to Passe Muraille in mink coats knew everything about Wallis Simpson, and the students and Queen Street types almost nothing. If I was playing to a certain niche, like regional theatre, I would assume they knew her. In this case the play is stuffed with information. I wanted to play with the time period and the enormity of the events which surrounded her. To do that, I had to teach the audience in a way that didn't repeat information some of them had but gave information others needed. There is fantasy—the jewels are personified. There is also a scene with Hitler because I wanted the audience reminded of her political alignments. But still, there was a challenge, a relationship with the audience based on their previous assumptions and information I chose to give. This was a bad woman and they expected her to be bad. In this case I chose to go toward those expectations—with various twists.

The whole process of *Jessica* is so complex. Maria Campbell and I wrote a whole book about it. *The Book of Jessica* is both a political and theatrical dialogue. Assumptions abound regarding the audience and both its creators.

I have taken enormous liberties with both the living and the dead. In *The Book of Jessica* there is a huge argument about this. We finally came to an agreement—true words of wisdom from Maria Campbell: *All artists are thieves. It is the artist's obligation to steal, but then to give back tenfold.* I feel enormous obligation and yet I am free with it—a contradiction. I always place, in my mind's eye, the people themselves in the audience. I played *Alien Creature* to Gwendolyn MacEwen's second husband, to her lovers and friends. I played *Maggie & Pierre* to Margaret Trudeau (but not Pierre). When other actors do my work, that basic connection between the material and the audience isn't there. They personally are not responsible. In a way, I'm surprised I've been allowed to get away with what I have, that I haven't been sued or beaten up. All I can think of is that I'm serious about giving back tenfold, and I'm not mean. Maybe that is the responsibility—not to be mean. I have gone too far at times, once basing not the writing but the performance on the character of a friend. The mimicry was a bit too on the money. I wouldn't do that again.

The differences between theatrical biography and written biography are as huge as the differences between the written word and theatre. Theatre is ephemeral and always will be, so open to interpretation that even historical truth is subject to it—to the subjective, physical nature of theatre itself. Yet to say the theatre must be free is to say that nothing should bind us, and that can't be. To say we have to be chained to someone else's idea of truth also can't be. I am a thief. Maybe an honest thief, a human thief, but still a thief. I'm not necessarily honourable either. I have to serve the theatre. I shouldn't be a model for anyone in this.

Fact Does Not Interest Me Near As Much As Fantasy

Tomson Highway

My process in writing these plays? Don't know. I just write. I find the whole process of writing just so excruciatingly difficult—it brings me close to tears many a day—that I just write whatever as an act of desperation. I just scrawl insanely, blindly away. All I have is a hunch of what, or who, I want to write about. There is no process; it's all just one goddamn mess. I wanted to write about these characters because I find them colourful, exciting, dramatic, unique. I do not do research; fact does not interest me near as much as fantasy. I ALWAYS start with monologues in whatever I do. And then build from there. Gets me going.

Generally speaking, I start with real people then fictionalize them draft by draft by draft so that, by the tenth draft, they are almost completely unrecognizable from the real people I started with. In the case of *The Rez Sisters*, it was my mother and six of her sisters, bingo-mad all. For instance, one of her sisters was famous (locally anyway) for being fast, for always doing everything fast—talking fast, walking fast, etc. And that was the sole characteristic I took for the character who eventually became Annie Cook, just for instance.

In the plays there is nothing of myself in the characters. The characters who are in them are, however, to an extent—to a very small extent—autobiographically based. As with Annie Cook, I take just a seed of their character and I build on that. And build and build and build ... until they are absolutely ridiculous, or mythical, in proportion.

Why am I not in the Rez plays [*The Rez Sisters*, *Dry Lips Oughta Move to Kapuskasing*, and *Rose*]? I don't know. Never thought of it at the time I guess. Just wasn't interested in me, at the time anyway. Just ... never thought about it. Has nothing to do with genres.

Audience? I generally think of entertaining my friends, the people I love. I think of making them laugh, of enthralling them, of giving them a good time. The race of my audience I never think about. You clarify characters and situations to the best of your ability no matter the racial background of your audience. You just gotta be clear. To everyone. Not just to whomever.

Figure 26. Anne Anglin, Sally Singal, Margaret Cozry, Gloria Miguel, Muriel Miguel, Gloria May Eshkibok, Monique Mojica, and Rene Highway in Tomson Highway's *The Rez Sisters*, produced by Act IV Theatre Company and Native Earth Performing Arts at the Native Canadian Centre, Toronto, 1986. Photograph by Adrian Oosterman, courtesy of Native Earth Performing Arts.

I think staying with the cultural truth of the characters and the situations comes naturally. You just write from the gut. You, as writer, are morally responsible to them, your characters, just simply from the viewpoint of making them as real as possible. You don't tell false stories. You don't lie. To your audience or to your friends or to anyone. Truth, that is the ultimate moral responsibility of the writer. That is what I think anyway.

I live winters in France, and probably will for the rest of my life. As a northern Canadian, I have, all my adult life, had to put up with insane travel costs just to be with my family, just to hear, and speak, my own language, etc. Just from Thompson, Manitoba to my home reserve of Brochet (even further north), a two-way plane ticket costs more than one from Toronto to Paris return. From Brochet to Toronto return? Think Sydney, Australia. Or Bombay. Or Buenos Aires, Argentina. So, in my old age, having lived through costs like that ever since high school, what is it for me to hop back and forth between Toronto and Paris? Nothing. By comparison, it's a joke. So I do it with great, immense, wonderful pleasure.

Having said that, we go to Barcelona a lot, my partner and I, principally because where we live is just over the French border from Spain and therefore only two and a half hours from that city. Which is where we go to the theatre, concerts, etc. So last March, for instance, we went to the Liceu Opera House there—Spanish equivalent of Milan's La Scala—and saw *Macbeth* by Verdi. Meaning we saw a Scottish story in a Scottish setting featuring Scottish characters originally set to words by an English playwright then set to music by an Italian composer. And of the seventy-two performers we saw on that stage (not to mention the sixty or so in the orchestra pit), not one—NOT ONE—was Scottish. They were all Spanish. Or Catalan. With a few Eastern Europeans thrown in for good measure (Lady Macbeth, for instance). Imagine, if you will: a bunch of black-haired—not red-haired but black-haired (i.e., they didn't even bother dyeing their hair)—Latinos running around in kilts singing merrily away in Italian AND in a style that had nothing—NOTHING—to do with Scottish music, of that period or of any other. But no one in the audience seemed to care. They loved it. WE loved it. It was a great show.

The same thing with a production of this same Verdi's *Aida* at Covent Garden in London a few years back. Of the eighty or so performers we saw on that stage (not to mention the sixty or so in the orchestra pit), not one—NOT ONE—was remotely Egyptian. They were all English. Or Scottish or Welsh or Irish. No one seemed to care. They loved it. WE loved it. It was a great show.

Let me ask you this: With the last production of *The Mikado* you saw in Vancouver a few years ago, produced (and toured) by the Manitoba Theatre Centre and our own venerable National Arts Centre, how many of those eighty or so performers (singer/actors and orchestra members) up on that stage were Japanese?

And so it goes ...

The Malcolm X School of Playwriting

Lorena Gale

I don't really have a process. It seems to vary greatly depending on the subject, what it is that has drawn me to it in the first place, how little or much is known about each character. Each figure demands that I deal with them on their own terms and, thus, treat each differently as a writer. And some characters are easier to work with than others.

The process for *Je me souviens* was very simple, quick and organic. I needed only to structure my thoughts, memories, and emotions, whereas with *Angélique* the process was lengthy, arduous, and frequently very turgid. I used a more academic approach. Far more deductive reasoning was involved as opposed to creative leaps of imagination. But then so little was known about Marie Joseph Angélique [a slave in 1730s Montreal] at that time that I had to reconstruct her story from tiny clues, provide her with a credible history in a believable context. It is hard to talk about my Darwin play. That process is still evolving. But I can say that it is difficult working with a figure who is so well-known and whose life and work are so intensely examined. The challenge is to find something new to say about him.

Research is key to all my work. I try to examine my subject from as many different perspectives as possible and saturate my mind with information drawn from many different sources: facts and fictions of all genres, music, poetry, visual arts, old love letters. Whatever is accessible to me. Even *Je me souviens* was extensively researched. Autobiography is meaningless without context. Then I wait to see what trickles down in writing in terms of stories, characters, and themes. Kinda like throwing all my cards in the air and then playing them as they lay—only somewhat more controlled because I have chosen the particular cards. The end result is always a surprise to me. The play I finish is never the play I start out writing. With *Angélique* I started out writing a one-person show. But after fifteen years of research, I ended up with a much, much larger play. *Je me souviens* began as an essay and turned into a one-woman play. Only time will tell what my Darwin play will be.

I do not begin my writing process with a monologue even though my plays are laden with them. But the monologue plays an important role in all my works. I do not know who my characters are until they talk to me directly. Essentially telling me who they are.

Figure 27. Lorena Gale as "Lorena Gale," ca. 2003. Resumé photograph by Tim Matheson.

Angélique is curious because I could not get her to speak for the longest time. Only monosyllables and short sentences came out. I tried to write around her. But when she did have more to say, it was startling and poetic. Certainly not what I was expecting. Then I understood what play to write.

I want to say there is no real difference writing about "real" people or about purely fictitious characters. Certainly all the characters in any play, whether based on real people or imaginary, are fictitious. After all, the writer can only present an interpretation of the life that they are examining. Not the real deal. Even me, Lorena, as presented in *Je me souviens*, is a fabrication. Lorena interpreting Lorena. But not my authentic self. All characters, even self-portraits, are contrived. Products of the writer's imagination.

Writing about myself was strange. Scary, really. As writer and performer I am naked because the material is extremely personal. I kept asking myself as I was writing, "What makes you think your life is so interesting?" I came to understand that my life was only as interesting as I could make it as a writer. That does not mean that I had to fabricate or embellish. Everything in *Je me souviens* was true. But as I said, context is everything. I placed my life in a context, selected those memories that best explored the chosen themes, and tried to approach the writing of those memories with an open mind and heart.

I create my characters as a writer in pretty much the same way I create them as an actor—from the inside out. I try to inhabit their emotional world and see what actions stem from there. I read aloud everything I write, over and over again for rhythm, flow, musicality. The words have to sit right in my mouth. I try to create characters that present challenges for the actor, roles that I would want to play. I try to create tension of opposites. So that there is always something going on underneath. I would like to think that smart actors know to play against the writing so that there are always dynamics in the character. Not to hit every word on its head.

I am one of those people who believe that all writing is autobiographical. We can only write what we know. Even non-fiction writing. What you get is the author's interests, opinions, and perspectives. My characters may be drawn from history, but everything they do and say in those two hours on stage comes from me or represents some aspect of myself, my life experience, relationships, people I know, or my intellectual understanding. I also believe that there is no real difference between the historical and the contemporary. The range of human action and emotion has remained the same across time. People behave the same in every country, culture, language, or time period. Our motivations and our responses have remained constant. The only thing that changes across time is how we dress our world up. The externals.

I think that knowing I will perform a character has no effect on my writing. It's like using two different parts of your brain. I am a much better actor than I am a writer and I'm extremely critical of my writing. If I let my actor take over, I could never write. I work predominantly in film and TV. It's my job to make shit sing. I take the same approach when acting my own words. And I surprise myself sometimes when the writing is really good. But I cannot tell you how many times I would turn to the director in rehearsals for *Je me souviens* and say, "Who wrote this crap?" As I said, I try to create challenging roles. Even for myself. To John's credit (my husband, John Cooper, directed), he would not let me off the hook as an actor or let me hang myself out to dry as a writer by allowing me to cut anything I found too difficult to perform. I tell you, some of the hardest acting bits were the best writing. Good for him.

My plays are written with a very conscious awareness of the audience. They are, in many ways, another character for me. Collectively they are the witness. But they are also the other voice in the writer's dialogue. The audience/reader is who I am trying to speak to. My plays are presentational in style or have presentational elements. I would like to think that it forces the audience to be more engaged, not to sit back and relax, zone out, or pretend they are watching television. I try not to lapse into realism for too long. I like to juxtapose scenes of different forms, styles, rhythms, and literary media, so the action keeps changing and spinning. I bring to my writing a complete knowledge and understanding of just about every element of the theatre. I have a pretty clear idea of how I would like my work to be staged for its best effect on the audience. I sometimes call this the Malcolm X School of Playwriting: tell the story by any means necessary.

I never assume that the audience knows who or what I am talking about. I knew that with Marie Joseph Angélique and myself, the audience would be in total ignorance. That is not quite the case with Charles Darwin. Everyone knows a little something. But I sincerely doubt that the things that are of interest to me about Darwin and his theories are the things that are popularly known and understood. I mean really, how many people know about Darwin's research into barnacles? Or that he remains the world's only authority on the subject. (Snore.) I know that whatever I write about Darwin, and my particular spin on it, will be fresh to the audience.

I think there is pressure on the writer of biographical theatre, especially when the subject is well-known, to conform to the popular conception of that character and to keep their story straight. I initially found working with the character of Darwin very intimidating. The man is an icon. Every aspect of his life is so well-documented, I could just imagine the outcry against every word I put in his mouth. Working directly with his theories and his life, I knew that there was very little I could say as a playwright that had not been said before. I had to cut Darwin out of the play and find a different way to work with the material. Now that I have come up with a story that allows me to focus only on those aspects of his life and his theories that are of interest to me, I feel somewhat liberated.

With Angélique, because history has failed to tell her story with any truth, it was very important to me to bring some form of truth to her life. Even if it was my own made-up truth. The result is a blurring of fact and fiction.

I do not feel compelled to recreate history on stage. That would be a waste of energy and creativity. I get really bored in so-called "historical dramas" that seek some form of verisimilitude. Besides, the theatre, by nature, is an artificial environment. There is no way that a theatrical biographer can present historical truth. That moment is well past. And the truth would have been filtered though their very modern sensibilities. But there are transcendent truths in every biography. I always ask myself, why do I need to tell this story today? Why is this story, this life, important now? When I can answer those questions, then I know that I have found the truth. My truth in history.

I do not see any ethical issues involved in portraying the lives of real people, dead or living, in the theatre. After all, as a writer and not a journalist, I am not telling their story but my own. All is fair fodder for the creative mill. I won't make up lies but I will certainly manipulate the facts in any way that I see fit to use them. It's interesting. I found out that a descendant of François Poulin de Francheville, the man who owned Angélique, lives in North Vancouver. He may have been a very nice man but I portray that character quite unfavourably. All I heard was that the descendant was thrilled that someone even thought enough to write about his great, great, great, great uncle or grandfather. Even the people I wrote about in *Je me souviens*, many of whom saw or read the play, were just happy to be remembered.

How in Hell Did She Do It?

Joy Coghill

Now, in my eightieth year, I look back on being fifty-six and think of it not as the beginning of old age but as a half-way mark only—*young*, in fact, as far as having a talent and lots of time to establish and develop a career of any kind.

However, many Canadian actresses of the first generation—i.e., women who were fifty-six in the 1980s—were in a state of panic about their opportunities in the marketplace, a marketplace fraught with ageism. I was one of them.

To create a play with Emily Carr as a heroine was a natural goal. Not only was she a famous writer and artist with box-office appeal but, most importantly, she reportedly did her best work after the age of fifty-six. Ah-ha! Many "leading ladies" looked for a playwright to write a Carr play for them. Joan Orenstein, the great Halifax actress, appealed to Sharon Pollock, the superb Alberta playwright, to write her. I went to P. K. Page, the prize-winning Canadian poet; Alice Munro, Ontario's beloved short story writer; and John Murrell, Alberta's internationally known playwright. They all had work that would keep them busy for years to come. They all said, "You must write this yourself." John Murrell invited me to do just that at the Banff Playwrights' Workshop.

By then, of course, I had done all the basic research that was possible at that time. I had spent days at the National Archives and at the British Columbia Archives. I had read all Emily's writing, both published and non-published. I had read all the biographies published to date (1983). Emily Carr was very much a part of my life. She had become a major passion, a constant irritant—a reality. I began to notice that none of the playwrights who had been approached had produced a play yet. I knew of four who made a start but something stopped them.

The plays that did appear before and during this time were charming and laudatory presentations of Carr's life, using words from her writing and slides of her paintings. The Emily I began to know would like that kind of presentation, I thought. I began to notice that Emily got dates wrong, lied about her age, compartmentalized her friends, and certainly preferred animals to people. I began to sympathize with her family, particularly the faithful, supportive sister, Alice.

314 / *Creating AutoBiography on Stage*

I created pages of diary entries for Emily and Alice. Alice was easier. How I wish I had kept those pages for this piece. However, some of it appears in *Song of This Place*.

It was at Banff, in the middle of the night, with typwriters tapping busily on either side (no computers then) that MILLIE—I had started to call her by the family's name for her—became a completely audible voice, a voice that resisted any attempt to put her life on the stage. The theatre was "second-hand living," it said, and "certainly not art!"

Perhaps the struggle to find the basic conflict, the basic relationship on which to hang the play, was solved. I had always suspected that it would have something to do with claiming that actors could be artists, that great actors could claim equality with great artists—that, indeed, Theatre was the way to popularize Art! It could serve the community with inspiration and with healing, much as Fine Art does.

The only other way I could find a conflicting relationship was to concentrate on sister Alice, who, I was sure, had had a hate-love relationship with Millie very like my own. How could Alice, lady that she was, have put up with this curmudgeon of a sister who swore and smoked, dressed in sacks, and pushed a monkey up Government Street, dear heaven, in a pram full of mud! And Alice with a private school to run. Yes, that was one way to go for my story. As a matter of fact there have been two Emily Carr plays since the first production of *Song* that are based on the Alice/Emily relationship.

But I decided in the end that the conflict between myself struggling to write this play and this creature Emily Carr—now my Millie—was the best and truest that I could find. I settled for it.

But now I had to create Frieda the Actress to battle things out with Millie the Artist. It was only practical to give Frieda some of my biography and all of my choices regarding Millie's life. But I also gave her a lot of the camouflage with which leading actors often protect themselves against the damage of opinion and exposure: all the affectations of voice and manner that used to be typical of the "theatah." I modelled her on people I knew. Frieda has been a star in the "golden years" of CBC radio drama. In spite of feeling old and confined to a wheelchair, she must find a way to present her Emily Carr play and still be the star, the only voice, the artistic director, the writer. She desperately needs a success. She uses puppets to tell her story because they are intensely theatrical and she can voice all the parts herself. In the end, Frieda, like me, has created a play to extend her career and prove that her artistry is relevant to her audience and to the art of Emily Carr. Nothing like taking on the impossible!

However, it so happens in the strange world of the theatre that Emily herself turns up both fascinated and disapproving. She intends to stop the whole process, but something about Frieda and about Frieda's choices in her puppet play—the lovely revelations of the puppets Harold, Sophie, and the Child—make her stay. When the young actors of Frieda's troupe give up their egos completely to little creatures that are obviously cloth and plaster; when, by their artistry, the audience starts to believe in the puppet world,

Figure 28. Joy Coghill played the role of Frieda (the playwright) in the
1987 premiere of her play *Song of This Place*. By the end of the play Frieda
successfully transforms herself into "Emily Carr." This image from the
cover of the published play illustrates the remarkable resemblance
between Coghill (as Carr) and Carr's *Self-portrait* (1938–39). Photograph by
David Cooper.

then even the cynical Millie is charmed. She decides to test this "actress person" by taking
her deeper into the experience of Millie's own incredibly difficult life. I was pleased with
the Millie that drove the action. She was very real to me. I made her wiser, I think, than
she was in life. I made her less of a curmudgeon, less subject to tantrums and jealousies.
That was left to the character SMALL, a puppet.

A note on this character, Millie's child self: I really do believe that an artist must retain
her/his child self or the work becomes artificial and lacks a rooted truth. This Small,
springing straight out of Emily's first literary success, *The Book of Small*, attacks Frieda

with "She can never never be a real artist. She has no Small." Frieda is forced to rediscover her child self left far behind in the artificiality of the theatre. Understandably, the Small that appears was born under the prairie sky and is mine. Only the magic of the puppet world makes this rebirthing of a child self possible.

The interesting thing about biography/autobiography and writing plays is that it is all, surely, autobiography. Because even as you take the breath, as the pen goes down on the yellow lined paper, you know what this character has to say. But it gets whirled around in the air somehow and when it gets down on the page, whether it is Millie or Frieda or Small, it's actually my understanding in that moment of her life and my own.

Acting in the play, playing Frieda, was extremely hazardous for me because I was a wet-behind-the-ears playwright. I mean I was suffering the fears of both the actor and the writer. The way through to safety was to bury myself deeply in the performance. Joan Orenstein was such an incredible Emily/Millie that I had to pay attention or she would have wiped the stage with me.

It is a great responsibility to bring alive on the stage a person that existed and was famous. You get weighed down with all the research, all the opinions of your director, the other actors, the many biographies. In the rehearsal process everyone fills you with ideas, with inspiration, with talk. But there comes a time when you must shed all your responsibilities and terrors, all the talk and opinion, and commit yourself to the moment. You make that stage your own; it is only you and that audience creating theatre. It is then that the artistry of the theatre is undeniable. I dared to create such a moment for Frieda. It is after that action of taking on the paternalistic world that Millie can say, "You are one of us." I must have been mad!

Theatre about Carr is, of course, about "how in hell did she do it?" How did she manage to overcome the isolation and alienation of this edge-of-the-world Western place? I know what helped. It helped to swear and smoke and push a monkey in a pram up Government Street! It was a good, defiant, demonic character to play until someone recognized her as an artist. No wonder all actors at fifty-six want to try and capture her. They want to be part of the Emily Carr parade. They want to be able to make it through in spite of age and heart attacks and critics and questioning. There is something important about who we are as Canadians that Emily understood—something about art and its importance to the human soul that she bet her life on. In *Song of This Place* we all wanted to contribute our refrain to the "Song" of Emily. We dared to try to do that.

I'm Not God's Gift to Black People

Andrew Moodie

Riot was the third play I had written. The first was a short one-man play called "Richard"; the second was *Hysteria*. For those plays, I just wrote whatever the hell I felt. For *Riot* I wanted to change my approach. I was largely influenced by Augusto Boal's work with the theatre of the oppressed: how he believed that every act a person performs is political and that theatre can be a forum for the people to see political ideas challenged. Basically, I focussed on a political idea that I wanted to communicate and then tried to figure out a way to communicate that idea through character, plot, and story.

I started by writing out character outlines for ten characters. I then took a look at all of them and whittled them down to six. Then I made a chart detailing which character liked which other character, and which character hated which other character. Their sympathy or antipathy was graded on a scale of five, so that some characters had a mild distaste for other characters, some were neutral to each other, and some had a full-blown dislike. I then took a stack of cue cards and just started making notes on possible scenes based on the like or dislike of the characters. How could they express their ideas through the conflicts they had with each other personally? The thing I love about Boal is his belief that the personal is always political. Then once I had all the cards I could think of, I tried to order them in some way. I tried to see if there was a hierarchy of ideas—if one idea naturally wanted to come before or after another. I then tried to prune out the issues that no longer seemed relevant or that were merely echoing the ideas of another scene. Then I sat in front of my word processor and began to write. From beginning to end the first draft took two weeks.

I have since tried to abandon this process and work in a less organized fashion because sometimes it can create something that feels too well-structured. But what I like about the process is that you really work the structure of the piece before you even know what the characters are going to say. It helps, I find, to keep the process moving.

With *Riot* I just basically took from the lives of my friends and myself. That was the point really. What were the issues that my African-Canadian friends were dealing with

Figure 29. Andrew Moodie as Robin, Derwin Jordan as Chris, and Andrew Jason Wade as Greg in Andrew Moodie's *A Common Man's Guide to Loving Women*, produced by the National Arts Centre and the Canadian Stage Company at the NAC, Ottawa, 1999. Photograph courtesy of Andrew Moodie.

during the Rodney King riots? That's what the play was about. But of course for other plays I have had to do much more research than that.

Each of the characters in *Riot* was an amalgam of so many people I knew. The character I played was Alex, a black male from Ottawa who had recently come out of the closet. I knew that people would think that the character was me. It wasn't a problem for me at all. I had a girlfriend and ultimately I would rather people think I'm gay than for people to know that deep down inside, I am so angry at the way young black men behave, choosing a life of violence and self-destruction, that I would prefer to just ship them out of the country. Make them somebody else's problem. Coming out of the closet is considered noble. Hating a fellow black person is not. I've never been interested in just saying things people want to hear.

I have been obsessed over my writing career with bringing contemporary Toronto to the stage. It's kind of essential if you want to talk about the modern African-Canadian experience. There's such a large population of blacks in Toronto but also, in English

Canada, it's our London, it's our Paris. It's the place where the extremes of life are at their most intense. I'm still working on liking Toronto more than my beloved Ottawa. (Slowly, as I get older, I realize there's really no point in not liking Toronto if I'm going to spend the rest of my life here.) But regardless of whether I like Toronto or not, it's the place that often inspires me.

I have always said and I will continue to say that I'm not really a playwright. I'm someone who can craft scenes for actors to perform. I'm not skilled enough to be called a playwright. Perhaps one day I will be. Until that time, I just try to make sure I can give the actors what they need on stage: a) a reason to enter the scene, b) a doable action and activity while in the scene, c) some kind of growth or transformation.

These are the things I want as an actor and I try hard to provide them for the actors in my plays. Of course some styles of theatre go against having a reason to enter the stage or having a doable action. And I enjoy performing in experimental theatre that challenges the rules of drama, so there are times when you don't give the actor what they want, you challenge them to change their perceptions of performance. But most of my work is pretty straightforward drama and I want to give the actors what I would want.

I never think about which character I want to play. The only reason why I act in my plays is because I'm out of work and need the money to pay my mortgage. And oddly enough, the money one earns as a playwright is often not exactly enough to pay the mortgage. If I need a job and if I'm right for the part, I'll do it. If I'm wrong for the part, I won't.

I used to be so concerned about writing for a black audience. I used to believe that theatre in Canada had to create plays that dealt with the lives of African-Canadians and then African-Canadians would feel welcome and come to the theatre in droves. The harsh, brutal reality is that black people are like white people. Most don't particularly want to see theatre in general; many can't afford the ticket price. Those that do want to see big-ticket items like *The Lion King* or *Mamma Mia*. Blacks do not feel beholden to me to come to my plays. As a matter of fact, black people shouldn't come to my plays because I'm black. They should come to my plays because they're good. Period. If they don't come, maybe it's because I haven't written a very good play. That's not their problem, it's mine. I'm not God's gift to black people.

The TRUTH. Ah yes. What is that exactly again? In my work there are three truths: the immutable truths (we all die, the sun always rises), the temporal truths (a tree existed on my front lawn, now it doesn't, the river I step into is not the river I stand in, yadda yadda), and the subjective truth (The Smashing Pumpkins is the greatest band in rock 'n' roll history). I think the only responsibility an artist has is to create a work of art. Period. Use whatever form of truth, in whatever fashion to do that. The work I have done, creating plays based on real people, has played fast and loose with the immutable truths of their lives. Elijah McCoy was not an only child, but I'm not interested in any of his brothers and sisters. They don't help me tell my story so they're gone. The real Macbeth probably didn't actually consult witches but damn, it's pretty entertaining to see him do it on stage. I really believe that one should only write about people who are long dead, and whose friends and family are long dead, so that you can make up whatever the hell you need to and you won't get sued. Sometimes the only way to express the true essence of a real person is through boldly creating your own immutable truths about the person. That way you can transcend the temporal truths of a person's life and hopefully communicate something that resonates as the audience's own subjective truth. If you want history, turn to the historian. If you want a story told through time and space that attempts to get at the essence of our experience on this planet and the nature of our souls and the mystery of our being, turn to the playwright.

I Always Stick to Facts

Sally Clark

I'm looking for a good story. I like true stories because they're usually more interesting than anything I could make up. All of my plays are based on some "true story" that I heard somewhere—whether it's documented history or some weird story that a friend has told me about someone they know. I try not to write "biographical" plays because they're a lot of work. I don't object to the research; I love the research. The hard part is finding the story when you've got a ton of information. It's easier to write a play when you've only got a few salient details.

I guess my first "biographical" play was *Jehanne of the Witches*. I was working for Theatre Passe Muraille as a playwright-in-residence. Clarke Rogers set me a challenge. He dared me to write a play about a woman with power. He seemed to think that I wrote only about women as victims! I had a vague idea that I wanted to write a play about Joan of Arc being a witch. Clarke wasn't too pleased with that idea. He figured I was heading into victim territory again. Anyway, I went to this occult bookstore and asked the man at the desk if he had any books on Joan of Arc. He looked at me and said, "Joan of Arc and Bluebeard were best friends," and I knew I had the story for my next play. Gilles de Rais, alias Bluebeard, was Joan of Arc's companion-in-arms. Their relationship was touched on in the book *The God of the Witches* by Margaret Murray, an anthropologist writing about the witch cults in Europe. I was fascinated by her theory about the relationship between Joan and Gilles. I did a lot of research on Joan's life and Gilles de Rais's life, but the inspiration came from a series of facts that were outlined in this book.

I always stick to facts. I use the facts as points on a line. My interpretation is finding the through-line between those points. What connects those facts? What truth is hidden underneath those facts? I think it's wrong to make up facts. To me, that's lying. I don't understand why someone would choose to write about a famous person and then write things that were patently untrue about that person. I don't get it. What's the point? And yes, I'm aware that Shakespeare did it with Richard III. And I still don't know why he would do that. Unless he was paid a large sum of money ...

With *Saint Frances of Hollywood*, I wanted to write about Frances Farmer because it seemed to me that her life had a perfect structure for tragedy. I spent many years working on this play. It had countless workshops. The first production was a dismal failure. I sent the script to Karl Siegler [publisher of Talonbooks], asking him what he thought. Was there a problem with the script or was it the production? Karl said, "Ah, you're trying to write a tragedy but the form's all wrong. You have to do this, this and this." He wrote me ten pages of notes, outlining what I should do. I sat in his office and stared at the pages for a long time. He thought I was angry at what he'd written. I was thunderstruck. I knew that he had put his finger on the problem and that now I had to rewrite.

Life Without Instruction came about after I had read about Artemisia Gentileschi in Germaine Greer's *The Obstacle Race* in the late 1970s when I was studying art. I liked her paintings because they were strong. The other paintings by famous women artists were very soft and feminine—flowers, portraits. Pleasant paintings. Suddenly, I go from a nice little portrait to a picture of a woman sawing a man's head off. I read the biography on Artemisia and it said that when she was fourteen, she was raped by a man who was giving her "lessons in perspective." The phrase haunted me. In about 1986, Nightwood Theatre commissioned me to write a play for them. Judy Chicago's *The Dinner Party* was in town. She had done a special plate for Artemisia and that reminded me to read more about her life. I discovered that the rapist was her father's best friend. That extra piece of information made me want to write the play.

There wasn't much written about Artemisia at that time. Roland Barthes had written "Deux Femmes" in a book that included the transcript of the trial (*Actes d'un proces pour viol en 1612* [1983]). It was in French (translated from Italian). For me, that was a stroke of luck. My French was rusty but I was able to translate it into English. Right after I wrote the play, Mary Garrard published her biography on Artemisia.

For me, plays are about discovering the mystery behind a story. The story has to be intriguing. There's always some buried secret that reveals why things happened the way they did. I don't always find the secret. Writing the play is simply a means of looking for it. The first scene I wrote for *Life Without Instruction* was the rape scene.

Michael Clark, the artistic director of Nakai Theatre in Whitehorse, Yukon asked me to write a play for his company. There was a historical story that involved a famous dance hall girl, her wealthy paramour, and a court trial. Michael thought it was a perfect "Sally Clark play." Well, I wanted to get as far away from that as possible. I was sick of writing about trials and really tired of writing about "real" people. So for *Wanted*, I read a lot of books about the Klondike, found the true event that grabbed my interest, and made up the rest. I did begin with a monologue which was an actual response to a want ad. It was such an odd response that it made me wonder who this person was. The character grew out of that.

Do I draw on my skill as an actor in the creating of A/B characters? Yes. How much of myself goes into them? I don't know. When I'm writing the play, I think all of me goes into them. But later I look at what I've written and think, "Who's that?"

I try never to make any assumptions about what an audience may think, say, or do.

Figure 30. Sarah Ireland as Frances Farmer in Sally Clark's *Saint Frances of Hollywood* at Manhattan Theatre Source, New York, 2005. Photograph by Daryl Boling.

Never Not Narrative

R. H. Thomson

Our universe was conceived. There will never be words to truly describe its inception. Even at the beginning it was dark. 400,000 years passed before the first radiation escaped the roiling, expanding gas of our beginnings in the Big Bang. We now detect the echo of that first radiation outburst that was the first signal of being. For the next 100 million years our universe took another dark path, a second dark age when no story of existence could be told. Only after the second darkness were stars capable of forming and there was at last light. The narrative had truly begun.

Light is the narrative by which we fathom existence. Light can be emitted either by a universe, a galaxy, a star, or a life. Narrative is the only tell-tale evidence by which we know existence.

Narrative and light have another mystery: within their individual frames time has no dimension. If you journey with a photon of light, neither you nor the light will experience time passing. Light does not know the dimension of time. Light experiences eternity since it knows no time and so too with narrative. Narrative is ageless. Once written, once on its journey, it does not suffer time. Both will eventually disappear with the disappearance of this universe. But now we live in an age of light. We live in an age of narrative.

In addition, what we have imaginatively yet to grasp is that 90 percent of the three-dimensional material precipitated by the Big Bang is dark. It is a mass called dark matter. Our matter, the visible matter of our lives, the matter capable of narrative, is a tiny minority of this universe. Dark matter gives no signs of existence. Dark matter is now segregated in our galaxies from matter that we see. Dead men, like dark matter and black holes, tell no tales.

In *The Lost Boys* I wanted to tell the tale of five dead men. I was drawn to their lives. They had been young as I had been. They had encountered the chaos, fear, and euphoria of the battlefields of 1914–1918 as I never had. They were five brothers. They were my great-uncles. What they had left behind were their letters: seven hundred of them over five years. Four of the five brothers had died from the wreckage of the First World War. I had known the fifth, the survivor, only as an old man.

Figure 31. R. H. Thomson and his great-uncle Arthur Stratford from the published text of Thomson's *The Lost Boys* (Playwrights Canada Press), first produced by the Great Canadian Theatre Company, Ottawa, 2001. Photographs courtesy of R. H. Thomson.

The letters were far-reaching. There were death notices and injury cables. There were letters from battlefields in Belgium, France, Egypt, and Portuguese East Africa. There were surrounding letters from their sister, from their aunt, from their mother, from their fellow soldiers, from officers who offered official condolences, and from strangers in France who had come to love a brother as they would their own child.

Yet what my father's uncles wrote from the killing fields, jungles, hospitals, and convalescent homes of the First World War was essentially dark. They told few tales. They wrote without context. They wrote endless and well meant details of trivia. They wrote of socks, food, leave, teas, horses, and reassurance. Five years of such letters begin to dull the reader and I thought that perhaps there wasn't a play in them at all. Could a narrative be found? Where was the war? Where was the journey amidst the four-year phenomenon of killing and stupidity? When men live with so much needless, pain-filled death, there is much to be written. But the dark enclosed the light, or so it seemed.

Narrative can often be revealed by the light and shadow of context. I assembled the brothers' war and medical records from the record offices in Canada and England. I read their regimental war diaries. I spent too long entombed in the collection of First World War photographs at the Imperial War Museum in London. I stood at night in the rain and mud of the fields of Flanders. Using military trench maps, I walked the route my great-uncle Art had walked in March 1915. He had had a bad flu and was on his way to the night convoy of ambulances behind the lines. Standing in winter mud, I saw the dim outline of Ypres on the horizon as Art might have seen it before he was hit by a sniper's bullet as he sat in that ambulance. I rode with him as he fainted repeatedly, travelling to the casualty clearing station. I had felt for that same bullet as a child since Art was the great-uncle who had survived and the surgeons were never able to remove what the sniper had left. My six-year-old fingers had felt for the bullet just beside the base of his spine. Art ached with it for the rest of his life.

Trivia can also be hints from a hidden world, a world shrouded purposely by my great-uncles. After all, they wrote to reassure those at home. I was also beginning to appreciate the intimacy they were protecting. The second youngest brother, George, wrote on 13 November 1917 of his regiment doing "the odd bit of fighting," a curious phrase in a four-year war. I read the regimental war diary. George was in the battle of Passchendaele, one of three major slaughters of that war: Passchendaele, the Somme, and Verdun. George continued in the darkness of understatement, "Again (the regiment) made a great name for themselves, maybe I wasn't lucky, as only one officer of this Company came out of it." George's understatement led only to horror—140,000 dead if you include German lives as well. It was a three-month battle in the autumn mud of Belgium that claimed 450,000 casualties overall. Military command had been warned that the mud would consume men and drown the battle. The warning was ignored. Three months later, the town of Passchendaele was finally taken by our Allied forces—a gain of seven kilometres. The grotesque irony was that, in March 1918, the military command that so many viewed as dysfunctional ceded the ground gained back to the Germans without a fight. The Passchendaele victory was declared redundant. The horror of the deaths was for nothing. George was amongst them.

In 1916 George endured six weeks in hospital. He wrote his mother that he was not wounded; rather he was in for his "feet." Looking for a crack, I read his army medical record. Again George was shielding the truth. Like so many soldiers, George was undergoing treatments such as "the hot umbrella" for the scourge of venereal disease. The Canadians had it in record numbers: 29 percent of the Canadian army in 1915. This statistical fissure led to a larger story about pay and prudery. Canadian troops attracted syphilis and gonorrhea like no others. There was more to this than Nature. They were paid more than their British army counterparts and therefore attracted more female companionship. At Victoria Station in London, trains that arrived with Canadian soldiers were often met by women crowding to sell at a better price. Our boys, still covered in mud and fatigue, were happy to buy. The prudery involved the Canadian citizenry safe at home. Too many good folk would not contemplate the idea that their fighting and dying boys were having sex. The French army had solved the challenge of desire and infection by licensing brothels. They were the *maisons de tolerance*. However, this solution was not to be contemplated by the Mrs. Grundys, as they came to be known in Canada. No safe sex please, since no sex was best sex. For the same reason the Canadian army was forbidden to procure prophylactics for the men. But towards the end of the war a concession was made. A blue cream was distributed that the soldier was to apply to his penis *afterwards*. If our happy Harry was so "blued" and inspected (in the dangle parade) to the army's satisfaction, his card was stamped for the record. If Harry then contracted venereal disease he would continue to receive full pay. The military reasoning was that VD was a "self-inflicted wound." Self-inflicted wounds meant a 50 percent pay cut while recovering. But if poor Harry had had his card stamped, he received full salary as he lay in VD hospital awaiting his dose of the "hot umbrella."

The process of writing *The Lost Boys* was unfurling the narrative that lay curled in cracks of trivia. With the light and shadow of context I believed I could hear the war. Pain, fear, anguish, depression, despair—these were the dark dimensions hidden by my great-uncles since their bleakness didn't bear telling. Yet the stories were all there curled up between the words in each letter. There was a sixth brother, Dave, who was nearing recruiting age. In the first years of the war his brothers wrote again and again, "When is Dave coming?" "Has Dave joined up yet?" By 1917–18 the refrain in the letters had shifted to "Don't send Dave." "Don't send Dave" ... a simple phrase with a far from simple story.

It was immensely fulfilling to write and perform *The Lost Boys*. It allowed me to complete part of my own journey. It gave voice to some very dear great-uncles I knew only through death. The echo of their voices remains with me still. I sensed that by speaking their words night after night we shared intimacies that lay beyond their words. There can be a cadence to language that only an actor comprehends. They are now my brothers. But perhaps most of all, the satisfaction was in the stories that arrived each night at my dressing-room door. So many wrote me letters after seeing the performance of *The Lost Boys*. So many others came backstage. Night after night my post-show wind-down was to listen to the narratives that poured from the hearts of my visitors in my dressing room. By unearthing my own I had a part in unearthing theirs. I never had to ask.

Inside each cell of our being lies curled a minute, miraculous protein strand called DNA. If the mystery of that protein sequence can be unfurled, the narrative of evolution lies before us. Each cell of our being carries hundreds of millions of years of evolutionary narrative. A concise, coded history of life is written within the nail of our smallest toe. Wherever we look there is narrative, if only we will see.

All lives are narrative. We are not human without narrative. If you are alive you cannot escape your own narrative. Whether we have the wit to fathom the structure within is another matter. Whether we personally are cognizant of our own journey is another matter. That is what the arts and religions attempt to do—give forms to the hidden journey. Glenn Gould taught me that through his music: to hear the silence in the music. Gould compelled me to listen to what lay between the sounding of the notes. Gould taught me to listen for the hidden story in the light and shadow of those silences. Gould encouraged me to hear the structure revealed by silence, structure that leads to the mystery of being.

The universe is light only if we let it. The universe is narrative only if we know it. When it all ends—when matter, both light and dark, and when our four dimensions of time and space collapse back to a singularity—narrative will again disappear from existence and with it existence itself. We are only the story that we tell. We are never not narrative.

In the End You Are Made Accountable

Marie Clements

I had had no intention of writing *The Unnatural and Accidental Women* until I read a four-page news story in the *Vancouver Sun* on Gilbert Paul Jordan and what his life's work had amounted to—the disappearance and drowning of a number of Native women in [Vancouver's] downtown eastside. I had heard about the case and people had approached me with articles, but I really thought this was just too horrifying to get into. What changed my mind was that there were three pages dedicated to this loser murderer but only a paragraph and a picture describing each woman he had victimized, their last known whereabouts, where they ended up—which was in hotel rooms, dying alone. They had no story as far as the world was concerned other than what Jordan had done to them. I started writing because I was angry that he had been allowed to kill Native women for over thirty years and he was still out there after a brief stay in jail asking women "if he could buy them a drink" and then killing them with alcohol. I looked into these paragraphs and their pictures, images started appearing, and I followed them into words.

It has always haunted me that he was and still is able to get away with it. I am not shocked politically or socially, or even that the justice system has failed … These aren't new things. I was astonished that he was able to kill these many Native women who, yes, were marginalized but who were also strong and had survived many things including incredible isolation, addiction, racism, and poverty. What I came to understand after reading his court documents and anything else in print was that he was able to become what they needed. So I went into their rooms and tried to imagine what they needed at that given moment—a lover, a father, a friend, a teacher, a companion—and in doing so, the writing began to come in waves. On a blood level the street research was already in me. I had grown up in Vancouver, my father was a logger; I knew Skid Row because that was where a girl could get a new pair of running shoes and a logger could get his chain sharpened and a few beers. Growing up, I knew some of the old loggers who lived in these hotel rooms, and I knew that isolation could amputate people who were already down. I also understood on a profound level that the only thing that separated me from the women I was writing about was privilege, and I don't mean money. I mean parents who loved me and were able to protect me, education, and a family that continued to always be there. If there are truly only six degrees of separation between us all, then I was only separated by one degree from the women I was writing about.

I think writing about real people has been a big part of my process. I don't think too many writers write purely fictitious characters anyway, but I think it is great to say that we do. The one thing that does impact the writing of a story that is based on true events and true people is the responsibility I feel to the people I have shared a room with. This is huge. I usually start writing from the ground up, building the environment, so that my characters are a part of it and the environment is a part of them. In this story it was explicit that it be set here in Vancouver and on Skid Row because this is the legacy of this land. We have left our most vulnerable people here to die or be killed: from the men who were handicapped by various industries, to our mentally handicapped, to those that suffer from addiction, to women who are poverty-stricken.

I think that for the most part the piece was written before I heard it out loud. What was and continues to be extraordinary is the guts and beauty actors bring to the piece and their ownership of it. I think this is partly because we know these women from the inside out. They are our sisters, our mothers, our aunts, and maybe parts of ourselves. They lived, had dreams, were perfectly imperfect, and loved like any other human being. A lot of myself went into the characters, or a lot of the characters went into me. I usually describe beginning a play by saying, "I'm going in," which is what I did. Reading aloud or performing a character is being whole in creation; it is the final dress. It allows me to express what has only been painfully internal and it also allows me as a creator to eat the words, meaning I will know what works and what doesn't by trying to articulate them, trying to be them.

I don't usually think about audiences, mostly because I believe I am a writer who is responsible to the story. Believe me, I love audiences. But for me it is a split focus to worry about what is or what isn't popular or acceptable for an audience to witness when I should be focussing on how to fulfill what the story demands. That being said, I'm sure the audiences came in for a good old-fashioned Native woman victim story and came out a little afraid, not because the women were frightful but because the Native women were just women, just like you and me, and had had "enough" ... and there is power in that.

I think, as a writer who creates theatrical AutoBiography, I have a huge obligation to write the voices I am given to write. You don't start a story like this because you think "wow, would this be a great story to put on stage!" It's too painful. You start it and end it because you don't have an alternative. Between the beginning and the end are so many questions. Are you doing the right thing? Are you respectful? Are you truthful? Is it your place? But the voices keep coming and it is your responsibility as a writer and a craftsperson to create a world for them to continue to live. Is that right? Should I have written it this way? Questions. That is the process, and in that process you will pay

Figure 32. Lisa C. Ravensbergen as Rebecca, Gene Pyrz as the Barber in the foreground; in the background Gloria May Eshkibok, Michelle Latimer, Sarah Podemski, Deborah Allison, Lena Recollet, Gail Maurice, Michaela Washburn, J. Patricia Collins, Muriel Miguel, and Valerie Buhagiar in *The Unnatural and Accidental Women* by Marie Clements, produced by Native Earth Performing Arts at Buddies in Bad Times Theatre, Toronto, 2004. Photograph by Nir Bareket.

for what will become your truth, the play, and the integrity with which it was created, because in the end you are made accountable personally, ethically, artistically, and professionally. You know what it cost them, and what it cost you, and after all that you better be able to stand.

Blahblahblahblah Memememememe Theatreschmeatre

Guillermo Verdecchia

Fronteras Americanas began as a letter (some fifteen to twenty pages, maybe more?) that I wrote to an Argentinian friend in Canada as I travelled through Argentina. The letter was an account of my wanderings but also an attempt to make sense of what I was seeing and feeling. In a sense this was a monologue, but one with a very engaged and familiar listener. You could also think of it as conversation in the sense that correspondence can be conversational: there are shared ideas, there is history, below the immediate monologic voice of the epistle.

I did a lot of research because I wanted to do more than simply articulate my feelings. I wanted to understand them, situate them, give them a context. Before it was a play, *Fronteras* was a condition, an uncertainty, that I wanted to understand. And when I realized it was going to be a play—a performance—I knew it had to have more going for it than just an accounting of my feelings. I mean, please ... *feelings*? Feelings do not a play (or much else) make. Research always suggests all sorts of theatrical ideas.

One of the very first things I came across—and I find this happens a lot when I'm "working": things come to me; materials I need cross my path and make themselves known to me—was an article in *Social Text* (#24, 1990) called "Living Borders / Buscando America: Languages of Latino Self-Formation" by Juan Flores and George Yudice. It opened up all sorts of things for me: introduced me to the work of Guillermo Gomez-Peña and Gloria Anzaldúa, introduced me to the U.S. debate around (Latino) identity politics (as distinct from the Canadian debate around multiculturalism), and helped me articulate the idea of living on and embodying a border.

As I read and researched I realized that my condition could be explored in a play and that my autobiography was simply a metaphor, a narrative, an example. An example of the problem/idea/proposal I was developing or elaborating in the play.

My research included cultural studies, history, media studies as well as music and lots of visual art. I didn't do any genealogical research. These choices (in terms of the research) have as much to do with my proclivities as any considered position about the play and what it might be. T. S. Eliot said, somewhere, something like "the ordinary

Figure 33. Guillermo Verdecchia as Guillermo in the premiere of *Fronteras Americanas* at Tarragon Theatre, Toronto, 1993. Photograph by Lydia Pawelak.

person reads Schopenhauer, falls in love, listens to music, and these remain discrete experiences or activities. For the poet these discrete experiences are always combining to form new wholes." I mention Eliot because he describes my method exactly: I read Octavio Paz, talk to my grandmother, and go to the doctor and these things come together to form a new whole. I've never been able to proceed in a purely linear, A-to-Z, focussed, cause-and-effect sort of way. I ramble, associate, annotate. I'm as interested in the footnote as in the main body of the text.

Research for *A Line in the Sand* [co-written with Marcus Youssef] covered a lot of territory as well. Media studies, Said and Orientalism, specific research on the Gulf War. We began *Line* with a two-pronged (research/creative) writing approach. Like *Fronteras*, the writing we pursued was personal and political (or contextual).

I don't think there are any major differences in my writing about "real" people as opposed to purely fictitious characters. The writing, whether it's autobiographical or not, is always constrained by, and organized and ordered according to, the imperatives of performance or narrative. And when I write a fictitious character, I am always drawing (to some extent) on my own experiences. And can you *write* a real person? You can BE a real person on stage, but can you write a real person?

I didn't really write *about* myself in *The Noam Chomsky Lectures*, not in any detail. Though we did spend a lot of time drawing attention to ourselves. Chomsky was worried that the play (before it was written) might trade on a cult of personality around him; Daniel Brooks and I did our best to make sure the only cult of personality in the play was built around us. *Chomsky* drew on my commitment to certain ideas, principles, drew on our (Brooks's and my) politics and convictions, our anger and youthful self-righteousness. In it we tried to avoid fiction and characters. (Joyce Nelson put it well: We reversed the typical theatre formulation. Instead of relying on illusions to reveal truths, we tried to use truth—our selves and fact—to reveal necessary political illusions.) *Fronteras* drew on many of the same ideas theatrically as well as the same convictions but also on my experiences, my inner life: more intimate aspects of my self.

Certainly my understanding of performance, of what it means to be live before an audience, informed the writing. I have a sense of what an audience expects, and some knowledge of how to play with that. For *Fronteras*, Wideload was created (or discovered?) through improvisation with an actor friend, Damon D'Oliveira. On tour, we started riffing on "TV Latino" characters, very tuff guys who had read a little Foucault and Marx, to amuse ourselves. Wideload came right out of those games.

Aspects of Marcus and myself went into the characters of *A Line in the Sand.* "Aspects" is perhaps too large. Certain personal details were dropped into all the fictional characters in *Line*, and many autobiographical elements inform the character of Marcus in the original second act (included in the published script but cut from the produced play).

Knowing that I will perform a character invites or allows me to use my rhythms. I write in a direct, immediate, and personal voice. I try to write in a manner that approximates how I speak. Where I am not writing for myself, I can use idioms, language, and rhythms that are not mine.

I am very aware of the audience. Of my presence before them. I don't necessarily assume they're going to know anything about me, but the use of autobiography is intended to alert/alarm the audience, to complicate matters for them. It's an attempt to make the theatrical experience more immediate, and to implicate/situate myself in the problem or politics of the piece. So much of theatre seems to me to be safe; the outcomes are, relatively speaking, known. By putting myself (or an aspect of it) on stage and making a point of it, I hope to disrupt or disturb that sense of safety, of familiarity that comes with being privileged voyeurs watching characters. I think the tension between presentation and representation is enormously productive. It keeps an audience alert. A kind of perpetual A-effect. In *Chomsky*, *Fronteras*, and *Line*, the autobiography makes the creators complicit, and (I hope) invites the audience to consider its own complicity with whatever idea/problem is under discussion.

(A great actor giving a great performance does something similar. S/he puts an aspect of her/himself on stage, dies a little bit before the audience's eyes, and upsets the safety, the nothing-will-really-happen feeling, that attends most theatrical performances.)

I believe there is such a thing as historical truth. I believe it is true, for example, that the U.S. waged a proxy terrorist war on Nicaragua in the 1980s, which was responsible for the deaths of thirty thousand Nicaraguans. I believe that this statement can be corroborated, proven to be true. I once told a Ph.D. student who interviewed me that I believed in facts, and realized when she raised her eyebrows skeptically that I was quaintly archaic. Nonetheless, I believe in facts.

Historical truth gets complicated when it meets theatre and performance. I feel I have a responsibility to the truth, but not necessarily to the literal, surface details of the truth. *A Line in the Sand* is based on the torture and murder of (Somali) Shidane Arone. We transposed the event to the Persian Gulf and made him Palestinian. Our audience is thus invited to make a connection—between Somalia, Canada, peacekeeping, and the Gulf—about another truth that is usually obscured.

I am especially interested in the way official truths are constructed. Truth is contextual. I am always trying to get to that which is not said, ignored, obscured, deleted, or denied by the culture generally and discourse elites in particular. That Canada is a nation of peacekeepers is not untrue, but it is not the entire truth. It is a partial truth that obscures other less flattering truths about ourselves. I see no point in repeating official and received truths (which is what much of our theatre seems to me to do; certainly what many of our reviewers expect of it). The theatre is the site (for a multitude of reasons) where I can best resist the official version of events. My autobiography or the very real fact of my presence is a fundamental element in that resistance.

In *Fronteras*, I distorted, embellished, and edited many (surface) details in order to get at what I held to be the *meaning* behind the truth of an event or moment. Writers do this all the time. Writers are always drawing on personal experience and disguising it, twisting it, changing it, and improving it for literary/dramatic/theatrical ends.

I realize there may be a contradiction here. (HEY! I'm an ARTIST, not an accountant; I don't have to be consistent.) On the one hand I say there is historical truth, but I admit to falsifying my autobiography, which I offer as a kind of fundamental truth—the thereness of me, the presence, *ecce homo*—with which an audience must contend. And I suppose that's the point. We must contend with the truth, with facts and appearances and statements and distortions and deceptions and history to get at the truth, uncover it a bit. And I suppose that's what I think I'm up to in the theatre when I mess around with presenting and re-presenting myself.

Ohmygod Jerry. Blahblahblahblah mememememe theatreschmeatre blahblahblah yaBrechtboo Fukiyamabut mostlyMMMMEEEMEMEMEMEMEME.

Playwrights' Selected Bibliography

Clark, Sally. *Jehanne of the Witches*. Toronto: Playwrights Canada, 1993.

———. *Life Without Instruction*. Vancouver. Talonbooks, 1994.

———. *Saint Frances of Hollywood*. Vancouver: Talonbooks, 1996.

———. *Wanted*. Vancouver: Talonbooks, 2004.

Clements, Marie. *The Unnatural and Accidental Women*. Vancouver: Talonbooks, 2005.

Coghill, Joy. *Song of This Place*. Toronto: Playwrights Canada, 2003.

Gale, Lorena. *Angélique*. Toronto: Playwrights Canada, 1999.

———. *Je me souviens*. Vancouver: Talonbooks, 2001.

Griffiths, Linda. *Jessica*. In *The Book of Jessica: A Theatrical Transformation*, by Linda Griffiths and Maria Campbell. Toronto: Coach House, 1989. 113–75.

———. *The Darling Family: A Duet for Three*. Winnipeg: Blizzard, 1991.

———. *The Duchess: a.k.a. Wallis Simpson*. Toronto: Playwrights Canada, 1998.

———. *Brother Andre's Heart*. In *Sheer Nerve: Seven Plays*. Winnipeg: Blizzard, 1999. 193–237.

———. *A Game of Inches*. In *Sheer Nerve: Seven Plays*. Winnipeg: Blizzard, 1999. 181–93.

———. *Sheer Nerve: Seven Plays*. Winnipeg: Blizzard, 1999.

———. *Alien Creature: A Visitation from Gwendolyn MacEwen*. Toronto: Playwrights Canada, 2000.

———. *Chronic*. Toronto: Playwrights Canada, 2004.

———, and Patrick Brymer. *O.D. on Paradise*. In *Sheer Nerve: Seven Plays*, by Linda Griffiths. Winnipeg: Blizzard, 1999. 35–94.

———, and Maria Campbell. *The Book of Jessica: A Theatrical Transformation*. Toronto: Coach House, 1989.

———, with Paul Thompson. *Maggie & Pierre*. Vancouver: Talonbooks, 1980.

Healey, Michael. *The Drawer Boy*. Toronto: Playwrights Canada, 1999.

Highway, Tomson. *The Rez Sisters*. Saskatoon: Fifth House, 1988.

———. *Dry Lips Oughta Move to Kapuskasing*. Saskatoon: Fifth House, 1989.

———. *Rose*. Vancouver: Talonbooks, 2003.

Moodie, Andrew. *Riot*. Montreal: Scirocco, 1996.

———. *A Common Man's Guide to Loving Women*. Montreal: Scirocco, 1999.

Pollock, Sharon. *Walsh*. Vancouver: Talonbooks, 1973.

———. *The Komagata Maru Incident*. Toronto: Playwrights Co-op, 1978.

———. *Blood Relations*. In *Blood Relations and Other Plays*. Edmonton: NeWest, 1981. 11–70.

———. *Blood Relations and Other Plays*. Edmonton: NeWest, 1981.

———. *Generations*. In *Blood Relations and Other Plays*. Edmonton: NeWest, 1981. 138–98.

———. *One Tiger to a Hill*. In *Blood Relations and Other Plays*, by Sharon Pollock. Edmonton: NeWest, 1981. 71–138.

———. *Doc*. Toronto: Playwrights Canada, 1984.

———. *Whiskey Six Cadenza*. In *NeWest Plays by Women*, ed. Diane Bessai. Edmonton: NeWest, 1987. 137–247.

———. *The Making of Warriors*. In *Airborne: Radio Plays by Women*, ed. Ann Jansen. Winnipeg: Blizzard, 1991. 99–132.

———. *Getting It Straight*. In *Heroines: Three Plays*, ed. Joyce Doolittle. Red Deer: Red Deer College Press, 1992. 85–126.

———. *Saucy Jack*. Winnipeg: Blizzard, 1994.

———. *Moving Pictures*. In *Sharon Pollock: Three Plays*. Toronto: Playwrights Canada, 2003. 13–94.

———. *Angel's Trumpet*. In *Sharon Pollock: Three Plays*. Toronto: Playwrights Canada, 2003. 159–224.

———. *End Dream*. In *Sharon Pollock: Three Plays*. Toronto: Playwrights Canada, 2003. 95–158.

———. *Sharon Pollock: Three Plays*. Toronto: Playwrights Canada, 2003.

Theatre Passe Muraille. *The Farm Show: A Collective Creation*. Toronto: Coach House, 1976.

Thomson, R. H. *The Lost Boys*. Toronto: Playwrights Canada, 2001.

Verdecchia, Guillermo. *Fronteras Americanas (American Borders)*. Toronto: Coach House, 1993.

———, and Daniel Brooks. *The Noam Chomsky Lectures*. Toronto: Coach House, 1991.

———, and Marcus Youssef. *A Line in the Sand*. Vancouver: Talonbooks, 1997.

Contributor Biographies

SUSAN BENNETT is Professor of English at the University of Calgary. She has published widely on a range of theatre and performance topics. She is the author of *Performing Nostalgia: Shifting Shakespeare and the Contemporary Past* and *Theatre Audiences: A Theory of Production and Reception*, and is an editor for *Theatre Journal*. She is currently completing research for a full-length study of British women playwrights in the 1950s.

SALLY CLARK, the Vancouver-born, critically acclaimed playwright, demonstrates her skill for dramatizing the lives of historical figures and for providing a feminist re-visioning of what it means to be a heroine in such plays as *Saint Frances of Hollywood* and *Life Without Instruction*. Clark has been playwright-in-residence at Theatre Passe Muraille, the Shaw Festival, Buddies in Bad Times Theatre, and Nightwood Theatre. She is also a painter, director, and filmmaker. When she was a resident artist at the Canadian Film Centre, she wrote and directed her award-winning short film "Ten Ways to Abuse an Old Woman."

MARIE CLEMENTS is an award-winning performer and playwright, director, and artistic director of urban ink productions. Her ten plays including *Burning Vision*, *The Unnatural and Accidental Women*, and *Urban Tattoo* have been presented on some of the most prestigious stages for Canadian and international work, including the Festival de Théâtre des Amériques (*Urban Tattoo* in 2001, *Burning Vision* in 2003) in Montreal, and the Magnetic North Festival (*Burning Vision* in 2003) in Ottawa. *Burning Vision* was awarded the 2004 Canada-Japan Literary Award, nominated for the 2004 Governor General's Literary Award and six Jessie Richardson Theatre Awards, and short-listed for the George Ryga Awards for Literary Arts.

JOY COGHILL, veteran actor and trail-blazer, is a consummate stage and screen performer, teacher, and director. In 1953 she broke new and innovative ground by founding the first Canadian professional theatre for children, Holiday Theatre, and she was the first female artistic director of the Vancouver Playhouse, where she commissioned such legendary plays as George Ryga's *The Ecstasy of Rita Joe* and *Grass and Wild Strawberries*. She went on to be the head of the English Acting Section at Canada's National Theatre School, and in 1994 she founded Western Gold, the first Canadian professional theatre for seniors. Among her many outstanding stage appearances are her recent performance of Lear in Jane Heyman's *Lear Project*, her portrayal of Frieda for the premiere of *Song of This Place*, and her creation of *The Alzheimer's Project*, including the play *Strangers among Us* for Western Gold. Coghill has received numerous honours, including two honourary degrees, four Jessie Richardson Theatre Awards, and a

Herbert Whittaker Critics' Award. She is a member of the Order of Canada, and in 2002 she received a Governor General's Performing Arts Award.

LOUISE FORSYTH, Professor Emerita, University of Saskatchewan, was Chair of the Department of French (University of Western Ontario), Dean of Graduate Studies & Research (University of Saskatchewan), and President of the Humanities & Social Sciences Federation of Canada. Her research specialization is Québec literature, particularly *l'écriture au féminin* and feminist playwrights. She has published extensively on the work of Nicole Brossard and edited *Nicole Brossard: Essays on Her Work*. Her current research involves a two-volume anthology of plays by Québec women in English translation, to be published by Playwrights Canada.

LORENA GALE, award-winning actor, director, and playwright, saw her first play *Angélique* produced internationally in 2002; and *Je me souviens* was nominated for the Governor General's Award in 2002. She is developing a new play titled *The Darwinist*.

MAGGIE B. GALE is Chair in Drama in the Department of Drama and Screen Studies at the University of Manchester, England. Recent publications include one book she has co-edited with Robert Gardner, *Auto/biography and Identity: Women, Theatre and Performance*, and another with John Stokes, *The Cambridge Companion to the Actress*.

SHERRILL GRACE teaches Canadian literature and culture at the University of British Columbia. She has published extensively on twentieth-century literature, theatre, and the arts, and her most recent books are a co-edited volume (with Albert-Reiner Glaap) on contemporary theatre, *Performing National Identities: International Perspectives on Contemporary Canadian Theatre*, a new edition of Mina Benson Hubbard's *A Woman's Way Through Unknown Labrador*, and a critical monograph about painter Tom Thomson, *Inventing Tom Thomson*. She is currently writing a biography of Sharon Pollock to be called *Making Theatre: A Life of Sharon Pollock*.

LINDA GRIFFITHS, playwright and actor, is the winner of five Dora Mavor Moore Awards, a Gemini Award, two Chalmers Awards, the Quinzaine International Festival Award for *Jessica*, and Los Angeles' A.G.A. Award for her title performance in the John Sayles film *Lianna*. She has twice been nominated for the Governor General's Award (*The Darling Family, Alien Creature*). Her nine published plays include *Chronic, Alien Creature, The Duchess: a.k.a. Wallis Simpson, Maggie & Pierre*, and *The Book of Jessica* (co-written with author and activist Maria Campbell). Her next play is inspired by a Victorian novel by George Gissing, *The Odd Women*.

TOMSON HIGHWAY is the proud son of legendary caribou hunter and world championship dogsled racer Joe Highway.

Born in a tent pitched in a snow bank (in December!), he comes from the extreme northwest corner of Manitoba, where it meets Saskatchewan, Nunavut, and the Northwest Territories. Today, he writes plays, novels, and music for a living. His best-known plays are *The Rez Sisters, Dry Lips Oughta Move to Kapuskasing, Rose*, and *Ernestine Shuswap Gets Her Trout*. As well, his first novel, *Kiss of the Fur Queen*, spent several weeks on Canadian bestseller lists. He has three children's books to his credit, all written bilingually in Cree (his mother tongue) and English. He divides his year equally between a cottage in northern Ontario (near Sudbury) and an apartment in the south of France, where he is currently at work on his second novel.

DENIS JOHNSTON holds a Ph.D. in theatre history from the University of Toronto, and has worked for the Shaw Festival since 1993. He has written or edited many books, articles, and reviews in the field of twentieth-century Canadian theatre, including *Up the Mainstream: The Rise of Toronto's Alternative Theatres* and two edited books of theatrical autobiography, *Also in the Cast* by Tony van Bridge and *A Thousand and One First Nights* by Leslie Yeo.

RIC KNOWLES is Professor of Theatre Studies at the University of Guelph, and editor of the quarterly journals *Modern Drama* and *Canadian Theatre Review*. He is author of *The Theatre of Form and the Production of Meaning, Shakespeare and*

Canada, and *Reading the Material Theatre*; editor of *Theatre in Atlantic Canada* and *Judith Thompson*; co-editor of *Modern Drama: Defining the Field* and *Staging Coyote's Dream*; and general editor of the Playwrights Canada Press series *Critical Perspectives on Canadian Theatre*.

RICHARD J. LANE is Professor of English at Malaspina University-College on Vancouver Island. He has published widely on contemporary British and Canadian literatures and twentieth-century theory. Recent literary-critical books include *Mrs. Dalloway: Literary Masterpieces*; *Beckett and Philosophy*; and *Contemporary British Fiction*; recent theory books include *Jean Baudrillard*; *Functions of the Derrida Archive: Philosophical Receptions*; and *Reading Walter Benjamin: Writing Through the Catastrophe*. Lane also writes the "Canada" section of *The Year's Work in English Studies* (Oxford University Press & The English Association). Forthcoming books include *Reading the Postcolonial Novel in English* and *Fifty Key Twentieth-Century Literary Theorists*.

LOUIS PATRICK LEROUX, playwright, director, and scholar, teaches playwriting and dramatic literature in the Department of English at Concordia University in Montreal. His undergraduate studies were in Theatre and French Literature at the University of Ottawa and his graduate studies were in arts management from HEC-Montréal and in Drama from the Sorbonne nouvelle in Paris. He is currently a doctoral candidate at the Sorbonne's Institut d'Études Théâtrales working on auto/biographical drama in Québec.

KATHERINE McLEOD is a Ph.D. candidate at the University of Toronto. At the University of British Columbia, she completed her SSHRC-funded Master's thesis, "Listening Out Loud: The Performance of Poetry in Robert Bringhurst's *Ursa Major* and George Elliott Clarke's *Québécité*," which explores how poets such as Clarke and Bringhurst, as well as Michael Ondaatje, negotiate the interactions between written and embodied performances. She presented a paper on Clarke's jazz opera *Québécité* at the 2004 Guelph Jazz Festival Colloquium and she continues to pursue interdisciplinary studies of performance and poetry at the doctoral level.

ANDREW MOODIE has performed in many theatrical, film, and television productions. Recently, he was seen in Roseneath Theatre's *Health Class* and Soulpepper Theatre's *Nathan the Wise* and *Hamlet*. He directed a production of Michael Miller's *The Power of Harriet T!* for Manitoba Theatre for Young People. He also directed *For Colored Girls Who Have Considered Suicide When the Rainbow Is Enuf* for the Coloured Girls Collective. His writing credits include the plays *Riot, Oui,* and *The Lady Smith*.

IRA NADEL, Professor of English and Distinguished University Scholar at the University of British Columbia, is completing a biography of David Mamet. His previous work includes biographies of Leonard Cohen and Tom Stoppard, as well as a brief account of Ezra Pound and a critical study of James Joyce.

ANNE NOTHOF is Professor of English and Chair of the Centre for Language and Literature at Athabasca University in Alberta. She has developed and tutored distance education courses in postcolonial literature and drama, women in literature, a history of drama, Canadian drama, and genre courses. She has published widely in international academic journals and texts, including *Theatre Research in Canada, Modern Drama, Mosaic,* and the *International Journal of Canadian Studies,* and presented papers at international conferences in Poland, England, Russia, Mexico, Israel, and the United States. Her research focus and publication have recently been on the plays of Sharon Pollock. She is a board member and editor for NeWest Press in Edmonton, and the past president of the Association for Canadian Theatre Research.

SHARON POLLOCK has written over fifty plays for stage, television, and radio, and her stage plays have been produced across Canada, in the United States, and around the world. She has won many prizes and awards for her work including Governor General's Literary Awards for Drama for both *Blood Relations* and *Doc*, and she is the recipient of four honourary degrees. Her plays have been translated into

French, German, Japanese, and Dutch. Her most recent published plays include *Moving Pictures, End Dream*, and *Angel's Trumpet*, and a three-volume collected works will be available in 2006. Pollock is also an award-winning actor, a director, and a theatre advocate, who has twice held the position of artistic director.

ANN SADDLEMYER, Professor Emerita of Drama and English at the University of Toronto, is the editor of letters and plays by J. M. Synge, Lady Gregory, and W. B. Yeats, and is currently much occupied with the plays of Bernard Shaw. She was founding president of the Association for Canadian Theatre History (now Research) and founding co-editor of *Theatre History (Research) in Canada*. Her most recent book is *Becoming George: The Life of Mrs. W. B. Yeats*.

PAULA SPERDAKOS is Associate Professor at the University of Toronto, where she teaches courses in acting theory and practice and Canadian theatre history. Her articles and book reviews have been published in *Theatre Research in Canada, CTR, Essays in Theatre, Modern Drama*, and *Queen's Quarterly*. She is the author of the Ann Saddlemyer Award-winning *Dora Mavor Moore: Pioneer of the Canadian Theatre*. Sperdakos has directed musicals, dramas, and opera in theatres across Canada.

R. H. THOMSON, actor and director, has been working for over twenty-five years in theatre, film and television. Winner of Gemini, Genie, and Dora Mavor Moore Awards in Canada, Thomson has achieved recognition through a series of diverse and memorable roles in theatre, film, and television. He has been hosting CBC's *Man Alive* series as well as advocating for cultural sovereignty and diversity on both national and international levels. He has recently performed in *No Great Mischief* at the Tarragon Theatre, and *Copenhagen* at Theatre Calgary. He recently directed *Romeo & Juliet* for ShakespeareWorks, *Of the Fields, Lately* for Theatre Calgary, and *Inexpressible Island* for the Great Canadian Theatre Company.

JOANNE TOMPKINS teaches at the University of Queensland, Brisbane, Australia. Her research interests include postcolonial, multicultural, and inter-cultural theatre, with a specific interest in Australian and Canadian theatre. She is completing a book on issues of spatiality in contemporary Australian theatre, and working on a project that uses virtual reality models of real theatres to investigate spatiality. With Helen Gilbert, she co-authored *Post-Colonial Drama*; with Julie Holledge, she co-authored *Women's Intercultural Performance*; and with Ric Knowles and W. B. Worthen, she co-edited *Modern Drama: Defining the Field*. She is also co-editor of the journal *Modern Drama* and author of articles on multiculturalism, postcolonialism, and interculturalism in theatre.

GUILLERMO VERDECCHIA, writer of drama, fiction, and film, and a director and actor, is a recipient of the Governor General's Award for Drama, a four-time winner of the Chalmers Canadian Play Award and sundry film festival awards. He is author, or co-author, of (among others) *Fronteras Americanas*, *Citizen Suárez*, and *The Adventures of Ali & Ali and the aXes of Evil*. His newest play, *bloom*, will be presented by Modern Times in Toronto. He is working on a documentary play about torture and the "War on Terror" with Marcus Youssef, as well as a new piece with long-time collaborator Daniel Brooks.

JERRY WASSERMAN is Professor of English and Theatre at the University of British Columbia and editor of the two-volume anthology *Modern Canadian Plays* as well as *Twenty Years at Play: A New Play Centre Anthology*. He has published widely on drama and theatre history, written and broadcast more than a thousand theatre reviews, and has over two hundred professional acting credits for stage, television, and film. He currently reviews theatre for the *Vancouver Province* and for his web site, www.vancouverplays.com.

CYNTHIA ZIMMERMAN has been a highly regarded commentator on Canadian playwriting and on the voice of women on the Canadian stage for her whole career at Glendon College, York University, where she is a professor in the English Department. Previously book review editor of *Modern Drama* and currently a member of its advisory board, Zimmerman has authored or co-authored four books, and produced numerous articles, chapters, and public papers. She recently completed her third annual comprehensive review of all drama publication in Canada for the *University of Toronto Quarterly*. An active member on the executive of the Association for Canadian Theatre Research, Zimmerman is currently completing a three-volume anthology to be called *Sharon Pollock Works* as well as a book on British Columbia playwright Betty Lambert.

Index

A Clash of Symbols: see La nef des sorcières
A Game of Inches: see Griffiths, Linda
A History of American Acting, 204
A Line in the Sand: see Verdecchia, Guillermo; *see also* Youssef, Marcus
A Streetcar Named Desire, 235–36, 239
A Very Long Engagement (film), 26
A Vision: see Yeats, W. B.; *see also* Yeats, George
Abbey Theatre, 23, 262, 263, 264, 268, 269, 270
Abbott, H. Porter, 154, 161
Acconci, Vito, 50
Ackery, Ivan, 236
Acorn, Milton, 304
Actresses As Working Women, 205
Actresses Franchise League, 189, 193
Adams, Maude, 206
Adams, Timothy Dow, 34
Adorno, Theodor, 77, 84
Aerial Letter, The: see Brossard, Nicole
Afrika Solo: see Sears, Djanet
After the Fall: see Miller, Arthur
Agnellus, 16
Aikens, James, 205
Aladdin (film), 131
Albee, Edward, 15; *Three Tall Women*, 15
Alien Creature: A Visitation from Gwendolyn MacEwen: see Griffiths, Linda
All That Fall: see Beckett, Samuel
Allan, Andrew, 215, 217
Allan, Martha, 204, 221
Allan, Maud, 204
Allen, Paula Gunn, 68
Allen, Viola, 203
Allgood, Molly, 263
Alpern, Sara, 14, 26
American Actress: Perspective on the Nineteenth Century, 205
American Buffalo: see Mamet, David
American Chestnut, The: see Finley, Karen
Amin, Idi, 60, 68
An Englishman Abroad; see Bennett, Alan
Anciennes odeurs, Les (Remember Me): see Tremblay, Michel
André, Francoise, 236–37, 247
Angel Street (film), 206
Angélique: see Gale, Lorena
Angélique, Marie Joseph, 309, 310, 312; *see also* Gale, Lorena: *Angélique*
Angel's Trumpet: see Pollock, Sharon
Anglin, Margaret, 203–04, 205
"Animal Spirits": *see* MacEwen, Gwendolyn
Anzaldúa, Gloria, 68, 332
Aristotle, 109

Arngrim, Thor, 226–48; *see also* Totem Theatre
Arone, Shidane, 124, 335
Artaud, Antonin, 78
Arthur, Julia, 203, 205
Ashwell, Lena, 189, 192, 193, 198, 203; *Modern Troubadours*, 189; *Myself a Player*, 189; *The Stage*, 189
Auden, W. H., 267
Augsburg, Tanya, 55
Augustine, Saint, 16, 52
Auslander, Phillip, 34, 50, 54
Autobiographics: A Feminist Theory of Women's Self-Representation: see Gilmore, Leigh

Baker, Stuart, 226–35, 240, 242–47; *see also* Totem Theatre
Bakhtin, Mikhail, 98–99, 101
Bal, Mieke, 17
Balzac, Honoré de, 257
Bannerman, Margaret, 202, 204, 213–15, 218, 219
Bareket, Nir, 331
Barker, Harley Granville, 189
Barlow, Sean, 270
Barrington, Josephine, 221
Barthes, Roland, 33–34, 322
Bataille, Georges, 77, 84
Bathroom: see Taylor, Emily
Beaudet, Louise, 203
Beaulieu, Victor-Lévy, 118
Beavington, Dorothy, 155, 164, 165
Beckett, Samuel, 15, 22, 73–75, 76, 77, 78, 80, 82, 83, 84, 85, 102, 154, 261, 262, 272, 273; *All That Fall*, 73; *Embers*, 262; *Film*, 81; *Krapp's Last Tape*, 15, 73, 262; *Not I*, 22, 73, 74, 75–78, 81, 83; *Unnameable, The*, 74; *Waiting for Godot*, 102
Begam, Richard, 76, 77
Beginner's Luck, 214, 215
Beil, Ryan, 147
Belasco, David, 206
Belles-Soeurs, Les: see Tremblay, Michel
Bellmer, Hans, 73, 76–78, 81, 82, 83, 84, 85
Benjamin, Walter, 84
Bennett, Alan, 256; *An Englishman Abroad*, 256
Bennett, Susan, 22, 51, 56, 150
Benston, Maggie, 163
Berd, Francoise, 172–73
Betrayal, The: see Pinter, Harold
Beuys, Buoys, Boys: see Garnhum, Ken
Bhabha, Homi K., 72, 79–80, 83, 84, 86
Billington, Michael, 153–54
Black Skin, White Masks: see Fanon, Franz
Blackburn, Marthe, 172–73
Blais, Marie-Claire, 176

Blake, Mervyn, 204
Blanchot, Maurice, 134
Blau, Herbert, 52
Blavatsky, Madame, 266
Blood Relations: see Pollock, Sharon
Boal, Augusto, 317
Boling, Daryl, 323
Book of Jessica, The: see Griffiths, Linda; *see also*
    Campbell, Maria
Book of Small, The: see Carr, Emily
Booth, John Wilkes, 217
Bosch, Hieronymus, 78
Boucher, Denise, 167, 168, 177; *Les fées ont soif*, 167,
    168
Boucicault, Dion, 215
Bowering, Elizabeth, 139, 143, 144, 150; *Talking to
    Trees*, 139, 143, 144, 145, 150
Brassard, André, 110, 111
Brater, Enoch, 75
Bratton, Jacky, 194, 196
Brawley, Tawana, 40
Breton, André, 76–77
Bring Down the Sun: see Lambert, Betty
Broadbent, Aida, 229
Broadfoot, Dave, 235
Brooks, Daniel, 53, 135, 334; *Here Lies Henry*, 53
Brossard, Nicole, 167, 171, 177, 178; *Aerial Letter, The*,
    167
Brother André's Heart: see Griffiths, Linda
Brown, Joe E., 240
Brown, Mary M., 205
Brustein, Robert, 276
Bryden, Ronald, 206, 221
Buckingham, Doris, 234
Buckley, Emily Ellen: see Van Cortland, Ida
Burden, Chris, 50; *Shoot*, 50
Burgess, Mary Ellen, 221
Burns, Diane, 68
Butler, Judith, 56, 57, 60, 66, 90, 100–01; *Gender
    Trouble*, 56, 67
Byatt, A. S., 137, 144, 284; *Still Life*, 137–38

Calder, John, 76
Calvary: see Yeats, W. B.
Cambron, Micheline, 115
Camerlain, Lorraine, 181
Campbell, Maria, 94, 301, 304, 305
Carlson, Lillian, 232
Carr, Alice, 144, 318
Carr, Emily, 18, 19, 22, 138–39, 143, 144–45, 146–47,
    149, 150, 262, 313, 314, 315, 316; *Book of Small,
    The*, 138, 146, 315; *House of All Sorts*, 138, 143, 145;
    Hundreds and Thousands, 138, 145
Carr, Lizzie, 144
Carroll, Lewis, 102
Carson, Linda A., 67; *Dying to Be Thin*, 67
Caruth, Cathy, 17

Cat and the Moon, The: see Yeats, W. B.
Cavell, Richard, 26
Chalmers, Eloise, 280–81, 282, 286
Chalmers, Everett, 280, 282, 284, 285, 286
Chalmers, Mary Branch, 285
Chalmers, Mary Sharon; see Pollock, Sharon
Chalmers, Peter, 280–81
Champagne from My Slipper: see Miller, Ruby
Chaney, Lon, Jr., 240
Chapman, Vernon, 205
Cheechoo, Shirley, 57; *Path with No Moccasins*, 57
Chicago, Judy, 322
Chitty, Mary Glen, 211, 212
Chomsky, Noam, 333–34
Christmas, Eric, 239
Chronic: see Griffiths, Linda
Chrystos, 68
Clapp, Susannah, 142–43
Clark, Sally, 24, 293; *Jehanne of the Witches*, 321; *Life
    Without Instruction*, 322; *Saint Frances of Hollywood*,
    321–22, 323; *Wanted*, 322
Clarke, David, 161
Claycombe, Ryan, 26
Clements, Marie, 292, 293–94, 331; *Unnatural and
    Accidental Women, The*, 293, 329–31
Cocteau, Jean, 112
Coeur à decouvert, Le (The Heart Laid Bare): see
    Tremblay, Michel
Coghill, Joy, 18–19, 22, 26, 139, 143, 145, 146, 147,
    148, 149, 160, 165, 268, 292, 293, 315; *Song of
    This Place*, 22, 139, 143, 145–49, 150, 314, 315, 316
Cohan, George M., 206
Collier, Constance, 190–92, 194, 197–98;
    Harlequinade, 191, 197–98
Come Good Rain: see Seremba, George
Connerton, Paul, 55, 56; *How Societies Remember*, 55
Conrad, Joseph, 102
Cooper, David, 315
Cooter, Verlie, 235
Copenhagen: see Frayn, Michael
Corbett, John, 96
Corbett, Mary Jean, 192
Coulter, Clare, 286
Coward, Noël, 188, 235, 256
Craig, Michèle, 173
Cranmer-Byng, John L., 217
Critchley, Simon, 74, 126, 134; *Very Little ... Almost
    Nothing: Death, Philosophy, Literature*, 74
Crossings: see Lambert, Betty
Cryptogram: see Mamet, David
Cusack, Cyril, 272

Damnée Manon, Sacrée Sandra: see Tremblay, Michel
Dane, Clemence, 185, 187–88; *London Has a Garden*,
    187; *Regiment of Women, The*, 187
Darewski, Max, 195
Darling Family, The; see Griffiths, Linda

Darwin, Charles, 312
Davies, Dorothy, 228, 234, 235, 240
Daviot, Gordon, 185
de Certeau, Michel, 35, 44
de la Roche, Mazo, 206
de Leeuw, Ronald, 139
de Sade, Marquis, 84
Death of Cuchulain, The: see Yeats, W. B.
Deleuze, Gilles, 80, 81
Democracy: see Frayn, Michael
Derrida, Jacques, 43, 45, 46, 51, 82; Glas, 72
Des nouvelles d'Édouard: see Tremblay, Michel
Desjardins, Pierre, 111, 114
Diamond, Elin, 15, 16, 26, 67
Diary of Anne Frank, The, 163–64
Dickens, Charles, 139, 142, 191
Disappearance of the Jews, The: see Mamet, David
Dobbie, Ian, 233, 235, 237, 241
Doc: see Pollock, Sharon
Dolan, Jill, 15, 16, 22, 26, 51, 52–53, 66, 67
Dominion Drama Festival, 225, 242
Doubrovsky, Serge, 108–09, 110
Douze coups de théâtre (Twelve Opening Acts): see
    Tremblay, Michel
Drainie, John, 204
Dressler, Marie, 203, 204, 205
Drover, Abby, 155–56, 158, 159, 162, 164
Drover, Ruth, 156, 157
Droy, Jack, 235, 241
Dry Lips Oughta Move to Kapuskasing: see Highway,
    Tomson
Duchess: a.k.a. Wallis Simpson, The: see Griffiths, Linda
Duchess de Langeais, La: see Tremblay, Michel
Duchesse et le roturier, La (The Duchess and the
    Commoner): see Tremblay, Michel
Duras, Marguerite, 108
Dussault, Louisette, 169, 172, 174–75
Dying to Be Thin: see Carson, Linda A.

Eakin, Paul John, 17, 26, 33, 285
Easthope, Anthony, 82
Eburne, Maude, 203
Edwardes, George, 190, 195, 197
Edwardes, Mae, 204
Edwards, Murray, 206, 208
Egan, Susanna, 19, 22, 89, 90, 99–100, 101, 116,
    118–19, 125, 135
Einstein's Gift: see Thiessen, Vern
E. J. P.: see Phillips, Elizabeth Jane
Eliot, George, 139
Eliot, T. S., 332–33
Ellington, Duke, 90
Ellis, Ed, 296
Ellmann, Richard, 268
Embers: see Beckett, Samuel
En circuit fermé: see Tremblay, Michel
Encore une fois, si vous permettez (For the Pleasure of
    Seeing Her Again): see Tremblay, Michel

End Dream: see Pollock, Sharon
Endgame: see Beckett, Samuel
Ends of Performance, The: see Orlan
Ensler, Eve, 168, 178; Vagina Monologues, The,
    168–69, 178
Epstein, William, 26
Esposito, Michele, 261–62, 263, 264
Esposito, Vera, 262
Euringer, Fred, 204–05
Evelyn, Judith, 202, 204, 206, 208, 211, 215, 217, 218
Everyman Theatre, 226, 228, 232, 239–40
Exorcist, The (film), 295

Fahrenheit 9/11 (film), 14
"Family Trappings": see Pollock, Sharon: Doc
Fanon, Franz, 84, 85
Farm Show, The, 303; see also Thompson, Paul
Farmer, Frances, 321–22
Féral, Josette, 51
Ferron, Marcelle, 171
Fighting the Waves: see Yeats, W. B.
Filewod, Alan, 26
Film: see Beckett, Samuel
Finley, Karen, 22, 24, 38–42, 44; American Chestnut,
    The, 38–40, 41; "Relaxation Room, The," 39; We
    Keep Our Victims Ready, 39–41
Firkins, Yvonne, 229, 233, 246
First English Actresses, The, 205
Fitzgerald, F. Scott, 275, 295, 299, 300; see also
    Pollock, Sharon: End Dream
Fitzgerald, Zelda, 275, 295, 300
Folkenflik, Robert, 116
Fontaine, Lynn, 206
Forgotten Leading Ladies of the American Theatre, 205
Forsyth, Louise, 23
Forte, Jeanne, 170
Forty Years On: see Bennett, Alan
Foster, Hal, 76, 77, 78, 81, 84, 85
Foucault, Michel, 50, 51; History of Sexuality, The, 50
Fraser, Kathleen, 205
Frayn, Michael, 15, 153; Copenhagen, 15, 153;
    Democracy, 15
French, David, 276
Frohman, Charles, 206
Frost, Anthony, 90
Frye, Northrop, 266
Fussell, Paul, 26

Gaboriau, Linda, 181
Gagnon, Odette, 174
Gaiety Girls, 190–91, 195, 197, 198
Gale, Lorena, 19, 22, 56, 57, 68, 276, 292, 293, 294,
    310; Angélique, 292, 309; Je me souviens, 56, 57,
    68, 292, 309, 310–11, 312
Gale, Maggie, 23
Gallagher, Kathleen, 90
Games, Alexander, 256
Gardiner, Robert, 26

Gardner, David, 205
Garnhum, Ken, 51–52, 53, 62; *Beuys, Buoys, Boys*, 51; *Pants on Fire*, 51–53, 62, 66; *Surrounded by Water*, 51
Geis, Deborah, 36, 40, 41
Gélinas, Gratien, 121
Gems, Pam, 15
Gender Trouble: see Butler, Judith
Generations: see Pollock, Sharon
Genet, Jean, 55
Gentileschi, Artemisia, 322
Gerussi, Bruno, 235–36
Getting It Straight: see Pollock, Sharon
Gill, Robert, 246
Gilmore, James, 302
Gilmore, Leigh, 13, 17, 26, 89, 101, 138, 153, 154, 168, 180, 192
Giraudoux, Jean, 110, 111, 112
Glas: see Derrida, Jacques
Glass Menagerie, The: see Williams, Tennessee
Glassco, Bill, 286
Gomez, Mayte, 68
Gonne, Maud, 265, 267
Goodman, Dean, 240
Gordimer, Nadine, 153
Goring, Marius, 188
Gould, Glenn, 328–29
Gould, Warwick, 26
Goulding, Dorothy Massey, 221
Grace, Sherrill, 23, 24, 26, 67, 72, 125–26, 149, 150, 248, 286
Graham, Elsie, 229
Gray, Spalding, 22, 24, 35–38, 44, 46; *Gray's Anatomy*, 36–38, 47; *Life Interrupted*, 46; *Morning, Noon, and Night*, 38; *Nayatt School*, 36; *Sex and Death to the Age 14*, 36; *Swimming to Cambodia*, 38; "Swimming to Macula Pucker," 38
Gray, Terence, 269
Gray's Anatomy: see Gray, Spalding
Greer, Germaine, 322
Gregory, Lady Augusta, 261–63, 264
Griffiths, John, 156, 164
Griffiths, Linda, 19, 22, 24, 89, 90, 91–97, 98, 101, 102, 150, 276, 292, 293, 294, 300, 302; *A Game of Inches*, 96, 301; *Alien Creature: A Visitation from Gwendolyn MacEwen*, 89, 90, 91–97, 98, 101, 102, 301, 304–05, 307; *Book of Jessica, The*, 94, 96, 301, 303, 304, 305; *Brother André's Heart*, 301, 303; *Chronic*, 301, 303, 304; *Darling Family, The*, 96, 301, 304; *Duchess: a.k.a. Wallis Simpson, The*, 96, 301, 304, 305; *Heartbreak Hotel*, 94; *Maggie & Pierre*, 94, 301, 302, 303, 304, 305; *O.D. on Paradise*, 94, 301, 303, 304; *Odd Women, The*, 303, 304
Griffin, Nonnie, 205
Grimson, Valdi, 229
Grosskurth, Phyllis, 272
Growing Pains: see Carr, Emily
Guattari, Félix, 80

Guilbeault, Luce, 171, 172, 176
Gunvordahl, Terry, 286
Gusdorf, Georges, 199
Gussow, Mel, 41

Haber, Fritz, 21
Hall, Amelia, 205
Hallam, Elizabeth, 127
Halliwell, Kenneth, 257
Hamilton, Cicely, 189
Happer, Martin, 141
Happy Days: see Beckett, Samuel
Harlequinade: see Collier, Constance
Harris, Geraldine, 16, 26
Harron, Don, 143, 204
Hart, Moss, 229
Hartman, Geoffrey, 82–83
Harvie, Jennifer, 98–99
Hawthorn, Pamela, 155, 164
Hay, Donald, 155–59, 163
Hay, Hilda, 155–57, 159, 164
Haynes, Elizabeth Sterling, 221, 246
Healey, Michael, 303
Heaney, Seamus, 272
Heartbreak Hotel: see Griffiths, Linda
Heble, Ajay, 90, 91
Helms, Gabriele, 19
Helms, Jesse, 41
Henderson, May, 148
Here Lies Henry: see MacIvor, Daniel; *see also* Brooks, Daniel
Hicklin, Ralph, 218
Highway, Tomson, 291, 292, 293; *Dry Lips Oughta Move to Kapuskasing*, 292, 306; *Kiss of the Fur Queen*, 292; *Rez Sisters, The*, 292, 293, 306, 307; *Rose*, 306
Hinz, Evelyn, 13, 18, 125–26
Hirsch, Marianne, 26
History of Sexuality, The: see Foucault, Michel
Hitchcock, Alfred, 206
Hitchman, Babs, 234
Hitler, Adolf, 302, 305
Hogan, Michael, 286
Holiday, Billie, 90
Holledge, Julie, 26
Hollingsworth, Margaret, 150
Hopkinson, William, 295, 297–98
House of All Sorts, The: see Carr, Emily
How Societies Remember: see Connerton, Paul
Huculak, Maggie, 161
Hugo, Victor, 76
Hundreds and Thousands: see Carr, Emily
Hunt, Hugh, 270, 271
Hutt, William, 204

I Am Nature (film), 39
Image(s) Nouvelle(s) Image(s): see Orlan
Indian Ink: see Stoppard, Tom

Inman, Derek, 243
Innocent Flowers: Women in the Edwardian Theatre,
    205
Invention of Love, The: see Stoppard, Tom
Ionesco, Eugène, 112
Ireland, Sarah, 323
Irwin, May, 203, 204

Jackson, Ian, 141
Jacobs, Tanya, 161
James, Henry, 152, 284
Jaspers, Karl, 84
Je me souviens: see Gale, Lorena
Jefferis, Nella, 204
Jehanne of the Witches: see Clark, Sally
Jennie's Story: see Lambert, Betty
Joffé, Roland, 38
John Bull's Other Island: see Shaw, George Bernard
Johnson, Dr. Samuel, 16
Johnston, Denis, 23
Johnston, James, 234, 235
Jones, Amelia, 126
Jordan, Gilbert Paul, 329
Jouvet, Louis, 110
Joyce, James, 261, 262, 276
Joyce, Nora, 268

Kane, Leslie, 250, 253, 254, 259
Kane, Margo, 67
Kelly, Katherine, 73, 74
Kennedy, Adam, 42, 44, 45
Kennedy, Adrienne, 15, 22, 42, 45; *Sleep Deprivation
    Chamber,* 42–45
Killing Fields, The (film), 38
King, Rodney, 318
Kinsman, David, 95
Kipling, Rudyard, 160; "The Ladies," 160
Kiss of the Fur Queen: see Highway, Tomson
Klebnikoff, Natalia, 261, 262, 272; *see also* Esposito,
    Michele
Klee Wyck: see Carr, Emily
Klossowski, Pierre, 77, 78, 84
Knott, Roselle, 203
Knowles, Ric, 22, 59, 68, 98–99, 101, 103
Knowlson, James, 75
Koenig, Elfi, 241, 247
Komagata Maru Incident, The: see Pollock, Sharon
Krapp's Last Tape: see Beckett, Samuel
Kristeva, Julia, 67, 82
Kushner, Rabbi Lawrence, 251

*La grosse femme d'à côté est enceinte (The Fat Woman
    Next Door Is Pregnant): see* Tremblay, Michel
La nef des sorcières (A Clash of Symbols), 23, 167–80,
    181
Lacan, Jacques, 61, 77–78, 80, 82–83, 126
"Ladies, The": *see* Kipling, Rudyard

Lafon, Dominique, 116
LaFontaine, Rita, 111
Lahr, John, 257
Lambert, Betty, 22, 153, 154–55, 156, 158–62, 163;
    Bring Down the Sun, 154; *Crossings,* 154, 165;
    Jennie's Story, 165; *Sqrieux-de-Dieu,* 154; *Under the
    Skin,* 22–23, 153, 154–62; *Visiting Hour,* 163
Lambert, Ruth Anne, 156, 163, 165
Lambrett-Smith, Frank, 234
Lamy, Suzanne, 181
Lane, Richard J., 22
Laplanche, Jean, 83
L'école des femmes: see Molière
L'État des lieux (Impromptu on Nun's Island): see
    Tremblay, Michel
LeCompte, Liz, 36, 47
Leeper, Trish, 26, 147
Le Grand, Margaret: *see* Bannerman, Margaret
Lejeune, Philippe, 16, 17, 108–09, 125, 127, 134, 179
Leroux, Patrick, 22
Le vrai monde? (The Real World?): see Tremblay, Michel
Les fées ont soif: see Boucher, Denise
Les vues animées (Bambi and Me): see Tremblay, Michel
Levin, Louis, 241
Levinas, Emmanuel, 126–27, 134
Life Interrupted: see Gray, Spalding
Light up the Sky, 229, 230, 233
Lill, Wendy, 22, 89, 90, 91, 98–101, 102; *Occupation
    of Heather Rose, The,* 89, 98–101
Lillie, Beatrice, 204, 243
Limbaugh, Rush, 40, 41
L'Impromptu de Paris: see Tremblay, Michel
L'Impromptu des deux "Presse": see Tremblay, Michel
L'Impromptu d'Outremont: see Tremblay, Michel
Lincoln, Abraham: assassination of, 217
Linson, Art, 250
London Has a Garden: see Dane, Clemence
Long Day's Journey into Night: see O'Neill, Eugene
Loot: see Orton, Joe
Lost Boys, The: see Thomson, R. H.
Lowry, Malcolm, 276, 284

McCance, Larry, 230
McCoy, Elijah, 319–20
MacDonald, Christie, 204
Macdonald, Sharman, 153
MacEwen, Gwendolyn, 18, 91–97, 98, 102, 150, 301,
    304, 305; "Animal Spirits," 97; "Magician, The,"
    96; "Past and Future Ghosts," 92
MacIvor, Daniel, 53; *Here Lies Henry,* 53
MacLeod, Joan, 22, 124, 126, 127, 128, 130; *Shape of
    a Girl, The,* 22, 124, 125, 126, 127–30, 134
MacLeod, Katherine, 22
Macmillan, Norma, 226, 234–35, 238–39, 242,
    243–44, 246
McNicholls, Learie, 53
McPherson, Thomas Shanks, 242

Macy, William H., 250
Maddox, Brenda, 268
Madness of George III, The: see Bennett, Alan
Maggie & Pierre: see Griffiths, Linda
"Magician, The": see MacEwen, Gwendolyn
Magny, Michèle, 177
Making of Warriors, The: see Pollock, Sharon
Malkin, Jeanette, 26
Mamet, David, 23, 24, 249–55, 257–58; *A Life in the
    Theatre,* 254; *American Buffalo,* 249, 250, 251;
    Boston Marriage, 251; *Cryptogram,* 250, 254;
    Disappearance of the Jews, The, 252–53; *Edmond,*
    254; *Faustus,* 252; *Five Cities of Refuge,* 251;
    Glengarry Glen Ross, 250; *Homicide* (film), 252;
    House of Games (film), 249; *Jafsie and John Henry,*
    250; *Lakeboat,* 250; *Lone Canoe,* 254; *Marranos,*
    253–54; *Old Neighborhood, The,* 250, 252, 253; *On
    Directing Film,* 249; *Sexual Perversity in Chicago,*
    250, 251; *Shawl, The,* 254; "Song of the Jew," 255;
    South of Northeast Kingdom, 251; *Spartan* (film),
    252; *Speed-the-Plow,* 250; *True and False: Heresy
    and Common Sense for the Actor,* 253
Mannering, Peter, 226, 234, 239, 241, 246, 247
Man Who Came to Dinner, The, 244
Mapplethorpe, Robert, 81
Marchessault, Jovette, 118, 143
Marcus, Laura, 17, 26
Marsh, Wally, 234
Mather, Margaret, 203
Matheson, Tim, 147, 312
Maude, Ulrika, 76
Maufort, Marc, 62
Maugham, Somerset, 197, 213; *Our Betters,* 213, 215
Medavoy, Mike, 249–50
Meisner, Sanford, 249
Mémoires affectives (film), 26
Menzies, Roderick, 26
Michelet, Jules, 140
Middleton, Peter, 26
Miller, Arthur, 15, 26, 276, 278; *After the Fall,* 15, 26,
    276
Miller, Ruby, 195–97, 198; *Believe It or Not!,* 195–96;
    Champagne from My Slipper, 195, 196
Mingus, Charles, 90
Mitchell, Betty, 221, 246
Mitchell, Ken, 17
Modern Troubadours: see Ashwell, Lena
Moiseiwitsch, Tanya, 268, 269, 270
Mojica, Monique, 22, 24, 56, 60, 307; *Princess
    Pocahontas and the Blue Spots,* 56, 60, 68
Molière, 112, 170; *L'école des femmes,* 170, 171, 176, 179
Moodie, Andrew, 292, 318; *A Common Man's Guide
    to Loving Women,* 318; *Hysteria,* 317; *Riot,* 317–18
Moon Is Blue, The, 238
Moore, Dora Mavor, 202–03, 204, 206, 246
Moore, Mavor, 5, 202, 204; *And What Do You Do?,* 5
Moore-Gilbert, Bart, 79

Moraga, Cherríe, 68
More, Robert, 18, 26, 146
Morra, Linda, 19, 21
Morris, Clara, 203, 217–18
Morris, Evelyn Mae: see Evelyn, Judith
Morris, William, 142
Morrison, Charlotte Nickinson, 202, 203, 209, 211,
    212, 215, 216, 219
Morrison, Daniel, 219
Moss, Jane, 181
Mostern, Kenneth, 45
Moving Pictures: see Pollock, Sharon
Munro, Alice, 313
Murray, Margaret, 321
Murrell, John, 313
Musikansky, Harry, 238
Myself a Player: see Ashwell, Lena

Nadel, Ira, 17, 21, 23
Nayatt School: see Gray, Spalding
Nelligan: see Tremblay, Michel
Nelson, Joyce, 334
New Play Centre, 154–55
New Play Society, 202, 206, 225; see also Moore,
    Dora Mavor
Nicholls, Liz, 137, 142
Nicholls, Sandra M., 141
Nickinson, Albert, 212
Nickinson, John, 209, 211, 212–13, 215, 217, 219
*Nineteenth-Century American Women Theatre
    Managers,* 205
Noam Chomsky Lectures, The: see Verdecchia,
    Guillermo
Nochlin, Linda, 81
Nothof, Anne, 22, 26, 62, 127, 150
Not I: see Beckett, Samuel
Novello, Ivor, 197

Obote, Milton, 57, 60
O'Casey, Sean, 272
Occupation of Heather Rose, The: see Lill, Wendy
O.D. on Paradise: see Griffiths, Linda
Odd Woman, The: see Griffiths, Linda
O'Gorman, Kathleen, 75
Old Neighborhood, The: see Mamet, David
Olney, James, 17
Oloagun, Modupe, 62, 68
On Baile's Strand: see Yeats, W. B.
O'Neill, Eugene, 109, 276, 278; *Long Day's Journey
    into Night,* 15, 276
O'Neill, Patrick, 205, 209
One Tiger to a Hill: see Pollock, Sharon
Only Jealousy of Emer, The: see Yeats, W. B.
Ontkean, Muriel, 235, 236, 247
Oosterman, Adrian, 307
Order of the Golden Dawn, 265, 266
Orenstein, Joan, 26, 148, 313, 316

Orlan, 24, 53–55, 67; Ends of Performance, The, 54; Image(s) Nouvelle(s) Image(s), 54, 67; Reincarnation of Saint Orlan, The, 54, 55, 57
Orton, Joe, 255, 257; Loot, 255
Our Betters: see Maugham, Somerset

Pachter, Marc, 26
Padden, Mayo, 144
Page, Malcolm, 154, 163
Page, P. K., 313
Pantages, Alexander, 242
Pants on Fire: see Garnhum, Ken
"Past and Future Ghosts": see MacEwen, Gwendolyn
Path with No Moccasins: see Cheechoo, Shirley
Pavis, Patrice, 109
Pawelak, Lydia, 333
Payne, Sam, 228, 235, 241, 243, 247
Pelletier, Pol, 169–70, 172, 176–77
Perrault, Jeanne, 168
Peter Wall Institute for Advanced Studies, 11, 18, 19, 67, 120
Petropoulos, Jacqueline, 98, 99, 102
Phelan, Peggy, 57
Phillips, Betty, 234
Phillips, Elizabeth Jane, 202, 203, 208–11, 212–13, 215, 217, 218, 219
Phillips, Stephen, 198
Piccione, Marie-Lyne, 107, 110
Pickford, Mary, 204, 205
Pinsent, Gordon, 204
Pinter, Harold, 153–54; Betrayal, The, 15, 154
Pitts, Zasu, 240
Plant, Richard, 205
Plath, Sylvia, 91
Player Queen, The: see Yeats, W. B.
Pollard, Barbara, 26, 149
Pollock, Amanda, 286
Pollock, Jackson, 39
Pollock, Sharon, 15, 23, 24, 137, 152, 268, 275–77, 280–85, 291, 292, 294, 296, 313; Angel's Trumpet, 275, 295, 300; Blood Relations, 275, 285, 295; Doc, 15, 23, 24, 275, 276–79, 281–85, 286, 292, 298–99, 300; End Dream, 275, 295; Generations, 296; Getting It Straight, 300; Komagata Maru Incident, The, 295; Making of Warriors, The, 295; Moving Pictures, 15, 275, 295, 296, 300; One Tiger to a Hill, 275, 296; Saucy Jack, 295; Walsh, 276, 295; Whiskey Six Cadenza, 295
Pominville, Francine, 286
Pontalis, J.-B., 83
Postlewait, Thomas, 26, 190–91, 192, 194
Pound, Ezra, 270
Pountney, Rosemary, 75
Price, Vincent, 206, 208
Princess Pocahontas and the Blue Spots: see Mojica, Monique

Prinsep, Anthony, 215
Proctor, Catherine, 202, 204, 206, 207, 211, 215, 218
Proust, Marcel, 109
Purgatory: see Yeats, W. B.
PWIAS: see Peter Wall Institute for Advanced Studies
Pyper, Nancy, 218, 221

Quarante-quatre minutes, quarante-quatre secondes: see Tremblay, Michel

Ragland-Sullivan, Ellie, 80
Rattigan, Terence, 257
Regiment of Women, The: see Dane, Clemence
Reincarnation of Saint Orlan, The: see Orlan
"Relaxation Room, The": see Finley, Karen
Resurrection, The: see Yeats, W. B.
Reynolds, John McCombe, 95
Reynolds, Kari, 95
Rez Sisters, The: see Highway, Tomson
Rhiel, Mary, 26
Richards, Sandra, 56
Richardson, Alan, 143
Richardson, Jessie, 246
Ricoeur, Paul, 109, 118
Riders to the Sea: see Synge, John Millington
Riendeau, Pascal, 110
Risk, Sydney, 228, 229, 232, 240
Roach, Joseph, 55
Roberts, Eloise: see Chalmers, Eloise
Robinson, Lennox, 269
Ronfard, Pierre, 119, 120
Root, Juan, 228, 234
Rosenstrasse (film), 26
Roy, Hélène, 169, 176
Ruskin, John, 142
Russell, Annie, 203, 206, 207
Rutherford, Dede, 229
Ryngaert, Jean-Pierre, 116

Saddlemyer, Ann, 23, 205, 273
Said, Edward, 131–32
Saint Frances of Hollywood: see Clark, Sally
Sainte-Carmen de la Main (Sainte-Carmen of the Main): see Tremblay, Michel
Sajnani, Nisha, 79
Saucy Jack: see Pollock, Sharon
Scarlatti, Domenico, 262
Schechner, Richard, 38, 47
Scott, Robert B., 205
Scott, Shelley, 127–28
Sears, Djanet, 56, 57, 59, 60, 62, 66, 68; Afrika Solo, 56, 57–60, 61
"Second Coming, The": see Yeats, W. B.
Seremba, George, 24, 57, 60–62, 63, 64; Come Good Rain, 57, 60–62, 68
Sex and Death to the Age 14: see Gray, Spalding

Sexual Perversity in Chicago: see Mamet, David
Shadow of the Glen, The: see Synge, John Millington
Shafransky, Renee, 47
Shakespeare, William, 45, 139, 142, 321; *Hamlet*, 45;
    Othello, 45
Shape of a Girl, The: see MacLeod, Joan
Shaw Festival, 247
Shaw, George Bernard, 189, 237, 261, 262, 263,
    264, 272, 273; *John Bull's Other Island*, 263
Shaw, Peggy, 67
Sherman, Cindy, 81
Shields, Carol, 284
Shipman, Nell, 295, 300; *see also* Pollock, Sharon:
    Moving Pictures
Shoot: see Burden, Chris
Shortt, Mary, 205, 208–09, 212, 216
Shuster, Frank, 239
Sidnell, Michael, 26
Siegler, Karl, 322
Simpson, Homer, 54
Simpson, Wallis, 301, 305
Skipsey, Eric, 236, 238, 245
Smart, Patricia, 174
Smith, Dodie, 187
Smith, Janet, 295, 299
Smith, Phoebe, 228, 229, 233, 235
Smith, Sidonie, 26, 33, 102, 125, 193
Somerset, Dorothy Maud, 221, 229
Song of This Place: see Coghill, Joy
Soules, Marshall, 90
Spence, Craig, 146
Spencer, David, 242
Sperdakos, Paula, 23
Spivak, Gayatri, 83–84, 85, 86
Sprung, Guy, 286
Sqrieux-de-Dieu: see Lambert, Betty
Stage, The: see Ashwell, Lena
Stahl, Rose, 203
Staley, Thomas E., 26
States, Bert O., 50
Stegeman, Charles, 236–37, 247
Stern, G. B., 185
Still Life: see Byatt, A. S.
Stoppard, Tom, 255–56, 258, 284; *Indian Ink*, 256;
    Invention of Love, The, 256, 258
Stovin, Jerry, 241
Stratford, Arthur, 325–26
Stratford, George, 326
Stratford Festival, 205, 235, 236, 247
Street, Brian, 127
Stuart, Aimee, 185
Stuart, Eleanor, 204
Sturkin, Marita, 26, 55–56
Suchoff, David, 26
Sullivan, Rosemary, 102, 306
Supersize Me (film), 14

Surrounded by Water: see Garnhum, Ken
Synge, John Millington, 261–64, 272; *Playboy of the
    Western World, The*, 262–63, 264; *Riders to the
    Sea*, 262; *Shadow of the Glen, The*, 263; *Tinker's
    Wedding, The*, 264;
Well of the Saints, The, 262, 263, 265
Sysak, Suzanne, 247

Talbot, Mary Ann, 219
Talking Heads: see Bennett, Alan
Talking to Trees: see Bowering, Elizabeth
Tandy, Jessica, 75
Tanguay, Eva 204
Taverner, Albert, 206, 212, 217
Taverner Company, 206
Taylor, Claire Drainie, 205
Taylor, Emily, 49, 50, 52, 53, 67; *Bathroom*, 49–51, 52
Taylor, Laurette, 206
Temple, Joan, 187
Testifyin', 60
*That Despicable Race: A History of the British Acting
    Tradition*, 204
Theatre Under the Stars, 226, 229, 230, 234, 237,
    238, 239, 241, 244
Thiessen, Vern, 21; *Einstein's Gift*, 21
Théoret, France, 173–74, 177
Thompson, Paul, 94, 293, 302, 303–04
Thomson, R. H., 19, 24, 137, 276, 292, 293, 325;
    Lost Boys, The, 19, 293, 324–27
Thorne, Ian, 242, 247
Till, Emmett, 43
Tinker's Wedding, The: see Synge, John Millington
Tobacco Road, 240, 247
Tompkins, Joanne, 22, 26, 59–60, 66, 68
Tony Draws a Horse, 238–39
Totem Theatre, 23, 226–48; productions at, 230,
    233–34, 235, 237, 238, 239–41, 243
Tournier, Michel, 116
Tree, Herbert Beerbohm, 194, 195, 197, 198, 264
Tremblay, Michel, 15, 22, 24, 107–19, 120, 121,
    276–78, 284, 286; *Anciennes odeurs, Les
    (Remember Me)*, 107, 114, 118; *Belles-Soeurs, Les*,
    108, 110, 112–13, 115–16, 117, 118, 119; *Coeur à
    découvert, Le*, 114; *Damnée Manon, Sacrée Sandra*,
    107, 110, 118, 120; *Des nouvelles d'Édouard (News
    from Édouard)*, 108; *Douze coups de théâtre (Twelve
    Opening Acts)*, 110, 117; *Duchesse de Langeais, La*,
    108; *Duchesse et le roturier, La (The Duchess and the
    Commoner)*, 108; *En circuit fermé*, 108, 115, 116;
    *Encore une fois, si vous permettez (For the Pleasure
    of Seeing Her Again)*, 107, 109–11, 117, 118; *L'État
    des lieux (Impromptu on Nun's Island)*, 108, 113,
    115, 116, 120; *L'Impromptu de Paris*, 110, 111;
    L'Impromptu des deux "Presse," 108, 113, 115;
    L'Impromptu d'Outremont, 108, 112, 115–16; *La
    grosse femme d'à côté est enceinte (The Fat Woman*

Next Door Is Pregnant), 114, 116; *Le vrai monde?*
(*The Real World?*), 108, 113–15, 116, 117–18,
276–78, 284, 286; *Les vues animées (Bambi and
Me)*, 110, 117; *Nelligan*, 118; *Quarante-quatre
minutes, quarante-quatre secondes*, 108; *Sainte-
Carmen de la Main (Sainte-Carmen of the Main)*,
118; *Un ange cornu avec des ailes de tôle (Birth of a
Bookworm)* 110, 117; *Ville Mont-Royal ou Abîmes*,
108, 112, 115, 120
Trotter, Kate, 286
Trudeau, Margaret, 301, 304, 305; *see also* Griffiths,
    Linda: *Maggie & Pierre*
Trudeau, Pierre Elliott, 304, 305; *see also* Griffiths,
    Linda: *Maggie & Pierre*
Turner, Victor, 67
TUTS: *see* Theatre Under the Stars
Tynan, Kenneth, 256, 276

*Un ange cornu avec des ailes de tôle (Birth of a
    Bookworm)*: *see* Tremblay, Michel
Under the Skin: see Lambert, Betty
Unnameable, The: see Beckett, Samuel
Unnatural and Accidental Women, The: see Clements,
    Marie
*Up the Mainstream: The Rise of Toronto's Alternative
    Theatres*, 225

Vagina Monologues, The: see Ensler, Eve
Vallières, Pierre, 181
van Bridge, Tony, 204, 225
Van Cortland, Ida, 202, 203, 206, 208, 211, 212, 217,
    218, 219
Vancouver Little Theatre Association (VLTA), 227,
    228, 229, 233, 234, 235
Van Duren, Catherine, 150
Van Gogh, Theo, 138, 139, 140
Van Gogh, Vincent, 22, 137, 138, 139, 140, 142, 143
Van Gogh-Bonger, Johannes, 139
Verdecchia, Guillermo, 22, 24, 26–27, 57, 62, 63,
    65, 66, 124, 126, 130, 135, 276, 292, 293, 294,
    333; *A Line in the Sand*, 22, 124, 125, 126, 127,
    130–34, 333, 334, 335; *Fronteras Americanas*, 24, 57,
    62–65, 135, 332, 333, 334, 335; *Noam Chomsky
    Lectures, The*, 135, 333, 334
Verdi, Giuseppe, 308
Vernon, Emma: *see* Esposito, Vera
Ville Mont-Royal ou Abîmes: see Tremblay, Michel
Virk, Reena, 124–25, 128, 129, 130
Visiting Hour: see Lambert, Betty
Vitez, Antoine, 111
VLTA: *see* Vancouver Little Theatre Association
Voaden, Herman, 143
Vyvyan, Frank, 234

Wagner, Richard, 262
Wagner-Martin, Linda, 26
Waiting for Godot: see Beckett, Samuel

Waldenfels, Bernhard, 127
Walsh: see Pollock, Sharon
Walsh, Major James, 295, 298, 299
Walters, Izzy, 240
Wansell, Geoffrey, 257
Wasserman, Jerry, 19, 21, 24, 67, 124, 127, 128, 130,
    248, 275
Watson, Julia, 26, 33, 102, 193
Watson, Lucile, 204
Wayne, Johnny, 239
Waxman, Al, 204
We Keep Our Victims Ready: see Finley, Karen
Well of the Saints, The: see Synge, John Millington
Wells, Alison, 144
Wertenbaker, Timberlake, 152, 161
West End Women: Women and the London Stage, 205
Whiskey Six Cadenza: see Pollock, Sharon
White, Donna, 26, 147, 149
Whitelaw, Billie, 75
Whitfield, Eileen, 143
Wilder, Billy, 250
Wilding, Dorothy, 213, 214, 215, 221
Williams, Tennessee, 109, 236, 238, 276, 278; *Glass
    Menagerie, The*, 15, 276, 277; *see also: A Streetcar
    Named Desire*
Williams, Vaughn, 262
Wilson, Ann, 50, 52, 53, 62, 63, 66, 67, 164
Women in American Theatre, 205
Wood, Brent, 102
Woods, Tim, 26
Woolf, Virginia, 16, 55, 257, 272
Words Upon the Window-Pane, The: see Yeats, W. B.
Worthen, W. B., 26, 54
Wright, Elizabeth, 78
Wright, Nicholas, 137, 138–39, 140, 141, 142; *Vincent
    in Brixton*, 137, 138, 139, 140–43, 150

Yarrow, Ralph, 90
Yeats, Anne, 269–70
Yeats, George, 23, 265–72
Yeats, Jack, 264
Yeats, W. B., 23, 137, 261, 262, 264–71, 272; *A
    Vision*, 265–66, 267; *Calvary*, 267; *Cat and the
    Moon, The*, 267; *Death of Cuchulain, The*, 267;
    Fighting the Waves, 269; *On Baile's Strand*, 269;
    Only Jealousy of Emer, The, 267; *Player Queen, The*,
    269; *Purgatory*, 269–70, 271; *Resurrection, The*,
    269; "Second Coming, The," 267, 271; *Words
    Upon the Window-Pane, The*, 267
Yeo, Leslie, 204, 225
Yorke, Alice, 204
Young, E. V., 234
Young, James, 26
Youssef, Marcus, 22, 124, 126, 130, 333, 334

Zimmerman, Cynthia, 22, 23

Lightning Source UK Ltd.
Milton Keynes UK
UKOW07f0810100915